The New York Times

CROSSWORDS FOR A LONG WEEKEND

First published by St. Martin's Griffin,
an imprint of St. Martin's Publishing Group

THE NEW YORK TIMES CROSSWORDS FOR A LONG WEEKEND.
Copyright © 2020 by The New York Times Company. All rights reserved.
Printed in the United States of America. For information, address St. Martin's
Publishing Group, 175 Fifth Avenue, New York, NY 10010.

www.stmartins.com

All of the puzzles that appear in this work were originally published in
The New York Times from March 4, 2016, to October 29, 2016, from January 2, 2017,
to March 7, 2017, or from March 5, 2018, to August 8, 2019.
Copyright © 2016, 2017, 2018, 2019 by The New York Times Company.
All rights reserved. Reprinted by permission.

ISBN 978-1-250-25312-5

Our books may be purchased in bulk for promotional, educational, or business use.
Please contact your local bookseller or the Macmillan Corporate
and Premium Sales Department at 1-800-221-7945, extension 5442, or
by email at MacmillanSpecialMarkets@macmillan.com.

First Edition: February 2020

The New York Times

CROSSWORDS FOR A LONG WEEKEND
200 Easy to Hard Crossword Puzzles

Edited by Will Shortz

ST. MARTIN'S GRIFFIN ⚏ NEW YORK

The New York Times

SMART PUZZLES

Presented with Style

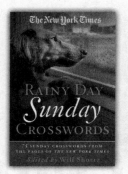
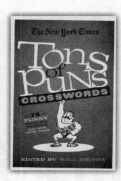

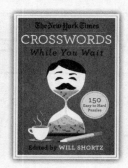

Available at your local bookstore or online at www.nytimes.com/nytstore

🦁 St. Martin's Griffin

f facebook.com/NewYorkTimesCrosswordPuzzle

ACROSS

1 33⅓ r.p.m. records
4 Cher or Adele, musically
8 Allude (to)
13 Annoy
14 Building for bovines
15 Mogadishu native
16 *Chief source of support
18 Self-centeredness
19 ___ fixe (preoccupation)
20 General Mills puffed corn cereal
21 Distances in Britain
22 *Chapel Hill athlete
24 Pyromaniacs' pleasures
25 Monogram for Long John Silver's creator
26 Cut (off)
27 Outbuilding for storage
30 Quarrel
33 Yankee great Yogi
35 Park or Madison, on an N.Y.C. map
36 Bouncy youngster in Pooh's crowd
37 Praise after a proper response to the end of the answer to each starred clue
39 Kesey who wrote "One Flew Over the Cuckoo's Nest"
40 Vow sworn at the altar
41 Round Mongolian tents
42 Wary
44 Spot for a teacher's apple or Apple
46 Virtuous conduct, in Confucianism
47 Dot follower in a website address
48 Pass, as a law
50 *"Why?"
54 Saudi city where Muhammad is buried
56 One running for office, informally
57 Noteworthy periods
58 First king of the Franks (A.D. 481)
59 *Tend an absent resident's property
61 M.L.B. division that includes the Astros
62 Prefix with tasse meaning "half"
63 Word before "blastoff"
64 Uptight
65 Harmonious, after "in"
66 Originally named

DOWN

1 Outer boundary
2 Devil's fashion choice, in a Meryl Streep film
3 Person on a slippery slope
4 Midsection muscles, briefly
5 Potato treats for Hanukkah
6 Backpacker's path
7 Black, banded gemstone
8 Radioer's "Got it"
9 Is melodramatic
10 *Equitable treatment
11 Otherwise
12 Edges, as of craters
15 Athlete getting part-time pay
17 India's first P.M.
23 Plaintive poem
24 Fiestas and Fusions
26 Resulted in
28 ___ and anon
29 Reject as false
30 Extremely dry
31 Went as a passenger
32 *Soft bedding material
33 Title character in a Sacha Baron Cohen mockumentary
34 Radiant
38 One rejected by a group
43 Roast host
45 Butchers' tools
47 Op-ed offering
49 Plant seed with a licoricelike flavor
50 Poppycock
51 "Citizen Kane" star Welles
52 State that's the largest U.S. producer of lobsters
53 Beauty mogul Lauder
54 Exam for a wannabe doc
55 Her: Fr.
56 Degrees after M.A.s
60 Error indicator in a quotation

by Lynn Lempel

ACROSS

1 "We should totally do that!"
5 Key of Beethoven's Symphony No. 7: Abbr.
9 Ain't I a stinker?
14 Energy field, in holistic medicine
15 Made-up story
16 Rub the wrong way
17 Metal that rusts
18 Coup d'___
19 What a tabloid may be sued for
20 Need for targeted advertising
23 Medium for modern matchmaking
24 Ghost in a haunted house, e.g.
25 '60s conflict site
28 "That sounds painful"
30 Ozs. and lbs.
31 Danson of "The Good Place"
34 Birdlike
36 A very long time
38 Neighbor of Pennsylvania
39 Netflix or YouTube
42 Online option that turns into "show" when clicked
43 Absence of complication
44 Profess
45 Sun or moon
46 UPS competitor
47 The longer of the two Morse symbols
49 "Hey" alternatives
50 Restaurateur Lagasse
53 Part of a headset
55 It settles a case
61 Classic hit
62 Catcher of counterfeiters, in old lingo
63 Retort to "Are not!"
64 Investigator
65 [Same source as before]
66 Like drone bees
67 Pizza size

68 Disadvantages found in this puzzle's three longest Across answers . . .
69 . . . and advantages found in them

DOWN

1 Concerning the nonordained
2 Franc's successor
3 Disney sci-fi classic
4 Eldest Stark daughter on "Game of Thrones"
5 "Resume normal speed," in a score
6 Each animal in Noah's Ark had one
7 First thing in the morning?
8 Like 747s
9 Beauty parlors
10 Butter spreader
11 "Occasion" celebrated 364 times a year in Carroll's "Through the Looking Glass"
12 "The First ___" (carol)
13 "South Park" boy
21 Leading by a single point
22 ___ Rizzo, hustler in "Midnight Cowboy"
25 Cheesy snack
26 French "to have"
27 Tough puzzle
29 Accepting destiny
32 Mi-mi-re-re-do, in a children's song
33 College accommodations
35 Got full, say
37 How a smartphone knows where it is, for short

38 De-squeak
40 So-called "architect of India"
41 TV programming filter
46 Option with a trash can icon
48 Making ___
51 Host's task, informally
52 Something to bend over backward for
54 Athlete's leg problem
55 West Virginia resource
56 Gymnast Korbut
57 Bigheaded
58 Actor Sharif
59 Scandinavian capital founded in the mid-11th century
60 Enemies

by Jake Halperin

ACROSS

1 Stitches
5 Old workplace sitcom with Danny DeVito as a dispatcher
9 Flashy effect
14 Honolulu's island
15 "Terrible" Russian despot
16 Many a New Year's resolution prescribes getting into it
17 Not strict adherence to what really happened, say
20 Convenience at a business that doesn't take credit cards
21 Confirmed the flavor of
22 Biblical garden
23 Surefire winner
25 Bewhiskered river swimmer
27 Touched down
29 "Be that as it may . . ."
33 When a fresh factory crew arrives
38 Singer Yoko
39 Elusive Tupperware components, often
40 Air quality watchdog created by the Nixon admin.
41 Norway's capital
42 Web address
43 Archipelago forming the southernmost part of the continental U.S.
47 Gloomy pal of Winnie-the-Pooh
49 Auditioner's goal
50 Newborn horses
53 Run for a long football pass
57 Singer Edith known as "The Little Sparrow"
60 Disappear
62 "Despicable Me" character voiced by Steve Carell
63 Member of an N.F.L. team transplanted to Los Angeles in 2017
66 "Could you, would you, with ___?" (Dr. Seuss line)
67 Black-and-white Nabisco cookie
68 Medics
69 Annual awards . . . like the one actor Shalhoub won in 2018
70 Fret (over)
71 Poker buy-in

DOWN

1 Fizzy drinks
2 Our planet
3 Company that makes Frisbees
4 Redundant word in front of "total"
5 Passenger ship in a 1912 calamity
6 Hertz rival
7 Hobbyist's knife brand
8 Cove
9 PC panic button
10 Upbeat
11 Touch down
12 Church recess
13 Someone who is not yet 20
18 Leaning
19 Canine collar dangler
24 Lummoxes
26 WSW's opposite
28 Letter you don't pronounce in "jeopardy" and "leopard"
30 Garden waterer
31 "It's ___ a matter of time"
32 Pursues romantically
33 Swivel around
34 Add to the payroll
35 Without really thinking
36 Mo. for fools and showers
37 Hair removal cream brand
41 Approved
43 To and ___
44 Order to party crashers
45 Annual Westminster event
46 Hawaiian greeting
48 Time of lackluster performance
51 Largest city and former capital of Nigeria
52 Derisive laugh sound
54 Prod
55 Standing upright
56 Where the endings of 17-, 33-, 43- and 63-Across are often found
57 Exam for sophs. or jrs.
58 "Othello" villain
59 In a little while
61 Drink that can cause brain freeze
64 "___ never too late to learn"
65 Abbr. on old vitamin bottles

by Brad Wilber

4 EASY

ACROSS

1 Simba's mate in 23-Down
5 Snoozefest
9 Not fully open
13 First mate?
14 "Runnin'" college team
15 "Call me the greatest!"
16 56-Across, roughly translated
18 Where to have your hair done
19 Song that opens and closes 23-Down and whose title is literally described in this puzzle's center
21 Fully
24 West Coast air hub, for short
25 Bastille Day season
26 "Can't be"
27 "Put a tiger in your tank" gas brand
30 Greek group that's not in Greece
32 Tries to lose some pounds
34 Actress Fanning
36 Seasoning that can lead to high blood pressure
39 Misfortunes
40 Show again
41 One who's looking
42 Only continent larger than Africa
43 Radio band options
44 Repeated "Survivor" setting
45 Globes
47 QB tackle
49 Slip-___ (shoes)
50 Dominate
52 Dug in, in a way
54 Enthusiastic
56 Song from 23-Down
60 Getting long in the tooth
61 23-Down setting
65 Gentrification raises them
66 Spill the beans
67 The "E" in HOMES
68 Best Picture winner based on events of 1979–80
69 College that awarded the first Ph.D. in the U.S.
70 23-Down villain

DOWN

1 One of the Bobbseys, in children's literature
2 Big fuss
3 Martial ___
4 1998 BP purchase
5 Pack animals
6 Suffix with hypn-
7 List quickly, with "off"
8 Valuable Scrabble tiles
9 ___ Sea (almost dried-up body)
10 Director of 23-Down on Broadway
11 Overhead
12 Fleming at the Met
15 Supports
17 Bar mitzvahs and the like
20 Job seeker's success
21 Neighbor of Nepal
22 Tough as ___
23 Disney movie released in June 1994
28 Appear to be
29 Five Norwegian kings
31 Not at the dock, say
33 Russian Revolution target
35 Bean type
37 British singer Lewis with the 2008 #1 album "Spirit"
38 It's worthless
40 Dreaded one?
44 Need for doing toe loops
46 Forehead covering
48 Baby rocker
50 2015 Tony winner Kelli ___
51 Bet
53 Evacuate
55 Long-eared lagomorphs
57 "Do ___ others as . . ."
58 Word after Bay or gray
59 Part of a cash register
62 Tolkien monster
63 Org. behind the Bay of Pigs invasion
64 Lead-in to plop

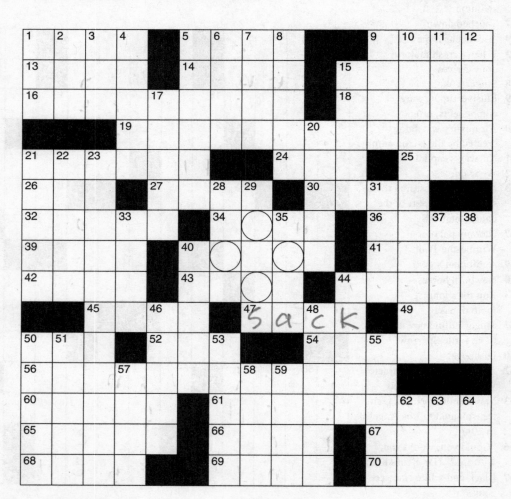

by David J. Kahn

ACROSS

1 Benchwarmer
6 Shut loudly
10 Calendar units: Abbr.
13 Dried plums
15 Part of a brain or a 59-Down
16 Cry at a fireworks show
17 Beach outing, say
19 Hit CBS forensics series
20 Movie filming locale
21 Merchandise
22 TV studio alert
24 Ice cream drink
25 Engender, as suspicion
26 High point of winter?
29 Sound of ice cream hitting the floor
31 On easy street
35 Raw metals
36 + or – particle
37 Stick in one's ___
39 Financially afloat again
44 Adds to the payroll
45 Comics' goals
46 Mother of Calcutta
49 Nota ___
50 Mobile app's clientele
51 Sweeping stories
53 Cry at a fireworks show
56 Instagram upload, informally
57 Traffic helicopter, e.g.
60 "Four score and seven years ___ . . ."
61 Landlord's due
62 Partner of "signed" and "delivered" in a Stevie Wonder hit
63 Anderson Cooper's channel
64 Utters
65 Wear down

DOWN

1 Coppertone stats, for short
2 Mötley ___
3 Peewee
4 Prefix meaning "one"
5 Most widely spoken native language of India, after Hindi
6 Toboggan, e.g.
7 L's meaning, in box scores
8 Aladdin's monkey sidekick
9 Hanukkah display
10 Asian gambling mecca
11 Refuge in the desert
12 Suffix in many English county names
14 Like a thief's loot
18 Like a thief's loot, slangily
23 "Beats me!"
24 Dutch artist known for his "impossible" drawings
25 Gore and Capone, for two
26 "I think," in textspeak
27 Low-___ diet
28 Brainchild
29 Drinks not meant to be savored
30 Phnom ___ (capital of Cambodia)
32 Fork prong
33 RuPaul's purview
34 A pop
38 Calendar units: Abbr.
40 Pieholes
41 Savings plan, for short
42 Votes into office
43 Gaelic spirit who wails to foretell a death in the family
46 Rapper Shakur
47 Provide one's digital John Hancock
48 Military info-gathering
49 Recycling receptacle
51 ___-weeny (small)
52 Very bad, with "the"
53 Nobel Peace Prize city
54 Ratified, for short
55 Jekyll's bad side
58 Senate assent
59 Place for a stud or a ring

by Erik Agard and Yacob Yonas

ACROSS

1 Science class adjuncts
5 Tyrannical
10 Losing casino roll
14 Double-apostrophe contraction
15 Tough watchdog
16 Old Italian capital
17 Autobiography of a "Star Trek" doctor?
19 Mental flash
20 Afternoon affair
21 Rib
22 Audre Lorde or Lord Byron
23 Kill off a major "Back to the Future" character?
27 Neighbor of Borneo
28 Zero
29 Pal for Pierre
30 Mates for does
33 Birthstone for some Scorpios
37 Typesetter's choice
39 Attach, as a button
41 Languish
42 English class assignment
44 Part of a baker's dozen
46 It might sit on a sill to cool
47 Brand of cooking spray
49 Lament about one's sorry appearance
51 Film star Danny hurriedly leaving the set?
56 Mayberry sot
57 Bemoan
58 Medit. country
59 Something to watch on the telly, with "the"
60 Help film star Steve recover from an action sequence?
65 Marine menace
66 Man in a cast
67 After-Christmas event
68 Bleacher feature
69 Impetuous
70 Give off

DOWN

1 Justin Trudeau's party: Abbr.
2 End of a sweet drink?
3 Niacin and riboflavin
4 Five Nations tribe
5 Lunch meat
6 Org. associated with the Westminster show
7 "___ and the Flash" (2015 Meryl Streep movie)
8 Stone-faced
9 New York's ___ Planetarium
10 Bygone street sound
11 No longer plagued by
12 Spinning
13 Like some fertilizer
18 Singer Brooks
23 Jumbo combatants
24 Some "traditional" investments, for short
25 Got along
26 Sch. on the bank of the Charles
27 Unlikely to cause controversy
31 Number of words in the shortest verse in the Bible (John 11:35)
32 Kind of boom
34 Wildly improbable goal
35 Ouzo flavor
36 Scrabble 10-pointers
38 Restaurant with small dishes
40 Like an arm that's been slept on too long
43 Pilot's problem
45 ___ Aziz, Iraq War figure
48 Singer Carey
50 Improper application
51 Unpaid factory worker
52 Wombs
53 Family girl
54 New Mexico's state flower
55 Assembles
61 "Bon" word
62 Show sorrow
63 ___ Lilly & Co.
64 Stocking material

by Jeff Stillman

ACROSS

1 Talks with a gravelly voice
6 Fastener with a twist
11 Brevity is said to be the soul of it
14 Sir John of London
15 Not get caught by, as a pursuer
16 Patient's insurance option, for short
17 "Affliction" suffered by Fab Four devotees
19 "The Simpsons" storekeeper
20 ___ stage left
21 Prefix with air or afternoon
22 Big person on the small screen
24 Prince Charles's onetime partner, affectionately
26 Removes from nursing, as a foal
27 "Affliction" suffered by bracketologists
32 Child, legally speaking
35 Villain's retreat
36 Quartet minus one
37 Has left the office
38 Triage locales, for short
39 Enjoy the taste of
40 Move like a butterfly
41 Green stone popular in Chinese craftwork
42 Woods who voiced Cinderella
43 "Affliction" suffered by clothes lovers
46 Track-and-field competitions
47 Insinuates
51 Person with a chrome dome
52 Cow's sound
54 "Gone With the Wind" plantation
55 Atty.'s org.
56 "Affliction" suffered by the winter-weary
59 Big part of a T. rex

60 What diamonds and straight-A students do
61 Gown
62 Commercials
63 Japanese port of 2+ million
64 "Same here"

DOWN

1 One in revolt
2 Amazon Echo persona
3 Reserved in manner
4 Spewing naughty language, as a child
5 Weekly show with a cold open, for short
6 Vehicle that can jackknife
7 Attired
8 Go for elected office
9 Tussle between wiki page modifiers
10 Bobbed and ___
11 "Well, I never!"
12 Fill with zeal
13 P.G.A. ___
18 Kuwaiti leader
23 Mail addressed to the North Pole
25 Missile aimed at a bull's-eye
28 Off drugs
29 The fourth letter of "circle," but not the first
30 Scrooge
31 Achy
32 Make peeved
33 Capital of Pakistan
34 Peace-and-quiet ordinances
39 Small, medium or large
41 Brooklyn's St. ___ College
44 "Quite correct"
45 Wide-eyed
48 Placed money in the bank
49 "Am not!" comeback
50 Ankle bones
51 ___ California
52 Stole fur
53 Prime draft status
57 Narrow waterway
58 Agcy. overseeing Rx's

by Ross Trudeau

Note: When this puzzle is done, read the dotted letters line by line from top to bottom to spell a title related to this puzzle's theme.

ACROSS

1 Book of the Bible after John
5 Like some high-end cigars
10 ___ vu
14 Russian rejection
15 Like about 60% of the world's population
16 Daredevil Knievel
17 Org. for the New York Cosmos
18 Alternative to a hedge
19 Answer to "Shall we?"
20 "Come in!"
22 Prez before J.F.K.
23 Bygone car model named for a horse
24 Technique employed in the painting hidden in this puzzle
27 What's far from fair?
29 ___ Fighters (rock band)
30 Counterpart of long.
31 One side of Niagara Falls: Abbr.
34 Had as a customer
36 Dijon darling
38 "Star Trek: T.N.G." character with empathic abilities
39 Bump up in pay
43 Impart
44 $15/hour and others
46 Suffix with elephant
47 Got ready to be photographed
48 Takes too much, in brief
49 What a Heisman winner might hope to become
52 "Le Comte ___" (Rossini opera)
53 Weaving machine
54 First small bit of progress
56 Artist who created the painting hidden in this puzzle
61 Crime scene clue
62 Rapa ___ (Easter Island)
63 Willem of "The Grand Budapest Hotel"
65 Tower-building game
66 ___ Radio Hour (NPR program)
67 Egg shell?
68 "Awesome!"
69 French religious title: Abbr.
70 Specialty

DOWN

1 Green Gables girl
2 Ink cartridge color
3 Aviators trying out new planes
4 Pope who negotiated with Attila the Hun
5 Half-___ (coffee order)
6 Did, once upon a time
7 Dot on a Hindu woman's forehead
8 Smallish battery
9 Fla.-to-Me. direction
10 Cold cut purveyors
11 With still greater intensity
12 Rocker Joan
13 Plus
21 Falling-out
23 Essential part
25 Koh-i-___ diamond
26 Doily material
27 Elroy's dog on "The Jetsons"
28 Missile detection org.
32 Forty-___ (old prospector)
33 All-in-one undergarment
35 Game cube
37 Chess rating system
40 Minor maladies
41 Counterparts of outs
42 Save for later
45 Dismiss with derision
47 Self-satisfied about
50 Harbor hazard
51 Took in some takeout, say
53 What the French pronounce "Louis" with that the English do not
55 "Well done!"
56 Increased
57 German article
58 Plum pudding ingredient
59 Beyond the horizon
60 Civil wrong
61 Cover of night?
64 Hurricane's center

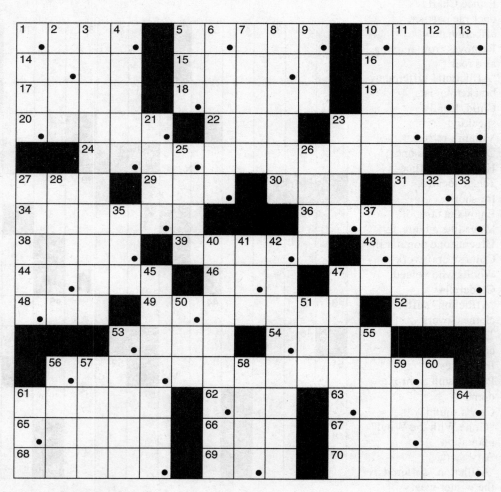

by Alex Eaton-Salners

ACROSS

1 Many flat screens
6 "Red, white and blue" land, for short
11 Zero, in soccer scores
14 Quintet followed by ". . . and sometimes Y"
15 Absolute minimum
16 Rocks sent to a refinery
17 Devil-may-care
19 Piece of lawn
20 Actor Guinness of "Star Wars"
21 Fashion line?
22 Summer romance, perhaps
24 Town crier's cry
28 Diamond great Ripken
31 Gives a red card, in short
32 Lerner's partner on Broadway
33 Carne ___ (burrito filler)
35 Broadband letters
36 Touch
39 Bar request . . . or hint to the letters in the circles
43 German auto sold mainly in Europe
44 Reaction to a body blow
45 Latches (onto)
46 Élan
48 Offering from Hertz or National
50 Message-spewing program
51 Rock drummer whose last name is the same as his band
55 Gift recipient
56 Eggs for fertilization
57 Petri dish medium
61 Hour after midnight
62 Accessing, as a password-restricted website
66 Race, as an engine
67 Pick up the tab for
68 Be of use
69 Slice of time
70 Dark wood
71 Midler of "Beaches"

DOWN

1 ___ funny (genuinely humorous)
2 "You're on!"
3 Goodyear product
4 Give personal assurance (for)
5 Total
6 Belly aches?
7 Run-down
8 Crew blade
9 The Seminoles of the A.C.C.
10 Charge to get cash from a bank, say
11 "Absolutely, positively not!"
12 Humor with a twist
13 Overhang
18 Basketball's O'Neal, informally
23 Permissible
25 Dutch cheese town
26 Disney snow queen
27 Wrestling maneuver
28 G.I. garb, for short
29 "Hurry!," on an order
30 Body of water between France and Switzerland
34 Of the highest quality
35 ___ Jam records
37 Falsetto-voiced Muppet
38 For fear that
40 Wee bit
41 Lunchtime, often
42 Fairy tale villain
47 Gracefully thin
48 Cause for a dental filling
49 Computer science pioneer Turing
51 Love to pieces
52 Recluse
53 Paul who played Crocodile Dundee
54 Easily fooled
58 Flying pest
59 Going ___ (fighting)
60 Part in a movie
63 Space ball
64 Nat ___ Wild (cable channel)
65 Yammer

by Damon Gulczynski

ACROSS

1 Starting players
6 Any classic vinyl record
11 On the ___ (fleeing)
14 Crown for Miss America
15 Satellite signals
16 ___ Jima
17 Actor with the same initials as Michael Rezendes, his role in "Spotlight"
19 Nuke
20 Sloth, for example
21 Have a go at
22 Put in a tandoor
23 ___ Mahal
26 Citrus garnish in a mixed drink
28 Used a riflescope, say
29 For fun
31 See 49-Across
33 Graphic representation of history
35 Fake ID user, often
36 Fruity drinks
37 Image on the back of a dime
39 Cell messenger
41 Serpentine letter
42 Strong string
43 Floating mass in the North Atlantic
45 Eye woe
47 Regularness
49 With 31-Across, actor with the same initials as Alfred Hitchcock, his role in "Hitchcock"
52 Performer with a baton
53 Construction girder
54 Didn't do takeout at a restaurant
56 Altar promise
57 Like lumber
58 Subj. involving telescopes or microscopes
59 Army NCO
61 Grassy field
62 Actor with the same initials as Jake Blues, his role in "The Blues Brothers"
67 Do the wrong thing

68 Fall bloom
69 Set of moral principles
70 Former fast jet, in brief
71 ___ nova (Brazilian music style)
72 "So I was wrong"

DOWN

1 It's stuffed with dough
2 Acapulco aunt
3 Musical sense
4 Temple cabinets
5 ___ status (survey information)
6 Not working
7 Southpaw punches
8 Lack
9 How doodles are generally drawn
10 What that is, in Tijuana

11 Actress with the same initials as Linda Marolla, her role in "Arthur"
12 Come to
13 Relatives of scooters
18 Oral only
22 Establishment that might have a lot of hogs in front
23 "Cheerio!"
24 Parenthetical comment
25 Actor with the same initials as Jefferson Smith, his role in "Mr. Smith Goes To Washington"
27 "You don't have to tell me"
28 Lummox
30 Symbol above the comma on a keyboard
32 Else

34 "___ go bragh!"
38 $100 bill, in slang
40 Took a parabolic path
44 Greek sandwich
46 ___ Kippur
48 Is sociable at a party
49 A wide-body plane has two of them
50 Cavs and Mavs, for example
51 Billionaires' vessels
55 Fork prongs
58 Mediocre
60 Ballerina's skirt
62 Quick punch
63 Bikini top
64 That woman
65 That man
66 Rink surface

by Peter Gordon

ACROSS

1 Al who created Li'l Abner
5 Chatting online, in brief
10 Almost any offer that's too good to be true
14 Doozy
15 "I swear!"
16 Robe in old Rome
17 The "A" of U.A.E.
18 *Basketball position for Magic Johnson or Steph Curry
20 *Level on the military wage scale
22 Player in front of a net
23 What sailors and beachgoers breathe
24 Uncouth person
25 Colorado summer hrs.
26 *Alternative to a brush when coating the side of a house
30 Things coiled on the sides of houses
33 With 44-Across, onetime British slapstick comic
34 Single-stranded genetic molecule
35 ___ and crafts
36 Consumer products giant, for short . . . or a hint to the answers to the eight starred clues
37 Tylenol target
38 "You got it now?"
39 Toyota hybrid
40 North Pole resident
41 *The Beach Boys or Backstreet Boys
43 Amusement
44 See 33-Across
45 Marx's collaborator on "The Communist Manifesto"
49 ___ Field, former home of the Seattle Mariners
52 *Shade akin to olive
54 *Sorority types who go out a lot
56 Eugene O'Neill's "___ Christie"
57 Help with a crime
58 Letter-shaped fastener

59 "Veni, ___, vici"
60 Hellmann's product, informally
61 Daytime or Primetime awards
62 Holler

DOWN

1 Applauds
2 Enveloping glows, old-style
3 ___ del Rey, Calif.
4 *Darts and snooker
5 Somewhat
6 An emoji may suggest it
7 1970s tennis champ Nastase
8 Writer Anaïs
9 Dig into work
10 E. B. White's "___ Little"

11 Unwanted stocking stuffer
12 Prefix with cultural
13 Prepared, as dinner or a bed
19 Foolish, informally
21 Frees (of)
24 Marching halftime crews
26 Fence in
27 Mom's mom, for short
28 The "U" of I.C.U.
29 Mom's mom
30 Lock securer
31 ___ O's (breakfast cereal)
32 One of 12 in Alcoholics Anonymous
33 Oksana ___, 1994 Olympic skating wonder
36 What may precede Chapter 1 in a novel
37 *Roast accompaniment prepared with drippings

39 $$$$, on Yelp
40 Like choir music
42 Run-down area
43 Lavish meals
46 Counting-off word
47 1980s tennis champ Ivan
48 Creature that leaves a slimy trail
49 What an email filter filters
50 Rhyme scheme for Robert Frost's "Stopping by Woods on a Snowy Evening"
51 Glenn of the Eagles
52 School event with a king and a queen
53 "For Better or for Worse" mom
55 Company that pioneered the U.P.C. bar code

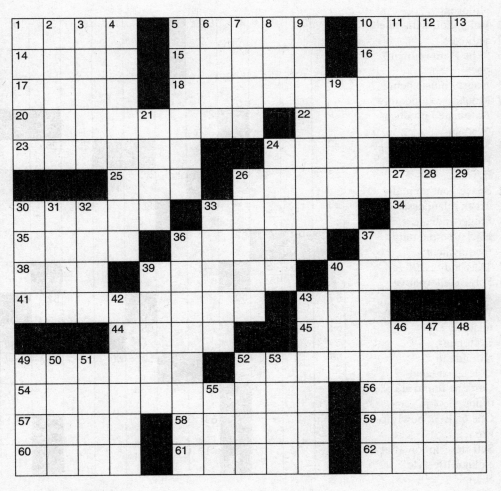

by Ned White

ACROSS

1 So far
6 Jazz style
11 Not an exact amount: Abbr.
14 Note from a 6-Down that might give you jitters
15 Plains tribe
16 To the ___ degree
17 Experience, redundantly
19 Opus ___
20 Prefix with tourism
21 Come after
22 "Victory is mine!"
23 Like some telephones and tires
25 Snitch, redundantly
28 Novelist Morrison
29 Dark force, in Chinese philosophy
32 Hoi polloi, with "the"
33 Smidgen
35 "The Highwayman" poet
37 Angsty music genre
38 Moolah, redundantly
41 Automated producer of spam
44 5/8/1945
45 Popeye's creator E. C. ___
49 Spaced out mentally
51 Track relentlessly
53 Singer India.___
54 Hack, redundantly
56 F equivalent
58 "Anybody ___?"
59 Folgers alternative
62 A/C meas.
63 Word in brackets after a mistake
64 Cottontail, redundantly
67 Get ___ on (ace)
68 Can't be found at the office
69 One of 10 in bowling
70 Pro ___
71 Self-description after a major lifestyle change
72 Exhorted

DOWN

1 Different sides to observe
2 Ship's galley worker
3 "Give me a simple answer!"
4 911 responder, for short
5 Giggle
6 Head honcho
7 Question to a backstabber
8 Rude person in the bleachers
9 Contraction sung twice in the first verse of "The Star-Spangled Banner"
10 College subj. that covers Freud
11 How train cars are linked
12 Feminist Gloria
13 "Really?"
18 ___ 500
22 Hypotheticals
24 The "D" of D.J.
26 "You got that right!"
27 Shocks, in a way
30 How many TV shows are viewed nowadays
31 Wanderer
34 Pandemonium
36 Quickly change one's mind back and forth
39 Video game giant
40 "You got that right!"
41 Goes for, as when bobbing for apples
42 Like laundry being dried outdoors
43 Subject of an I.R.S. consumer warning
46 Potpourri
47 Broadcast slot
48 Said (to be)
50 Shakespearean cry before "What, are you mad?"
52 One of 10 in a ten-speed
55 At this point
57 Problem that has ballooned
60 E pluribus ___
61 Memory unit
64 Recycling container
65 Not let go to waste
66 "I'm f-f-freezing!"

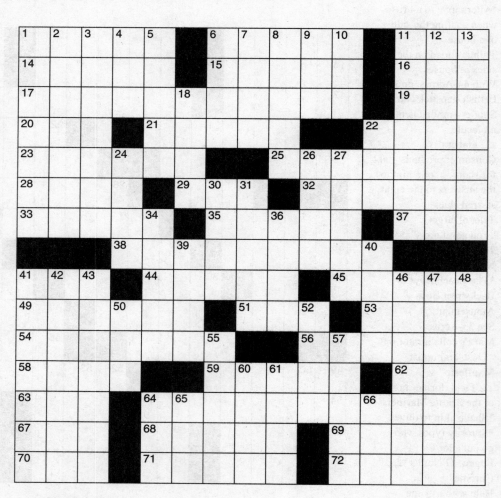

by Bruce Haight

ACROSS

1 Cow's newborn
5 Upbeat, as an outlook
9 SWAT team actions
14 Singer India.___
15 Aunt Bee's charge on "The Andy Griffith Show"
16 Disney attraction in Florida
17 Trendy terms
19 Ragú rival
20 Palestinian territory bordering Israel
21 Busybody, from the Yiddish
23 ___ Dhabi, part of the United Arab Emirates
24 Most unspoiled
26 First host of "America's Funniest Home Videos"
28 "Haste makes waste" and similar sayings
30 "Venerable" monk of the Middle Ages
31 "Able ___ I ere I saw Elba"
32 Ship's wastewater
35 State led by Lenin, in brief
36 Magical powder in "Peter Pan"
39 "I do solemnly swear . . . ," e.g.
42 Browned bread
43 "Fee, fi, fo, ___"
46 Stick back in the microwave
49 Going from two lanes to one
51 Style of collarless shirt
54 ___ Pieces (candy)
55 Nonkosher meat
56 Say "Nyah, nyah," say
58 Snow queen in "Frozen"
59 To any degree
61 Timesavers . . . or the starts of 17-, 26-, 36- and 51-Across?
64 Scalawag
65 Peace Nobelist Wiesel
66 Length × width, for a rectangle
67 Opening golf shot
68 Pepsi, for one
69 Hang in the balance

DOWN

1 Taxi
2 Peppery salad green
3 Chameleons, e.g.
4 Some Moroccan headwear
5 Aussie marsupial, in brief
6 Grand Ole ___
7 Lesser-played half of a 45
8 Like some straightforward questions
9 Meal
10 Its showers bring May flowers: Abbr.
11 Periods with the largest glaciers
12 Places for pooped pooches
13 Having a heavier build
18 Sushi bar condiment
22 Atlanta-based channel
24 Sound effect on "Batman"
25 Candy bar packaged in twos
27 Touch geographically
29 Open with a letter opener
33 Prefix with cache
34 Cheese from the Netherlands
36 "Glad that's over!"
37 Addict
38 Word before map or smarts
39 Apple production site
40 Aquarium accessory
41 Biblical group bearing gifts
43 Opening, as after an earthquake
44 Like leftovers
45 British sports cars of old
47 "Crouching Tiger, Hidden Dragon" director
48 ___ Aviv
50 Tablet alternative
52 Trig ratio
53 Mexican artist Frida
57 Hard labor
60 Sentiment on a candy heart
62 Stephen of "The Crying Game"
63 Unhappy

by Ed Sessa

ACROSS

1 Start of an incantation
6 Up to the task
10 Landlocked Asian country
11 DuVernay who directed "Selma"
13 One with a feather duster, maybe
14 'Vette option
15 Speedy Amtrak option
17 Yours, in Tours
18 Grp. that combats smuggling
19 Land made for you and me, in a Woody Guthrie song
21 Demo material for Wile E. Coyote
22 Entertained with a story, say
24 Print media revenue source
26 Copenhageners, e.g.
28 Oasis beast
29 Lawn game banned in 1988
30 In the manner of
32 ___ Amidala, "Star Wars" queen
34 "___ quote . . ."
35 Oakland's Oracle, for one
37 Diez minus siete
38 Born
39 Insect feeler
41 The "e" of i.e.
42 The Kennedys or the Bushes, so to speak
44 As a group
46 Country singer ___ James Decker
47 Very wee
48 Embarrassing fall
52 Structures illustrated twice in this puzzle through both black squares and letters
58 Male buds
59 Nae Nae or cancan
60 Captain who circumnavigated the globe
61 Flue buildup
62 "Come in!"
63 Influence

DOWN

1 Setting for a classical sacrifice
2 Flinched
3 Adjuncts to some penthouses
4 Nile viper
5 State as fact
6 Org. for docs
7 Military field uniform
8 World's highest-paid athlete in 2019, per Forbes magazine
9 Drops (or adds) a line
11 Got 100 on
12 Et ___
15 Iowa college town
16 "Hells Bells" band
19 Bottles that might be marked "XXX" in the comics
20 "Stat!"
23 Not pro
25 Amo, amas, ___
27 Sheltered at sea
29 Maker of "No more tears" baby shampoo, for short
30 Pretentious
31 Hathaway of Hollywood
33 Alternative to Chanel No. 5
35 Predate
36 Glassworker, at times
39 "Take me ___"
40 Modify
43 Equally speedy
45 Shenanigans
49 Abba of Israel
50 Fourth-and-long option
51 Subject of a school nurse's inspection
52 Targets of plank exercises
53 Do that might block someone's view, for short
54 Pooh's pal
55 When repeated, calming expression
56 Smallest state in India
57 Wild blue yonder

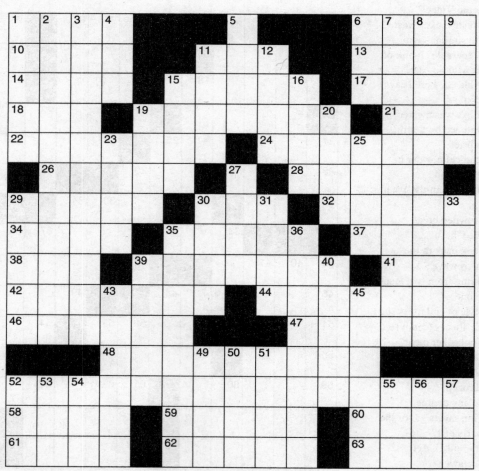

by Ross Trudeau

ACROSS

1 Mushroom part
4 ___ Xing (road sign)
8 Managed to avoid
14 South America's Carnaval city, informally
15 Not doing anything
16 Baltimore bird
17 Psychic ability, in brief
18 Yard event to clear out the attic
20 Manage to avoid
22 Big coffee holder
23 Applaud
24 Louisiana's avian nickname
28 Giant in health insurance
29 Mortal dangers
33 "Phooey!"
35 Commotions
38 Provide with continuing funds
39 Athlete who said "Silence is golden when you can't think of a good answer"
40 Strong-smelling cheese made in England
42 Investment for the golden yrs.
43 Cook's workspace
45 Enroll for another year of duty
46 Work by Wordsworth or Whitman
47 Coughed (up)
49 Ledger entry on the minus side
51 One barely in the water?
56 German carmaker
59 ___ Paulo, Brazil
60 Big name in mattresses
61 Fairy tale question whose answer is spelled out in the starts of 18-, 24-, 40- and 51-Across
65 Fast asleep
66 Mythical beauty who lent her name to a continent
67 Oil producers' grp.

68 "___ to Joy"
69 Singer/songwriter Crow
70 Shipped
71 Gave a meal to

DOWN

1 Slimeball
2 Supermarket section
3 China's is around 1.4 billion
4 Without stopping en route
5 Part of a campus URL
6 "Slippery" tree
7 Co-founder of Rome with Romulus
8 Run off with a boxer, maybe?

9 Gold waiting to be discovered
10 Recognize, as differences
11 Objective for a soccer player
12 Fitzgerald of jazz
13 Profound
19 The "A" of MoMA
21 Conks out
25 Med school subj.
26 Low point
27 Juliet Capulet or Holden Caulfield, agewise
30 Impossible to mess up
31 Set of traditional beliefs
32 Got one's kicks at the pool?
33 Hoarse voice
34 Voice above tenor
36 Grand ___ Opry

37 Prepare for a hard test
40 Search for
41 Coup for a newspaper freelancer
44 Someone dropping by
46 Something that might spring a leak
48 Dreary
50 Cut in half
52 Vote that cancels out a yea
53 Unacceptable actions
54 Musical practice piece
55 Given a PG-13, say
56 Bowls over
57 Thumbs-down response
58 Show gumption
62 Someone not likely to show off intelligence?
63 "Great" hominid
64 Word on a restroom door

by Lynn Lempel

ACROSS

1 Missing school
7 Cousin of a lark
14 Nonsense word repeated in Stephen Foster's "Camptown Races"
15 Literally, "empty orchestra"
16 "Spare me your lame reasons!"
18 Home of Wall St. and Fifth Ave.
19 "Chicago ___" (NBC drama)
20 With 24-Across, food coloring in Twizzlers
21 Compound with a fruity scent
24 See 20-Across
26 Roman emperor who wrote "Meditations"
32 Waiting for a pitch
33 Siesta, e.g.
34 Michael of "Weekend Update" on "S.N.L."
35 Pull an all-nighter
36 Expand
38 Giggle
39 Be laid up in bed
40 Call to a lamb
41 Garden plant also called stonecrop
42 Facial hair for Sam Elliott and Wilford Brimley
46 Equipment hauled by a roadie
47 Course covering axons and dendrites, for short
48 Maple product
50 Chinese zodiac creature for 2019
51 Consumer safety org.
54 1981 hit with the lyric "We can make it if we try" . . . or a possible title for this puzzle
59 So far
60 Getting some shut-eye
61 Composer Bizet
62 Alternatives to Ho Hos

DOWN

1 Mideast's Gulf of ___
2 Squarish
3 Necessity for achieving one's goals?
4 Ending with "umich." or "upenn."
5 Rapper Lil ___ X
6 Topics for book clubs
7 Slated events, in brief
8 Material for Icarus' wings
9 Circle segment
10 Branch of the Olympics?
11 Misplace
12 Gave the go-ahead
13 Anderson who directed "The Grand Budapest Hotel"
17 "Buona ___" (Italian greeting)
22 Rip-off
23 Famed child ruler, informally
24 Compete in Pictionary
25 "You betcha!"
26 Colorful parrot
27 Some heart chambers
28 Card game with suits of four different colors
29 Caffeinated summer drink
30 "You betcha!"
31 Teacher's note that makes one go [gulp]
36 [Oh. My. God!]
37 Piece of siege equipment
38 Get wind of
40 Wander here and there, with "around"
41 Disco ___ ("The Simpsons" character)
43 Any member of the 2019 N.B.A. championship team
44 Meter or liter
45 Mall cop's transport
48 Apartment building V.I.P., in slang
49 Regarding
50 Benches along an aisle
52 "Hamilton" climax
53 Nile biters
54 Put a cork in it!
55 "Star Trek" spinoff series: Abbr.
56 It's groundbreaking
57 Spanish for "bear"
58 Timeworn

by Kyle Dolan

ACROSS

1 Major uncertainty
6 Canvas for a tattoo
10 Mae who said "I used to be Snow White, but I drifted"
14 "You ___ Beautiful" (Joe Cocker hit)
15 Mexican entree in a shell
16 Large fair, informally
17 Athlete with a mitt
19 Bridle strap
20 Poker stake
21 Bill Clinton's was in the 1990s
22 ___ Haute, Ind.
23 One going for a stroll among urban greenery
26 "Quit wasting time!"
30 Abba of Israel
31 Even a little
32 ___-haw
33 Plumbing woe
37 Official hearing a case
41 Fish that wriggle
42 What's dropped off a cigarette
43 Words of empathy
44 Weights that may be "short" or "long"
46 Tevye's occupation in "Fiddler on the Roof"
48 Herbie Hancock or Chick Corea
52 "Later, amigo!"
53 Employ
54 Bleats
58 William with a state named after him
59 Place where 17-, 23-, 37- and 48-Across might be found
62 Sheltered from the wind
63 Parks in civil rights history
64 Language family of Africa
65 Loch ___ monster
66 "That's enough!"
67 Adventurous journey

DOWN

1 "Ali ___ and the 40 Thieves"
2 Land with an ayatollah
3 Hanukkah "moolah"
4 ___ of Capri
5 Dandyish dresser
6 Van Gogh's "The ___ Night"
7 Boat you might shoot rapids in
8 What a "neat" drink doesn't come with
9 Word paired with "neither"
10 "How fortunate for us!"
11 Apply, as force
12 Former vice president Agnew
13 Printer cartridge contents
18 Meadows
22 Airport screening org.
23 Tug on
24 Turn sharply
25 Skeptic's sarcastic comment
26 Racehorse's starting point
27 Raison d'___
28 Pin the ___ on the donkey
29 Bomb testing areas
32 "Come again?"
34 Semihard Dutch cheese
35 City that's home to the Taj Mahal
36 Sharp-witted
38 "Is it O.K., mom?"
39 Peak near Olympus
40 Leave at the altar
45 Special ___ (military missions)
46 Event that's an "Oops!"
47 "Ah, makes sense"
48 Where Honda and Mazda are headquartered
49 Grammy-winning singer of "Hello"
50 Fan publications, informally
51 Bonkers
54 Lover boy
55 Youngest of the Brontë sisters
56 Things passed in Congress
57 "___ your piehole!"
59 Surgery sites, for short
60 Word after waste and want
61 Cookout, briefly

by Bruce Haight

ACROSS

1 What a coin may go in
5 ___ & Allies (classic board game)
9 Lies lazily in the sun
14 Stun with a gun
15 Brad of "Fight Club"
16 Someone's in the kitchen with her, in an old song
17 Wreck
18 Petty set of procedures
20 Woman who's bid good night in an old song
22 "___, old chap!"
23 "With this ring, I thee ___"
24 Local officials in dioceses
28 Seats in many bars
29 Car
32 Car with a meter
35 Sites of biceps and triceps
36 More cunning
38 With 40-Across, money required to open a business . . . or a hint to 18-, 24-, 47- and 57-Across
40 See 38-Across
41 Permeates
42 Feature of many an old car
43 Cunning
44 Some beans
45 "Here's how experts handle this"
47 Longest-serving Independent member of Congress in U.S. history
53 Vaccine target
55 Greeting in Guatemala
56 Generate by dubious means
57 Part of a Juliet soliloquy
61 Crème ___ crème
62 Juiced (up)
63 Noted terrier in a 1939 film
64 Scott of an 1857 Supreme Court case
65 Inventor with a coil named after him
66 Lead-in to chat or dragon
67 Time long past

DOWN

1 Unit of bacon
2 Actress Linney of "The Truman Show"
3 Common basket-weaving material
4 Something you'll have to go to court for?
5 Financing letters
6 Midnight, on a grandfather clock
7 Edie Sedgwick and Kendall Jenner, for two
8 Condition of inactivity
9 They're almost always shared by twins, informally
10 Televise
11 Winter play outfits
12 Leafy vegetable that can be green or purple
13 Place to store a lawn mower
19 Fannie ___
21 Locale for a manor
25 Falcon-headed Egyptian god
26 Circumstance's partner
27 Car with a meter
30 Blue-green shade
31 Alternative to Charles de Gaulle
32 Some CBS police dramas
33 Prefix with sphere
34 Obvious signs of pregnancy
36 Fruity soda brand
37 Selecting, with "for"
39 Ploy
40 Tops of corp. ladders
42 "That'll never happen!"
45 Ones doing loops and barrel rolls
46 Onetime stage name of Sean Combs
48 "The Mary Tyler Moore Show" spinoff
49 ___'easter
50 Month after diciembre
51 Side of many a protractor
52 Garden tool
53 ___ row (some blocks in a college town)
54 Togolese city on the Gulf of Guinea
58 Fish that can be electric
59 Second letter after epsilon
60 "Alley ___!"

by Christina Iverson

ACROSS

1 Group in a play
5 Plasterwork backing
9 Bracelet securer
14 Arthur with a stadium named after him
15 Feeling fluish, in a way
16 "___ me" ("Go along with it")
17 ___ the Man (old baseball nickname)
18 Be overrun (with)
19 "E" on a gas gauge
20 Pre-snap powwow
22 Garden munchkin
24 "How was ___ know?"
25 2012 Best Picture winner set in Iran
27 Kind of toy that moves when you turn a key
31 Semiaquatic salamanders
33 Flowers on trellises
35 Bill in a tip jar
36 Slangy "sweetheart"
37 Horace, as a poet
38 Barrister's headgear
39 Scrub vigorously
41 Manipulate
42 Littlest ones in litters
44 Contagious viral infection
45 Cross ___ with
47 Side-to-side nautical movement
48 Plural "is"
49 First appearance, as of symptoms
50 Toronto N.H.L. team, for short
53 Common ankle injury
55 Biggest bear in "Goldilocks and the Three Bears"
57 "V for Vendetta" actor Stephen
58 Grind, as teeth
60 Withstands
62 Gemstone measure
65 Chopped down
67 3:1 or 4:1, e.g.
68 Superior beef grade
69 They're mined and refined

70 Large, scholarly book
71 "For ___ waves of grain" (line in "America the Beautiful")
72 Water swirl
73 Elderly

DOWN

1 Redeem, as a savings bond
2 Uncommonly perceptive
3 Air-punching pugilist
4 Manage, as a bar
5 "Ciao"
6 Unreturned tennis serve
7 2006 Matt Damon spy film
8 Song sung on Sunday
9 Place with beakers and Bunsen burners
10 Measure of light's brightness
11 Electric guitar accessory
12 Drunkard
13 Jimmy (open)
21 Lecturer's implement with a light at the end
23 Is indebted to
26 Fills, as tile joints
28 Popular yoga pose . . . or a literal hint to the ends of 3-, 7-, 9- and 21-Down
29 The "U" in I.C.U.
30 Cribbage scorekeepers
32 Letter after sigma
34 Nap south of the border
39 Pampering places
40 Bus. concern
43 Persian Gulf country, for short

46 Actress Kendrick
51 What "woof" or "meow" may mean
52 Talked back to with 'tude
54 Best effort, informally
56 Colorful flower with a "face"
59 Pump or oxford
61 Smidgen
62 Helper during taxing times, for short?
63 Triceps location
64 Poke fun at
66 Marry

by Tracy Gray

ACROSS

1 Means of surveillance, for short
5 Co-conspirator with Brutus and Cassius
10 Banter jokingly
14 "I got it! I got it!"
15 What's standard, with "the"
16 ___ breve
17 Litter noises
18 Bottom coat?
20 Slammer
21 Word before and after "à"
22 Had people over for dinner, say
23 Habitat for a walrus
27 "___ seen worse"
28 Actor Dennis or Randy
29 Sports org. that plays in the winter
30 Co-workers of TV's Don Draper
32 Spending jags
34 Locale of the anvil and stirrup
36 Cincinnati sluggers
37 Its motto, translated from Latin, is "If you wish for peace, prepare for war"
40 Fill with cargo
43 A.M.A. members
44 Messed with, with "around"
48 Avoid the clutches of
50 Early nuclear org.
52 Esther of "Good Times"
53 TV show set in Westeros, for short
54 Drill bit alloy
57 Untouched, as an artifact
59 Slack-jawed emotion
60 Good name for a girl born on December 24?
61 1963 Bobby Vinton hit . . . or a hint to both halves of 18-, 23-, 37- and 54-Across
64 Surgeons' subj.
65 Focusing aid
66 Something to believe in
67 Ballet leap
68 Whence the Three Wise Men, with "the"
69 Defeated by a hair
70 Fired

DOWN

1 Pioneering personal computers
2 "Come on, things aren't so bad"
3 Limousine
4 Bygone kind of tape
5 Like the numbers 8, 27 and 64
6 How one's much-loved nephew might be treated
7 Periscope site
8 Low island
9 Leader of Athens?
10 Thriller set around Amity Island
11 Quaint
12 Like LPs and some dresses
13 Coagulates
19 Actress Chaplin of 53-Across
21 YouTube upload
24 Like wedding cakes, typically
25 Posh neighborhood of London or New York
26 Spirit
31 Problem in an old wooden building
33 Guitarist Barrett
35 British rule over India, once
38 Spirited steed
39 Part of a biblical citation
40 Unlike most physicians' handwriting, stereotypically
41 Home of Anne of Green Gables
42 Old Nissan autos
45 Something that may be used before a blessing
46 Put on a pedestal
47 Struck out
49 Outside: Prefix
51 A dependent one might start with "that"
55 Unit of measure with the same Latin origin as "inch"
56 Jacket material
58 Superlative ending with grass or glass
62 Reprimand to a dog
63 Big galoot
64 Best-selling Steely Dan album

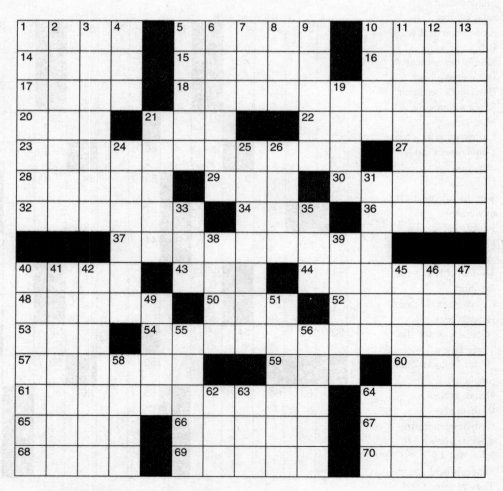

by Jon Olsen

ACROSS

1 Snake charmer's snake
6 Pushy
11 Coquettishly playful
14 First zodiac sign
15 Highway
16 Network of medical providers, in brief
17 Country bumpkin's counterpart
19 Oil-drilling apparatus
20 Weed-whacking tool
21 Assists
22 Prius maker
24 Following
26 From Shanghai or Mumbai, say
27 Woman having literary interests
31 Hosts for roasts
34 Carried the day
35 Corporate head, for short
36 Group choosing a 35-Across
37 Smucker's product
38 Grew ashen
40 Hit on the head
41 Ad exhortation
42 Solitary sorts
43 Pompous person
47 Usually spicy Indian dish
48 Disheveled
52 Lou on six winning World Series teams
54 Soup can painter Warhol
55 Motorists' org.
56 "How __ doing?"
57 Know-it-all
60 Smith & Wesson product
61 Swimming phenom Ledecky
62 Fjord, e.g.
63 He hee-haws
64 Slammin' Sammy of golf
65 King on "CBS This Morning"

DOWN

1 Hidden stash
2 Hunter in the night sky
3 What fishermen want from fish but not from mosquitoes
4 Heroine of "Star Wars: The Last Jedi"
5 Attacked vigorously
6 What you might come across at a river?
7 Fierce fliers of myth
8 Diving bird of the Arctic
9 High, wide-brimmed hat
10 Brave
11 Historical account
12 Skip
13 Hindu-inspired exercise
18 "Peanuts" boy with a security blanket
23 Shaggy Tibetan beast
25 Cab company competitor
26 Elemental bit
28 Persuades
29 __-do-well
30 Mount Olympus residents
31 Subsides
32 No longer relevant
33 Monkeys named for monks
37 Children's writer Blume
38 Looney Tunes character who says "Th-th-th-that's all, folks!"
39 Card game stake
41 Ingmar who directed "The Seventh Seal"
42 Lucky __ (nickname for the Spirit of St. Louis pilot)
44 Taboo for PETA
45 Pats down, as a suspect
46 Pursued, as prey
49 Virile
50 Dev who starred in 2016's "Lion"
51 One of the five senses
52 Infatuated
53 Birds on Australian coins
54 Operatic solo
58 Cleaned one's plate
59 Santa __ winds

by Lynn Lempel

ACROSS

1 French clerics
6 Resource in the Mesabi Range
9 Lacking any tread
13 Florida's Key ___
14 Fruit center
15 Official state sport of Wyoming
16 Forced walk with arms pinned behind the back
18 Relating to element #76
19 Something "lost" in the highest-grossing movie of 1981
20 Precalculator calculators
21 Grace under pressure
22 "Hogwash!"
24 Hit 2000 animated film set on a farm
26 Specialties
28 State with conviction
29 Test, as 6-Across
30 Seriously injure
33 ___ Moines, Iowa
34 Core-strengthening exercise performed on all fours
38 Death on the Nile cause, perhaps
41 Commend
42 Swine
46 Muss, as the hair
49 Young raptor
50 Old ragtime dance
54 Cockney greeting
55 Courtyards
56 Trickled
58 Bit of a draft?
59 Fire department V.I.P.
60 Straight-kneed military movement
62 Any of eight English kings
63 "Barbara ___" (Beach Boys hit)
64 Hunger for
65 Physics units
66 "Get it?"
67 Propelled a boat

DOWN

1 Cattle or horse feed
2 New York's Spanish Harlem and others
3 Employees at Re/Max and Coldwell Banker
4 Bad thing to have on one's face
5 "Brave New World" drug
6 Who said "I'm black. I don't feel burdened by it. . . . It's part of who I am. It does not define me."
7 Christina who played Wednesday Addams
8 Honesty and hard work, e.g.
9 Particles in quantum mechanics
10 Looked up to
11 Sports & ___ (Trivial Pursuit category)
12 Museum guides
15 Borders of boxing rings
17 Some kindergarten instruction
23 Attack as Hamlet did Polonius
25 ___ Sutra
27 Hurricane's center
30 Noninvasive diagnostic procedure, for short
31 One of two in "Waiting for Godot"
32 Ill temper
35 ___-deucey (card game)
36 Org. awarding titles to Mike Tyson and Tyson Fury
37 Balcony section
38 Embassy worker . . . or something that worker might carry
39 Wind that typically brings warmer air
40 Operating smoothly, as an engine
43 Kareem Abdul-Jabbar, for a record 19 times
44 Take over for
45 Clogged (up)
47 Super G competitors
48 Like lettuce, spinach and kale
49 French summers
51 Coverage of senators in ancient Rome?
52 Onetime news exec Arledge
53 O_3
57 Art ___
61 Mme., in Madrid

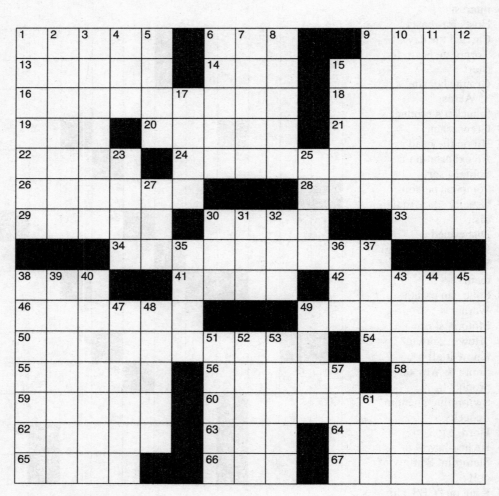

by Bruce Greig

ACROSS

1 Parts missing from the Venus de Milo
5 Ancient Greek market
10 What hairy dogs do in the spring
14 Boyfriend
15 Toilet paper layers, e.g.
16 Architect Saarinen
17 Complain querulously
18 *Monster outsmarted by Odysseus
20 Drivers doing 90, say
22 With mouth wide open
23 Indian queen
24 Tin lizzies
26 *Rat Pack member who sang and danced
30 Parts with irises
31 Actor Morales of "La Bamba"
32 See 39-Across
35 Dawn, to Donne
36 Like clothes in the hamper
38 Servant in "Young Frankenstein"
39 With 32-Across, what the answers to the starred clues each have
40 Brief moments, briefly
41 Frighten
42 *Black face card whose face is seen in profile
45 Indy or Daytona
48 What two fives are change for
49 Cancel at Cape Canaveral
50 "Star Wars Episode IV" subtitle
54 *Comic character on a gum wrapper
57 Satanic
58 Part of a list with bullets
59 Scam
60 Swimmers' units
61 Hawaiian goose
62 "Two mints in one" sloganeer
63 Nolo contendere, e.g.

DOWN

1 Things learned in "The Alphabet Song"
2 Harvest
3 Stallion's mate
4 Hero who's neither a bird nor a plane
5 Tack on
6 Steinem who co-founded Ms. magazine
7 Classic paintings
8 Spanish king
9 Biter of Cleopatra
10 Folk legend Pete
11 Blood-related
12 Blow, as a volcano
13 Amounts in a hypodermic needle
19 Pilgrim to Mecca
21 February has the fewest of them
24 Aerosol spray
25 Start of "The Star-Spangled Banner"
26 Sport originally part of a Shinto ritual
27 Shakespeare's stream
28 Parisian mother
29 Left page in a book
32 "Heavens to Betsy!"
33 Bygone times
34 "___ Tú" (1974 song)
36 Ten: Prefix
37 Highly off-putting
38 "Allow me"
40 Handled, as a task
41 Blow, as from a volcano
42 Saint known for translating the Bible into Latin
43 Spread, as people in a search party
44 The Lone Ranger's Silver and others
45 Former Israeli P.M. Yitzhak
46 Lessen
47 Cheat
50 "When it's ___" (answer to an old riddle)
51 Squished circle
52 Prop for Sherlock Holmes
53 Two-time Oscar-nominated actress Lanchester
55 The Colonel's restaurant
56 "I am, you ___, he is"

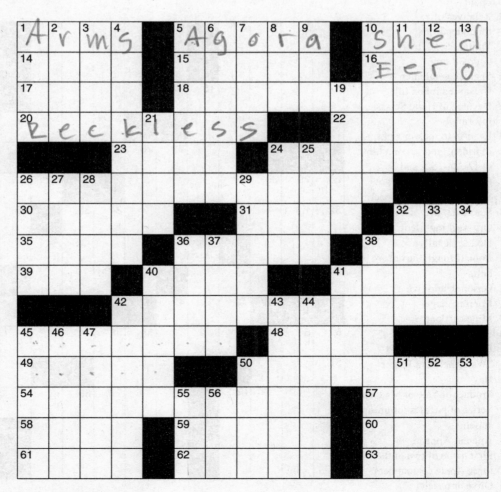

by John R. O'Brien

ACROSS

1 Slightly open
5 Overhead
10 Approximately
14 What you might do to a turtle that's withdrawn into its shell
15 Theater, for a Broadway show
16 Rod's mate
17 Change one's approach
19 Things that bottles and snow-covered mountains have
20 Boredom
21 Societal problems
23 Some do it through their teeth
24 Metallica hit with the lyric "Sleep with one eye open"
28 Relatives of rhododendrons
31 Young friend, to a good ol' boy
32 Spanish gentlemen
33 Unwanted inbox filler
36 Devotee of Haile Selassie, informally
40 Lead-in to rock or right
41 Florida island . . . or a hint to 17-, 24-, 52- and 65-Across
43 Soda brand, or its opener
44 See 53-Down
46 Org. seeking life in space
47 De ___ (legally)
48 Look through the cross hairs
50 Gasoline additive
52 Micromanager
57 Mine cartload
58 Soprano's solo
59 Frank who performed "Watermelon in Easter Hay"
63 Product of Yale or Medeco
65 Series of puzzles for group solving
68 Ancient Andean
69 First name of two of the three Apple co-founders
70 Olive or peach
71 Codger
72 Big name in kitchen appliances
73 Abbr. before a memo recipient's name

DOWN

1 Church recess
2 Loo
3 Similar (to)
4 Makes a pit stop, say
5 Part of G.P.A.: Abbr.
6 Harper who wrote "Go Set a Watchman"
7 TV studio sign
8 Rolls up, as a flag
9 Model S, Model X and Model 3
10 Tolkien monster
11 Ruler's domain
12 Digital photo filter
13 Jimmy of the Daily Planet
18 One of four on a fork, often
22 Derisive sound
25 Zap, in a way
26 Awards show for top athletes
27 Double-helix molecule
28 First among men
29 Émile who wrote "J'accuse"
30 Opposed to
34 Feeling upon meeting an idol
35 Poetic rhythm
37 Zap, in a way
38 ___ chips (trendy snack food)
39 Victim of the first fratricide
41 Actress Knightley
42 Something pinned on a map
45 Singer ___ King Cole
47 Capital of the world's largest island country
49 Beyond that
51 Mental blur
52 Source of a baby's (and parent's) discomfort
53 With 44-Across, home of a major Northeast university
54 Wafer brand
55 Grocery shopping aids
56 Side of a gem
60 Cruise ship stop
61 Keats or Yeats
62 "You said it!"
64 Kit ___ bar
66 "___ Maria"
67 Each

by Carl Worth

ACROSS

1 Radical Hoffman who wrote "Steal This Book"
6 Stimulating quality
10 Huff and puff
14 John who married Pocahontas
15 On the briny
16 Opposite of "on tape"
17 *Garnish for a cocktail
19 Takes advantage of
20 The "A" of A.D.
21 Zipped along
22 Tin Man's desire
23 *Bureaucratic rigmarole
25 Place for drinks
26 *"Closer to Fine" folk-rock duo
32 How some home videos are stored
36 Disney World transport
37 53, in old Rome
38 Father, to Li'l Abner
40 Russian legislature
41 Dole out
43 Bit of land in the ocean
44 *Caution to slow down
47 Very long time
48 What the starts of the answers to the seven starred clues constitute
53 Fountain drinks
56 Letters suggesting "I'll just go ahead and throw this out"
58 Anise-flavored liqueur
59 Taiwanese computer brand
60 *DC Comics superhero with the sidekick Speedy
62 "30 Rock" star Fey
63 Shipwreck site, perhaps
64 Chili con ___
65 Circular water current
66 Exerciser's sets
67 Did a blacksmith's job on

DOWN

1 Loud, as a crowd
2 Carried
3 Flavorless
4 "Otherwise . . ."
5 Hosp. readout
6 Heated in a microwave
7 "Uh-huh"
8 Requirement
9 Cowpoke's sweetie
10 *Symbols of happiness
11 Simpson with a high I.Q.
12 So last year, as a fad
13 Sunset's direction
18 "Monday Night Football" channel
22 Victor who wrote "The Hunchback of Notre Dame"
24 Earthquake relief, e.g.
25 Small equine
27 Louvre Pyramid architect
28 Lincoln was its first successful standard-bearer, for short
29 ___ Julia, actor who played Gomez Addams
30 Tart, green fruit
31 Shutter strip
32 Neutrogena rival
33 Cairo's river
34 It's in a pickle
35 *Antique medical device used for electrotherapy
38 Lowly chess piece
39 Home of the Braves: Abbr.
42 Dove sounds
43 "Lord, is ___?": Matthew 26:22
45 Intense sorrows
46 Actress Goldie
49 "Don't Know Why" singer Jones
50 Beast of burden
51 Layer of the upper atmosphere
52 Superimpressed
53 One sock, to another
54 Gastric ___
55 Supply temporarily
56 They say there's no such thing as this kind of lunch
57 Shed tears
60 Watchdog's warning
61 Cooling units, for short

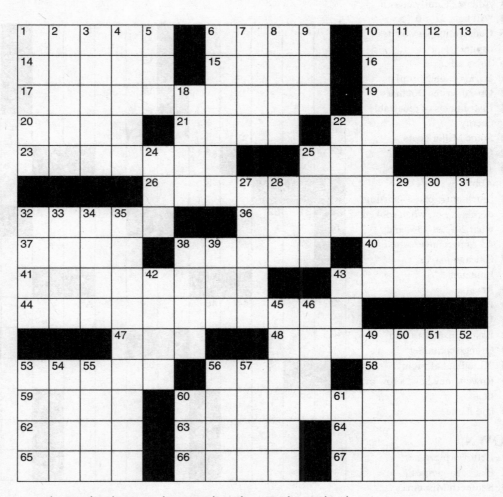

by Michael Wiesenberg and Andrea Carla Michaels

ACROSS

1 Put a cork in
6 "___ pass"
10 Girl-watch or boy-watch
14 Leveled
15 Queens stadium that was 14-Across in 2008–09
16 Recess in a room
17 Prized taste in ramen
18 Rocks whose names often end in "-ite"
19 Feeling sad
20 Part of a fire safety system
23 Critical cluck
24 Wait awhile
25 Dance place that might have a revolving ball overhead
28 Flipped
31 Peter the Great, for one
33 Addams Family cousin
34 "All bets ___ off"
35 Constantinople was its capital
40 Tulsa sch.
41 ___ Ep (college frat)
42 Op-ed writer Douthat
43 Instruments of renewable energy
48 Some Miller beers
49 Egyptian sacred bird
50 1, along the East Coast: Abbr.
53 Much-anticipated sporting events . . . or, when spoken, what 20-, 28-, 35- and 43-Across have?
57 Chicago mayor Emanuel
59 Reverse
60 Pitch-perfect?
61 Edible succulent
62 Easily pushed around
63 Orange container
64 "Good ___ almighty!"
65 Rowers may have a row of them
66 Old flame?

DOWN

1 Leftover pizza part
2 Places for genies
3 Southern Missouri's ___ Mountains
4 Game before the final
5 Pennsylvania university that's home to the Fighting Scots
6 Tristan's love, in legend
7 Loose-leaf sheet holder
8 Creepy look
9 Unit of corporal punishment
10 How a suspect might be released
11 Elementary school honors
12 Reed with a guitar
13 Barely get (by)
21 Most common Korean surname (22%)
22 Alternative to .com
26 Largest object in the asteroid belt
27 Work of Horace
28 Perched (on)
29 ___-Foy, Que.
30 Deposit site, for short
31 Traditional Japanese gate
32 "Don't try this at home" spectacle
36 Spartans of the Big Ten Conf.
37 Precious supply on a spaceship
38 ___ of mind
39 What 46-Down runs on
40 Symbol of wisdom
44 Judged
45 3-1-1 liquids rule enforcer, for short
46 Apple reading app
47 Light bite
50 Help for an addict
51 Like the expressions "a dime a dozen" and "a penny for your thoughts"
52 Ending with poly-
54 Sport conducted in a dohyo
55 Prime draft category
56 Standard
57 Car wash aid
58 Pie ___ mode

by Andrew Zhou

ACROSS

1 Sassy
5 "Ooky" TV family name
11 "___ the Force, Luke"
14 Bell-ringing cosmetics company
15 Cash alternative
16 Pester no end
17 Site of a postrace celebration
19 Yank (on)
20 Caribou kin
21 Without ice, at the bar
22 ___ acid (protein component)
24 Snarling dog
26 Director of "Lawrence of Arabia" and "Doctor Zhivago"
29 Snoopy's comic strip
32 Neighbor of Ben & Jerry's in the freezer section
33 Tolkien language
34 Corporate boss, briefly
35 Salem or Marlboro, slangily
38 Follow one's political group
42 Bro's sibling
43 Still in the shrink-wrap
44 Body of work
45 Does in, in mob slang
47 Military forays
48 Helping hand for a low-income entrepreneur
52 Investigator, in old film noir
53 Common last option on a questionnaire
54 One-third of a hat trick
56 Lightly apply
59 Popularizer of the Chinese tunic suit
60 Classic Debussy work that translates as "Light of the Moon"
64 "I have a dream" orator, for short
65 Shot two under par on
66 Tallest active volcano in Europe
67 "Yes, captain!"
68 Does 50 in a school zone, say
69 Like Easter eggs

DOWN

1 Finish a drive?
2 Fiendish
3 Things spelunkers explore
4 Detonation producer, for short
5 Field measurement
6 Wood nymphs, in myth
7 "Keep climbing" sloganeer
8 Abbr. on toothpaste tubes
9 Max's opposite
10 Like a good surgeon's hands
11 Loosen, as shoelaces
12 Finnish bath
13 Goad
18 Deluge
23 Seattle Sounders' org.
25 Syllabus section
27 Zig or zag
28 "Same here!"
29 Dogs, cats and gerbils
30 "The Time Machine" race
31 Org. featured in 2015's "Concussion"
34 Crow's call
35 Voting or jury service, e.g.
36 About, at the start of a memo
37 Bee ___ ("Night Fever" group)
39 Cuban currency
40 Turtle in a Dr. Seuss title
41 Renaissance stringed instrument
45 Shipment to a smeltery
46 Troops
47 Sawed logs
48 "Throw ___ From the Train" (1987 Danny DeVito comedy)
49 Where the Renaissance began
50 Snatch defeat from the jaws of victory
51 Nimble
55 Puts two and two together, say
57 Name shared by two of Henry VIII's wives
58 Droplet of sweat
61 One of 200 in the Indy 500
62 What the number of birthday candles represents
63 Went first

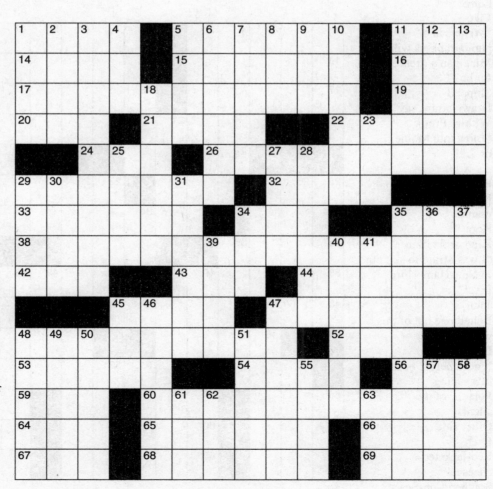

by Andy Kravis

ACROSS

1 Fellows
6 Mystic in a turban
11 Fixer at a horse race?
14 Leader in a turban
15 Less risqué
16 "Black-___" (ABC sitcom)
17 Alternative to National or Enterprise
18 Luxury handbag maker
19 Magpie relative
20 "Explore Alaska! It's ___!"
23 Sack
24 A fleur-de-lis is a stylized one
25 Wine server
28 Kuala Lumpur's home
32 Like
33 "Writers and photographers will find Michigan a great place for ___!"
35 Shipped
37 Drawn straw, say
38 Within: Prefix
39 "Blow into Maine on ___!"
44 ___-X
45 Breastbones
46 In a mischievous manner
48 Hoot
49 Kind of fixation
50 "I was afraid to ski, but in New Hampshire I ___!"
56 John
57 Belted one out of this world?
58 Implied
59 It goes before beauty, in a saying
60 Pola ___ of the silents
61 Other side
62 Each
63 Red-jacketed cheeses
64 Southend-on-Sea's county

DOWN

1 Finally hit the books
2 Xbox space-war franchise
3 Nearly closed
4 Actress Anderson
5 Launched, as a missile
6 Green party honoree, briefly?
7 Put on guard
8 Key with three sharps: Abbr.
9 Section of the brain
10 Citizen of a theocratic republic
11 Fijian-born golf Hall-of-Famer
12 Isaac's firstborn
13 Possessive in the Ten Commandments
21 Gardener, often
22 "Family Ties" mom
25 Parts of barrios
26 Northern archipelago dweller
27 Luxury S.U.V. import
28 Alley sounds
29 Harmonizers with soprani and bassi
30 What drones collect
31 What waiting for overdue results can be
34 Ancient civilization around Susa
36 Shroud of ___
40 Treat with one's choice of syrup
41 Taught privately
42 ___ a one
43 Conscript
47 What a janitor does
49 Some upscale chain hotels
50 Protection for a shark diver
51 Baltic city where Baryshnikov was born
52 Housing that's often empty in the summer
53 The best, in slang
54 Hoarfrost
55 River to Hades
56 Baby sitter?

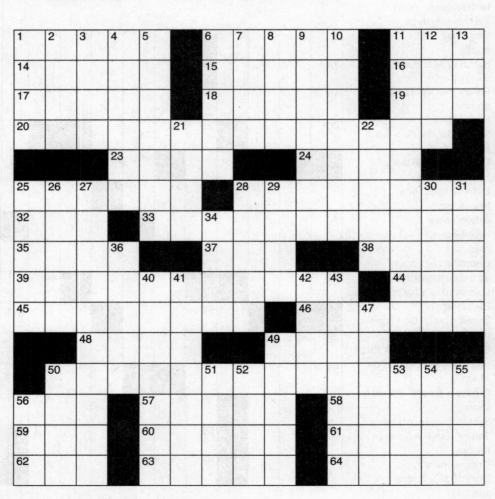

by Peter Koetters

ACROSS

1 Arnaz of "I Love Lucy"
5 Skewered meat dishes
11 Col. Sanders's restaurant
14 Muscat's land
15 Battery terminals
16 Not feeling well
17 62-Across landmark
19 Siegfried's partner in Vegas
20 Laurence who wrote "Tristram Shandy"
21 Vietnamese holiday
22 What's thrown in a cafeteria fight
23 Blue Jays' home, for short
24 62-Across museum
26 Turn down, as an offer
29 N.B.A. coach Steve
30 62-Across bridge
32 "I know! I know!"
36 Opposite of WSW
37 Basketball venue
40 Roadside bomb, for short
41 Artoo-___ of "Star Wars"
44 62-Across school
47 Clutch
50 Toy that shoots foam darts
51 62-Across cathedral
55 ". . . or so ___ told"
56 ___ vera
57 Airport guess, for short
58 Exile
61 Family members
62 World capital that's the theme of this puzzle
64 She tasted the forbidden fruit
65 Many
66 One of three in a hat trick
67 Dôme ___ Invalides (historic church)
68 Extends, as a lease
69 Abbr. on many a cornerstone

DOWN

1 Bucks' mates
2 Let out
3 Social Security, Medicare, etc., collectively
4 Leading the pack
5 Green vegetable with tightly curled leaves
6 Suffix with differ
7 Diner seating option
8 Trade publication read along Madison Avenue
9 Ladybug or scarab
10 Ukr., e.g., once
11 Big name in Russian ballet
12 Elevator stop
13 Bonnie's partner in crime
18 Scandal-ridden company of the early 2000s
22 Pelts
24 Grand ___ (cultural trip around Europe)
25 ". . . man ___ mouse?"
26 Zoomed
27 Top-notch
28 Drink that's often iced
31 Second-largest city of Morocco, after Casablanca
33 Mythical ruler of Crete
34 List of options
35 Genesis garden
38 ___ of the above
39 "Vous êtes ici" ("You ___ here")
42 Shrek, e.g.
43 Galena or bauxite
45 Hide-out for Br'er Rabbit
46 At the point in one's life
48 Think up
49 St. Genevieve, for 62-Across
51 Like a jaybird, in an idiom
52 Shade of green
53 Shades of color
54 State formed as part of the Missouri Compromise
58 Bosom buddies, in modern lingo
59 Sing like Ella Fitzgerald
60 Clutched
62 Golf course standard
63 Strew, as seed

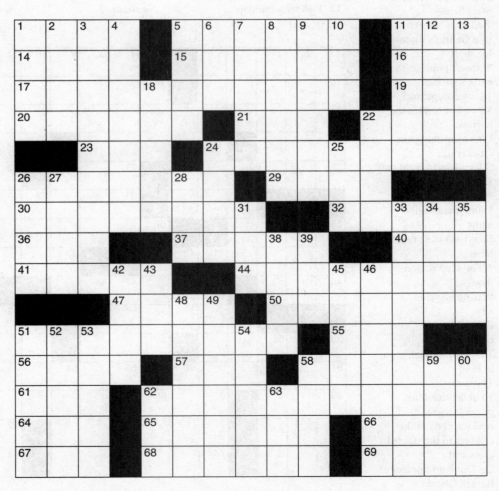

by Jason Mueller

ACROSS

1 10% donation
6 Makes a to-do about this and that
12 Air ticket abbr.
15 Disney mermaid
16 Because
17 "Seinfeld" uncle
18 *List for some binge watchers
20 Bit of a comic
21 Bearded beast
22 Freeze over
23 Setting of Kubla Khan's palace
25 *Response to "Who, me?"
27 Body blow reaction
29 *"Balderdash!"
30 Much-used Twitter symbols
31 Line around the globe
33 State firmly
36 "Gil Blas" writer
37 Lou Gehrig's disease, for short
40 *Lowest point on the earth's surface
43 *Avon competitor
45 Move low toward the horizon
46 Like a curmudgeon
49 Quaker ___
50 Sticky-leaved plant that feeds on insects
51 "Six-pack"
53 *Superman's alien name
56 Longtime U.K. record label
57 *"For what reason, though?"
61 War-torn Syrian city
63 Flexible conjunction
65 Tow job provider, in brief
66 Thither
67 To understand this puzzle's theme, read the ends of the answers to the starred clues and . . .
70 ___ Dunham, mother of Barack Obama
71 Marked down
72 First-stringers
73 Crucial
74 Excited, as a crowd
75 "Chocolat" director Hallström

DOWN

1 Having a zesty taste
2 Cara who sang "Flashdance . . . What a Feeling"
3 Emperor who finished the Colosseum
4 Mag mogul with a mansion
5 Mama Cass
6 Prix ___
7 Ending "
8 Drunken dazes
9 Ship's pronoun
10 French waters
11 More passionate
12 Fish tank buildup
13 Having bags all packed, say
14 Animal that has strayed from the herd
19 Hosp. areas
24 Big Apple inits.
26 Almost a meter
28 Like whitecaps
32 Org. concerned with eagles and birdies
33 First few minutes of many podcasts
34 Geese formation
35 Sup
36 Summa cum ___
37 Rap sheet letters
38 Muscle below a delt
39 Lead-in to "ops"
41 Rodin, for one
42 Suffix with north or south
44 World Series-winning manager Ned
47 Spanish weeks
48 When repeated, what little stars do
50 Equinox mo.
51 "___ Ben Adhem" (Leigh Hunt poem)
52 Interment
53 Alternative to Travelocity or Orbitz
54 Without assistance
55 Comedian Bruce
58 Boat trailers?
59 Papa Bear of Chicago Bears history
60 "I rule!"
62 "Egads!"
64 Tossed out of the game, informally
68 The Cyclones of the Big 12 Conf.
69 Windy City rail inits.

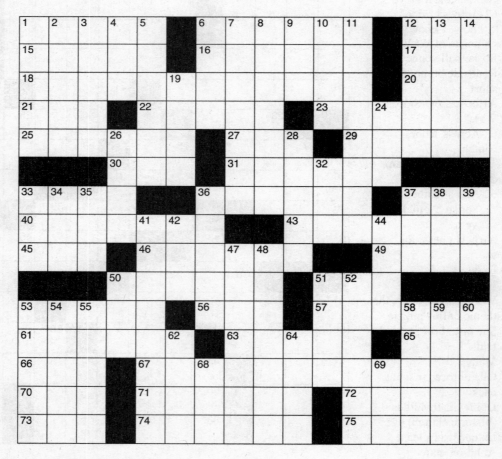

by Damon Gulczynski

ACROSS

1 Address including "www"
4 Doctors' org.
7 Small computer program
13 Biblical sister of Rachel
15 Purr-fect pet?
16 Succeed greatly
17 Get 10%-15%, say
19 Signaled, as a cab
20 *Actor in "The Bridge on the River Kwai" (1957)
22 Where Seoul and Pyongyang are: Abbr.
23 "Encore!"
27 *Actor in "Ocean's Eleven" (2001)
32 Mets' old stadium
33 In ___ straits
34 ___-de-sac
35 Gchat exchange, for short
36 All ___ (what a G rating means)
37 Freshman, sophomore, etc.
40 Here's the kicker!
41 Photos, informally
42 Unprocessed, as data
43 Part of the roof with the gutter
44 Number between dos and cuatro
46 *Actress in "Mogambo" (1953)
49 Fourth letter of "business"
51 "___ whiz!"
52 Setting for the answers to the three starred clues - appropriately enough, given their initials
58 New York home to Cornell University
61 Not meant to be thrown away
62 Tinklers on porches
63 Rower's blade
64 Scottish girl
65 Aficionado
66 Letters on a beach bottle
67 "Are we there ___?"

DOWN

1 Big name in beauty supplies
2 Genuine
3 "Go jump in the ___!"
4 What typists and archers are judged on
5 Second-largest Hawaiian island
6 Memo heading abbr.
7 Greek goddess of wisdom
8 New or full moon, e.g.
9 Light-refracting objects
10 Rapper ___ Wayne
11 Preholiday night
12 Cruz in the news
14 Enthusiastic agreement
18 Wide-eyed with excitement
21 "There's ___ in team"
24 From Columbus or Cleveland
25 Take away
26 Holiday with an egg hunt
27 Turns from a book into a movie, say
28 Sushi consisting of thin slices of fish over rice
29 University in Philadelphia
30 Regret
31 Nurse Barton
38 Old washcloth
39 Rhythmic group dance of the 2010s
40 Bigger than local or state
45 "___ Street"
46 "I thought this day would never come!"
47 Woman's palindromic nickname
48 Letters of support, for short
50 Less of a jerk
53 Greek equivalent of Cupid
54 Collect in the field
55 Auction service since 1995
56 Besides that
57 Place for baby birds
58 It goes "clink" in a drink
59 Quick expression of appreciation
60 Culturally conversant

by Erik Agard

ACROSS

1 Cold-shoulder
5 Opinion pieces
10 Brand of tea
14 ___ Grey tea
15 Russian ballet company
16 Score before deuce, maybe
17 The online world
19 They help you access 17-Across, for short
20 Commotion
21 Actress Ward of "Sisters"
23 King topper
24 Ending with east or west
26 Song whose first verse ends "Sleep in heavenly peace"
30 Pioneering building game for computers
32 Graceland's home: Abbr.
33 Japanese farewell
35 Woody Allen emotion
39 Court fig.
40 Grub or maggot
43 Top-notch
44 "Whoopee!"
46 1948 Triple Crown winner
48 Mrs. Addams, to Gomez
51 Star's spot at Christmas
52 Big school event attended by parents
56 Source of PIN money?
57 Spasm
58 Marx who co-wrote "The Communist Manifesto"
59 Manhattan, for one: Abbr.
61 One-half base × height, for a triangle
63 Undermined the confidence of
68 Volunteer's offer
69 Start of a kid's choosing rhyme
70 "Puppy Love" hitmaker, 1960
71 On deck
72 Church council
73 Sharp

DOWN

1 Jiffy
2 "I vote no"
3 Story debunked on Snopes.com
4 Ran, as fabric dye
5 Signs off on
6 Backup singer for Gladys Knight
7 Wipe the board clean
8 Museum guide
9 Gracefully thin
10 Greek letter shaped like a cross
11 "What ___ it is getting old" (Rolling Stones lyric)
12 Nothing, informally
13 Beginning
18 Bagful on a pitcher's mound
22 Fashion's Wintour
24 Optional part of the SAT
25 Cowboy's lasso
27 Slanted type: Abbr.
28 Constellation named for a stringed instrument
29 Present at birth
31 Wild animal that yips
34 Path followed by a shooting star
36 Eschew help
37 Supercilious sort
38 Local news hour, on some stations
41 "La Dolce ___"
42 Longfellow's bell town
45 Sound on Old MacDonald's farm
47 High home for a hawk
49 Scenic vistas, briefly
50 "Hiroshima" author John
52 Blemish on one's reputation
53 "Odyssey" temptress
54 Alpine climbing tool
55 Swashbuckling Errol
60 Badlands locale: Abbr.
62 Picnic pest
64 Grp. in a 1955 labor merger
65 "If only ___ listened . . ."
66 Luau instrument, familiarly
67 Shade darker than beige

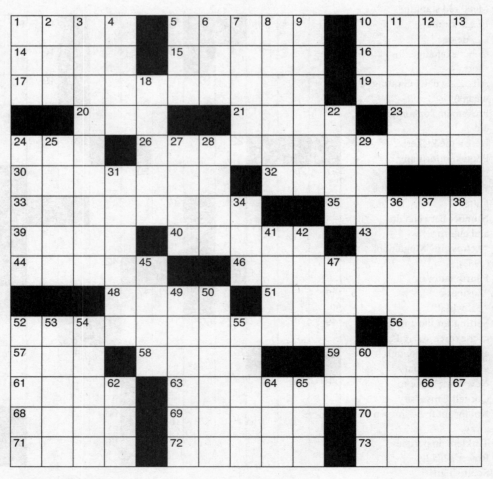

by Alan Arbesfeld

ACROSS

1 Crudely sexual
5 Orange-yellow
10 Quick and not well thought out
14 Creative start
15 Longest river in France
16 "Sesame Street" monster
17 World's largest religious denomination
19 Matty or Felipe of major-league baseball
20 Play a role
21 Org. for the Suns and the Heat
22 Inuit homes
24 Org. looking for aliens
28 Ink problem
30 End of a business's email address
31 Tales set on Mount Olympus, e.g.
32 Say "No, thanks" to
35 Baby's starting place
37 Supporting nativist policies
43 Cow sounds
44 Device behind a deli counter
45 Dog on "The Jetsons"
49 Moon vehicle, for short
51 Supermodel Banks
52 One teaching pizza slices and S-turns
56 Make blue
57 Partner of the Father and Holy Ghost
58 Musical Yoko
61 Gas or electric: Abbr.
62 Asset for a public speaker . . . or a hint to 17-, 24-, 37- and 52-Across
66 Philosopher Descartes
67 Hole in one on a par three
68 Move text here and there
69 Avant-garde
70 Radioer's "Got it"
71 Old U.S. gas brand still seen in Canada

DOWN

1 Crossword-solving girl on "The Simpsons"
2 Cabinet dept. concerned with schools
3 Became lenient
4 Roseanne's hubby on "Roseanne"
5 Accused's line a judge might not believe
6 Artwork with tiles
7 Cartoonist Keane
8 End of an ___
9 Send, as payment
10 Property in buildings and land
11 "110%"
12 Alternative to chunky, for peanut butter
13 Purchases before hotels, in Monopoly
18 Bad throw for a QB: Abbr.
23 Stabilizing part of a ship's compass
25 Needle case
26 Still uninformed
27 Urban air pollution
28 Upper half of a bikini
29 ___ Goodman, longtime judge on "Dancing With the Stars"
33 Gymnast Biles with four Olympic gold medals
34 Offshoot of punk rock
36 ___ Fields cookies
38 Shed, as feathers
39 One of the Jackson 5
40 Winter driving hazards
41 "___ the ramparts we watched . . ."
42 Gun enthusiast's org.
45 Guarantee
46 Glided on ice
47 Satisfying until later, with "over"
48 Daisy who plays Rey in "Star Wars" films
50 Brawn
53 Make a nasty face
54 One making dove sounds
55 Channel that became Spike TV in 2003
59 Long-running CBS police drama
60 Good name for a chauffeur?
63 Ming worth millions of dollars
64 ___ McMuffin
65 Item in a caddie's bag

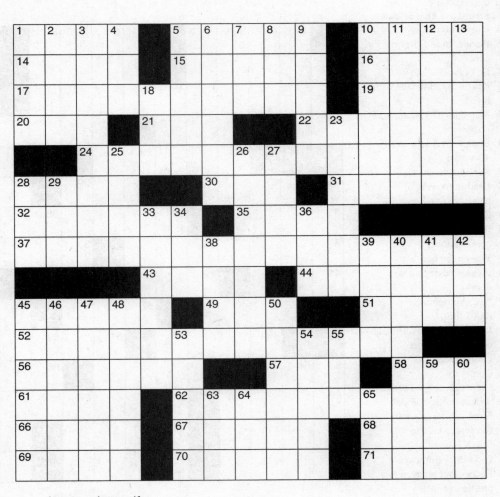

by David Woolf

ACROSS

1 Rock singer who was a Time co-Person of the Year
5 Poland/Germany border river
9 Pizza party drink
13 West Indies native
14 Hurled weapon
15 God depicted with a spear
16 Like a life that's not worth living, per Socrates
18 ___ Strauss & Co.
19 Picasso daughter known for her fashion designs and perfumes
20 Alligator pears
22 Really bother
24 First field in an online form, often
25 Makes weary through overexposure
28 Meditative kind of state
30 Pan, in myth
33 Pioneer in self-driving cars
34 Be beaten by
36 Kitchen brand made with love?
37 Map with a "You are here" arrow
39 Book with Adam and 41-Across
41 See 39-Across
42 Lead-in to army or band
44 Despicable
45 Bud ___, former M.L.B. commissioner
47 Was on the bench
48 Figures posted on taxi doors
49 "___ Almighty" (2007 film)
51 Loosening of government controls, for short
53 Lantern fuel
56 Comes to
60 Giant four-legged combat walker in "Star Wars" films
61 Car with a bubble
63 Lug
64 Food-thickening agent
65 Every other letter in this puzzle's grid(!)
66 Lacking width and depth
67 Stories passed from generation to generation
68 With 1-Down, star of Spielberg's "Munich"

DOWN

1 See 68-Across
2 Cy Young winner Hershiser
3 1969–74, politically
4 White House family after the Bushes
5 Sash worn around the waist
6 Contributes to a Kickstarter campaign, say
7 Mountain fig.
8 Gas that home inspectors check for
9 Pizza topping
10 Lode
11 Rock band known for its "energy domes"
12 Sign suggesting "caveat emptor"
13 Recipe unit
17 People or Us, for short
21 Chicken for cooking
23 Archipelago west of Portugal
25 Author Verne
26 Like the sky (unless you're an astronaut)
27 Slow down
29 Nullify
31 Napoleon, when on St. Helena
32 Kentucky Derby prize
34 Scary Chaney
35 Base ___
38 Attire on ancient statues
40 "Green Acres" co-star in 1960s TV
43 Did better than bogeyed
46 Sticker worn proudly in November
48 Fixed, as a tapestry
50 Home to Tenzing-Hillary Airport
52 One making a ewe turn?
53 Bruce Lee role based on an old radio character
54 Rival school of Harrow and Radley
55 Canceled, as a launch
57 New Zealand bird
58 "Juice": Abbr.
59 Salt, in France
62 "But I heard him exclaim, ___ he . . ."

by Wren Schultz

ACROSS

1 Engaged in country-to-country combat
6 Dance movement
10 Story about Zeus and Hera, e.g.
14 Be dishonest with
15 Language of Bangkok
16 Salmon variety
17 Small floor covering
19 Witticism
20 Gummy gumbo vegetable
21 "Winnie-the-Pooh" baby
22 Irene of old Hollywood
23 Standard breakfast order
27 Johnny who sang "Chances Are"
29 Toward shelter, at sea
30 White as a ghost
31 Legacy student's relative, for short
33 Friendly
37 Nintendo game console
38 Lead off . . . or a hint to the circled letters
41 Aye's opposite
42 Makings of a castle at the beach
44 Gyro wrap
45 Waste maker, in a saying
47 At any time
49 Entries in the minus column
50 Passover no-no
55 Holder of unread emails
56 Savings plan for old age, in short
57 Kudrow of "Friends"
60 Cut and paste text, e.g.
61 Play H-O-R-S-E, say
64 Michelangelo's "David," for one
65 German luxury carmaker
66 Arctic people
67 Put the pedal to the metal
68 Get over a sunburn, maybe
69 Green pasta sauce

DOWN

1 Likewise
2 Sound of a watch
3 Diminishes, as patience
4 Embassy staffer
5 "Poppycock!"
6 Longtime senator Thurmond
7 Pulsate
8 French water
9 Big Bad Wolf's target
10 Steve who directed "12 Years a Slave"
11 The "Y" of Michael Jackson's "P.Y.T."
12 The "T" of Michael Jackson's "P.Y.T."
13 "High" feelings
18 Timeline periods
22 J.F.K.'s predecessor
24 Age indicator in a tree trunk
25 Actress Linney in "Kinsey"
26 Trees attacked by bark beetles
27 Cavernous openings
28 Home to 48 countries
31 Blazing
32 Blazing
34 Sneakily dangerous
35 Suffragist Carrie Chapman ___
36 Baby blues, e.g.
39 Like most businesses from 9 to 5
40 "Get ___ to a nunnery": Hamlet
43 Totally loyal
46 Sea snail with a mother-of-pearl shell
48 Annoy
49 "Shucks!"
50 Creditors' claims on property
51 Ultimately become
52 Bear patiently
53 Semiconductor device with two terminals
54 Swelter
58 Barbecue rod
59 Concerning
61 Source of maple syrup
62 Choice from a painter's palette
63 Belly dancer's gyrating body part

by Lynn Lempel

ACROSS

1 Johnny of "Chocolat" and "Charlie and the Chocolate Factory"
5 Pieces in the game Rummikub
10 Lose control on ice, say
14 Unit for surveyors
15 "Fear of Flying" author Jong
16 Dubliner's home
17 Author of "American Psycho"
20 Magnificent
21 Polish seaport
22 Yoga surface
24 Charlemagne's domain: Abbr.
25 "Jerry Maguire" Oscar winner
32 Teri with a big "Tootsie" role
33 Company with numbered sheep plush toys
34 Southernmost team in the American League
36 Eldest of Chekhov's "Three Sisters"
37 The year 205
38 Furniture superstore
39 Dos × 5
40 Bracelet fastener
42 Piquancy
43 Star of "Mandela: Long Walk to Freedom"
46 Approach furtively, with "to"
49 Machine that produces power
53 Patti Page song that begins "It was winter when you told me you were leaving"
54 Continues
55 John Donne quote disproved by 17-, 25- and 43-Across?
59 Ever's partner
60 Mortise's partner
61 13th-anniversary gift
62 Belief systems
63 What birthday cake candles represent
64 Passed with flying colors

DOWN

1 Brylcreem amounts
2 Stationery color
3 Ready for surgery
4 Sessions of Congress
5 They're likely to get into hot water
6 Form letters?
7 Hammered
8 Green: Prefix
9 Drink made with red wine and fruit
10 Emmy winner Ward
11 Oven for pottery
12 Apt name for an ophthalmologist
13 Rolltop, e.g.
18 Humor columnist Bombeck
19 Genesis garden
23 Pedal attachment on a racing bike
24 Modern hotel room item
25 Colombian city that hosted the 1971 Pan American Games
26 Impulse
27 Largest group of Portuguese speakers
28 Menaces of the deep
29 "Memory" singer in "Cats"
30 Hunky-dory
31 Deli loaves
32 One of two words added to the Pledge of Allegiance in 1954
35 Wasn't a straphanger
40 Primitiveness
41 Software add-ons that offer extra features
44 Paula who wrote "It Ain't All About the Cookin'"
45 Some sibs
46 Egyptian peninsula
47 Mao and Xi, in China
48 She might check for a fever with her hand
50 Fashion designer Mizrahi
51 Time being
52 Over and done
56 Visualize
57 Santa ___, Calif.
58 Negative conjunction

by Peter Gordon

ACROSS

1 Quick drinks, as of whiskey
6 What one might be after doing 1-Across
11 "___ be my pleasure!"
14 Trunk of the body
15 Run off to the preacher
16 Neither's partner
17 Underwear for judges?
19 Ginger ___ (soft drink)
20 Singer Grande with the #1 albums "Yours Truly" and "My Everything"
21 Terminates
22 The "O" of B.Y.O.B.
24 Underwear for Frisbee enthusiasts?
28 Feeling of a person stranded in the desert
30 Silvery hair color
31 Mediocre
32 Who says "To be, or not to be: that is the question"
34 Underwear for beginners?
39 Soap operas, e.g.
40 What "I" or "me" refers to
42 Belgian diamond center
45 Fixed charge
47 Underwear for actors?
50 "Gross!"
51 One direction for an elevator
52 Romantic hopeful
54 Nasty Amin
55 Underwear for tycoons?
60 Furry sitcom alien
61 Like the moon landing, according to conspiracists
62 ___ Marie, singer of the 1985 hit "Lovergirl"
63 Director Spike
64 "Woo-hoo!"
65 English class assignment

DOWN

1 Cardinals, on scoreboards
2 Soil tiller
3 Any living thing
4 Romanov ruler
5 Opponent of stripes in billiards
6 Shore fliers
7 Relating to part of the pelvis
8 Who wrote the line "Once upon a midnight dreary . . ."
9 Rating on a Coppertone bottle, for short
10 "Indubitably!"
11 More ridiculous
12 "See, I was right!"
13 Like formal clothing
18 Worms for fishing
21 Heart health evaluation, for short
22 Extra periods, in brief
23 "Stop right there!"
25 Doorframe parts
26 Nobel Peace Prize city
27 Cereal in a party mix
29 Victory in an away game
32 "Well, I never!"
33 Notre Dame's Parseghian
35 Part of an arbor
36 Distinctive features of Mr. Spock
37 Whistle blowers
38 Whole bunch
41 Small bunch
42 It goes from about 540 to 1700
43 Casserole bit
44 Laura vis-à-vis Rob Petrie, on "The Dick Van Dyke Show"
45 Use a swizzle stick
46 Property in a will
48 Actor Milo
49 Rosy-cheeked
53 Has bills
55 Corp. money honcho
56 "How relaxing!"
57 Where clouds are
58 Genetic stuff
59 Second word of "The Star-Spangled Banner"

by Bruce Haight

ACROSS

1 Tests the weight of by lifting
6 Sot's woe, for short
9 Welcome sight in a desert
14 Dole out
15 Slip of paper in a poker pot
16 Thin pancakes with sour cream
17 Work like a dog
18 Mexican state that touches Texas
20 "___ Last Bow" (1917 Sherlock Holmes story)
21 Caboose, for a train
23 Alliance
24 Utopia
27 Aids for butterfly collectors
28 "The Simpsons" girl
29 Cream ___
31 Busy bees during tax season, for short
33 Figures on a spreadsheet
35 Macaroni or ravioli
40 Meandering
42 "Rock-a-bye Baby" setting
44 Push away
45 Yen
47 Gait faster than a walk
48 More than none but less than all
50 Morrison who wrote "Beloved"
52 Word stamped on an invoice
56 Good place to fish from
59 Salient
61 Kovalchuk of the N.H.L.
62 African game
64 Obstacle . . . or any one of four black squares in this puzzle?
66 Bishop's headdress
68 Polynesian land east of Fiji
69 Greek letter that represents the golden ratio
70 Figure in many a sci-fi film
71 Part of a cattle roundup
72 Perfect diving score
73 Winter Olympics equipment

DOWN

1 Corned beef dish
2 Perry of fashion
3 Early means of providing light for a photograph
4 "Mazel ___!"
5 Backs of ships
6 Currency of Tunisia
7 Reader of a Fodor's guide
8 "So ___ me!"
9 One of two to four in a standard orchestra
10 Poe's middle name
11 Long, drawn-out fight
12 Two-way, as doors
13 Certain math ratios
19 Infamous impaler
22 "Good gravy!"
25 Bride's path
26 Unwilling
30 Play "monkey see, monkey do"?
31 Airport rental
32 ___ chart
34 "Same here"
36 Corporation named after a mountain
37 Bit of wear for Colonel Sanders
38 As well
39 Prone (to)
41 Harlem sights
43 Take another crack at
46 Latin American seafood dish
49 Pitcher Hershiser
51 White House family with the dog Bo
52 Strong wines
53 Going on
54 Vapid
55 Word before City or after Fort on Midwest maps
57 Stanley who wrote "The Magic Kingdom"
58 Hit below the belt
60 Skier's convenience
63 Large coffee holders
65 Go (for)
67 Under the weather

by Jacob Stulberg

ACROSS

1 Peak near Tokyo: Abbr.
7 Facts and figures
11 Guy's date
14 Stuff that may make you go "Ah-choo!"
15 Actor Wilson of "Midnight in Paris"
16 Cheer at a bullfight
17 Group preparing a ball field for a game
19 Homes on wheels, for short
20 Slippery fish
21 Like Monday crosswords, relatively speaking
22 Protection
24 Blown away
26 DuPont fiber
27 1972 platinum album by the Allman Brothers Band
31 "___ out of it!"
33 Opposite of a liability
34 Window section
36 Bit of acne
37 Globe: Abbr.
38 Locale of all the circled items in this puzzle
41 Suffix with pay
42 Running total at a bar
43 Apartment building overseer, informally
44 Gets whiter
46 Not working
48 Doesn't get near
51 Peter who compiled a book of synonyms
53 James of jazz
54 The Audi symbol has four of them
55 Fly high
57 Musical cousin of calypso
60 Ancient
61 Japanese delicacy served in thin slices
65 Hearty brew
66 Send off, as rays
67 One always making adjustments on the job?
68 ___ Moines, Iowa
69 Releases of Drake and Cardi B
70 Tune out

DOWN

1 Fuel economy measure, for short
2 Ripped
3 Ice sheet
4 Wail in grief
5 Actress Aniston, to friends
6 Seriously involved
7 E.R. figures
8 Off-kilter
9 Shirt that might have a slogan on it
10 Egypt's Sadat
11 Blue-veined Italian cheese
12 American Dance Theater founder
13 Not so much
18 "Smooth Operator" singer, 1985
23 Aboveground trains
25 Light bulb units
26 "Say it isn't so!"
27 Shoe that ties around the ankle
28 Some women with light-colored hair
29 Cop ___ (confess in return for lighter punishment)
30 Taxi
32 School grps.
33 Sparkling Italian wine
35 One living abroad, informally
39 Boot out
40 Make a choice
45 Completely covered with
47 Shape of a Silly Putty container
49 Affirmative votes
50 Sheetlike gray clouds
52 Ending with poly-
54 The Beatles' "Abbey ___"
55 Scissors sound
56 Honey Bunches of ___
58 About 2.2 pounds, for short
59 Latin love
62 Actress Thurman
63 What shoulders may do after a disappointment
64 Fury

by Julie Bérubé

ACROSS

1 Bunch of wolves
5 Book composed of 10-Across
10 See 5-Across
14 Word after computer or fashion
15 Port-au-Prince's land
16 Satan's doings
17 "What's there to lose?"
19 Ankle-length dress
20 Sleep disorder
21 Patriotic finger-pointer
23 Way to run or ski
26 Sauce in a Bloody Mary
29 Radiate
30 Tortilla sandwich
31 Bunny action
33 Wastes time, with "off"
37 Not feeling well
38 Band with the 12x platinum album "Slippery When Wet"
41 2016 Olympics locale
42 "I kid you not!"
44 Pronoun for a ship
45 Concert venue
46 Singer McEntire
49 Board game with black-and-white pieces
51 Like some August sales
55 Comment made while covering someone's eyes
56 67–69, gradewise
60 West Coast gas brand
61 Ignite something . . . or what the first words of 17-, 23-, 38- and 51-Across do?
64 Seriously wound
65 ___ point (concise)
66 Sch. that plays home football games at the Rose Bowl
67 "Legally Blonde" girl
68 Satirical news site, with "The"
69 Minus

DOWN

1 City with a noted tower
2 "And we'll tak' ___ o' kindness yet": Burns
3 Ears that can't hear
4 Patella
5 Sound of contentment
6 Scotland's Firth of ___
7 "Peanuts" boy with a blanket
8 Immediately
9 "Parks and Recreation," e.g.
10 Keepsake
11 Sailor's cry
12 Animation studio with a lamp mascot
13 Morally reprehensible
18 Hawks push them
22 Nintendo brother
24 Tres y cinco
25 Procrastinator's promise
26 Certain bed size
27 Folk singer Guthrie
28 Event for Cinderella
32 Nighttime attire, briefly
34 Kind of exam
35 Occupy completely
36 Han who's the title role of a 2018 film
38 Borscht ingredients
39 "Pick me! Pick me!"
40 Presidential prerogative
43 Irritating
45 Lending a hand
47 Greets respectfully
48 Kutcher of "That '70s Show"
50 "Today" co-host Kotb
51 Not one's best effort, in sports
52 Hearing-related
53 The "C" of C. S. Forester
54 Relative of a raccoon
57 Canine woe
58 Web addresses
59 Wet septet
62 Letter after pi
63 Full count

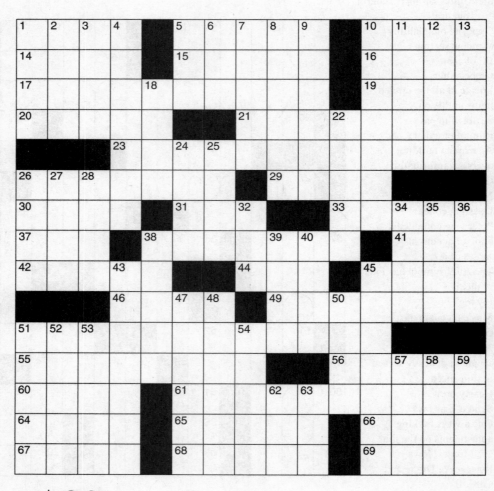

by Ori Brian

ACROSS

1 Wolfish look
5 Lead-in to "di" or "da" in a Beatles song
9 Fowl raised for food
14 Commedia dell'___
15 Gas, oil or coal
16 Port St. ___, Fla.
17 End of a drinking hose
19 Rand McNally volume
20 Diving gear
21 Get going, as an old motorcycle or a new company
23 Spheres, in poetry
25 Angsty music genre
26 Rapper with the 1996 double-platinum album "Hard Core"
29 Handyman's inits.
31 What sirens do
35 Enero begins it
36 Certain red dye
38 Having a high metallic sound
39 Like some magazine perfume ads
42 Ill-tempered
43 Borden milk's cow
44 6-3 or 7-6, e.g.
45 Cy Young Award winner Hershiser
46 Faux ___
47 Tribal leaders
49 Like non-Rx drugs
51 Female friend of François
52 Party vessel with a ladle
57 "There ___ to be a law!"
61 Loud, as a crowd
62 1999 Brad Pitt movie hinted at by the beginnings of 17-, 21-, 39- and 52-Across
64 Planet demoted to "dwarf planet" in 2006
65 Woman of the Haus
66 Fishes that may shock you
67 Good ___ (repaired perfectly)
68 Appear (to be)
69 Go bananas

DOWN

1 Parts of science courses
2 "Spamalot" creator Idle
3 Caesar's rebuke to Brutus
4 Nike competitor
5 Birds ___ feather
6 Gains muscle, with "up"
7 Blue jeans pioneer Strauss
8 Trump portrayer Baldwin
9 Blood fluid
10 Not just playing for fun
11 The N.C.A.A.'s Bruins
12 Word repeated before "pants on fire"
13 Word repeated while tapping a microphone
18 Magazine of show business
22 Code breaker
24 Fellow who might be senior class president, for short
26 Rope in a Wild West show
27 Run up, as expenses
28 Peter of "The Maltese Falcon"
29 Uses a rotary phone
30 Bed-and-breakfasts
32 Licorice flavoring
33 Derive by logic
34 Alternatives to Ubers
37 Mets' former ballpark
38 Poet whose work inspired "Cats"
40 Distribute, as resources
41 Carpe ___ (seize the day: Lat.)
46 Banned pollutant, in brief
48 Cards that may be "wild" in poker
50 Lose on purpose
51 Fish tank gunk
52 "___ Was a Rollin' Stone" (Temptations hit)
53 Addresses that may be linked on the web
54 Person, place or thing
55 Murders, mob-style
56 Hide a mike on
58 Campbell who sang "By the Time I Get to Phoenix"
59 Hawaiian dance
60 Recipe measure: Abbr.
63 Vocalize on a kazoo

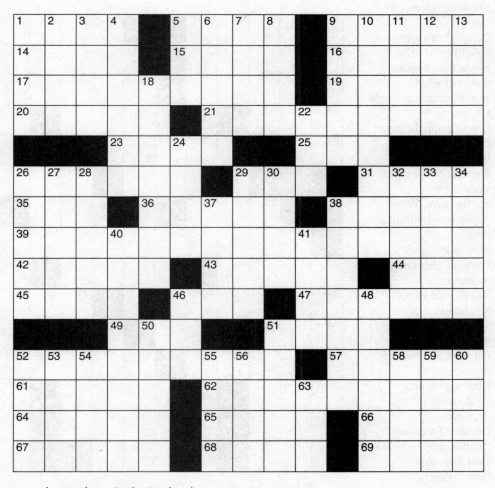

by Andrea Carla Michaels

ACROSS

1 Pioneering game company behind Tank and Tank II
6 Music genre for Tokyo teens
10 Contribute
13 By the clock
14 Good: It.
15 Coif that gets squished by headphones
16 "Uncle!"
17 Jargon
18 Fib
19 Something to stand on
20 H.S. science course for college credit
22 Tequila plant
24 Relatives of cable cars
26 Actress Dash of "Clueless"
27 Showbiz reference site
28 Critical, as a situation
29 Neighbor of Miss.
30 Something to pour dans votre café
32 A philanthropist might set one up
33 Dave Chappelle and Dane Cook . . . or a literal hint to the answers to the eight starred clues
36 ___ Ewbank, 1969 Super Bowl-winning coach
37 Schlemiel
38 Cartoon response to a rodent
39 Big Florida export
41 Kitchenware brand with a hyphenated name
43 Fix with a blowtorch, say
44 Classic Pontiacs
48 Drum used for a drumroll
49 Cousin of a chimp
50 "Runaround" girl in a 1961 Dion hit
51 Barn bales
52 Certain jelly

54 Like a red-faced cartoon character
56 Neighbor of Mont.
57 Timid
58 Smallest pups
59 Stroke
60 The "S" of GPS: Abbr.
61 Smallest

DOWN

1 Slanted
2 *Feline in a zoo
3 Mexican friend
4 Minister: Abbr.
5 Perfect guy
6 The "J" of J.D.
7 *Bounce on a stick
8 Lennon's love

9 Food famously misspelled by Dan Quayle
10 Noted "spokesfowl"
11 Alfresco theaters
12 Innocent-looking
14 *Dreamy eyes, informally
21 ___ Xing
23 *President between Hayes and Arthur
25 *1959 film set in Dogpatch, U.S.A.
26 ___ speak
28 *Detective who wore a two-way radio
29 Eroded
31 Earth Day's mo.
33 Croon beneath a balcony

34 Played at work, informally?
35 Rachel McAdams or Amanda Seyfried role in a 2004 comedy
36 Deify
40 Shines, as silver
42 Devoted follower
44 Material for a mill
45 Sitting position in yoga
46 *Mongrels
47 Look at, as thou might
49 *Magnum ___
53 Protein source in a vegan diet
55 French street

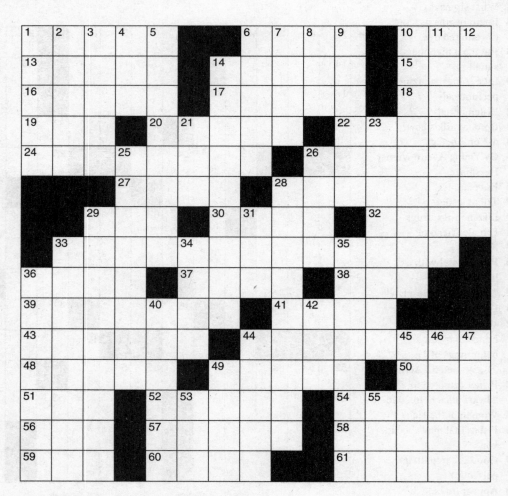

by Garry Trudeau and Ross Trudeau

ACROSS

1 Levi's material
5 Coconut tree
9 Lacks, in brief
14 The sun and the moon
15 ___ facto
16 Women's golf star Lorena
17 Holder of some precious memories
19 Transports between airport terminals
20 Position for a baseball batter
21 What sending someone to Mars would be
22 Wunderkind
26 Recede, as the tide
29 1960s-'70s Ford named for an Italian city
30 Fashion magazine spinoff
33 "Here's to you!," e.g.
38 Turn at high speed
39 "As American as apple pie," for example
40 Jokes and such
41 Popular Cartoon Network programming block
44 The "M" of NASA's LEM
46 Smartphone download
47 Temporary mental lapse
53 Squirrel's stash
54 ___ Herman (Paul Reubens character)
58 Insinuated
59 Place where no one lives anymore
62 Bring joy to
63 Actress Hatcher
64 Crucifix
65 Philadelphia N.B.A. player, informally
66 Plow pullers
67 Inquires

DOWN

1 Steve who once headed Apple
2 The "E" of Q.E.D.
3 Swedish pop quartet that won the 1974 Eurovision contest
4 Justin Timberlake's original group
5 Assign two projects, a long reading and several writing assignments, say
6 Police alert, for short
7 Baton Rouge sch.
8 Dad's partner
9 Run fast
10 Having a burning smell
11 Puppeteer Lewis
12 Request to a waiter
13 Yummy
18 German's "Oh!"
21 Prince Valiant's son
23 Item in a grate
24 ___ Hill (R&B group)
25 Chart type
26 Write on metal, say
27 Lover boy
28 Road shoulder
31 Prefix with liberal
32 Bernie Sanders, for one
34 Meditation sounds
35 Onetime electronics giant
36 Lose one's footing
37 Worker hired for the day
39 Has a lazy Sunday morning, say
41 Naval chief: Abbr.
42 Batman and Robin are a "dynamic" one
43 Einstein's birthplace
45 Where surgeons do surgery, for short
47 Wise ones
48 Bacterium that can help or hurt
49 Levy-free
50 Furious
51 Alternative to .com
52 Prefix with -hedron
55 Tries to win, as a damsel
56 Furry "Star Wars" creature
57 Kills
59 Sporty Pontiac
60 Bewitch
61 It's mined

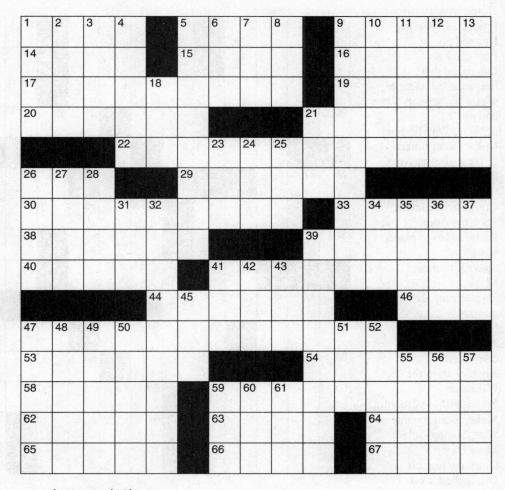

by Hannah Slovut

ACROSS

1 Sonata finale
5 Fateful day
9 Noted tower setting
14 Villain's hangout
15 City on the Seward Peninsula
16 Habituate
17 Constellation next to Draco
19 Subtly suggested
20 1962 Paul Anka hit
21 Widely adored woman
23 Part of a gig
24 Garr of "Tootsie"
25 Original of an old photo, informally
26 "You don't say!"
28 2008 Benicio Del Toro title role
30 Diminutive swimsuit
32 Indo-__ languages
35 Hopped up
37 Calf catcher
38 Language that becomes the name of where it's spoken if you add an "s"
39 __ Gay, 1945 bomber
43 Gofer's assignment
45 U-Haul alternative
46 Part of NATO
49 Outdo
51 Gut-punch reaction
52 Took the cake
53 Dame Myra of piano fame
55 SpaceX founder Musk
58 How lemmings migrate
60 Held in contempt
63 Authoritative command
64 Another term for 17-Across
66 Prefix with -hydrozoline
67 Make, as an income
68 "Casablanca" role
69 More foxy
70 Drain decloggers
71 Dispatched, as a dragon

DOWN

1 What this is for 1-Down
2 Galley equipment
3 Doesn't mind
4 Sheik's land, in poetry
5 "Just hang on!"
6 Martial arts school
7 Music genre with confessional lyrics
8 Twilled fabric
9 Part of 17-Across . . . and what the circles from A to G depict
10 Give __ of approval
11 Compound in synthetic rubber
12 Wiped clean
13 "Come on already!"
18 Assembled
22 Approximately
24 Lease signatories
26 Hoedown partner
27 Victorian __
29 Hi, on Hispaniola
31 Start of a decision-making process
33 What landlubbers don't like to be
34 Thing located in the night sky by extending a line from circle F past circle G
36 Numbskull
40 Former co-host of "The View"
41 Zodiac constellation
42 Lab warning?
44 Bakery loaves
46 Responsibility for a social media manager
47 14-line verse with only two rhyme sounds
48 Antagonism
50 Flavorers of some pies and ice cream
54 Jason of "I Love You, Man"
56 Auction grouping
57 Caesar's world?
59 Real estate unit
60 Dried up
61 Heart's-__ (pansy)
62 Tournament director's responsibility
65 Laser output

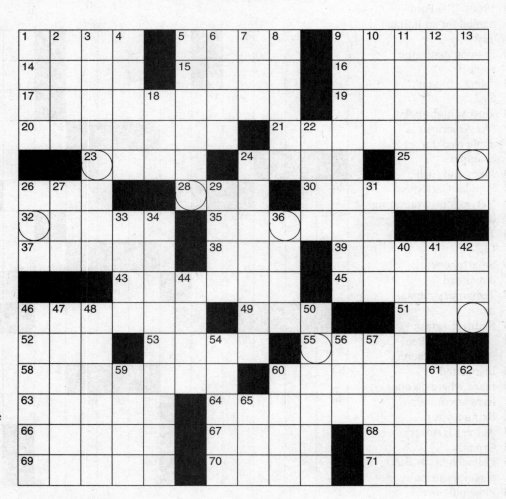

by Jeff Stillman

ACROSS

1 Trudges
7 Billboard Hot 100 and others
13 Language spoken by Jesus
14 Hinged part of an airplane wing
16 "Bye Bye Birdie" song
18 Partner of his
19 Untagged, in tag
20 "Star Trek" lieutenant
21 Ore-___ (frozen taters brand)
22 Inflatable item for water fun
24 Bon ___ (clever remark)
25 Russian cottage
27 Philosopher ___-tzu
28 Humiliate
30 Super bargain
31 Internet connection faster than dial-up, for short
32 More Solomonlike
33 ___ roaming (smartphone setting)
35 "Well, shoot!"
37 What you might do if you sing 16-Across
44 500 sheets of paper
45 Most deals that sound too good to be true
46 1 1 1
47 Units of farmland
49 Before, in poetry
50 Elizabethan neck decorations
51 Florida's ___ National Forest
53 ___ four (small pastry)
54 How you might feel if you sing 16-Across
59 Prefix with center
60 Show hostility to, as a dog might a mail carrier
61 Powerful cleaner
62 Medium strength?
63 No-goodnik
64 Girl at a ball, in brief

DOWN

1 Slangy "Amen!"
2 Corporate hustle and bustle
3 "Famous" cookie name
4 Fellow
5 It has 88 keys
6 Prom, e.g.
7 Washington image seen on the back of a $50 bill
8 Aware of, informally
9 Prince ___ Khan
10 Ones whistling while they work?
11 Shocks with lasting impact
12 "Almost got it that time!"
13 Pests in the garden
15 Spay, e.g.
17 Travel aid made obsolescent by GPS
22 ___ paneer (Indian dish made with spinach)
23 Expressions of boredom
26 Ate substantially
29 One who blabs
34 "My country, ___ of thee . . ."
36 Some small batteries
37 Undergarment with straps
38 Makes back, as an investment
39 Bit of jewelry on the side of the head
40 Roofing sealant
41 Area for six of the nine baseball positions
42 Part of the head hidden on the jack of spades
43 Curvy letter
48 Long, tiring jobs
50 Right-hand page in a book
52 Big top?
53 BlackBerrys, e.g., in brief
54 Lawyer's charge
55 ___ long way
56 Possess
57 Antiquated
58 Yank's Civil War foe

by Alex Eaton-Salners

ACROSS

1 Idiosyncratic sorts
9 J. J. ___ , director of "Star Wars: The Force Awakens"
15 Irrational suspicion
16 Unpleasant accompanier of a headlock
17 "M*A*S*H" star
18 Cosmic order, in Hinduism
19 Her first scene is with R2-D2
20 Google or Yahoo offering
22 Payroll ID, for short
23 FedEx alternative
25 Aries animal
26 Betty White's role on "The Mary Tyler Moore Show"
32 Knight's steed
35 Choreographer Alvin
36 Baseball's Felipe, Matty or Jesus
37 Many a word ending in -gon
40 NBC's "The More You Know" spots, e.g.
41 Place for a sweater
43 Craftsmanship from a barista
45 Moniker of an 18th-century British statesman
48 Answer to "Who is?"
49 AOL alternative
50 Engine part
53 Sorting criterion at the women's department
58 Massive
59 Vegetable with a pungent taste
60 Teaches
63 Word in 17 Monopoly property names
64 Short piano piece
65 Indulges in too much Netflix, say
66 Certain spears . . . or a curious spelling feature of 1-, 20-, 26-, 45- and 53-Across?

DOWN

1 October birthstones
2 Broad valleys
3 Deplete, as savings
4 Fox News host Perino
5 Spanish article
6 Rank above maj.
7 Speedy DC Comics sidekick
8 German coal district
9 From the mountains of Peru
10 European region that lent its name to a nonconforming lifestyle
11 Wander
12 Taj Mahal city
13 "Rent" role
14 Certain Navy specialist
21 Sea eagle
23 Rock's White Stripes, e.g.
24 His and ___
26 Railroad switch
27 Writer Zora ___ Hurston
28 Dodge model named after a snake
29 "Let It Go" singer in "Frozen"
30 In the neighborhood
31 Part of GPS: Abbr.
32 Stinger with a slender "waist"
33 Jai ___
34 Lopsided game
38 Highest prize at the Cannes Film Festival
39 Snow may push them back, for short
42 Under discussion
44 Number of sides on a decagon
46 Corned beef dishes
47 Big initials in the recording industry, once
50 Interrupt
51 Hollywood power player
52 Tablelands
53 Visually uninspiring
54 Sitarist Shankar
55 Genesis locale
56 Snitch
57 Piquancy
58 "Cherish those hearts that ___ thee": Shak.
61 Lead-in to code, on a computer
62 Heel

by John Lieb

ACROSS

1 Leatherworker's tool
4 Wrath
7 Sauce often used in a Bloody Mary
14 Port-au-Prince resident
16 "Um-hmm, O.K."
17 Call from a football referee
18 "Please! Anything but!"
19 Onion relative used in soups
20 Little troublemakers
22 Charged particles
23 M.R.I. orderers
24 Versatile bean
25 Texas site of a 1993 siege
27 Itsy-bitsy branch
29 Some DVD players
31 Caustic agent
34 Japan's largest company by revenue
36 Crops used in making cigarettes
38 Ready, willing and __
39 Classic Eric Clapton song about unrequited love
41 Statutes
42 Loses one's hair
44 Hold back, as a yawn
46 Moment, informally
47 World's fair, e.g.
48 Wish
49 Like the water in a baptism
51 Get bent out of shape
53 __ talks (lecture series)
56 Busy time at the drive-thru
58 Nay voter
59 It's made up of DNA
60 Message that might end "R.I.P."
63 Invaded in large numbers
65 17-year insects
66 Standards by which things are measured

67 Follows, as a schedule
68 Monterrey Mrs.
69 Consumed

DOWN

1 Get __ of (grasp)
2 Communion tidbit
3 Vegetarianism or bohemianism
4 Three on a grandfather clock
5 Source of faraway X-rays
6 Foe
7 Pantry containers
8 Long, long __
9 Web crawler, e.g.
10 Web-filled room, often
11 Spot for a food fight

12 Jackie of "Shanghai Knights"
13 Honey Bunches of __
15 "Shameful!"
21 Really revel . . . or a hint to the words formed by the circled letters
24 Take a chair
25 Indiana/Illinois separator
26 White __ sheet
28 Troubles
30 Kurtz's rank in "Apocalypse Now": Abbr.
32 Mournful cry
33 To be, to Tacitus
34 Little things that say "To" and "From"
35 Orchestra reed

37 Scissor cut
40 Swiss mount
43 __ Paese (variety of cheese)
45 Spinning toy
50 Like beer that's not in a bottle
52 Things split in fission
54 Make into 41-Across
55 Not the brightest bulb on the Christmas tree
56 Part bitten by a vampire
57 Mayberry boy
58 "I understand," facetiously
59 Hound's warning
61 Many online banners
62 Bit of butter
64 When a plane is due in, for short

by Chuck Deodene

ACROSS

1 Misgiving
6 Small quarrel
10 Leader from the House of Pahlavi
14 Eating pork, to an observant Jew or Muslim
15 Pac-12 hoops powerhouse
16 __ Alto, Calif.
17 Not be inert, as two chemical compounds
18 Cognitive scientist Chomsky
19 10-Across's land
20 Puerto Rico clock setting
23 Resealable bag
26 Chair with two hyphens in its name
27 Apple that might be seen on a teacher's desk
28 __-oriented
32 W.W. II spy org.
33 Genre for Mötley Crüe
35 Incendiary weapon
37 Fitness pro
42 Ohio city on Lake Erie
43 Czech-made auto that's part of the Volkswagen Group
44 "Yes . . . ri-i-i-ight there!"
47 Airplane's direction
49 Like custard
50 Adopted
52 Chain of children's stores founded by the Kaufman brothers (hence its name)
54 Basis of particle physics
58 Nothin'
59 Relative of fake news
60 Ghostly white
64 Fashionable Christian
65 Including all grades, briefly
66 "Bear" that's actually a marsupial
67 Gait faster than a walk
68 Baby's crib part
69 "Bon appétit!"

DOWN

1 Three months: Abbr.
2 Neighbor of Oman, for short
3 Atty.'s org.
4 Neighborhood buzz?
5 "Veritas" for Harvard or "Veritas vos liberabit" for Johns Hopkins
6 Sushi fish
7 Trash bin on a computer screen, e.g.
8 Dead-tired?
9 Acquainted (with)
10 Pointy-eared dog
11 Big maker of gummy bears
12 Los __ National Laboratory
13 Sweetie pies

21 Like some digital clocks, for short
22 Maria known as "La Divina"
23 Bygone alcopop
24 TV's "How __ Your Mother"
25 Way
29 "Giant Brain" introduced in 1946
30 Not expressly stated
31 Abbr. in many an urban address
34 Pope said to have died from a heart attack while in bed with his mistress
36 Former heavyweight champion with a tattooed face
38 Soldiers' digs?

39 Canceled, as a mission
40 Tense
41 They may be caught at the beach . . . or out at sea
44 Communications giant . . . or a possible title of this puzzle
45 All talk, no action
46 Bringer of bad luck
48 __ Pictures (bygone studio)
51 Store known for its Blue Light Specials
53 Stopper
55 Bridge charge
56 "The joke's on you"
57 Off-ramp sign
61 Trek to Mecca
62 Band with the 1977 hit "Telephone Line," in brief
63 Yea's opposite

by Michael Shteyman

ACROSS

1 Puts on TV or radio
5 Ending on several central Asian country names
9 Meanie in "Jack and the Beanstalk"
14 U.S. weather agcy.
15 Zeus' wife
16 ___ and wiser
17 1990s TV series about a murder in a town in Washington
19 Film director Kurosawa
20 Made smooth, as wood
21 Part of the conjugation of the French "avoir"
23 And others, for short
24 Bump fists
25 K-K-K-5-5, e.g., in poker
28 Exhibit in an anatomy class
31 Guided
32 Is sick
33 Four-baggers: Abbr.
34 Like favorite stations on a car radio
38 Pie ___ mode
39 Result of failure to comb the hair after sleep, maybe . . . or a feature of 17-, 25-, 49- or 61-Across?
41 School grp.
42 Young male viewed as a sex object
44 Black ___ (covert doings)
45 ___ Ticonderoga
46 Apr. 15 mail addressee
47 Place to pull over on an interstate
49 English monarch with a "lace" named after her
53 ___-rock (music genre)
54 Land between Can. and Mex.
55 Inits. at the start of a memo
56 "You ready?"
59 Drilling tool
61 Hooded snake
64 Thin pancake
65 Place for the banjo in "Oh! Susanna"

66 Exposition
67 N.B.A. star ___ Irving
68 Freezes, with "over"
69 Worry

DOWN

1 Picnic pests
2 State that produces the most corn
3 Weather-related stoppage in baseball
4 Beach footwear
5 Tool building
6 Lipton offering
7 Genesis vessel
8 Word before congestion or spray
9 Job that might involve watching the kids?
10 Variety
11 French farewell
12 "Rats!"
13 Use a stencil on
18 Amorous cartoon skunk
22 "No thanks"
25 President after Nixon
26 Like a sheep with all its wool
27 Praiseful poem
28 Onetime Volvo competitor
29 K, in the NATO alphabet
30 "According to conventional wisdom . . ."
35 Place to drink lined with TVs
36 French "to be"
37 "So long!"

39 Joy Adamson book about Elsa the lioness
40 Fencing sword
43 Coat and ___
45 Decrease
48 Soft mineral
49 Phony doc
50 Unscrupulous moneylending
51 Rarin' to go
52 Republican pol Haley from South Carolina
56 Gets 16-Across
57 Buffalo's lake
58 Sour
60 Prefix with dermis
62 "Monsters, ___" (2001 movie)
63 Word before a maiden name

by Neville Fogarty

ACROSS

1 *One side of a 23-Across piece
6 *Leeway
11 Tolkien's Treebeard, e.g.
14 Switch from plastic to paper, say
15 Hedren of "The Birds"
16 Actress Vardalos
17 Aggregate
18 Buildings in a Washington, D.C., "row"
20 Widespread
21 Julio is part of it
22 *Formation of poker chips
23 Disc-flipping board game hinted at by a word ladder formed by the answers to the nine starred clues
25 Slaps with a court fine
27 Where "Hamlet" opens
29 *Celery unit
33 Largest U.S. univ. system
37 Baltic capital
38 *Hackneyed
40 Not just bite and swallow
41 Haphazard
43 *Sedimentary rock
44 Dollar bill, e.g.
47 Moves heavenward
50 Another name for 23-Across
55 *Pinocchio swallower
56 Part of L.G.B.T.
57 The Panthers of the A.C.C.
58 Twosome in a Shakespeare title
61 Nut jobs
62 Fair-hiring letters
63 Mimic's ability
64 Creator of a logical "razor"
65 Coastal raptor
66 *"___ England Slept" (1938 Churchill book)
67 *Other side of a 23-Across piece

DOWN

1 "Congratulations!"
2 Actor Paul of "American Graffiti"
3 Embarrass
4 Social standing
5 Metric measures: Abbr.
6 Trial figures
7 Prom night rental
8 Police dept. alert
9 H&R Block V.I.P.
10 Mouths, slangily
11 Pioneering computer of the 1940s
12 Eleanor Roosevelt, to Theodore
13 Items on a to-do list
19 Something to do immediately after waking up
21 The whole ball of wax
24 Albanian currency
25 Way too uptight
26 Insider informant
28 Corporate raider Carl
29 H.S. students getting ready for college
30 Up to, informally
31 ___ Khan
32 Airplane seat restraint
34 "Now I get it!"
35 ___ Aviv
36 Farm female
38 Composition of dunes
39 Sounds of disapproval
42 Rules in force in England before the Norman conquest
43 A few: Abbr.
45 Grand Marnier flavor
46 Josephine who wrote "The Daughter of Time"
47 "Shucks!"
48 See-through
49 Big name in cameras and copiers
51 Notable time period
52 Perfumer Nina
53 Brown ermine
54 "Who's there?" response
56 Robt. E. Lee, e.g.
59 Book between Galatians and Philippians: Abbr.
60 The year 1002
61 Setting for simmering

by David Poole

ACROSS

1 "Penny Dreadful" channel, for short
4 ___ Longstocking, girl of children's literature
9 Poet Robert who spoke at J.F.K.'s inauguration
14 Highly classified
16 Like four-leaf clovers, supposedly
17 Somehow
19 Nut popular in ice cream
20 Apparatus pulled by oxen
21 Have a mortgage, e.g.
22 Intestinal fortitude, informally
25 "Ah, now it's clear"
27 Play about Capote
30 Walkie-talkie
35 Something that may be hidden behind a framed picture
37 Mixes
38 Ancient Peruvian
39 Stairs
42 Eye part with the iris
43 Odor
45 Table tennis
47 Rare occurrence on "Jeopardy!"
50 Prop for a golf ball
51 Sheet on a mast
52 Co-ops, maybe: Abbr.
54 Abbr. before an alias
57 Pizazz
59 Nut-bearing tree
63 Completely . . . with a summation of 17-, 30- and 47-Across
67 Larsson who wrote "The Girl With the Dragon Tattoo"
68 Sign of a beaver's activity, maybe
69 Exams
70 "Alas . . ."
71 Dove's sound

DOWN

1 "Halt!"
2 Sharpen, as skills
3 Grp. that includes Iraq and Qatar
4 Alternative to bubble wrap
5 Slippery, as winter roads
6 One who gives tips (and gets tips?) at a country club
7 Arrested suspect, informally
8 Roma's country
9 Daisies and dahlias
10 Sign of a well-worn trail
11 Eight: Sp.
12 Polling bias
13 Lebanese city that was once the center of Phoenician civilization
15 Lavish party favors
18 Inquisitive
23 "___ the night before Christmas . . ."
24 Cushiony
26 Readily accept
27 1960s dance craze
28 Cowboy's workplace
29 Stomach woe
31 Given to crying
32 Golfer's gouge
33 "Goodnight" girl of song
34 Missouri river or tribe
36 10 things in an Olympic swimming pool
40 Falafel bread
41 Scissor cut
44 Lipton products
46 "Hop to it!"
48 Thin but strong
49 Most-wanted groups for parties
53 Transmitted
54 Aide: Abbr.
55 Toy on a string
56 W.W. II foe
58 Other: Sp.
60 Common Core dept.
61 Duck-hunting attire, informally
62 Syringe, for short
64 Freshly painted
65 British ref. work
66 French seasoning

by John Wrenholt

ACROSS

1 When Polonius says "Brevity is the soul of wit"
6 Tusked beast
10 Kind of threat
14 Swoon
15 Alan who played Captain Pierce
16 Essential point
17 Agonizes (over)
18 With 61- and 37-Across, famous line by 53-Across in [see circled letters]
20 The "E" in HOMES
21 Nubian heroine of opera
22 Family member who was probably adopted
23 Hairstyle for 53-Across, colloquially
28 Place where trials are conducted
29 Hitting blackjack after blackjack, say
33 Michelangelo masterpiece
36 A few
37 See 18-Across
43 Ambience
44 "Same here!"
45 Is victorious in
48 Swindles
53 Iconic role for 2-/51-Down
56 "What have we here?!"
59 Knock 'em dead
60 Online crafts seller
61 See 18-Across
64 Like old, neglected sweaters, maybe
65 Renaissance Faire instrument
66 Sign of things to come
67 Tree-lined walkway, in France
68 Make slo-o-o-ow progress
69 Concealed mike
70 Entitled sorts?

DOWN

1 Influence
2 With 51-Down, late, beloved actress
3 Certain marketing gimmicks
4 Hell-bent (on)
5 "___ a trap!"
6 "Harrumph!"
7 Brand of artificial fat
8 Deal with a broken teleprompter, say
9 Rae Sremmurd, e.g.
10 Makeup of the planet Hoth
11 Nosedive
12 Squeak stopper
13 Turnoff for drivers
19 "Doctor Faustus" novelist Thomas
24 Mont Blanc, e.g., to locals
25 Cripple
26 Heeds
27 Merit badge displayer
30 Figure on an Aussie Xing sign, perhaps
31 World Series official
32 Formerly named
34 "___ late!"
35 Tennis champ Agassi
37 Deviate during flight, as a rocket
38 Non's opposite
39 Coffee container
40 Speak with a gravelly voice
41 Amy Adams's "Man of Steel" role
42 Puppy sounds
46 British derrière
47 So far, informally
49 Chant after a fútbol goal
50 In fine ___ (healthy)
51 See 2-Down
52 Agree to a proposal
54 Country singer Judd
55 Modern lead-in to space or security
56 Real head-turners?
57 Drag
58 Not deceived by
62 Beer barrel
63 Having four sharps
64 Reference in "Treasure Island"

by Timothy Polin

ACROSS

1 "Winnie-the-___"
5 "Kisses, dahling!"
9 Recorded on a cassette
14 Something cleared up by Clearasil
15 Akron's home
16 To whom Butler said "Frankly, my dear, I don't give a damn"
17 Slow-cooked beef entree
19 Used a light beam on in surgery
20 Samuel of the Supreme Court
21 "How do you ___?" (court query)
23 Indenting key
24 Indian tribe that lent its name to two states
26 Fabled city of wealth sought by conquistadors
28 Before, to Byron
29 401(k) relative
31 Versatile piece of furniture
32 Put into law
34 Detroit factory output
35 One with a leg up in the circus business?
39 Trig or calc
41 October birthstones
42 Tel Aviv native
46 Sch. run by the Latter-day Saints
47 Have bills
50 Gambling scam
52 High on pot
54 Bottle alternative
55 Laughs loudly
57 Big name in retail jewelry
58 "Shucks, you shouldn't have!"
60 What the starts of 17-, 26-, 35- and 50-Across are
62 ___ Ste. Marie, Mich.
63 Regarding
64 List-ending abbr.
65 Writers' wrongs?
66 Container for eggs
67 Cincinnati team

DOWN

1 Macy's Thanksgiving event
2 Eye-related
3 Like a live radio announcer
4 Aware of, in cool-cat slang
5 Cow sound
6 Fly swatter sound
7 Passage in a plane
8 Red Monopoly purchases
9 Described, as something in the past
10 "So THAT's the story here!"
11 Carb-heavy buffet area
12 Kindle or Nook
13 Some pudgy, middle-aged physiques, informally
18 Corkscrew-shaped noodles
22 Commotion
25 Asia's ___ Sea
27 Off to the ___ (starting strong)
30 Coll. entrance exam
32 Actor Hawke of "Boyhood"
33 What it takes to tango
35 Hang, Wild West-style
36 Alert to squad cars, for short
37 Big name in potato chips
38 All thumbs
39 Wrong for the role
40 "Go ahead, shoot!"
43 Long-necked waders
44 Language in Vientiane
45 "Your work is wonderful"
47 Airing after midnight, say
48 Little shaver, to a Scot
49 '50s Ford flops
51 Clear the blackboard
53 Many a John Wayne film, informally
56 Takes a chair
59 "Evil Woman" rock grp.
61 "Balderdash!"

by Bruce Haight

ACROSS

1 Harley-Davidson bike, in slang
4 Assume the role of
9 Like Vatican affairs
14 Plains tribe name
15 Emulate Picasso or Pollock
16 "Too rich for my blood"
17 Place to pay the going rate?
19 Skin abnormalities
20 Dummies
21 Dennis the Menace, for one
23 Former G.M. compact
24 Margarine
25 Put at risk
29 Affectedly polite
31 Exactly right
32 Former Nevada senator Harry
34 How Lindbergh crossed the Atlantic
35 Something that might be thrown behind a teacher's back
40 Bowling venue
41 Input for fivethirtyeight.com
42 Like Baroque architecture
44 Purchase payment plan
49 In all probability
52 Add punch to, as the punch
53 ___ pro nobis
54 Cardinal's insignia
55 Florida senator Rubio
56 "O death, where is thy ___?": I Corinthians
58 Masterpiece waiting to be found . . . or a hint to the words in the circled letters
61 Right-hand page of an open book
62 People eaters, maybe
63 Work of Horace
64 Namely, in Latin
65 "Toodles"
66 Room with an easy chair

DOWN

1 "Oh, goody!"
2 Peter with eight Academy Award nominations (and, sadly, zero wins)
3 ___ Globes
4 iPad downloads
5 "Silent" prez
6 ___ Maria
7 W.W. II Allied landing site in Italy
8 Philatelist's buy
9 Polaroid, e.g.
10 Part of the brain believed to control emotion
11 Neptune's Greek counterpart
12 Big name in car parts
13 Capts.' inferiors
18 Booty
22 Rocket launch site
25 Taunt
26 "On the Waterfront" director Kazan
27 "I'm not kidding!"
28 Cincinnati-to-Philadelphia dir.
30 1974 top 10 foreign-language hit
33 Double-___ recession
35 Repeated word for word
36 "The Vampire Chronicles" author
37 The "them" in "Let them eat cake"
38 Restaurant freebie
39 The "thing," to Hamlet
40 Cut (off)
43 Letters on many ambulances
45 King of comedy
46 Mars, for example
47 Give in (to)
48 Guards at Buckingham Palace
50 One of the Three Musketeers
51 Singer Mary J. ___
55 ___ Verde National Park
56 Guru's title
57 Tricked but good
59 "Dr." who co-founded Beats Electronics
60 Actress Susan

by John R. O'Brien

ACROSS

1 Views as
6 Place, as a wager
9 Hate with a passion
14 Yank living overseas
15 Gibbon or gorilla
16 Bête ___ (pet peeve)
17 City in upstate New York
18 Got stuck in a rut
20 Time before dinner for socializing
22 Santaland worker
23 Where clouds are
24 Venerable London theater
28 Hero war pilots
31 Source of most of Google's revenue
32 2004 event for Google, for short
33 Polygraphs
36 "Be ___!" ("Help me out here!")
37 Protection for a police officer
40 Heavy burden
41 Repeated parts of songs
42 Sarcastic laugh sound
43 Stand-up comic Schumer
45 Med. school subject
46 Maker of Mashed Potato Bites
48 Colorado winter hrs.
50 Massage
53 Ohio's nickname
57 Certain Hollywood stars . . . or an apt title for this puzzle
60 Companion ship for the Niña and Santa Maria
61 Swell up
62 Locale of Phelps's last five gold medals
63 Like chip shots
64 Targets for a college fund-raising drive, informally
65 Swimming unit
66 Fortunetellers

DOWN

1 Card with two pips
2 Praise enthusiastically
3 Huge blunder
4 "___ the Knife"
5 "Right away!," in the E.R.
6 Vision-correcting procedure
7 In a fitting manner
8 "Woo-hoo!"
9 Declares invalid
10 What chess is played on
11 Top 10 song, say
12 Valuable mine rock
13 Color of beets
19 Well-behaved
21 Something in the plus column
25 Special access for celebs
26 "No bid from me"
27 Stallion-to-be
29 Cartoon frames
30 Summer, in Soissons
31 Starting on
33 Like the Chinese and Hebrew calendars
34 Agile for one's age
35 Uno + due
36 Reebok competitor
37 ___-chic (fashion style)
38 Give out one's address?
39 Whirrer on a muggy day
43 Whom R-rated movies are intended for
44 Spray for self-defense
47 Letter-shaped girder
48 Newspapers, magazines, etc.
49 Online network admin
51 Say
52 Items on an Indian necklace
54 Marx who wasn't one of the Marx Brothers
55 Luxury resort amenities
56 Spare change?
57 Univ. degree for Romney and Bloomberg
58 Every last bit
59 "Skip to My ___"

by Zhouqin Burnikel

ACROSS

1 Pulling a rabbit out of a hat, e.g.
6 Kazakhstan's ___ Sea
10 Computer company with the slogan "Explore beyond limits"
14 Embarrass
15 Was a passenger
16 It's always getting stepped on
17 Sign of life
18 *Vessel with a large hold
20 Camera part
22 "Seinfeld" stock character?
23 *What a family spends together at the dinner table
26 Competitor of Secret
27 Predecessor of the CW
28 Mauna ___
29 Scout's shelter
31 Back on a boat
32 Hilarity, in Internet-speak
34 One side of the Pacific
38 *Branches in a storm?
43 6'11" Channing of the N.B.A.
44 Partridge's tree, in a Christmas song
45 Color TV pioneer
46 Put together, as a team
50 Ham on ___
51 Singer Scaggs with the 1976 hit "Lowdown"
52 Front of a boat
55 *Its arrival may be signaled by a ding
58 So-called "house wine of the South"
60 What you might use when you say "Giddyup!"
61 Words that can follow the ends of the answers to the starred clues
63 Sean who played Mikey in "The Goonies"
66 Band with the hit "Whip It"
67 Pope who excommunicated Martin Luther
68 Elbow, maybe
69 Garden of ___
70 Puzzlemaker Rubik
71 Strength

DOWN

1 Help at the entrance to a mall
2 Aladdin's monkey
3 Courage in battle
4 Basketball Hall-of-Famer Dan
5 Plush fabric
6 Eyebrow's shape, roughly
7 Criticize severely
8 Skillful
9 Peanut, for one
10 One of the A's in N.A.A.C.P.: Abbr.
11 Roomie
12 Woman who sings "Burn" in "Hamilton"
13 Affix again, as a badge
19 Word before air, fire or water
21 Tolerated
23 Hearty drink
24 Willing to do
25 Everyone, in Dixie
30 Give a lickin'
33 "___ your lip!"
35 First winner of horse racing's Triple Crown, 1919
36 Disguised, briefly
37 Staring
39 Item that might be fervently wanted by a prisoner
40 Start of an idea
41 President after Grant
42 Encroach on someone's land
47 "The Simpsons" bus driver
48 "That's a fine ___ of fish!"
49 Devon cathedral city
52 Rod Stewart's "Maggie May," e.g.
53 Had title to
54 Work on a loom
56 Hawk's hook
57 Maki, temaki or uramaki
59 Black, in poetry
62 Prefix with planet
64 "Now ___ seen it all!"
65 Just-minted

by Neil Padrick Wilson

ACROSS

1 Submissive
5 Heading on a list of errands
9 Moon-related
14 Church recess
15 Iris's place in the eye
16 Make amends (for)
17 Food grown in a paddy
18 Transport for Huck Finn
19 Days of the week in a calendar heading
20 "Keeping my fingers crossed"
23 Chilled jelly dishes
24 Philosopher and social activist West
28 Follow
30 Gabriel García Márquez novel "Love in the Time of __"
31 Chunk of ice in the ocean
33 Exercise area for convicts
35 Prefix with skeleton
36 Dictator __ Amin
37 __ v. Wade
38 First satellite to orbit Earth
43 Swiss capital
44 Attaches by rope, as a ball to a pole
45 Rolling Stones album "Get Yer __ Out!"
47 Place to wear one's heart, in a phrase
48 Employee at a perfumery
51 Common security device . . . or a feature of 20-, 33- or 38-Across
55 Edible mushroom
58 Out on the ocean
59 Graph line
60 Dentist's tool
61 Book between Matthew and Luke
62 Color shade
63 Recurrent theme
64 Naked
65 "__ small world after all"

DOWN

1 Santa __ (one of Columbus's ships)
2 "Iliad" and "Odyssey," for two
3 Means of getaway
4 Loudly lamenting
5 Appears after being lost
6 Egg-shaped
7 Challenge
8 Inauguration recitation
9 National __, bygone humor magazine
10 Downright
11 Immediately
12 Aardvark's morsel
13 Coin flipper at the Super Bowl, informally
21 Mil. training academy
22 Spanish eight
25 Something to look for in an emergency
26 Goof
27 Weighed down (with)
29 Actor Estrada and others
30 TV procedural set in the Big Apple
31 Defeats
32 Kick out of school
34 Words at the altar
39 2011 Oscar-nominated picture set in 1960s Mississippi
40 1930s British P.M. Chamberlain
41 Ticked off
42 What Marie Antoinette supposedly said to "let them" do
43 Indian variety of 17-Across
46 Nay's opposite
49 Brockovich and Burnett
50 Many a reggae musician, informally
52 Send to hell
53 Biblical son of Isaac
54 Jock's antithesis
55 Summer hours in Denver: Abbr.
56 Bobby who played 10 seasons with the Boston Bruins
57 __ Grande

by Andy Hinz

ACROSS

1 Bear whose bed was too hard for Goldilocks
5 With 15-Across, "Don't delay!"
8 First coat for a painter
14 At any point in history
15 See 5-Across
16 Chest of drawers
17 Repeated word before "pants on fire"
18 Queen's place
20 Mexican dish served in a shell
21 Villain's vanquisher
22 On edge
23 Queens' place
26 Loser to the tortoise, in fable
27 Lovey-dovey sound
28 "Let's Get Loud" singer, affectionately
31 People often caution against reinventing it
34 "The ___, the Proud, the Marines"
35 Oafish sort
36 Queens' place
40 In
41 Broadcast
42 Broadcast part
43 Muscle toned from push-ups, informally
44 Comic strip sound from a drunkard
45 Make bread
47 With 57-Across, Queen's place
51 Many a Donald Trump announcement
54 Snowman in "Frozen"
55 Common street name
57 See 47-Across
59 Off-roaders, for short
60 Debonair
61 Fish eggs
62 Place divers explore
63 Hung around
64 Title for two Clue characters
65 Annual Austin festival, for short

DOWN

1 Animal hide
2 Bird-related
3 "See ya"
4 Pointy stone used in early Native American weaponry
5 TV news deliverer
6 Hold together
7 Shake one's booty
8 "Masterpiece Theatre" network
9 In a relaxed rhythm, musically
10 Twisted humor
11 Heart of the matter
12 Prominent Dumbo features
13 1993 football movie starring Sean Astin
19 World Cup sport
24 Asian river whose name is one letter away from an Ivy League college
25 Site of the first-in-the-nation caucuses
28 "The Grapes of Wrath" surname
29 Central points
30 Cookie that's often pulled apart
31 "That's a ___!"
32 David ___, philosopher influenced by Locke
33 Grander than grand
34 Four-term prez
35 2014 Super Bowl performer
37 Secular
38 So done with
39 Teri who played Phoebe's mother on "Friends"
44 Scorcher
45 Inflame with love
46 Charges for some Madison Avenue firms
47 Track-and-field event
48 Bedside buzzer
49 Condom material
50 A cat is said to have nine of them
51 "Ergo . . ."
52 Blemish
53 First place where Napoleon was exiled
56 Warning initials above an Internet link
58 Interest rate setter, with "the"

by Finn Vigeland

ACROSS

1 Name of five Norwegian kings
5 Words after work or museum
10 Former Iranian leader
14 How Charles Lindbergh flew across the Atlantic
15 French department capital known in Roman times as Nemausus
16 __ Nostra (crime group)
17 Rock and roll has one in Cleveland
19 Pro's opposite
20 Org. that monitors gun sales
21 Reached
22 Shop employee
23 Words of greeting
26 Chandon's partner in Champagne
27 Blossom-to-be
28 October birthstone
30 Play, as a guitar
33 Dem.'s counterpart
36 1980s cop show that TV Guide once ranked as the greatest TV drama of all time
40 Dollar bill
41 Robber
42 Singer Fitzgerald
43 Battery for a TV remote
44 Window unit
46 James Earl Jones or Tommy Lee Jones
53 Zones
54 String quartet instrument
55 An evergreen
57 Gentlemen
58 Ruckus
60 Made off with
61 Freezing rain
62 Mexico's __ California
63 One-named New Age singer
64 Succinctly put
65 What the Ugly Duckling became

DOWN

1 Worker protection org.
2 Reluctant (to)
3 Like the band Josie and the Pussycats
4 Stereo control: Abbr.
5 Walking
6 Saks __ Avenue
7 Former Italian P.M. whose name means "beloved"
8 Cut again, as grass
9 China's Mao __-tung
10 Reduced, with "back"
11 Beehive product
12 Houston player
13 Poem like "The swallow flies up / Into a blue evening sky, / Summer's small herald"
18 Devour with the eyes
22 Cookie morsel
24 Laze
25 Share a border with
28 "Well, what have we here!"
29 Brooch
30 __ Lanka
31 Item in a golfer's pocket
32 B-ball official
33 Alternative to arbitrary governance
34 Wriggly fish
35 Smokey Bear ad, e.g., for short
37 Doesn't leave
38 Deice
39 Gave for a while
43 State that the Arctic Circle passes through
44 Aesthetic taste
45 "Call me __!" "O.K., you're . . . !"
46 Proverbial waste maker
47 Heavenly hunter
48 "Bad, bad" Brown of song
49 Small egg
50 Houston player, once
51 Metes (out)
52 Spanish wine region, with "La"
56 Horse whose coat is sprinkled with white hairs
58 F.D.R.'s successor
59 "Six-pack" muscles

by Brent Sverdloff and Michael Blake

ACROSS

1 Helps
5 —-size model
9 Things
14 Licentious man
15 Paying close attention
16 — congestion (cold symptom)
17 Small, cute residence?
19 Bygone Toyota sports car
20 Music with conga drums
21 500 sheets of paper
23 Moral toughness
24 Device for killing mosquitoes?
27 Annie who was nicknamed "Little Sure Shot"
31 Like a well-worn dirt road
32 Pouring into a shot glass, e.g.?
36 Come to earth
37 Fair-hiring inits.
38 Stars and — (Confederate flag)
42 Relatives of slack jaws?
46 Delilah was his undoing
50 "Stop joshin' me!"
51 What wakes everyone up in the morning at the duck pond?
55 Sch. for future admirals
56 Like books and tea leaves
57 Host at a roast
62 "Ad — per aspera" (Kansas' motto)
64 Archenemy of Bugs Bunny . . . who might say things like 17-, 24-, 32-, 42- and 51-Across
66 Wail of an ambulance
67 Den
68 Not — deal
69 Having an exhilarating effect
70 Trig function
71 Leave completely filled

DOWN

1 Counterpart of sciences
2 Des Moines's home
3 Fight at 20 paces, say
4 Lays eyes on
5 Expert
6 Advice-giving "Dr." of radio
7 Surprise victory
8 Sauna feature
9 Shoo-— (overwhelming favorites)
10 Instructed
11 — de corps
12 Jarhead
13 On the schedule
18 Goalie Dominik with 16 seasons in the N.H.L.
22 Man's nickname that's just wonderful?
25 Letter before zee
26 Signal from offstage
27 — exams (tests at the end of a student's fifth year at Hogwarts)
28 "Eureka!"
29 Family relations
30 "Acid"
33 Wood for archery bows
34 One of the Stooges
35 U.K. lexicon
38 Software problem
39 From — Z
40 Letter before sigma
41 Fig. on an application
42 Stir-fry vessel
43 — about (approximately)
44 Gaping opening
45 Proprietor
46 Racket sport
47 Sydneysider, for one
48 Words said over and over
49 Chicken
52 Believes
53 — Lama
54 PC network overseer
58 Degs. for creative types
59 Country with which the U.S. re-established diplomatic relations in 2015
60 Toolbar heading
61 Narrow advantage
63 "— last words?"
65 Before, to poets

by Daniel Larsen

ACROSS

1 Sunrise
5 Musial in the Baseball Hall of Fame
9 High in the air
14 Soil-related prefix
15 Diva's solo
16 Stubble remover
17 Only president to scale the Matterhorn
19 Love, to Lorenzo
20 Temporary
21 Fine, thin cotton fabric
23 Bill __, the Science Guy
24 Cheer (for)
26 Women's stockings
27 Only president whose grandfather was also president
29 Move like a bunny
32 Space streakers
35 Moms
36 Had on
37 Only president born outside the continental United States
38 Bo or Checkers
39 Only president to have 15 children
40 Photos, informally
41 Make a quick note of, with "down"
42 Writer Hemingway
43 Airport pickup driver's info
44 Only president to be a lifelong bachelor
46 Mend, as socks
48 Cheerleader's cheer
49 Lead-in to historic
52 Washington's Union __
55 TV ratings name
57 Former Afghan leader Karzai
58 Only president to be married in the White House
60 Submit a tax return online
61 End in __ (require overtime)
62 Marc Antony's lover, informally
63 Sports figures?
64 Building annex: Abbr.
65 Eurasian duck

DOWN

1 "Mack the Knife" singer Bobby
2 Excruciating pain
3 Worked on an essay or novel
4 Scent picker-upper
5 Redeemers
6 Sign of an earthquake
7 Be sick
8 Defense alliance since 1949, for short
9 Catherine of __
10 Tibetan priests
11 Seasonal thinning in the atmosphere over Antarctica
12 Only president to serve as both vice president and president without being elected to either office
13 Card that just beats a deuce
18 Printing mistakes
22 Greek P's
25 Dalton who played 007
27 __ and haws
28 Give in to gravity
30 Iron and tin sources
31 Saucy
32 Deal (with)
33 Last words?
34 Nut from Hawaii
36 Vegas casino developer Steve
38 Bespectacled Disney dwarf
39 Tourist destination in County Kerry, Ireland
41 Roman goddess, protector of women and marriage
42 Jazz up
44 Wedding figures
45 Epic poem starting with the flight from Troy
47 Slanted
49 Sacred song
50 Soprano Fleming
51 Fund, as a university chair
52 Tom Jones's "__ a Lady"
53 Only president to administer the oath of office to two other presidents
54 March Madness org.
56 Legal entities for partnerships: Abbr.
59 Inc., overseas

by Ed Stein and Paula Gamache

ACROSS

1 Plants used to make tequila
7 Health resort amenity
10 Penne ___ vodka
14 Flying insect with prominent eyespots
15 University address ender
16 Painful muscle injury
17 Frozen CO_2, familiarly
18 Grooming accessory that may be stuck in the hair
20 Classic American dessert
22 Lays out neatly
23 Granola morsel
24 Tenant
26 "___ already said too much"
28 Smaller cousin of the double bass
30 Would-be attorneys' hurdles, briefly
34 Qatari capital
36 Like some profs.
37 Frame job
38 Cass of the Mamas & the Papas
40 Obi-Wan ___ (Jedi knight)
41 Taking no guff
42 Spitting sound
45 Federal tax agts.
46 Rain delay covers
47 Undergoes oxidation
49 Driver's licenses and such, for short
50 BlackBerry alternative
52 Sans prescription, in brief
54 Washington and environs, informally
57 Material to sketch on
61 Michael Corleone player in "The Godfather"
63 Relating to songbirds
64 Take care of, as the bill
65 Ornamental pond fish
66 Trade associations
67 Genre
68 "www" address
69 Exam for an ambitious H.S. student . . . or what this puzzle has been?

DOWN

1 Opera set in Egypt
2 Trail mix
3 "Parks and Recreation" star
4 "And there it is!"
5 "And so on and so forth"
6 Generic name for a herding dog
7 Congers, e.g.
8 Sharable PC file
9 Invisible emanations
10 Currently
11 ___ Organa ("Star Wars" princess)
12 Having an open, delicate pattern
13 Chests in synagogues
19 Ultimatum's end
21 Societal troubles
25 Barfly
26 Explanatory Latin phrase
27 Physicist Alessandro, inventor of the electric battery
29 Grab a bite
31 Nuclear reactor
32 Went leisurely downriver, perhaps
33 Recasts damaging information in a favorable light, say
35 Plane hijacker
39 How freelance work is typically done
40 Pup : wolf :: ___ : fox
42 Expert
43 Source of healthful fatty acids in a StarKist can
44 Exploiter
48 Absorbs, as gravy
51 5-7-5 verse
53 Wordlessly implied
54 Batty
55 Sicken with sentiment
56 Per person
58 Garment draped over the shoulders
59 Draws to a close
60 Be at leisure
62 Neither here ___ there

by Timothy Polin

ACROSS

1 "No problem for me!"
6 Peru's capital
10 Omar of Fox's "House"
14 Dickens's "__ House"
15 Per item
16 Hand lotion ingredient
17 Intimidates, in a way
19 Crime scene barrier
20 Goes to, as a meeting
21 Not as hard
23 Airport up the coast from LAX
24 Flash mobs, once
25 "Science Guy" Bill
26 Jean __, father of Dadaism
29 "Oh, darn!"
32 Fired (up)
34 Period between wars
36 Goat's cry
37 World's fair, for short
38 Circus animals that balance beach balls on their noses
40 "When You Wish __ a Star"
43 Manning who was twice Super Bowl M.V.P.
45 Watch or clock
47 Showed in syndication, say
49 Justice Kagan
50 Numbered hwy.
51 Abbr. before a credit card date
52 Feeling blue
54 __ card (cellphone chip)
56 Exercise in a pool
58 Cross-reference for further information
62 Male deer
63 On a lower floor
66 "__ kleine Nachtmusik"
67 "Ars Amatoria" poet
68 Foe
69 Ones in suits?
70 Big name in pet food
71 Aid in storm-tracking

DOWN

1 "2 Broke Girls" airer
2 Ski area near Salt Lake City
3 "Cool!"
4 Pub game
5 Artist Georgia who is known for her flower canvases
6 Cheryl of "Charlie's Angels"
7 Wall St. debuts
8 Trim the lawn
9 Sleeper's problem
10 Has supper
11 Unlined sheets without any writing
12 Sailor who's smitten by Olive Oyl
13 Get angry
18 Pig noses
22 Name first encountered in Genesis 2
24 "Understand?," slangily
26 Big galoot
27 Tyrannosaurus __
28 Classroom missile
30 Followed a weight-loss plan
31 Alternative to AOL or Yahoo
33 Island ESE of Oahu
35 Pepsi, for one
39 Just knows
41 Month before Nov.
42 Born: Fr.
44 Police dept. figure
46 Van Gogh or Van Dyck
47 Moses parted it
48 Beautifully strange
53 "Me, too"
55 2016 Disney film set in Polynesia
57 10 and 8 for Bart and Lisa Simpson, respectively
58 Do the breaststroke, e.g.
59 Terminals
60 Like the score 7-7
61 Humorous Bombeck
64 Lab eggs
65 Damascus's land: Abbr.

by Zhouqin Burnikel

ACROSS

1 ___ jacket (bit of casualwear)
5 Dish that's sometimes rated in "alarms"
10 Curds and ___
14 Wagon part
15 Like much music
16 In fine fettle
17 Widespread
18 1960s activist Hoffman
19 Has
20 ___ friends (not having to be on one's guard)
22 Quaint inn, informally
24 Cry after "Ready!"
25 Muffed one
27 Bearlike
29 Powerful Renaissance family
32 A book collector might seek a first one
33 Available
34 Spanish girlfriend
35 Italy's shape
36 Setting for much of the movie "Lion"
38 Zippo
42 People encountered by Pizarro
44 Things ghosts lack
46 Riga native
49 Charms
50 In addition
51 What tryptophan is said to induce
52 Place to go for a "me day"
53 Munchkins
55 Nash who wrote "Parsley / Is gharsley"
59 Turner or Fey
61 Bother greatly
63 Tell to "Do it!"
64 Lead-in to a conclusion
65 Movie, informally
66 Class with mats
67 Feature of a late-night show set
68 Words to live by
69 Catch sight of

DOWN

1 Morning joe
2 Start of many a doctor's visit
3 In addition
4 Outcome that's overall unfavorable
5 Windy City 'L' overseer
6 Imaginary tiger friend in the comics
7 Not on good terms (with)
8 Done nothing
9 Infamous prison featured in the 1969 best seller "Papillon"
10 "___ knew?"
11 Southernmost U.S. state
12 Weather concern in 11-Down
13 Lackeys
21 Sheepish look
23 Two-masted vessel
26 Socialist Workers Party's ideology
28 Honest sorts . . . or what the circled squares contain?
29 Palindromic boy's name
30 "Be My Yoko ___" (first single by Barenaked Ladies)
31 Pi's follower
32 Former Big Four record co.
34 They're taken out in newspapers
37 Palindromic girl's name
39 Lungful
40 Hollywood ending?
41 Nincompoop
43 River that feeds Lake Nasser
45 Topping in kosher restaurants
46 Didn't run out
47 Have dreams
48 Features of some country singers
49 Region on the Rhine
51 Took effect
54 Area between mountains
56 Plunge
57 Breakfast food with a rhyming slogan
58 In order
60 Totally fine
62 Box office purchase: Abbr.

by Jacob Stulberg

ACROSS

1 Medicine-approving org.
4 Wine barrel
8 Awards in the ad biz
13 Rainbow shape
14 Opera melody
15 Quick look
16 Paving goo
17 Article of outerwear for an urbanite?
19 Too many of them "spoil the broth"
21 Bunny's movement
22 Component of a science course
23 Article of outerwear for a champagne drinker?
26 Done: Fr.
27 Having a ho-hum attitude
28 Warm greeting
29 Justice Sotomayor
30 Leave full
31 Common weather phenomenon in San Francisco
32 Ankle-high work shoe
33 Article of outerwear for a candy lover?
36 Potato chips, to Brits
39 ___-rock (music genre)
40 Entree that may be slathered in barbecue sauce
44 "Grand" women
45 Classic muscle car
46 Removes the rind from
47 Inlets
48 Article of outerwear for a housekeeper?
50 Lee who directed "Life of Pi"
51 ___ Harbour, Fla.
52 Newspapers, collectively
53 Article of outerwear for a General Motors employee?
57 Bird that gives a hoot
59 Gold standards
60 ___ lily
61 Chinese leader with a Little Red Book
62 Panache
63 Rat or roach
64 No. after a main telephone no.

DOWN

1 What the "Gras" of Mardi Gras means
2 Count with fangs
3 Circus tumbler
4 Witch's laugh
5 Crop up
6 Command to a dog
7 Mary ___ cosmetics
8 Bit from a movie
9 Fond du ___, Wis.
10 Faintest idea
11 Easter Island locale
12 Belgrade native
15 Unappetizing food that might be served with a ladle
18 Carpet variety
20 Thinks, thinks, thinks (about)
23 Small ammo
24 Command spoken while pulling the reins
25 Rambunctious little kids
26 200- or 400-meter run, e.g.
29 Madrid Mrs.
31 N.F.L. three-pointers: Abbr.
32 Droid
34 Alternative to FedEx
35 Thicken, as blood
36 Holders of some music collections
37 Headgear for a drizzly day
38 Descriptive language
41 Annoying
42 Honeycomb product
43 Retired jet, for short
45 Shorebird with a distinctive shriek
46 Caged talker
48 Painters' touches
49 Some computer picture files
51 Memory unit
54 Kilmer of "Top Gun"
55 Nile viper
56 Middle of Arizona?
58 Auction grouping

by Susan Gelfand

ACROSS

1 Things that may be displayed on a general's chest
7 "Oh no!," in comics
10 Old Testament prophet
14 "Leave this to me!"
15 West who said "It's better to be looked over than overlooked"
16 Foreign Legion hat
17 Famously unfinished 14th-century literary work, with "The"
20 Hotel name synonymous with poshness
21 Org. whose motto is "We are their voice"
22 Historical period
23 "Happy Days" diner
24 "How cheap!"
27 Exam for the college-bound, for short
29 Reggae relative
30 What one might start over with
35 Arthur Ashe Stadium org.
39 Prevents litter?
40 Beverage that may be 41-Across
41 Alternative to "bottled"
42 "Shame on you!" sounds
43 Losing crunchiness, as chips
45 Ukr., e.g., once
47 Org.'s cousin
48 Historical figure played by David Bowie in "The Prestige"
54 Narcotics-fighting grp.
57 Rapid-fire gun
58 Embellish
59 Uphill aid for skiers
60 "Finally . . ."
64 Cut with a beam
65 Sighs of relief
66 Some family reunion attendees
67 ___ terrier
68 Tennis do-over
69 Like wind chimes

DOWN

1 Millionths of a meter
2 Spam medium
3 "Shhh!"
4 Movie that came out about the same time as "A Bug's Life"
5 Emulate Pinocchio
6 Orch. section
7 Something necessary
8 Gripes
9 It's just for openers
10 Letters on a "Wanted" poster
11 Major scuffle
12 Sydney ___ House
13 Agave fiber used in rugs
18 Sheep sound
19 Job to do
24 Catches some rays
25 Altitudes: Abbr.
26 Gibes
28 States positively
30 Winter hrs. in Texas
31 The Stones' "12 × 5" and "Flowers"
32 Chinese philosopher ___-tzu
33 "___ Baba and the Forty Thieves"
34 Full complement of bowling pins
36 "Give him some space!"
37 Chess champ Mikhail
38 Copy
41 Bones, anatomically
43 Done bit by bit
44 Half of a square dance duo
46 Chunk of concrete
48 Makes void
49 ___ Walton League (conservation group)
50 Given to smooching
51 ___ nth degree
52 Dadaist Max
53 Lead-in to Cat or cone
55 Prop found near a palette
56 ___-craftsy
59 27-Across taker, typically
61 Shape of a three-way intersection
62 Channel with explosive content?
63 52, in old Rome

by Freddie Cheng

ACROSS

1 Projects, with "out"
5 Hans Christian Andersen, by nationality
9 "Whatever You Like" rapper + Gets some color at the beach
15 Queens stadium name
16 Comic book legend Lee
17 Wild cat
18 Root on
20 Beliefs
21 Massive lang. reference
22 Arabian land near the Strait of Hormuz
23 Like a tightrope, more so than a slackline
24 Frat dude + Cpls. and sgts.
26 Actor Lundgren + Elected officials
30 Something often inflated and rarely appreciated
31 Inner things that may be suppressed
33 "Terrible" czar
34 Willem of "Spider-Man"
36 ". . . man __ machine?"
37 Take a stand by not standing
38 Goal for six answers in this puzzle?
41 Expels, as lava
43 Tolkien tree being
44 Particle with a negative charge
46 Garfield's frenemy
47 Jordan Peele's directorial debut
49 Final, in a math series
50 Butter square + Hilarious people
52 London's Big __ + Ladies
55 Pairs
56 Reign
57 Course overseer, for short
58 Sentimentality
61 Concerning both the moon and sun's motions
63 Cosmopolitan
64 Abbr. on an envelope
65 Malek of "Mr. Robot"
66 U.S. soldier + Little scurriers

67 "CSI" actress Elisabeth
68 Snake eyes

DOWN

1 "Twilight" werewolf
2 Led down the aisle
3 Classic schoolkid's alibi
4 "Understand?"
5 Internet link?
6 Drill sergeant's command
7 Bread often served with curry
8 Finish
9 Bottom rows on spreadsheets
10 Freeze over, as a windshield
11 Bonus in baseball
12 Bottle marked "XXX," maybe
13 Do __ Call Registry
14 Ave. crossers
19 Mythical bird in the "Arabian Nights"
23 Like Mandarin
25 At least
26 Popular corn chip
27 "Hmm, leave this to me"
28 Scot's refusal
29 Show filmed weekly in N.Y.C.
32 Steeds
35 Western Hemisphere grp.
37 Kith's partner
39 Sugar sources from a farm
40 It runs down the middle of the Pacific

41 Soak
42 "Get a room" elicitor, for short
45 Stanley Cup matchup, e.g.
47 Gives a boost
48 Operating system in the Linux family
51 Possible reply to "Don't forget!"
53 "Super" gaming console
54 Hindu dresses
56 Book after Judges
58 Snug rug inhabitant
59 "Exodus" hero
60 Course list abbr.
61 __ Vegas
62 Obsession of el rey Midas

by Amanda Chung, Karl Ni and Erik Agard

ACROSS

1 City where you can view Edvard Munch's "The Scream"
5 Japanese roadster
10 Images on Australia's 50-cent coins
14 Dweller along the Don
15 Shades for many window shades
16 Mom's mom
17 Success for a closer in baseball
18 ___ and Link (popular online comedy duo)
19 Compact arms
20 Mosque of ___ (shrine in Jerusalem)
21 "Check it out for yourself!"
22 Keepsakes for March Madness victors
23 So-called "Goddess of Pop"
25 Idle on the set
27 Ribs
30 "Heck if I know"
34 Apex predators of the deep
35 Phishing target, for short
38 Sticks, as a landing
39 Peter or Paul
40 Tasted
42 Sub
43 Major ___, "Dr. Strangelove" character who rides the bomb
44 Blather
45 Exchange of swear words?
46 Literally, "a hopeful person"
49 It may involve dips, in two different senses
52 Nickname
53 Ingredient in black jelly beans
57 Culinary phrase
58 Ones reading the Book of Shadows
61 Kind of operation in number theory, for short
62 Hidden trouble indicator . . . or what you'll need to finish this crossword?

65 Superhero's defining quality
66 Recount
67 It's between an A and a B
68 Yoga poses

DOWN

1 ___ buco
2 It's symbolized by a star and crescent
3 It flows and glows
4 Entry fees
5 Comes out
6 Blood of the gods, in Greek myth
7 Exposes
8 Alexander the Great, to Aristotle
9 Like Confucianism or Taoism
10 Formal rejection
11 Puzzle in which people take turns solving
12 Put the pedal to the metal
13 Stylishness
24 Fathers and sons
26 F–, e.g.
27 Athletic type . . . or athletic wear
28 Pasta common in minestrone
29 Digitize
31 Word on a gravestone
32 Muppet who refers to himself in the third person
33 The snakes in the movie line "Snakes. Why'd it have to be snakes?"
35 Like one-size-fits-all garments

36 The Admiral's Cup, e.g.
37 Words after "Oh, no!"
40 Waze or WeChat
41 Bog
47 Deemed appropriate
48 Shockers
49 Leader of the land down under?
50 Out
51 Rabbit fur
54 "Let me clarify . . ."
55 In a way
56 Nips
59 Teensy
60 Indianapolis-based sports org.
63 "Hurrah!"
64 No ___ Day (October 13)

by Jeff Chen

ACROSS

1 North Carolina county . . . or lead-in to "-ville"
5 Family member, endearingly
9 Produced
14 Keep away from
15 Attribute for "my girl" after "Five Foot Two" in a 1920s tune
17 Notable feature of Chicago
18 *Literally, "small ovens"
19 Pricey bar
21 CPR provider, for short
22 "That's quite a trick!"
23 Philosopher Lao-___
24 Throw in
27 Its first vol., A-Ant, was published in 1884
29 Slick
30 *Literally, "outside the works"
34 Toward the rudder
35 ___ Cruces, N.M.
36 Eponymous naturalist of a California woods
39 *Literally, "boil and lower"
43 Slips up
44 Sir, to a Brit
45 Ad follower
46 *Literally, "thousand-leaf"
51 Succor, briefly
54 ___ Paulo, Brazil
55 Notable feature of San Francisco
56 Org. that monitors gas prices
57 Prefix with -nautic
59 What the V sign can also represent
61 Question after a bad pun
63 Julia Child's PBS show, with "The" . . . or one associated with the answers to the starred clues
67 Example of change
68 Ritzy hotel accommodations
69 Ending with evil
70 Actress Spacek
71 Contemptible sort
72 Capp of classic comics

DOWN

1 Just like
2 Historic political visitor to Pearl Harbor on 12/27/16
3 Want really badly
4 Inner: Prefix
5 Energy
6 "Roger" in the Navy
7 Rose no longer seen in fields
8 Writer after whom an asteroid and Mars crater are named
9 #1 pal
10 Jet-black
11 Secures, as scrapbook photos
12 Like an otologist's exam
13 Irascible
16 River gamboler
20 Small amount
25 "Guest" at a child's tea party
26 Negotiation goal
28 50% to start?
31 ___ und Drang
32 Grammarian's concern
33 Food that comes in rolls
37 A quarantined person is kept in it
38 Like about 17% of the land in Holland
40 Org. with a feared black-and-white flag
41 Muscular
42 Old Chevy model renamed the Sonic
47 Certain trellis components
48 Revealing, in a way
49 Big name in comfy footwear
50 Cafe
51 White House family of the early 1910s
52 "Vive ___!"
53 Work groups
58 Word sometimes substituted for "your"
60 Interstates 70 and 71 cross in its capital
62 Ancient Icelandic literary work
64 "___ 'Havoc,' and let slip the dogs of war": Mark Antony
65 J.F.K. stat
66 Provided sustenance

by Jeffrey Wechsler

ACROSS

1 Interrogate
5 Leave flabbergasted
10 IV units
13 French 101 verb
14 Fermented milk drink
15 Pre-snap signal
16 Made a false move?
18 Finding fault with
20 Word with sauce or milk
22 Some R.S.V.P.s
23 Bears: Lat.
24 "Fire away!"
27 Trader ___
29 They can be taxed like partnerships, for short
30 Goal for Ponce de León
35 Give the silent treatment?
36 Stops partway through
37 Bon ___
39 Costumes
43 Actor Mark
45 Tatooine has two of them
47 Incensed
52 Successor of Carson
53 "___ of Dogs" (2018 animated movie)
54 Univ. department
55 "Um, don't look now, but . . ."
56 Vietnamese new year
58 Still
60 Colorful food fish
63 Beach house?
67 Key for exiting full-screen mode
68 Carafe size
69 Where work piles up . . . with a hint to this puzzle's theme
70 "Please keep it down"
71 Radiate
72 Where finished work goes . . . with a hint to this puzzle's theme

DOWN

1 The end of mathematics?
2 Western native
3 Tick off
4 Middle of a puzzle?
5 Org. concerned with good breeding
6 Will, if one can
7 Start of some hybrid music styles
8 Speeds (along)
9 "Dancing With the Starts" co-host Andrews
10 Oscar-winning Cliff Robertson title role
11 One in a blue-and-yellow uniform
12 Somewhat stocky
17 Place to get one's kicks?
19 Wide divide
21 Question to a returning pest
24 Cash cache, for short
25 Gang weapon
26 ___ sabe
28 Sportscaster Dick
31 Fairylike
32 Jargons
33 One way to stare
34 German direction
38 "That feels so-o-o good!"
40 Put into service
41 What you might do with gas or a fist
42 Features of tapirs
44 Headwaiter
46 Prone to blushing, say
47 Skirt features
48 Go over anew
49 Three barleycorns, as defined by Edward II
50 Sepulcher
51 Partners of haws
56 Mars candy
57 Roman rebuke
59 Become less crowded
61 "Hurrah!"
62 Weird
64 Go back
65 John of Cambridge
66 70, in old Rome

by Alex Eaton-Salners

ACROSS

1 Hosp. hookups
4 Sneaky scheme
8 Two-by-four, for one
13 Part of XXX
14 Churchill prop
15 Not so cordial
16 Knickknack
18 Painter's primer
19 Accustom (to)
20 Excessive sentimentality
22 The Falcons, on a scoreboard
23 Some steak orders
24 Shameless audacity
29 Yes, to Yvette
30 "Frank, __ & Sammy: The Ultimate Event" (1989 documentary)
31 Response to an affront
33 Follower of "Twice-Told" or "old wives'"
37 Sí, at sea
38 Source of the six longest Across answers in this puzzle
40 One of the Gulf states: Abbr.
41 Italian city known for its cheese
43 Girl or boy intro
44 Rose Bowl, e.g.
45 Severe displeasure
47 "Jeez!"
49 Two- or three-ring holder
52 "Cool" amount of money
53 Long, involved account
55 Mount that Moses mounted
57 Suspect's out
58 Choked up with emotion
61 Backless sofa
62 Naïvely optimistic Muppet
63 For whom the Edgar Award is named
64 John who invented the steel plow

65 Old TV's "Guiding Light," for one
66 W-2 datum: Abbr.

DOWN

1 Cousin of Gomez Addams
2 End of Caesar's boast
3 Dog with a bearded muzzle
4 Crosstown rival of the University of Houston
5 "That's disgusting!"
6 Noted Fifth Avenue emporium
7 Standing tall
8 Sort who can't keep a secret
9 Locale of Tuvalu and Nauru
10 Separator of some rows
11 Snoozes, e.g.
12 Physician who was once a regular on "The Oprah Winfrey Show"
14 "Undo" shortcut in Microsoft Word
17 "I'm __ here!"
21 TV debut of 1972
24 Give someone a hand
25 Informal greeting
26 Tire gauge meas.
27 Actor nominated for 34 Emmys
28 Couldn't help but
32 "Too bad!"
34 1960s fad light sources
35 Alternative to Israir Airlines
36 What "S" may stand for on a dinner table
38 Gridiron marker
39 Yield to gravity
42 Fancy hotel room amenity
44 Sheeplike
46 Sushi roll fish
48 Author Zola
49 Misrepresent
50 "Uncle!"
51 Opposite of pans
53 Org. advocating highway safety
54 Bolívar, in much of South America
55 Problem with a 45-r.p.m. record
56 Major N.Y.S.E. events
59 Genetic inits.
60 Half a score . . . or a perfect score

by Scot Ober and Jeff Chen

ACROSS

1 African menace
6 Opening between the vocal cords
13 Six-time M.L.B. All-Star Rusty
14 Outing at which participants go hog-wild?
15 Run out, as a well
16 Place securely
17 Series of exchanges in a chat window
19 Longtime parent of Parlophone
20 Gross figure
24 "Ciao!"
26 Part of a Disneyland postal address
30 "Jay Leno's Garage" channel
31 They're connected to arteries
32 Hosp. procedure with a readout
34 Woven into
38 ___ soda
39 Rodenticide
42 Catches
45 1950s title lyric after "When we are dancing and you're dangerously near me . . ."
46 One from the Land of Cakes
47 Group that bows onstage
48 For all ___
50 Trophy
55 Completely fall apart
58 In a frenzy
60 Without intermission
61 First fill-in on many a form
62 Contributor to a locker room odor
63 Door

DOWN

1 Venue near Penn Station, for short
2 Alter ego for Lex Luthor
3 Improved the situation
4 Prickly plant parts
5 You'll never get to the bottom of this
6 Rotted
7 In the cellar
8 Fantasy creature spawned from mud
9 "___: Ragnarok" (2017 film)
10 Wine vessel
11 Worshiper of the sun god Inti
12 Part of an office building address: Abbr.
14 Brightly colored perennial
18 "___, 'tis true . . ." (start of a Shakespearean sonnet)
19 Series finale?
21 Drives in a field
22 Corresponding need?
23 Jet (off)
25 Stomach
27 Half a laugh
28 In-state attendees of Drake University, e.g.
29 Summer hrs. for 28-Down
33 Something it's bad to pull
34 The rainbow personified
35 Badger or hound
36 Top
37 Associate in finance, say
40 Blue-green?
41 Tiny amount of time: Abbr.
43 Nightclub hiree
44 Brand at a garage
49 Hackneyed
51 Fashionably high-class
52 Makeup of some sci-fi beams
53 Some dip, informally
54 "Let's do this thing!"
55 Tour division
56 Barnyard male
57 ___ Speedwagon
59 Only 5-point tile in Scrabble

by Sam Ezersky

ACROSS

1 Deg. for a museum worker
4 Loll
8 Elapse
14 Dashboard part
16 Musical run with four sharps
17 Part played by women and girls?
18 Have hot cocoa on a winter day, say
19 U.S. president with a Nobel Peace Prize
20 Take a breath
22 Had for dinner
23 Blue ___ (Duke mascot)
25 Use a lot?
27 Overhaul
29 Area below "To:" in an email?
32 Land in a Beatles song
35 Tide alternative
36 "Ghost" psychic Oda ___ Brown
37 Ones on set with 2009's "Star Trek" director?
40 Any one of the 12 steps?
42 Grant with the 1991 #1 hit "Baby Baby"
43 Battery size
45 "This round's ___"
46 Group of buildings housing a King?
49 Recedes
53 What Lot's wife became
54 Common bacterium
57 Go bad
58 Group in the original "Ocean's 11" movie
61 "Sure, that works"
63 Harrowing experience
64 Lover of Cummings's poetry?
66 Sasha ___, Beyoncé's alter ego
67 Speedster's undoing
68 Owns (up to)
69 Money to belong
70 Green-minded org.

DOWN

1 Freight train part
2 Dwell (on)
3 Bruce Wayne's butler
4 Intertwined
5 Eccentric
6 "Million Years ___" (Adele song)
7 Irony?
8 Places for parishioners
9 "Now!"
10 Libretto, for example
11 "Spider-Man" director, 2002
12 Horse with evenly mixed black-and-white hairs
13 "Indeedy"
15 Gang pistol, in old slang
21 Jewelry designer Peretti
24 Obsolescent TV attachment
26 Place to bounce a baby
28 "___ House," 1970 Crosby, Stills, Nash & Young hit
30 Panache
31 Quahog or geoduck
33 Where clothes often rip
34 Trade
37 Nasty comments
38 Pan creator
39 Island group in the Aegean Sea
41 Spike who directed "BlacKkKlansman"
44 Smart fellow?
45 Tic-tac-toe loser
47 Bewhiskered mammals
48 ___ College, liberal arts school in St. Petersburg, Fla.
50 Subject of a New York Times column until 2015
51 Study, informally
52 Chest bones
55 Feminist writer Audre
56 Giant furniture stores
59 Tempo
60 Hoppy mediums?
62 With 63-Down, distant
63 See 62-Down
65 What's found in the French rivière?

by Melinda Gates and Joel Fagliano

ACROSS

1 ___ bar
5 Substance
9 Zombie's domain
14 Kind of rinse
15 Nose (along)
16 Coverage of the Senate?
17
20 Draw upon
21 Word that sounds like a state when accented on the second syllable rather than the first
22 Place
23 Noted Warhol subject
24 Spotted
26 Cause for a shootout
27 Gives, as roles
31 Packing
33
36 Brand name derived from the phrase "Service Games"
37 Sign of summer
38 Iraq's ___ City
42
47 Crowd, they say
49 Good standing in the Navy?
50 Break up a plot?
51 In times past
54 Munchkin
55 "'Tis sad"
57 Hyundai model
59 Rejuvenation station
62
65 Bean sprouts?
66 Lambchop
67 Bellyache
68 Stuff from which some suits are made?
69 Some overhead light covers
70 Dr. Foreman player on "House"

DOWN

1 Vegetarian choice
2 Early-blooming ornamental
3 Moolah
4 "___ see you"
5 Highest-grossing animated film of 2015
6 Tolkien tree creatures
7 Pays for a workout, say
8 "Hah! Done!"
9 Card letters
10 Kind of black
11 Light
12 Help in getting past a bouncer
13 Immigration or health care
18 Brand concern
19 One way to play something
23 During flight
25 Org. whose first-ever presidential endorsement was Ronald Reagan
27 Hoofed animal
28 ___-bear
29 Dip
30 Songs for one
32 Walt Whitman's "Song of ___"
34 Added fuel to
35 Leaves
39 Fiver
40 Follow relentlessly
41 Scripts, informally
43 Lead-in to Latin
44 Awareness
45 Rocks on the edge
46 Permissible to be eaten, in a way
47 Spanish city where El Greco lived
48 Fastball, in baseball
50 Something you might kick after you pick it up
52 Complex purchase, in brief
53 Word next to an arrow
56 Thwack
58 Starbuck's order giver
59 [Just like . . . that!]
60 One in custody, informally
61 African menaces
63 Part of a dollar sign
64 Chill

by Daniel Kantor

ACROSS

1 The challengers
5 Sailor's quaff
9 Presidential perk until 1977
14 Speck
15 Roof feature
16 Jibe
17 Roald who wrote "James and the Giant Peach"
18 Sea nymphs, in Greek mythology
20 Like Edward Snowden
22 Tear in two
23 Rank for Jay Landsman on "The Wire": Abbr.
24 Munch Museum city
25 Gives comfort
27 Generation ___
29 Had by heart
32 1,000 in a metric ton
33 Certain operating system
35 Check closely
37 Gobble down
39 Muckraker Tarbell
40 An American abroad
44 Like Brutalist architecture
47 Top-notch
48 Utah's ___ Canyon
50 Annual Austin festival, for short
52 Prince George, to Prince William
53 Like a dog on a walk, usually
55 Haul
57 Tuna type
58 Nonhumanities subjects, for short
60 Immature
63 Vain queen who boasted that she was more beautiful than 18-Across
66 Object of worship
67 "Don't Cry for Me Argentina" musical
68 Actor Epps
69 Chasers in many a chase scene
70 Mails
71 Upscale
72 Place to play musical spoons

DOWN

1 It ebbs and flows
2 Hoodwink
3 Where 63-Across ruled prior to her banishment
4 Locales for many food courts
5 Finish
6 "Go, team!"
7 Finished
8 Big factor in longevity
9 Football field marking
10 Mature
11 Shortening brand
12 Garden dividers
13 Lab work
19 Long, thin mushroom
21 Herd at Yellowstone
26 "She" responds to voice commands
27 Director Van Sant
28 Writer Beattie
30 One end of a maze
31 Moves like a heron
34 Checks for a fracture, perhaps
36 "Das Kapital" author
38 Purplish-red flowers
41 God who banished 63-Across to the sky, as depicted by the constellation formed by the X's in this puzzle's finished grid
42 Year abroad
43 Base ___
45 Handle
46 Where a river meets the sea
48 Sit quietly, perhaps
49 Cereal fruit
51 Took gold
53 Gets ready to play hockey, with "up"
54 Train stop
56 Guessing a number an audience member has thought of, e.g.
59 Office note
61 Alexander who wrote "The Dunciad"
62 Besides
64 Norm: Abbr.
65 English novelist McEwan

by Jennifer Nutt

ACROSS

1 Pride Month inits.
5 Org. defending 1-Across rights
9 At full speed
14 This and that
15 "Yay!"
16 1930s vice president John ___ Garner
17 It might pop out of a kid's mouth
19 Thus far
20 Seven-time All-Star Dave, who pitched for the Toronto Blue Jays
21 Wind instrument
23 Heavy metal band whose name is a euphemism for "Jesus Christ!"
27 Notable times
31 Pacific Northwest hub, informally
32 Main connections, of a sort
34 Going rates?
39 Touching
40 Carefully explained
42 Profundity
43 Fashion designer whose namesake brand features a rhinoceros in its logo
44 "Count me in!"
47 Distort
48 Swinger's club
53 Eponymous regatta-winning yacht of 1851
54 Bumbling
59 Occupy, as a table
60 Ingredient in some cocktails . . . or a hint to the last words in 17-, 23-, 32-, 43- and 48-Across
64 Occupied
65 Long nap?
66 Actress Dobrev of "The Vampire Diaries"
67 Bounded
68 "This is probably dumb but I'm doing it anyway" hashtag
69 Online handicrafts marketplace

DOWN

1 High shots
2 Overabundance
3 Benjamin Netanyahu's nickname
4 Choice A for Hamlet
5 Flabbergasted feeling
6 Minor player, metaphorically
7 Comedian Costello
8 Greatest extent
9 Southern, and then some
10 An official language of New Zealand
11 2014 movie musical starring Quvenzhané Wallis
12 Phone tapping targets?
13 Unused to
18 Great Society prez
22 Audit expert, for short
24 "We deliver for you" org.
25 Off! ingredient
26 Penlight powerers, often
27 "My word!"
28 Fury
29 Rush order
30 Stick in the fire?
33 Under restraint
35 "To . . ." things
36 Stone-cold cinch
37 Gospel with the Prodigal Son parable
38 Put in a hold
40 Epitome of gentleness
41 Calculus calculation
43 Evil, in Laval
45 High Sierra runner
46 Like a blank stare
48 Herb with "sweet" and "holy" varieties
49 ___ acid
50 Institute
51 Wipe away
52 Senator Kaine of Virginia
55 Soccer striker's jersey number, traditionally
56 Out
57 Female swans
58 Server load?
61 "Well, what have we here?!"
62 Indian lentil dish
63 Before this time

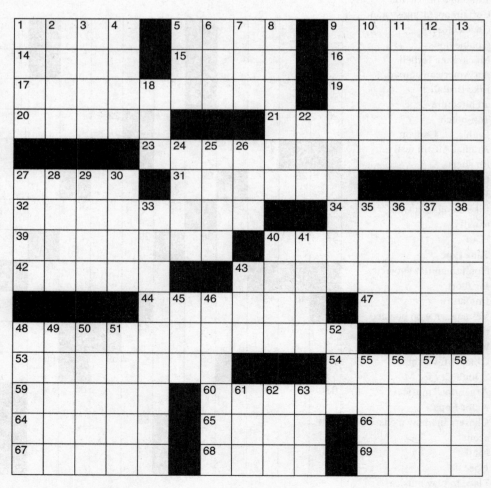

by Joon Pahk

ACROSS

1 Quickly take down
4 UV rays, to the skin
8 Alternative to paper
15 Singer whose name sounds like a cry of dismay
16 Highlands hillside
17 One-named singer whose real first name is Robyn
18 Onetime resident of Mauritius
20 Here and there
21 Former Hawaiian senator Daniel
22 "Um, sure"
24 Pant-leg tugger, perhaps
25 Sea cave dwellers
26 They might have 2½ or 3 stars
30 Partner of yon
32 YouTube offering
33 Deep voices
34 Suffix with cannon or block
36 Behind bars
40 Pantry pest
41 2016 Best Picture "winner" (for about two minutes)
44 Thurman of "Even Cowgirls Get the Blues"
45 1950s Corsairs, e.g.
47 Fashionable letters
48 Podded plants
50 An addict may go into this
52 Summer cover-up
54 Swear words?
58 Elisha in the National Inventors Hall of Fame
60 Gasteyer of "Mean Girls"
61 Put on board
62 Part of la península ibérica
64 Carpenter's tool
67 Series whose first seven members are sung to the starts of 18-, 26-, 41- and 54-Across
69 To eat a late lunch or wait until dinner, say
70 ___-tiller
71 Majors in film
72 Gets the wrinkles out
73 Annual Austin music-and-media festival, briefly
74 Settings for some TV dramas, for short

DOWN

1 ___ Whittaker, player of the first female Doctor on "Doctor Who"
2 How you can count up to five
3 Sheets that might have check boxes
4 "Dear" one
5 Super Bowl-winning QB Bob
6 Canal zone?
7 Second chances
8 A ___ (independent of experience)
9 Networking site
10 Cries of surprise
11 Drain
12 U.S. govt. security
13 Getting pulled along
14 Finds a part for
19 Dethrones
23 Squalid shelters
27 Unwritten
28 One setting up at a flea market
29 Apple creation
31 Jewish campus group
33 Sweetheart, in modern lingo
35 Piece of multifunctional furniture
37 Record holder
38 Designer of attractions at Walt Disney theme parks
39 Dorm watchers, in brief
42 Volcanic discharge
43 Plus
46 'Fore
49 ___ Troopa (Mario foe)
51 Some stoves
53 Skilled sorts
54 ___ 500
55 Live
56 Selassie of Ethiopia
57 The ten of a ten-speed
59 Leaves full
63 Finish third
65 "___ Misérables"
66 Diamond V.I.P.s
68 Jewish deli supply

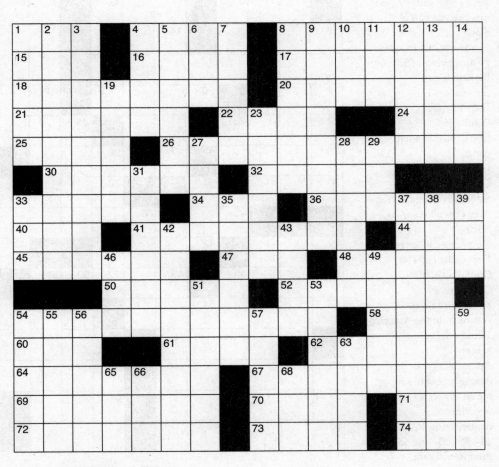

by Alex Eaton-Salners

ACROSS

1 Keeps in the loop, in a way
4 Ones making passing judgments, for short?
7 Witty
13 Genre at the Grammys
14 Its capital is Abu Dhabi, for short
15 ___ Sea, body of water between Sicily and Greece
16 Picking out of a lineup, e.g.
18 Sign at some beaches
19 Doctrine
20 Lamb in literature
21 Not pay taxes by mail
22 Upper body muscles, for short
24 Extremely
26 Pulitzer Prize winner for "A Death in the Family"
27 Animated Princess of Power
29 James who sang "At last, my love has come along . . ."
30 Headwear in a Prince hit
32 Posting on an office bulletin board
34 ___ sauce
35 Didn't delete
39 Potus #36
42 One choice in a party game
43 Home pages?
47 Car named after an automotive competition
49 "I'm Down" vis-à-vis "Help!"
52 Climber's challenge
53 First name in "The Godfather"
55 Chess piece
57 Mantelpiece, e.g.
58 Award from the American Theater Wing
59 Mix in
60 Apartment type
61 Annual event to support breast cancer awareness . . . or a hint to answering 16-, 22-, 24-, 35-, 53- and 55-Across
63 Producer of rain
64 Prompt

65 About
66 Dampened
67 Letters for college applicants
68 Result of imperfect service

DOWN

1 Wrist attachment
2 Scale awkwardly, with "up"
3 Go downhill fast
4 Collections of patches, say
5 Exile
6 Company in the book "Console Wars"
7 Precursor to IMAX
8 Bathtub item
9 Salad green
10 State flowers of Rhode Island, Illinois and New Jersey
11 Enthusiastically gonna
12 Co-workers of M.D.s
13 Facility at Quantico
17 Govt. agency that combats smuggling
23 Stagger
24 ___ Fox
25 "Woo-hoo!"
28 Journalist in a military unit
31 Colleague of Mary, Murray and Lou on "The Mary Tyler Moore Show"
33 Application for the Mr. Universe contest?
36 Burgers and fries, typically
37 Donald Duck's nephews, e.g.
38 Make out
39 Tyler of "The Lord of the Rings"
40 Visibly take offense
41 Activity for many a senior
44 She helped Theseus navigate the Labyrinth
45 Seaside sculpture, say
46 Easter supply
48 Give recognition
50 Flow away from the shore
51 Payments made with a wink, maybe
54 Dress style
56 ___ Lingus
58 Start of a reminiscence
60 Darn, e.g.
62 Be in bad shape

by Johanna Fenimore and Jeff Chen

ACROSS

1 Sorcery
6 Serving of butter, as might go on top of several answers in this puzzle
9 Welds
14 "Let's see what you've got," in poker
15 Linguistic ending
16 Menace in the 1957 film "The Enemy Below"
17 Car company headquartered in Palo Alto, Calif.
18 Cancel
19 1992 Joe Pesci title role
20 Kitchen shortening?
21 Kind of makeup
24 Instrument with a notable solo in Springsteen's "Born to Run"
25 Keeps it together
27 Hearing-related
28 Christianity, for one
30 Swim with the fishes, maybe
32 Internet messaging pioneer
34 One of 18 French kings
37 Mama lobster
38 Flatten
41 Vane dir.
42 ___ noche (tonight: Sp.)
44 Spot for a flowerpot
45 "Love It or List It" channel
46 Hospital patron
48 Opposite of paix
50 Siri's digital cousin
51 Carrier to Oslo
54 Assess, as a dress
55 On the ___ (fleeing)
56 Breakfast food item
59 Au ___ (how a French dip is served)
60 Like a superfan
62 "Later!"
63 Broccoli ___ (leafy vegetable)
64 10 bucks, in slang
65 Totally committed
66 Sch. whose colors are "true blue" and gold
67 Info for a graduate
68 Item that might go under several answers in this puzzle
69 Gets by on, with "out"

DOWN

1 Ball catcher
2 Terrific, in slang
3 [Horrors!]
4 "Licensed to ___" (1986 Beastie Boys album)
5 Nonsense
6 Place that's "beneath the blue suburban skies," in a Beatles song
7 Big name in athletic shoes
8 Banner with a single star
9 Minor
10 Tie that binds, in Japan?
11 Charged particles
12 "Peter Pan" dog
13 River in which Achilles was dipped
22 Designation for the Buffalo Bisons and the Durham Bulls
23 Snake in "The Jungle Book"
25 Footlong, for one
26 W.W. II arena
27 Syrup brand
29 Syrup brand
30 1971 Tom Jones hit
31 "Them's the breaks," genteelly
33 Hoarder's possible condition, briefly
35 Imperiled
36 All the oceans, colloquially
39 With 40-Down, something tapped at a pub
40 See 39-Down
43 "La Cage ___ Folles"
45 Nameless woman
47 Fist-bump
49 Great Basin people
51 Fishhook line
52 Train from Boston to Washington
53 "Don't hold back!"
57 "Stat"
58 Title film character based on William Randolph Hearst
61 ___ Spiegel
63 Regret

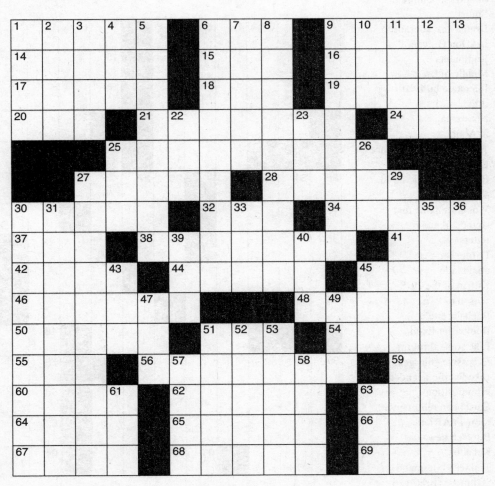

by Patrick Blindauer and Tony Orbach

ACROSS

1 American dance move that, for whatever reason, is illegal in Saudi Arabia
7 Fictional Charlie
11 Milk ___
14 Disney princess in "Brave"
15 Palmist's reading
17 Small burger
18 Lady Gaga or Judy Garland
19 ___ Park, Calif.
20 Big chin-wag
21 20 under 30
22 Try to swat
23 Flair, informally
26 Traits that clash
28 Looney Tunes surname
32 Nickname of the singer of 2007's "Umbrella"
33 Squirt
34 Donna ___, soprano in "Don Giovanni"
35 Rudiments
36 Middle of time?
38 Interstate billboard info
39 Not casual
41 8: Abbr.
42 The Owls of Conference USA
43 President who lived in 47-Down
44 Woman's name that sounds like two letters
45 Datum for a car aficionado
46 Kufrin of the 2018 season of "The Bachelorette"
48 Book after Exod.
50 Like some thinking
53 Excessive enlargement
56 Like Pacific Islanders
58 Film position
60 Caribbean religion with roots in Africa
61 Big tech news website
62 Trainer's command
63 "Gilmore Girls" girl
64 So hot right now

DOWN

1 Symbols in superscript, for short
2 Position of command
3 Home to Bessie, a lake monster in American folklore
4 Said something in response almost immediately
5 Singing superstar born in Tottenham
6 Noble domain
7 Gridiron org. with the Grey Cup
8 Savory Scottish pudding
9 Turn up
10 Let, maybe
11 Things blown on for luck
12 Spanish for "some"
13 Bit of initial progress
16 So-called "black national anthem," informally . . . or what 4-, 6-, 22- and 34-Down do, in part?
22 Volcano's spew
23 Some May celebrants, informally
24 Sign of balance?
25 Like the path of the sun in the sky
27 Halloween "blood," e.g.
29 Fairy
30 Writer Jong
31 Designated driver's order
34 German composer Humperdinck
37 Non's opposite
40 More flinty
44 Patisserie offering
47 See 43-Across
49 Person with seniority
50 Insurance estimate
51 Purplish berry
52 Fair sight
54 Super-often
55 Newsman Chuck
57 And more than that
59 Tutee of Luke in "The Last Jedi"

by Erik Agard

ACROSS

1 Discuss, as an issue
8 Internet nuisance . . . or a hint to four answers in this puzzle
15 Birthstone for most Leos
16 Noted piranha habitat
17 Shade of green
18 Rambles
19 Classic strategy in the boxing ring
20 -
22 What inmates do until they're released
23 Your: Fr.
24 It's off the beaten path
27 "How cool!"
28 Hedonistic
29 -
32 Ankle-related
35 Burgundy or claret
38 Secret DC headquarters
39 Crateful from Florida
40 Like many chicken cutlets
41 Most welcoming
42 Like seven teams in the N.H.L.
43 -
45 French word on some wedding announcements
46 Better than expected
49 Unruly head of hair
52 Labor
54 Where you may be going nowhere fast
55 -
56 More bananas
58 Fictional African kingdom in "Coming to America"
61 Bubble gum brand
62 Stretchy
63 Epic quest
64 Gander

DOWN

1 Not together
2 R&B trio Bell Biv __
3 Releases, as new music
4 Crop in a paddy
5 Author LeShan
6 Lawn order
7 Got ready to sing the national anthem
8 Launched a tech start-up?
9 __ pro nobis
10 One of a famous seafaring trio
11 Loosened, as laces
12 "The Star-Spangled Banner," basically
13 Zoning unit
14 Fashion mag suggestions, in two senses
21 __ Xing
24 "How tragic"
25 "Eureka!"
26 Ancient relative of a flute
27 It's black and white and wet all over
29 Tiny bits of work
30 Bygone Nair rival
31 Some N.F.L. highlights
32 Reid of "American Pie"
33 "Do you have two fives for __?"
34 Misguided
36 Sped
37 Perch for a bouncing baby
38 Original airer of "The Office"
44 It may be found between "here" and "there"
46 Mujer's boys
47 Jambalayas
48 Ring around a watch face
49 Bowlful next to a restaurant cash register
50 "Golden" song
51 Finish second at the track
52 Warty creature
53 Like mud
55 Pioneer in commercial spaceflight
56 Bit of news in the W.S.J.
57 Squeeze (out)
59 Teléfono greeting
60 China's __ Zedong

by Michael Paleos

ACROSS

1 Actor Hemsworth
5 Where chapeaux go
10 Greek house, for short
14 Rough spots?
15 ___ Lodge
16 Top-notch
17 Footnote info
18 See 17-Across
20 Looks beneath the surface, in a way
22 Not real emergencies
23 Night school subj.
24 2010 health measure, in brief
25 John who founded a Fortune 500 company
26 See 29-Across
29 Common article
32 Something that's tailor-made
33 Shooting game
35 Stage name of rapper Sandra Denton
38 Seasoning for un oeuf
39 Prefix with nautical
40 What may blossom from buds?
43 Worker in a chamber: Abbr.
45 Oft-repeated words
46 See 45-Across
51 That's an order
53 Trail
54 German opposite of alt
55 Pat who played filmdom's Mr. Miyagi
57 Vented, say
59 See 61-Across
61 Bed selection
62 Garden crawler
63 Not yellow
64 Neighbor of a Jayhawker
65 Tears for Fears, e.g.
66 Disseminated
67 Have (to)

DOWN

1 Ran out
2 Firm affirmation
3 African country that's a member of OPEC
4 Dutch artist Jan van der ___
5 Verizon, e.g.
6 Anti-fracking legislation, e.g.
7 Part of a tennis serve
8 Sinusitis treater, for short
9 Bond producers
10 Muslim ascetic
11 Rigged game in "Casablanca"
12 Deep blue dye
13 "Bill & ___ Excellent Adventure"
19 Adler in "A Scandal in Bohemia"
21 Popular smoothie ingredient
25 Twofold
27 Fraud
28 Censor
30 Sarcastic laugh syllable
31 Freudian subject
34 Cape Town coin
35 "Masterpiece" network
36 Slice of history
37 Boots
38 Rabbit's tail
41 Result of stress, maybe
42 One dieting strategy
43 Gobbled (up)
44 Lucky thing to get in Ping-Pong
47 Nook
48 Like a live radio announcer
49 Dog, slangily
50 Physically prompted
52 San ___, Calif.
55 Waterfall feature
56 Exclusively
57 "Saint Joan" playwright
58 One-named singer with the 2006 hit "Smack That"
60 ___-Magnon man

by Neville Fogarty

ACROSS

1 ___ rug
5 Audibly horrified
10 Quarrel
14 Stephen King title about a dog
15 Cabaret show
16 A transcontinental traveler might go by this
17 Saint who lent his name to a Minnesota college
18 Justice Kagan
19 It's not a good look
20 Listings in the Internal Revenue Code
22 C.I.A. infiltrator during the Cold War
24 Part of I.P.A.
25 Sound at a séance
26 Savings for a rainy day
30 Not self-parked
34 Afore
35 A. A. Milne character
36 Drips in the O.R.
37 Biblical judge
38 Nabokov title
39 ___ turkey
40 Goddess: Lat.
41 Toward the most common part of a boat to fish from
42 Prize on "The Bachelor"
44 Wooden rod
46 Story of a lifetime, for short?
47 Public ruckus
49 P, for Plato
50 Like the ocean
51 Groups that typically meet weekly for lunch
54 Drug also called angel dust
56 Language spoken by Jesus
57 Lincoln or Ford
60 Visa alternative
62 Discovering the word at 67-Across, for this puzzle
63 Place underground
64 Pay (up)
65 Baltic capital
66 Animated film of 1998
67 Resting place hinted at by 28-, 5-, 45-, 9- and 31-Down, in that order
68 Oodles

DOWN

1 Macbeth, e.g.
2 Dance with percussion accompaniment
3 Battler of Hector in the "Iliad"
4 Lose carbonation
5 "Do you still like me?"
6 Comes together
7 N.Y.C.'s Park or Fifth
8 Destroyed, as an armada
9 Walkway option in lieu of paving
10 ___ l'oeil (illusion)
11 Rival of Cassio, in Shakespeare
12 Truckload at a garbage dump
13 Get out of Dodge
21 Tip off
23 Material for Thor Heyerdahl's Kon-Tiki
26 Becomes imminent
27 Worker in a trauma ward, for short
28 Image on an ancient mariner's map
29 Symbol of depravity
30 Security device, informally
31 Serving at a 4:00 social
32 Pixielike
33 Jingle, e.g.
43 "Music for Airports" musician
45 "What did I do to deserve this?"
46 Image on the king of clubs
48 When one is expected, for short
50 Tampa Bay pro, informally
52 It is "either plagiarism or revolution," per Paul Gauguin
53 Be horizontal
54 ___ John
55 "You're pulling my leg!"
58 Hit 2012 movie whose plot involves a plan to make a movie
59 House leader after Boehner
61 ___ Affair
63 Playtex product

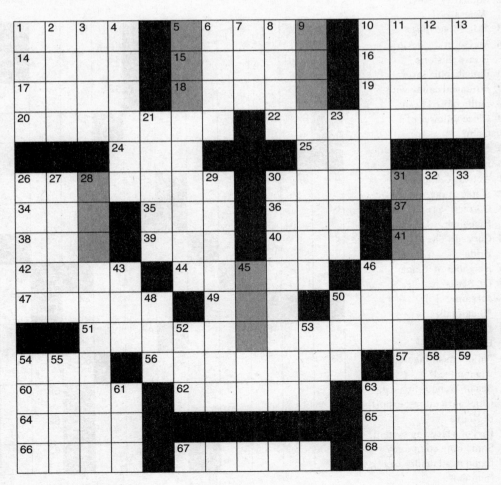

by Bruce Haight

84 MEDIUM

ACROSS

1 Something you must be willing to leave?
7 Them's the breaks!
10 River past Orsk and Orenburg
14 Add to in haste
15 Snake genus, or one of its members
16 Pet form of José
17 *Sound of little feet
18 Shade of deep purple
20 Custom-fit
22 *Tycho Brahe contemporary
23 Bridge player's combo
25 Deprive of courage
26 3.3, give or take
29 Without a downside
31 A lot
32 Solidarity leader Walesa
33 *Mr. Moneybags
36 McGillin's ___ Ale House (historic Philadelphia tavern)
37 *Branded candy with multicolored beans
39 Close follower of a team?
40 *Woman's young lover, in slang
41 Actress Campbell
42 Staple of ragtime music
43 Corrects, as an ID on Facebook
45 Cary of "The Princess Bride"
46 Neighbor of Tonga
49 Dr. Seuss' real surname
51 *Small talk
53 Leapt
56 Bossed around
58 *Idiom meaning "guaranteed"
60 Sea of Tranquillity, e.g.
61 Chief agricultural export of Kenya
62 Part of a steering system
63 Something commonly found in a laundry bag
64 Remnant
65 Wholly absorbed

DOWN

1 Picking up things?
2 Louver feature
3 "See ya!"
4 Ability
5 Like sandals
6 ___ Field, former home to the Houston Astros
7 Figure seen on the National Mall, informally
8 Writing on many a greeting card
9 Frank Herbert's "Dune" series, e.g.
10 What you need to talk to a satellite
11 Sphere
12 Nocturnal affliction
13 Admitted
19 Richly luxurious
21 Did one leg of a triathlon
24 What's helpful to a degree?
26 Ink stain, e.g.
27 Explorer whose name is a sport
28 Word in many Catholic church names
30 Frigid
33 Scratch, say
34 Tops
35 Groups on Noah's Ark
37 Take a flier
38 Bond girl in 2006's "Casino Royale"
39 Visigoth vis-à-vis Rome
41 "Cool beans!"
42 Uses a keyhole, perhaps
43 Scoundrel, in Britain
44 Girl in the fam
46 Loser
47 Up
48 Prefix with economics
50 Rush
52 One-named French designer
54 "The Thin Man" role
55 Sticky stuff
57 One who might explain the birds and the bees
59 Debugging aid?

by Matt Ginsberg

ACROSS

1 "Caught you!"
7 Rapidly increase in size
15 Britain, Spain or France, once
16 Shrub used to make tea
17 Bachelorette party attendee
18 *Seek surreptitiously
19 Author Kingsley
20 Under the weather
22 Faculty heads
23 Mormon's donation
25 Got ready to run?
28 Woman's name that's an anagram of a European native
30 Stylish, '60s-style
31 All the rage
34 Maker of Team USA swimsuits
37 Nada
38 Comic strip opossum
39 *Fight imaginary enemies
42 "Such a shame!"
43 Clearance item holder
44 "For sure!"
45 Deep desire
46 Ashen
47 Occasion to dress up
48 Intestines' locale
50 Airheaded
54 Hard effort, metaphorically
57 "The Cask of Amontillado" writer
59 "Toodle-oo!"
60 *Baseball throw that might thwart a squeeze play
63 Captain Ahab, e.g.
65 "Regrettably, it's true"
66 Coleridge's "The ___ Harp"
67 Get wasted
68 Commoners' superiors

DOWN

1 Sired
2 So-called "fifth taste"
3 Tricky bowling situation
4 *Bettors' aids

5 ___ of Good Feelings
6 New York's Katz's, for one
7 Burn with water
8 Indian flatbread
9 "U can't b serious!"
10 Joined with a torch
11 Not be colorfast
12 ___ Romeo
13 Meaning of "Simba" in Swahili
14 Film director ___ von Trier
21 Grassy expanse
24 Source of medieval Norse poetry
26 Declaration made while anteing up
27 "What'd I say?!"
29 Halfway decent

31 Fit to be canonized
32 Eye hungrily
33 Throw out
34 Bit of training accompanying "Sit!" and "Speak!"
35 Stack (up)
36 Verve
37 Diarist Anaïs
38 Home to this puzzle's featured structure, as hinted at by the starts of the answers to the starred clues
40 Improvise, with "it"
41 Gin rummy combo
46 ___ reason
47 1960s muscle car
48 Former colony that's a gambling mecca

49 Supermodel and actress Kate
51 Shire of "Rocky"
52 Total bargain
53 Exaggerated accounts
54 Dustup
55 Surfing aid
56 Raison d'___
58 Wide-mouthed jug
61 Tribute that may be urned?
62 Nonprofit grp. that works with the Defense Department
64 "Boo-___!"

by Timothy Polin

ACROSS

1 Put at sea
6 "As a result . . ."
11 Birthed
14 Ira who wrote "The Stepford Wives"
15 South American forest dweller
16 Hoarfrost
17 Many a hit by Def Leppard
19 Grp. that's well-financed?
20 N.F.C. North team, to fans
21 Bit of crab house attire
22 "You've got to be kidding me!"
23 Stored away
25 Like medieval knights
27 Screwy
28 Response to oversharing
30 Hang tight
31 Religiousness
34 A shore thing to happen
37 Horace Greeley's advice, as followed by 17-, 25-, 50- and 60-Across?
41 Working harmoniously (with)
42 Home of Spaceship Earth
44 Baja blast
47 Sound of a leak
49 #Me___
50 Meal served in an edible bowl
53 Follow, as a moral code
56 Tag line?
57 Ending with polypropyl-
58 Lacking joie de vivre
59 Montenegro joined it in 2017
60 Famously expensive commercial
64 Mushy mass
65 "Sounds good," in informal pronunciation
66 Part of the unconscious
67 Military term of address
68 N.F.L. quarterback Drew
69 Long-limbed

DOWN

1 Nothing but
2 Arm for taking needles, for short?
3 Format that preceded Blu-ray
4 Fatty compound
5 Japanese mushroom
6 Air Medal recipients
7 Negative operation in computing logic
8 "Yabba ___ doo!"
9 Unadventurous
10 Notable feature of North Dakota and Texas
11 Kendrick Lamar's genre
12 Egyptian "king of the gods"
13 Boil down
16 Around 70°F, informally
18 Took one's turn
23 Cut
24 Take ___ at (insult)
25 Benghazi's land
26 Feature of a forehead or fingerprint
29 Crystal ___
32 Bottle cap type
33 Gossip
35 ___ nova
36 A school yr. often begins on one
38 Site of zero-gravity experiments
39 Played the tough guy
40 Beginner, in video game lingo
43 Item in a claw machine
44 One-night stands, say
45 2014 boxing documentary
46 Person at a desk
48 Swat
51 Live in a studio
52 Marsh plant
54 It doesn't get any better than this
55 Actor Troyer of the "Austin Powers" movies
58 Protrudes
61 Spanish : ella :: English : ___
62 Texter's "No 63-Down!"
63 See 62-Down

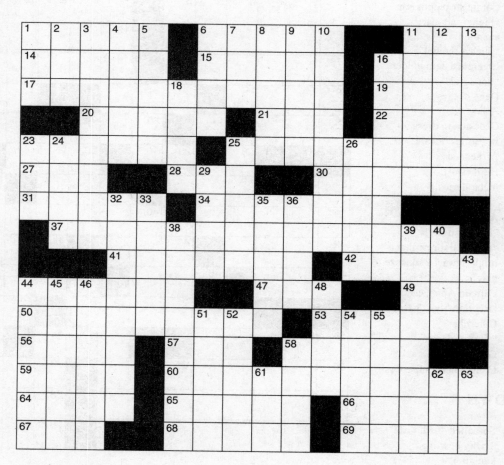

by Sam Ezersky

ACROSS

1 Mag for docs
5 Absorbs, with "up"
9 Attire that may include covering for the feet, in brief
12 Old enough
14 Cool, in dated slang
15 Boy's name that's an anagram of 18-Across
16 Key for five Mozart piano concertos
18 Girl's name that's an anagram of 15-Across
19 Its worship is condemned in the Bible
20 The ___ things in life
21 Intentions
22 "Just act natural!"
24 Letter-shaped beam
26 Waves may convey a message in this
27 Be an agent for, informally
28 Many-time Grammy-winning cellist
33 Struck (out)
34 "The Golden Girls" actress
36 Initiation, e.g.
39 Bad, bad boss
40 Fairy queen in "Romeo and Juliet"
43 "The party can finally start!"
45 Muse featured in "Xanadu"
47 Worrisome sign around a campsite
52 Fitzgerald known as the Queen of Jazz
53 Get clean
54 Fighting words
56 Swenson of "Benson"
57 Do the opposite of shave . . . as suggested by the circled letters
58 Letter-shaped fastener
59 User-edited web page
60 Mom on "The Simpsons"
61 ___ milk
62 Sweeties, in modern slang
63 Angry, with "off"

DOWN

1 Event for college seniors
2 ___ de coeur (French romance)
3 Plan for shoppers
4 Longtime Sampras rival
5 Heart beater, in bridge
6 "How wonderful!," sarcastically
7 Paul : U.S. :: ___ : Italy
8 Orch. section
9 Hypothetical body in the solar system beyond Neptune
10 "Hidden Figures" co-star Monáe
11 Inhaled, as food
13 Summer in Paris
15 Much-sought-after celeb
17 Will Smith/Tommy Lee Jones film franchise, for short
20 Big do
23 German rapid transit system
25 Ingredient in a drain declogger
29 Western flick, in old parlance
30 "That's terrific!"
31 Bruins great Bobby
32 Underground org. in N.Y.C.
34 Drinker's party headgear
35 Sport-___ (vehicle)
36 Sounds heard at night near a pond
37 Resolute refusal
38 Fellow you don't want to be, in a phrase
40 It might require antiviral treatment to beat
41 Still wanted by the police
42 Got on
44 Highway: Abbr.
46 Move into or from an exit row, perhaps
48 Fancy hotel lobbies
49 Strangle
50 New Zealanders
51 Govt. org. dating from the 1930s
55 Big name in cloud computing
57 Potus #43

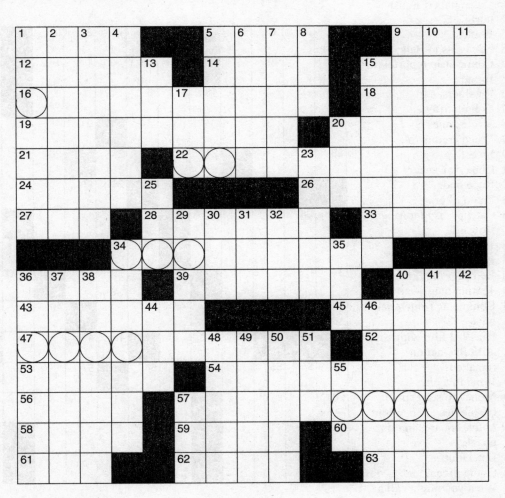

by Sam Trabucco

ACROSS

1 Real lifesaver
5 Cloned machine of old
10 Something to hold near a skunk
14 Matty who once had a National League batting title
15 Bit of regalia
16 Repulsive
17 Making a "Top Party Schools" list, e.g.
19 Precisely
20 "Outrageous Acts and Everyday Rebellions" author
21 Iconographic image in Catholic art
23 One of the Kennedys
24 Zeno's birthplace
26 ___ anglais (English horn)
27 Bounce
28 "Heavens to Betsy!"
33 Comic strip reporter Brenda
36 Retainers, e.g.
37 Collar stiffener
38 Strike zones?
39 When credits roll
40 Invective, e.g.
41 Choice of juice?
42 Rude dudes
43 Photo filters
44 Catchphrase for Moe Howard
46 1990s game disk
47 Plethora
48 Reindeer in "Frozen"
50 Texting qualifier
53 Comments from quick wits
57 Hit 1992 film with a 2019 live-action remake
59 Wind in a pit
60 Money to start small businesses . . . or a hint to five squares in this puzzle
62 Bawl (out)
63 Going green?
64 What you might call a Friend
65 $$$ holders
66 Martini & ___ (vermouth)
67 Word processing function

DOWN

1 Possessed, biblically
2 Wash out with a solvent
3 Like Druids
4 "Certainement!"
5 What the Genius Bar provides
6 Wetland or rain forest
7 "Holy Toledo!"
8 Party that often has an after-party
9 Santiago de León de ___ (formal name of a world capital)
10 Noted artist on Bad Boy Records, with "the"
11 Take too much of, in brief
12 Winnebago, for one
13 "Cómo ___ usted?"
18 Shows of contempt
22 E.N.T., e.g.
25 Well-run meetings have them
27 Contents of a treasure chest
29 1970s N.L. powerhouse
30 Dumbfound
31 It may be rigged
32 Surveys
33 Deli dish
34 Instrument with a needle, for short
35 First name in pop art
36 Bowling a 300, e.g.
40 Keyless
42 Many a con artist
45 "Is that so . . ."
46 House speaker after Hastert
49 Sundry
50 Home of Shoshone Falls
51 One who's gone underground?
52 It's a start
53 Author ___ Neale Hurston
54 "Likely story!"
55 Linguist Chomsky
56 ___-Japanese War
58 Parts of colons
61 ___ Health (corporate giant)

by Mary Lou Guizzo and Jeff Chen

ACROSS

1 Emanuel of Democratic politics
5 Titles for attys.
9 Alternative to a float
14 Curved molding
15 Dogs that take YOU for a walk?
16 Dealer's query
17 *Principle of international economic pacts
19 Fred ___, lead vocalist for Limp Bizkit
20 Setting for the first panel of Bosch's "The Garden of Earthly Delights"
21 Victory, in German
23 Most arias
24 Old Chrysler
26 Tailor, at times
28 Big Ten sch.
29 Tube travelers?
30 *Neanderthal
31 Six-time N.L. home run leader in the 1930s and '40s
32 Indie singer ___ Case
34 Bus stop: Abbr.
35 Applesauce eponym
37 Water hazards
39 Cuisine with tom yum soup
43 Nile biter
45 Executes
47 Choose
48 *Noted Vegas entertainers of the 1960s
52 Deli offering
53 British pols
54 Like some dogs in dog parks
55 In very few words
57 Mom-and-pop grps.
58 Spotted
60 "No food needed for me"
61 Island north of Australia
63 Questionable political moves suggested by the answers to the nine starred clues
66 Run ___ of

67 This: Sp.
68 Tit for tat?
69 St. ___ (Caribbean getaway)
70 Title
71 Novelist Seton

DOWN

1 Nonsense
2 Goes along with
3 *Half of a 1990s cartoon duo
4 Euripides tragedy
5 Scrabble 4-pointer
6 Source of a venomous underwater bite
7 Role for Helen Mirren, informally
8 Watch via HBO Now, e.g.
9 Barrett of Pink Floyd
10 *Informal term for a brothel
11 Night lights?
12 Ninth month of the Hebrew calendar
13 Full
18 Company that's the subject of "The Smartest Guys in the Room"
22 *Mr. Peanut accessory
24 Machine with a treadle
25 *Spring festival
27 Stock for Wile E. Coyote
33 A heart symbol, meaning "love," was its first graphical entry, for short
36 *Bloopers, typically
38 Popular battle royale video game
40 *Residence in a row
41 Digital wallet choice
42 Lilliputian, to a little 'un
44 Spanish Mrs.
46 Sans-___
48 Can opener
49 Modern protest group
50 Hubbub
51 Special interest group?
56 Guacamole go-with
59 Alternatively
62 "Treasure Island" monogram
64 "___ Save America" (popular downloadable political show)
65 Place to treat yourself

by Brandon Koppy

ACROSS

1 Green rock
8 Goes down a steep rock face, in a way
15 Danger for sailors
16 "Fake news!"
17 OWARD
19 Playground retort
20 Distress signal?
21 Talk up
22 Neighbor of Moldova
25 QUARR
31 Bygone orchard spray
32 Worker in a garden
33 Some lumps
35 Superior floor, e.g.
37 To each accordingly
39 Combat zone
40 Concept embodying yin and yang
41 John, abroad
42 SEASO
46 Without attention to detail, say
47 Environmental concern
51 Swimmer Torres with 12 Olympic medals
52 Advances
57 IKINI
60 Blood drive donation
61 Simultaneously
62 John in the Clinton and Obama administrations
63 America's Cup participant

DOWN

1 K-12
2 Hangout for Homer
3 Quod ___ faciendum
4 Overhaul
5 With full effort
6 Linda ___, Supergirl's alias
7 Took the heat off of?
8 Friend of the Fonz
9 2004 Olympics site
10 Letter that appears twice in the Schrödinger equation
11 Hostilities ender
12 Nevada county or its seat
13 Place
14 On its way
18 Step on it
23 Kind of beef
24 Gas station in Canada
25 Roar
26 Like many chardonnay barrels
27 Statistician's observation
28 Jewish holiday with costumes
29 Comment when turning down a charity appeal
30 Golden Horde member
31 Resembling
34 Published
36 So-called "Island of the Gods"
37 Expire
38 Drubbing
40 Peter and Paul
43 Breaks off a relationship
44 California forest name
45 Home planet of TV's ALF
47 Check
48 Like early recordings
49 Like some columns
50 Sticker
53 O.T. book read during 28-Down
54 Ravel's "Gaspard de la ___"
55 Small change
56 Suffix with trick
58 Starfleet Academy grad.
59 Spanish diminutive

by Randolph Ross

ACROSS

1 Roast a bit
4 Tee off
8 Called on
14 Roast bit
16 Words in a threat
17 Contents of a football "shower"
18 Echelons
19 As many as
20 Last readout before an odometer rolls over
22 Kobe cash
23 Juillet's season
24 Accordingly
25 Church recesses
27 A. A. Milne hopper
29 Self-help genre
31 Miscreant
35 Peddled
39 One of Snoopy's brothers, in "Peanuts"
40 Surfing moniker
42 Wrath
43 Actress Adams
44 Strawberry, e.g.
45 Numerical prefix
46 "Little" one of old TV
48 Witness
50 Staggering
52 "The Simpsons" clerk
53 Beat
56 Noted Hungarian puzzler
59 Inflate, as a bill
62 Oaxaca whoop
63 2014 Rock and Roll Hall of Fame inductee John
64 "I am not what I am" speaker
65 Exerts
68 How some deposits are held
70 Fragrant compounds
71 Public
72 Contemporary of Pizarro
73 Da's opposite
74 Course of action

DOWN

1 Good-for-nothing
2 Not pertinent
3 What things on the downslide may have "seen"
4 Old space station
5 Ludicrous
6 Provided, as data
7 Historical event suggested by each of the six groups of circled letters
8 Coin ___
9 "What you can get away with," according to Andy Warhol
10 For each
11 What Ascap counts for purposes of royalties
12 First name in skin care
13 Emory board feature?
15 Lav, in Leeds
21 Abbr. in help-wanted ads
24 Ad ___ committee
25 Not much
26 Punch line?
28 Big lug
30 Attempt, informally
31 Wild pig
32 President Coin in the "Hunger Games" series
33 Veil material
34 Spanish she-bear
36 Start some trouble
37 Harper's Bazaar cover designer
38 Pricey
41 Darling of baseball
44 Betting game popular with Wyatt Earp and Doc Holliday
45 Alley-___
47 Limit
49 Symbol of durability
51 Big time
53 Like most repos
54 Beethoven honoree
55 Pool competitions
57 Andersson of Abba
58 It merges with the Rhone near Valence
60 Old Greek square
61 Old-fashioned in attire
63 ___ buco
64 Govt. watchdog until 1996
66 Sign of summer
67 Richard Gere title role
69 Goal for one trying to "collect 'em all"

by David J. Kahn

ACROSS

1 Maximally
7 Team that moved to the American League in 2013
13 Nuclear energy source
15 Patsy
16 President in the 2009 film "Invictus"
17 Trail mix alternative
18 "___ rise"
19 "Huh, interesting . . ."
21 Tailor
22 They might be painted in a bathroom
24 Gift from Hawaii
25 Frothy beverage
27 Start of creation?
29 Afrikaans "farmer"
32 *Become angelic, figuratively
33 Mauna ___ Observatory
34 Something found in a rush
35 *Reason for resetting a digital clock
39 California's ___ Valley
41 Native of New Mexico
43 ___ Hand (name used for some prank calls)
45 Actor Sheridan of "X-Men: Apocalypse"
46 Command following a countdown
47 Court do-over
48 Seasonal migrant worker from Mexico
51 25-time Rose Bowl winner, for short
52 Kind of spray used for goggles and windshields
54 Actress Lyonne of "Orange Is the New Black"
56 Deadline info
57 Goads
58 Light at a dance party
59 Beat badly

DOWN

1 First living designer exhibited at the Guggenheim
2 Beverage server in Britain
3 More virile
4 Condition for some germophobes, briefly
5 Some slow-cooked meals
6 Painted tinware
7 Prefix with -polis
8 Serape, e.g.
9 Old channel that showed "Hee Haw"
10 Setting for an urban garden
11 Minerals also known as egg stones
12 Figure eight figure
14 *"Vive la France!" or "Free Tibet!"
20 Place for a cowherd
23 Blockhead
26 Something simple
28 Indirectly . . . or how some of this puzzle's answers should be entered?
30 "Never thought of that!"
31 N.H.L. great Bobby
35 Pesto ingredient
36 One leaving something out
37 Fourth U.S. state capital alphabetically
38 Deli turnovers
39 Some light bites
40 Home of the F.D.R. Drive and J.F.K. Airport
42 Direct way to be paid
44 Britcom made into a 2016 film, informally
46 Mess up
49 Going over something again and again and again
50 Go on a tirade
53 "Who wants one?" response
55 Melody
57 *"Whew, that's enough for now!"

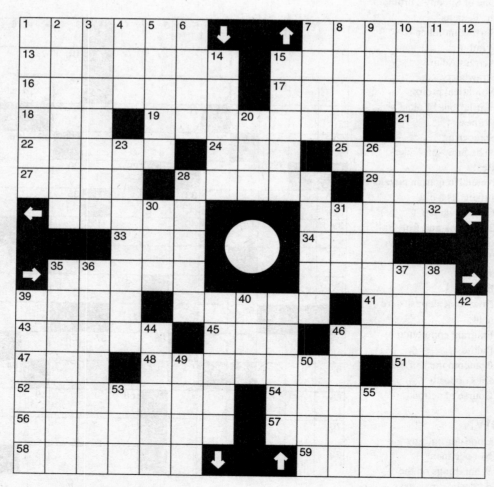

by Herre Schouwerwou

ACROSS

1 Sabbath service site
5 Title woman in a 1976 Dylan song
9 Couples
14 ___ Millions (multistate lottery)
15 Aberdeen resident
16 "Yippee!"
17 "You can't bring in a crazed antelope, Mr. Glass!"?
20 Picker-upper
21 House, as soldiers
22 Put under wraps
23 Wrigley Field's beer boycott goes into effect?
28 Shoulder bone
30 Call for help
31 Stat for which lower is better
32 One may be red
34 "Mayor" memoirist
35 Organization honored on October 24 . . . and the theme of this puzzle
40 Melee memento, maybe
41 Early spaceman
42 Clay, after 1964
43 Guitarist Paul
46 Amusement park attractions
50 Mother isn't straight with actress Vardalos?
53 Mich. neighbor
54 Venetian basilica eponym
55 Western band
57 Suffering caused by reader prejudice?
61 Slave in "Uncle Tom's Cabin"
62 Let off some steam
63 Breakfast brand
64 Ability to effect change
65 One of 12 on a cube
66 It helps you focus

DOWN

1 Workers at forges
2 Lifesaving, say
3 Landlocked African country
4 Civil rights activist Guinier
5 Suffix with ideal
6 One close by a swordsman's side
7 Ancient land on the Aegean Sea
8 Shots from movies
9 Nerdy sorts
10 Big Three conference site
11 "Gotcha!"
12 Put on
13 Means of putting down roots?
18 Like Hogwarts courses
19 Jazz singer Laine
24 Beekeeper of filmdom
25 Element between helium and argon on the periodic table
26 Middle-earth menaces
27 "Don't think so"
29 Part of a full house
33 "Star Trek" sequel, briefly
34 Big Island coffee
35 Jackie Robinson's alma mater
36 Get perfectly
37 Comic who said "If you want to read about love and marriage, you've got to buy two separate books"
38 Garr of "Tootsie"
39 PRINTED SO AS TO SHOUT
40 Rick's Café Américain employee
43 Sics on
44 Name in a Salinger title
45 Eschew rather than chew?
47 Rx info
48 Flag
49 Pool members of old
51 Japanese import
52 Spherical
56 Volkswagen competitor
57 Toning target, for short
58 90° turn
59 Kia model
60 Polished off

by Alan Arbesfeld

ACROSS

1 Things driven on ranches
5 Three-time Best Director of the 1930s
10 Gazillionaire
14 Father of Deimos and Phobos, in Greek myth
15 Put on
16 Baldwin of "The Boss Baby"
17 You may use a roller to get rid of it
18 Reluctant
19 Deep cut
20 Cereal bit
21 What thirsty flowers do
22 Small and delicate
24 Sings the praises of
27 Single-stranded building block
28 Bustle
29 Co. with a striped logo
31 Effect of a sac fly
34 Places where some house pets "go," in both this puzzle and real life
39 Hobby shop buy
40 "So it goes"
41 1990s commerce pact
42 Number two
43 Kind
44 Diagonally . . . or a hint to four of this puzzle's squares
46 Ingredient in many a breakfast cereal
47 When doubled, dance of the 2010s
48 Row maker
49 French word that's a homophone of 47-Across
51 "Stay calm!"
57 Eat quickly, with "in"
60 Johns across the pond
61 My Chemical Romance genre
62 ___ Caesarea, original name of New Jersey
63 Create, as a chair
65 Fellow
66 Premiere
67 Squeak or creak

68 Host
69 Provides food for
70 Fortify
71 Mideast capital

DOWN

1 Mailing from Lands' End or Williams-Sonoma
2 High point of "To Kill a Mockingbird"
3 Slowly
4 Loose fig.
5 The world's fifth-largest economy
6 Sauce with a vowel-heavy name
7 Babble
8 No longer working: Abbr.

9 Reason for an Adderall prescription, for short
10 Bad role model for Oliver Twist
11 Best Supporting Actor nominee for "Argo"
12 Beta ___
13 Like the hook of a good pop song
21 Vast
23 Regenerable parts of a sea star
25 "Goshdarnit!"
26 Cruising speed, maybe
30 Sunbather's accessory
32 ___ one's time
33 Roman road
34 Put down
35 Poorly
36 No longer independent

37 Held, as breath
38 Many times, in poetry
42 Surveyor's finding
44 Part of the body to slap
45 "My bad!"
50 Lily Potter's maiden name in the Harry Potter books
52 Song from a "Best of" album, maybe
53 Alternative to a guillotine
54 Kind of jacket
55 Muslim leaders
56 Imitator
57 Ski resort vehicle
58 2008 political catchword
59 It may be labeled 2× or 3×
64 "I think ___"
65 Engine part

by Sophia Maymudes

ACROSS

1 Baja resort
5 Prefix with cycle or sphere
9 Choice words
14 Informed about
15 Big publisher of romance novels
16 Tour leader
17 Debate venues
18 Nickname of an Israeli leader
19 What Fortune magazine called "America's most innovative company" for six consecutive years
20 With 58-Across, iconic frontman of 39-Across
22 25-Down, notably
24 ___ of Hormuz
25 Words in an old French cheer
26 Manhattan Project physicist Bruno ___
28 Many a decal
32 Home run, in slang
35 June Cleaver or Marge Simpson
37 Bedazzle
38 1977 album with a palindromic title
39 British rock band that gave an iconic performance at 25-Down
40 Subject of a spot check?
41 Easygoing, and then some
42 Darfur's locale
43 Exclaims
45 Sevastopol's locale
47 Something to debate
49 Softened
51 Service, maybe
55 25-Down, notably
58 See 20-Across
59 White mushroom
60 River in W.W. I fighting
62 Sting, e.g.
63 April Fools' Day birth, e.g.
64 Make silent
65 "Where ___?"
66 One of three biblical gifts
67 Part of a dog breed's name
68 Went platinum?

DOWN

1 Police officer's equipment
2 Left on a ship
3 Hole maker
4 How you might go zip-lining
5 Things that are kicked
6 Wilcox daughter in "Howards End"
7 Flash ___
8 How fish on a fishing boat are stored
9 Benchmark figure given how old a person is
10 Vatican diplomat
11 Urgent
12 Fragrance
13 Hit musical set in 1990s New York
21 Designer who said "My dream is to save women from nature"
23 Hunter in the heavens
25 1985 fund-raising event watched by 1.5+ billion people
27 Tuxedo shirt attachment
29 "Life Is Beautiful" extra
30 Baby's boo-boo
31 Clears
32 Rash decision?
33 Cracked a little
34 Lyft alternative
36 Kind of store or chorus
39 Somewhat
42 Haddock or hake
43 One who might work in the wings of a theater
44 Flinched or blinked
46 Not as assertive
48 Two-channel
50 Root words
52 Bad-tempered and unfriendly
53 Leave no trace of
54 Entered (in)
55 Radiant smile
56 Professor Higgins, to Eliza
57 "Strangers on a Train" film genre
58 2015 World Series team
61 Bro hello

by David J. Kahn

ACROSS

1 Vessel for frying food
9 Variety of green tea
15 Word with power or zero
16 Having win after win
17 Beer you make yourself
18 Get cell service?
19 Lovelace of computing fame
20 Some West Point grads
22 Non-PC?
23 Is an agent for, informally
25 One end of a kite string
26 Genuflect, e.g.
27 Indian state known for its tea
29 The moon, e.g.
30 Book leaf
31 Two, to Teo
33 N.F.L. star who was a Sports Illustrated Sportsperson of the Year in 2017
34 Who said "If you're not ready to die for it, put the word 'freedom' out of your vocabulary"
37 Accept the sudden loss of, as an opportunity
38 Children's author Beverly
40 "Duuuude!"
41 Flute, e.g.
42 One doing cat scans?
44 "Finished!"
48 Lift
49 Mother-of-pearl
51 Zippo
52 "Here Come the Warm Jets" musician
53 Butts
55 Lead-in to X, Y or Z
56 Lose fizz
58 Classic declaration in Gotham City
60 Burning
61 Not closing before 10 or 11 p.m.
62 Back from a vacation, say
63 Acceptance from fellow brainiacs, in slang

DOWN

1 Name that comes from Arabic for "desert"
2 Dwellings
3 Many graphics on election night
4 Use it for kicks
5 Italy's third-largest island, after Sicily and Sardinia
6 Engine sounds
7 At the original speed, in music
8 Publishing debut of 1851, with "The"
9 Lead-in to T, A or X
10 In short order
11 Bit of ink
12 What might have a large collection of prints
13 What Gandhi once likened to an ocean
14 Opening of many a speech
21 Swarm
24 Pathetic one
26 College in Brunswick, Me.
28 Ties up, in a way
30 Oslo setting
32 Furtive
33 LinkedIn listing
34 Mixed martial arts champion Conor __
35 Multipurpose
36 First ones to bat
39 Representative sample of a larger group
42 Acid holder
43 __ l'oeil (illusion)
45 One-named 1950s TV sex symbol
46 Imagine
47 Back from a vacation, say
49 "Gotcha"
50 Old flame?
53 Like Old Mother Hubbard's cupboard
54 Smooth
57 Burning
59 Spa offering, briefly

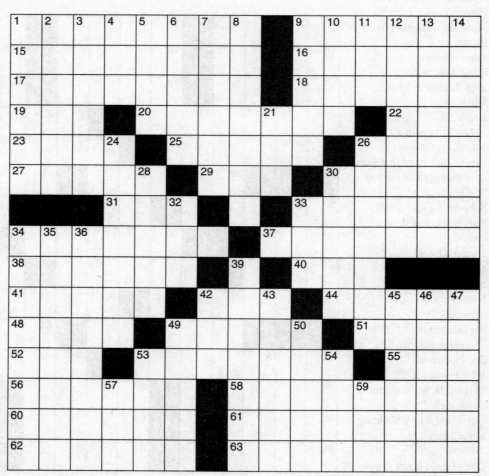

by John Westwig

ACROSS
1 Hit hard
5 Beats it
11 Org. with the Wizards and Warriors
14 Prefix meaning "wine"
15 Pub spigot
16 Path of a blooper
17 Rating for many a sitcom
18 Ahab's inspiration?
19 Give a whuppin'
20 *Acts phony
22 Chopin piece
24 Sweat units
25 Beehive contents
26 Carl who wrote "Contact"
29 "WTF With Marc Maron," for one
32 Industry kingpin
33 2002 animated film with a woolly mammoth
36 Warm, action-oriented sort, they say
37 Part of S O S, in popular usage
38 Each asterisked clue vis-à-vis its answer
39 Little trickster
40 Scepter's go-with
41 Like an evangelical Christian
42 Phrase on a yard sale tag
43 Kitchen gadgets for mixing
45 Unable to sit still
46 Mother that might have a beard
47 Fast-food utensil
50 2000s teen drama set in California
52 *Hint: hotel
56 Sharpshooter's asset
57 Kevin ___, investor on TV's "Shark Tank"
59 As a result
60 Rx watchdog
61 Sweetums
62 Alaska, before 1959: Abbr.
63 Start of many CB radio codes
64 Stands in a studio
65 "So it may ___"

DOWN
1 Ones always tossing things back?
2 Impose, as a tax
3 Potentially offensive, in brief
4 Relative of a discotheque
5 One of the Obama daughters
6 Implore
7 Slants
8 "Let's leave ___ that"
9 Mai ___
10 Order from a police officer
11 *A trails nut
12 Thin fastener
13 Target of an astringent
21 "The tongue of the mind," per Cervantes
23 Little jerk
25 Paul of "Crocodile Dundee"
26 Cartoon uncle of Scrappy-Doo, informally
27 Bright blue
28 *Bag manager
29 Catherine who married Henry VIII
30 Big rigs
31 Young slave girl in "Uncle Tom's Cabin"
33 Like gases in the rightmost column of the periodic table
34 They measure miles in meters
35 "I" strain?
38 One of seven for New York City
42 Common wear for female tennis players
44 Besides
45 Shapiro of NPR
47 Social media button
48 Danger
49 "Absolutely!"
50 President who later served as chief justice
51 Cry to guests at a surprise party
52 Twinings products
53 One leaving in the spring?
54 Brutish sort
55 Average guy?
58 Pasture

by Seth A. Abel

ACROSS

1 Prophet who said "The Lord roars from Zion and thunders from Jerusalem"
5 E-tail icons
10 Upscale hotel features
14 ___ Sweeney, leading character in "Anything Goes"
15 Actress Aimée
16 Approach in handling something
17 Afternoon affairs
18 Place for a picnic along a highway
20 Choice of routes?
22 See 21-Down
23 From birth
24 Result of some sunburn I had?
30 Mr. Potato Head part
31 "Ready about! Hard ___!"
32 "According to the grapevine . . ."
35 With 38-Across, what a two-letter answer is in a crossword, usually . . . or a hint to 20-, 24-, 44- and 51-Across
36 Home to the Rohingya
38 See 35-Across
39 Like lizards and fish
42 River through Flanders
43 Pouch holder, for short
44 Declaration concerning British geography?
48 Ancient markets
50 Egg ___
51 Nitrous oxide?
57 Time of valor, in a Winston Churchill speech
58 Big cheese?
60 Hgts.
61 Stand and deliver?
62 Org. behind the InSight mission
63 Part of iOS: Abbr.
64 Some greens
65 An aye for an eye, say?

DOWN

1 Biblical verb
2 What parallel lines never do
3 Because why not?
4 "Already?!"
5 Home to Castro
6 Suffix with expect
7 Tobiko and ikura, on a sushi menu
8 Common casserole ingredient
9 Certain attire when hitting the slopes
10 Steadfast
11 Not teetotal, say
12 Nail the test
13 Variety of ray
19 1997 Nicolas Cage thriller
21 With 22-Across, a triumphant cry
24 Comic ___ (typeface)
25 Ray of fast-food fame
26 Wray of "King Kong" fame
27 Whips
28 Gatherer of intelligence?
29 Country where camel jumping is a sport
33 Shortly, quaintly
34 Where one might find Jesus
36 Chatty ones
37 The Cardinals, on scoreboards
40 Six of one and half a dozen of the other, say?
41 Like the outer matryoshka doll
43 Time for a mint julep in Louisville
45 "Do you mind?"
46 Concorde, e.g., for short
47 Dormant
48 Sporty Spiders, informally
49 In a cheery manner
52 Drag racing org.
53 Top of a fund drive thermometer
54 Trumpet accessory
55 "Wonder Woman" antagonist
56 Carpentry tool
59 Revolutionary figure

by Ruth Bloomfield Margolin

ACROSS

1 Shoo-in
6 "That is really unpleasant," tersely
9 Rho follower
14 Island greeting
15 Word with small or fish
16 Animated singer of "Part of Your World"
17 Movie that really should have featured Anne Archer?
19 Greek-born New Age musician
20 Cheese from cow's milk
21 Miner matters
23 Ride associated with low m.p.g.'s
24 ___ Talks
25 Movie that really should have featured Nicolas Cage?
28 They play for pay
29 Little untruth
30 Coffee grown on the Big Island
33 Red, perhaps
36 It's kept by a metronome
40 Movie that really should have featured Tom Cruise?
43 Balboa's film foe
44 Opening of a classic Langston Hughes poem
45 "Yipes!"
46 Pencil after lots of crosswords, maybe?
48 Told a 29-Across
50 Movie that really should have featured Vin Diesel?
55 Business card abbr.
58 Balance shower, for short
59 Overflow (with)
60 Una corrida figure
62 ___ Osaka, 2018 U.S. Open tennis champion
64 Movie that really should have featured Sigourney Weaver?
66 Town where Grey Poupon originated
67 1/3,600 of an hr.
68 Pokey or Pee Wee of Major League Baseball
69 Cast replacement
70 Eponymous ice cream maker
71 One going downhill in a hurry?

DOWN

1 Diamond unit
2 "You got me this game"
3 Like a contract awarded without competition
4 ___ Pet
5 Plane storage site
6 1950s Project Blue Book subject, for short
7 Figure on top of some cakes
8 Multiheaded monster of myth
9 Greets informally
10 Lyricist Gershwin
11 Kind of knife in old infomercials
12 Maître d's handful
13 Not yet out of the game
18 "May I do the ___?"
22 Part of Santa's workshop
26 Famous query in Matthew 26
27 Followed instructions
28 Entrepreneur's protection
30 One of the Yum! brands
31 Tool sometimes used with two hands
32 Boise-to-Missoula dir.
34 Orchestra's place
35 Unpleasant strain?
37 GQ or O
38 Org. whose members are teed off?
39 Ref. that added "cruciverbalist" (a person who does crosswords) in 2006
41 Doing grown-up tasks, in modern lingo
42 Performed, as in an animated film
47 Pollinator
49 Conger catchers
50 America, Asia and Europe (but not Africa)
51 Amazon's biz
52 Bit of graphic language?
53 Williams of "Grey's Anatomy"
54 Worked behind the plate
55 Actress Marisa
56 Clear the boards
57 Introverted sort
61 Long trip
63 Fellow in Jamaica
65 Supercool?

by Howard Barkin

ACROSS

1 ___ billiards, game on a pocketless table
6 Mount whose name means, literally, "I burn"
10 Something with teeth
13 In the course of
14 Detached
15 Fed. science org.
16 Family symbol
17 Flier with a message
19 Monomaniac of fiction
20 Divisions in the Congressional Record
21 View remotely?
23 Sunroof alternative
26 "You sti-i-i-ink!"
27 Follower of clear or cross
29 "Forever, ___" (1996 humor book)
30 Drone's job
33 Rod's partner
34 Realm with an Imperial Diet: Abbr.
35 Rods' partners
37 Rival of Cassio
38 One might have a wink or a smile
41 Foreign-born musician with a Presidential Medal of Freedom
43 Trough filler
44 Tin or glass
46 Business meeting that participants dial into, informally
48 Bunch of lovers?
49 "Just like that!"
52 Gray
53 Words before "a good night"
55 Author Calvino
57 Former Yankees manager Joe
59 Crafty person?
61 It helps keep the machinery running
62 Does something to a T
63 Clichéd
64 "A tyrant's authority for crime and a fool's excuse for failure," per Ambrose Bierce

DOWN

1 Carolina tribe that allied with the colonists in the American Revolution
2 Song sung by Elvis in "Blue Hawaii"
3 Muscle with a palindromic name
4 End of an era?
5 Company that released "2001: A Space Odyssey"
6 ___ Club
7 Department store department
8 "___ get it"
9 It was once big for Aretha Franklin
10 It's indicated by arrows on a map
11 Parody, in a way
12 Newspaper headline of 12/8/1941
14 Alternative to "Sincerely"
18 Department with a buffalo on its seal
20 One frequently pictured in GQ or Vogue
22 Symbol on many a bumper sticker
24 Rolex rival
25 Texas' ___ Duro Canyon
28 Radiation cleanup, briefly
31 "Fingers crossed!"
32 Brooklyn attraction
36 Acoustic measure
38 Sad songs
39 Burrowing rodent
40 Follower of a plane . . . or a hint to this puzzle's theme
42 "Most definitely!"
43 Amos Alonzo ___, coach in the College Football Hall of Fame
45 I.S.P. option
47 Dominate
49 Lowest parts
50 Author Locke of the Harlem Renaissance, the first African-American Rhodes scholar (1907)
51 Hall of fame
54 Comic strip canine
56 Bias
58 Celestial altar
60 Norma ___ (Oscar-winning role of 1979)

by Mary Lou Guizzo and Jeff Chen

Note: In the newspaper version of this crossword, the clues appear in a single list, combining Across and Down. When two answers share a number, they also share a clue.

MEDIUM 101

ACROSS

1 It emerges at dawn
4 Prometheus' gift
8 May honoree
14 "Either you do it __ will"
15 Russia's __ Mountains
16 Source of some pop-ups
17 Contribution of Gilbert, but not Sullivan
19 Give a hand to
20 Implore
21 "__ from that . . ."
23 Presided over
24 Word of greeting
26 Help for a star witness?
28 Underground rock
29 Dawn's direction
30 Sound from a rowdy crowd
31 Like Ganymede among Jupiter's moons
34 Light beige
37 Classify by type
38 "Otello" and "Pagliacci"
42 Many a character in Ann M. Martin's "The Baby-Sitters Club"
44 Language of the answers to this puzzle's uniclues
45 Urban area
48 British bottom
50 Cpl. or sgt.
51 Comment made while yawning
54 Prime-time time
56 Miley Cyrus's "Party in the __"
57 One of Donald Trump Jr.'s parents
58 World Smile Day mo.
59 Hair-coloring technique
61 Fight finisher
65 Any of the Magi
66 Nessie's home
67 Where you might get into hot water
68 Dissuades
69 "When all __ fails . . ."
70 How many feet are in a fathom

DOWN

1 [See note]
2 Sch. with a campus in Providence
3 Dainty eaters
4 [See note]
5 N.Y.C. subway letters
6 Rapping sound
7 Runs off to a justice of the peace
8 [See note]
9 "Awake and Sing!" playwright Clifford
10 Bygone Pan Am rival
11 Call to the hounds
12 Port up the lake from Cleveland, O.
13 Clarify, as butter
18 Seminary subj.
22 Old person, in Oldenburg
24 [See note]
25 Notable stretches
27 Sadistic
29 [See note]
32 "Somebody That I Used to Know" singer, 2011
33 Byron's "before"
35 Alternative to a cup
36 Dungeons & Dragons, for one, in brief
39 Carnival game with bottles
40 Author Sholem
41 Drinking game penalty, perhaps
43 "Peter Pan" dog
44 [See note]
45 [See note]
46 Good place to be during a blizzard
47 It might be left holding the bag
49 Annoy
52 One practicing self-help, informally
53 Declares with confidence
54 [See note]
55 __ factor
60 Dr. of rap
62 Facility at Quantico, Va.: Abbr.
63 News inits. since 1958
64 Line on a receipt

by Queena Mewers and Alex Eaton-Salners

102 MEDIUM

ACROSS

1 Wrangler, for one
5 Things kids sometimes draw
9 Carriages in Kew Gardens
14 Band with a slash in its name
15 Occur to, with "on"
16 ___ Cinemas, second-largest theater chain in the U.S.
17 Be hot under the collar
18 Snap, Crackle and Pop, e.g.
19 Dweller on the Arabian Sea
20 "No one can get in a fight by himself," informally
23 Rum cocktail
25 Robert Burns's "since"
26 Starting point for a platypus
27 Steam
28 Some Windows systems
30 Is nostalgic for
32 Classic song with the lyric "I'll see you in my dreams"
36 What you may call it?
37 S. Amer. land
38 Air condition?
42 World traveler since 1985
47 What's honed on the range?
50 Put pressure on
51 Downed a sub?
52 Goethe's "The ___-King"
53 Like the German article "der": Abbr.
56 Welled (up)
58 Flip out . . . or a hint to eight answers in this puzzle
61 Diamond datum
62 Adjutant
63 Progenitor of the Edomites, in the Bible
66 Old Scottish title
67 What optical readers do

68 Staples of "Poor Richard's Almanack"
69 Sir William ___, medical pioneer
70 Far from subtle actors
71 Pro side

DOWN

1 Dig, in a way
2 Writer Umberto___
3 Where Copy and Paste appear
4 School tech class site
5 Some expensive dental work
6 Rows
7 Jerks
8 Having a white blanket
9 Body building block
10 San ___, Italy
11 Banded stones
12 Get along
13 Babies in a pond
21 Powerful checker
22 "I'll spring for it"
23 National park in Utah
24 Latin word on a dollar bill
29 Pipe part
31 Basted, e.g.
33 Indigenous Peruvian
34 Whack
35 Littlest piggy
39 "My assumption is . . ."
40 Time of day, in ads
41 Archived document
43 Current device
44 Delivery door location, often
45 Silky cottons

46 Fired
47 Opposite of staccato
48 Foams
49 Universal
54 Supply that no one's supposed to find
55 Second-longest-running Broadway musical ever (after "The Phantom of the Opera")
57 A very long time back
59 Provider of directions to a farmer
60 Mild cheese
64 Wow
65 ___ Constitution

by Morton J. Mendelson

ACROSS

1 Bridge
5 "I'll take care of that"
9 American Girl products
14 Jai ___
15 Common blessing
17 Undercover buster
18 Rhyming description for IHOP's "Fresh 'N Fruity" pancakes
19 Safety warning for some kitchenware
21 Born
22 ___ Park, Calif.
23 Jots
26 Outer thigh stabilizers, in brief
29 See in court, say
30 Art Spiegelman's Pulitzer-winning graphic novel
31 Craze
34 Road Runner cartoon sights
38 Goof
39 Warm and cozy spots
41 Manning with two Super Bowl M.V.P. awards
42 Homeland of many 2010s refugees
44 What bugs are found in
45 Bug on a hook, maybe
46 Ctrl-___-Del
48 On the loose
50 Big news involving extraterrestrials
54 Caddies' suggestions
55 Some four-year degrees, for short
56 Kangaroo's pouch
59 Loudly angry, as a group
62 Flight part
64 Rolls the dice and moves one's token
65 Perfect dives
66 Parts of porch chairs
67 Airport postings, in brief
68 Italian wine region

DOWN

1 Lead-in to Francisco or Pedro
2 With 36-Down, astronomical rarity . . . or a hint to the circled letters
3 Alexander Hamilton's nemesis
4 ___ Maduro, successor to Venezuela's Hugo Chávez
5 Fairy tale baddie
6 Sign gas
7 Gets tagged, say
8 Rwandan minority
9 Banned insecticide
10 "Well, well, well!"
11 Sierra ___
12 Some Millers
13 Bad eye sight?
16 Nabokov's nos
20 Part of many German names
22 They act in silence
24 Big name in antacids
25 Meade's opponent at Gettysburg
27 "Dr." of hip-hop
28 Onetime Volvo alternative
32 Master's seeker's hurdle, for short
33 Suffix with oper-
35 Shipping lanes
36 See 2-Down
37 Browser history contents
39 "Freeze!"
40 Fedora, for one
43 McKellen who played Gandalf
45 One who won't serve the average joe
47 Florida city on a bay
49 Back talk
50 Ear passage
51 Japanese city on a bay
52 ___ blanche
53 Prey for a brown bear
55 Smithereens
57 Actress Ramirez of "Grey's Anatomy"
58 Cremation containers
60 Pull in
61 ___ Intrepid (New York City tourist attraction)
63 Letter after "X"

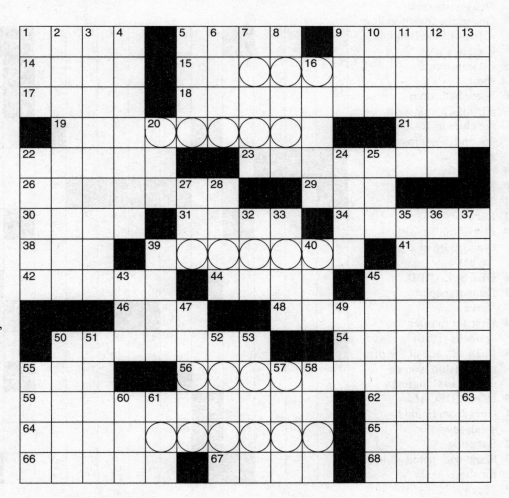

by Ross Trudeau

ACROSS

1 Flip (out)
4 Dandy neckwear
10 "___ NewsHour"
13 Opera that famously ends with the line "La commedia è finita!"
15 Potion container
16 NOTED TENOR
17 "Dark Angel" star Jessica
18 Advantage
19 Kickstarter figure
20 Desk tray labels
21 SIMPLE DIET
24 "Dallas Buyers Club" Oscar winner
26 Apprehend
29 Something checked on a questionnaire
30 One of the five founding nations of the Iroquois Confederacy
35 Fat remover, for short
36 Some bathroom postings . . . or what the clues to 16-, 21-, 46- and 59-Across are?
39 Not stuffy
40 Mason's tool
41 "Watch it!"
42 Puzzle
44 Part of the Spanish conjugation of "to be"
46 GET SPEARED
51 Dune transport
53 Verve
54 First car to offer seatbelts (1950)
58 Ilhan ___, one of the first two Muslim women elected to Congress
59 DOOR DECALS
61 Goes from liquid to solid, say
62 Babbling
63 Show with noted alumni, for short
64 "See ya!"
65 Off-roader, in brief

DOWN

1 Out of the strike zone, in a way
2 Product whose introduction was music to people's ears?
3 Group of friends
4 Abbr. in a cockpit
5 The Alamo had a famous one
6 "Can you ___?" (classic cologne catchphrase)
7 The planets, e.g.
8 Immune system defender
9 ___ Toby, character in "Twelfth Night"
10 Part of a stove
11 Pakistani restaurant owner on "Seinfeld"
12 Blind spot?
14 "Whither ___ thou?": John 16:5
15 Milli ___ (1980s–'90s pop duo)
20 "Methinks," in texts
22 [It's gone!]
23 Words of empathy
24 When repeated, a classic of garage rock
25 Teeny-tiny
27 Nighttime woe
28 Like the dawn sky
29 Lead-in to load or lift
31 Our: Fr.
32 Overthrow, e.g.
33 Court oath affirmation
34 Morning coat
37 ___ Rockefeller
38 Where to see two runners side by side
43 Serpentine swimmer
45 What to call un hombre
47 State flower of Indiana
48 Candied
49 Heaviest of the noble gases
50 Pepper used in mole sauce
51 Teeth not connected to jaws
52 "And how!"
55 On the briny
56 Elated
57 LG product
59 "Spare" part
60 ___ Wallace, "Ben-Hur" author

by John E. Bennett and Jeff Chen

ACROSS

1 "Not so!"
8 Modifier for "film" or "pinot"
12 *Instructions for premade dinner rolls
14 *Noble couple
15 With 4-Down, each year
16 Election day in the U.S.: Abbr.
17 Workplaces for scrub nurses, for short
18 Wrestling combos
21 Come through in the ___
24 Completely mistaken
25 With 38-Across, hex that's hard to shake
26 Cotton gin inventor Whitney
27 Have the wheel
28 Holier-___-thou
30 Partiality
31 *Latin American side dish that combines two food staples
34 *Title pair in a 2004–07 Nickelodeon sitcom
37 Practically an eternity
38 See 25-Across
39 Set aside for later
43 Bath tissue layer
44 Earth Day's mo.
45 Word of caution
46 Items scattered on bridal paths
48 Almond-flavored liqueur
50 Cool, in dated slang
51 Ancient kingdom in modern-day Jordan
52 Sn, to chemists
53 *Eponymous founders of a Massachusetts-based firearms manufacturer
58 *Duo of magicians who are the longest-running headliners in Las Vegas history
59 Bit of pond scum
60 Mark ___, longtime game show partner of Bill Todman

DOWN

1 Rankle
2 Sock tip
3 Try to hit, as a fly
4 See 15-Across
5 Fills a cargo hold
6 Unaffiliated voters: Abbr.
7 URL ending associated with the beginnings of the answers to the six starred clues
8 P.M. who inspired a 1960s jacket
9 Trilogy of tragedies by Aeschylus
10 I.C.U. drippers
11 Hi-___ monitor
12 Enter to steal from
13 Upbraid
14 Gave out hands
15 School support grps.
19 Shakes one's booty
20 Unnervingly strange
21 Positive kind of attitude
22 Extended family
23 Sound of contemptuous disapproval
25 Hootenanny instrument
28 Barbershop quartet voice
29 Pilgrimage to Mecca
30 "Act like you're supposed to!"
32 Sleeps in a tent, say
33 Rigel or Spica, by spectral type
34 Johnny of 2005's "Charlie and the Chocolate Factory"
35 Part to play
36 "Can I get you ___?"
40 Casino patron
41 Language of 15-Across 4-Down
42 School founded by Henry VI
44 ___ male
45 Caravan animals
47 Insurance giant based in Hartford
48 Supplement
49 Cut the lawn
51 Prefix meaning "within"
53 Employer of a masseur
54 Brooks with Emmy, Grammy, Oscar and Tony awards
55 "Brokeback Mountain" director Lee
56 ___-pitch softball
57 One of 100 in D.C.: Abbr.

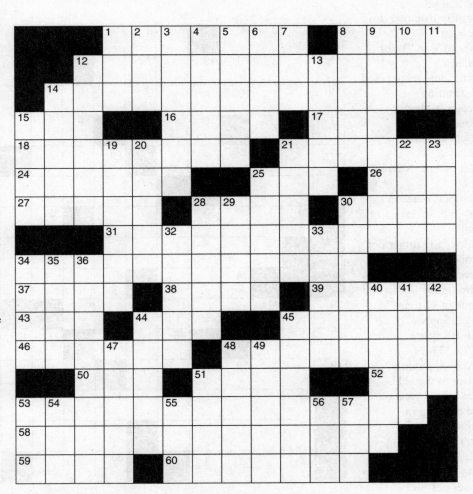

by Byron Walden

ACROSS

1 Precursor to riches, it's said
5 "A Farewell to Arms" subj.
8 Snide chuckle
12 Unalaskan, e.g.
14 Hide-y holes?
15 Player of X in "X-Men"
17 Alternatives to texts
18 Squeeze (out)
19 Frequent favorite
21 Scotch brand
23 Courtroom V.I.P.s
24 Part of some future planning, for short
25 Like many of Pindar's works
26 Player of M in "GoldenEye"
29 Carefully listening (to)
32 Screw up
33 Player of V in "V for Vendetta"
36 Cabinet dept. concerned with farming
37 Chicago landmark nicknamed for its resemblance to a legume
39 Player of J in "Men in Black"
43 Urban portmanteau
45 Lead-in to -cide
46 Equal
47 Would really rather not
49 Member of a fratlike Silicon Valley work environment
52 "Game of Thrones" role ___ Snow
53 Cardi B's genre
54 15-, 26-, 33- or 39-Across, punnily?
57 Answer to the old riddle "What wears more clothing in summer than in winter?"
58 What Dante wrote in
59 Try to get a good look
60 Crosses out
61 A really long time

DOWN

1 Spanish fleet?
2 San Francisco Bay city
3 Becomes involved in
4 Big ___
5 Ones going down in flames?
6 Shake, maybe
7 Walk-___
8 Julia Ward ___, writer of "The Battle Hymn of the Republic"
9 Really long times
10 Contained by this text
11 Ph-neutral vitamin brand
13 Mezzanine, e.g.
14 Magical basin used to view one's memories in the Harry Potter books
16 Disgusting sort
20 "Lah-di-___!"
22 Honest-to-goodness
23 Cool woman, jocularly
26 Typical Seder attendee
27 Tiny amount
28 Rutherford known as "The Father of Nuclear Physics"
30 Popular boots from Australia
31 Title role for Sally Field
34 "How relaxing!"
35 Online handle for an Xbox player
38 Zero
39 Drippy, say
40 Geographical feature of Mars
41 12-time Olympic swimming medalist Ryan
42 Classic Camaro, informally
44 Action-documenting cameras
47 Some circle dances
48 Super-uptight
50 Title creature in an Aesop fable
51 Title in Uncle Remus stories
52 "Black Swan" jump
55 Two for the show, informally?
56 Org. concerned with bugs and plants

by Sam Trabucco

ACROSS

1 Do some digging
6 "Good joke!"
10 Phishing scheme, e.g.
14 City whose cathedral is the subject of a series of Monet paintings
15 "Good gravy!"
16 Target of the U.S.-backed Radio Martí
17 Exuded
18 Was afraid of losing
20 Pre-22-Across
22 Go for a stroll
23 Indian bread
24 One who gets booked, informally
26 Pre-29-Across
29 Subject in acting school
32 Features of leopards
33 Noted family of German composers
34 Ceiling
36 Some Craigslist listings: Abbr.
37 Red Scare epithet
38 Animal also called a Nittany lion
39 '70s rock?
40 Some Spanish murals
41 Bud of baseball
42 Pre-44-Across
44 Job in a monastery
45 Inauguration recitation
46 Enjoy a nice long bath
47 Pre-50-Across
50 How emotionally developed people handle things
54 One cabinet in a kitchen, typically
56 Douglas ___, author of "The Hitchhiker's Guide to the Galaxy"
58 ___ boots
59 Pod creature
60 Regal maker
61 Flabbergast
62 "All right already!"
63 Skunk's defense

DOWN

1 Positive
2 Thatcher's creation
3 Anise-flavored liqueur
4 Bar snack
5 Causes (oneself) to be cherished
6 Long-beaked bird
7 Soup thickener
8 Doesn't just choose randomly
9 Autoplaying annoyances, sometimes
10 Dish that can give you garlic breath
11 Park place?
12 Ferrara who directed "King of New York"
13 Wasn't late for
19 Supermarket aids
21 Extremely, informally
25 Auto-reply?
26 "Stat!"
27 Increased
28 The Teflon Don
29 Virgil's fellow traveler
30 Eyelike openings
31 Desert in southern Africa
33 Prominent Gorbachev feature
35 Part of a website
37 Scotch flavorer
38 Suddenly got excited
40 Hotel sojourns
41 Pharaonic symbols
43 ___ Whitehead, author of the 2017 Pulitzer-winning novel "The Underground Railroad"
44 Tiny amount
46 Brunch partner of 47-Down
47 Brunch partner of 46-Down
48 Very often
49 Italian word with a grave accent that becomes a brand name with an acute accent
51 With the bow, in music
52 Where a supervillain schemes
53 Gay anthem of 1978
55 Romantically pursue
57 Where a telescope points

by Will Nediger

108 Medium

ACROSS

1 Crowd on the move
6 Valuable paper
14 Crossing the keel
15 It holds water
16 Blue jays
18 "Watch out!"
19 Game with 501 points
20 ___ plate
21 Temple title
24 Bygone compacts
26 Honey bees
30 "I can see clearly now"
31 Second-largest moon of Saturn
32 Alternative to AOL
33 Dry eyes
38 Abbr. at a tire shop
41 To boot
42 Autobahn auto
46 High seas
51 Candy bar with chocolate and caramel around a wafer
52 Tributary of the Rio Grande
53 Gandhi and others, for short
54 Much of the back of a baseball card
57 Follower of debate in the General Assembly, in brief
59 Green peas
63 AA and AAA
64 Farm refrain
65 Parts of tourist guides
66 Jobs at a body shop

DOWN

1 Leon Uris novel, with "The"
2 Shortest Old Testament book
3 Smooths over
4 Very, informally
5 Albert Einstein, notably
6 'L' train overseer, for short
7 Caterer's container
8 Funny Foxx
9 Indian chief
10 Surface
11 Thunder, but not Lightning
12 Bleeps
13 QB's accumulation: Abbr.
15 Nikola Tesla's countrymen
17 ___ miss
20 Not yet on the sched.
22 Without exception
23 Like a crisp picture, say
25 Private info, for short
27 "There but for the grace of God ___"
28 Opus ___
29 Kick out for good
34 Real heel
35 Seat of White Pine County, Nev.
36 "Now!"
37 China's Chiang ___-shek
38 Election fig.
39 Unlikely source of a silk purse
40 Mirror
43 Lots of
44 Teacher's punishment
45 Magazine no.
47 Tough-to-win horse racing bet
48 Certain intimate apparel sizes
49 Traffic director
50 Got back (to)
55 Abound
56 Tegan and ___ (pop duo)
58 Andy Taylor's kid on old TV
59 Keglers' org.
60 Quick drink
61 Paris's Jardin ___ Tuileries
62 Kind of pad

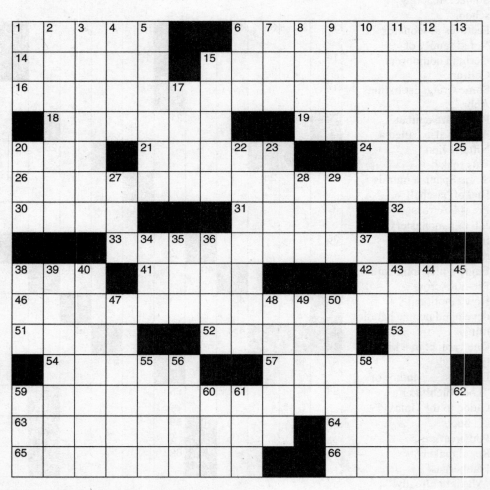

by Randolph Ross

ACROSS

1 Caprice
5 Rung #1 of an apt word ladder
9 "Too frustrating for me!"
14 Michael who played the title role in 2014's "Cesar Chavez"
15 Melville work following "Typee"
16 Exploding stars
17 History moving forward
20 Bring up . . . or something brought up
21 Same-___ marriage
22 "Phooey"
23 Canine command
25 "The Amazing Spider-Man" director, amazingly enough
28 Trade show
30 Alternative to Target
32 Rung #2 of the ladder
34 Ire
38 Actress Falco
39 Supermarket section
40 Readily open to change
41 Snowy expanse
44 In a nervous manner
45 Lowest number not found on a grandfather clock
46 Woman's name that's a city in Oklahoma
47 Takes five
48 Rung #3 of the ladder
49 "And yet . . ."
50 Quench
52 Italian province where Moscato is produced
54 Follower of crack or crock
55 Shadow
58 Where Hawks soar: Abbr.
60 South side?
62 Cry when warmer weather returns
67 Taqueria option
68 Jai ___
69 Funny Samberg
70 Subscription option
71 Rung #4 of the ladder
72 Not nice

DOWN

1 Typist's stat: Abbr.
2 Experience auditory hallucinations
3 Latin phrase on memos
4 New World parrots
5 English head
6 Global financial org.
7 "Didn't intend for that!"
8 Irish girl's name related to the word "honor"
9 Dutch banking giant
10 Stuffed with ham and Swiss cheese
11 Allege
12 Big employer in Huntsville, Ala.
13 Try
18 Charlemagne's domain: Abbr.
19 Losing line in tic-tac-toe
23 Spit in the food?
24 I-, in chemistry
26 Gusted
27 City just east of Gulfport
29 1950s–'60s TV emcee Jack
31 Not be bothered by something
33 Lower limits, in math
35 National Zoo animal on loan from China
36 Current event?
37 Hindu's bindi, traditionally
39 Needing moisturizer
40 Gift for a ukulele player
42 To whom "Do You Want to Build a Snowman?" is sung
43 "It's mine!"
48 Deadly
49 Style of yoga in a heated room
51 Identify
53 Best
55 Peter or Paul
56 Area abutting a transept
57 Country with a Supreme Leader
59 ___ land
61 Part of a Viking message
63 "Uh-uh"
64 Singer/songwriter Smith
65 One you might squabble with in the back seat
66 OB/___

by Mary Lou Guizzo and Erik Agard

ACROSS

1 Forest hatchling
6 Home of Hells Canyon and Heavens Gate Lookout: Abbr.
9 Root site
14 Chitchat
16 St. ___, only nation named for a woman
17 1968 Clint Eastwood western with six nooses on its poster
18 Much-trapped animal in wilderness America
19 It's hardly a Champagne cooler
20 "Why ___?"
21 Highest peak in N.Z.
22 "Sick, dude!"
23 Cheer at a Texas football game
26 Exclamation usually made in a high voice
29 Enemy agency in "Get Smart"
30 Cleaner brand with the slogan "Hasn't scratched yet!"
32 Dead spot
34 91, in old Rome
37 Toy boxer in a classic two-player game
40 Something much sold on St. Patrick's Day
41 PBS series since 1974
42 Some long sentences
43 Emcee's need
45 Be all thumbs?
46 "Show the world what you've got!"
52 Short-term job
54 Rob who directed "This Is Spinal Tap"
55 15-time N.B.A. All-Star Duncan
57 This, that or the other
58 Combine
59 "Hands in the air!" . . . or a literal hint to 17-, 23-, 37- and 46-Across
62 Tall, slender wineglass
63 Shapes of many car air fresheners
64 Like computer data, with "in"
65 London ___
66 Cheeky

DOWN

1 Fall color
2 "Some jerk he is!"
3 Cha cha slide, e.g.
4 Lang. of 16-Across
5 Counterfeiter trackers, in old lingo
6 "Does this seem fine to you?"
7 Jab
8 German cry
9 Dillydallier
10 Kitchen utensil brand
11 Best ___
12 Use for a bed
13 Partner of recreation
15 [Gulp!]
21 Eponymous hypnotist
24 Classic Scottish breakfast item
25 Nut
27 ___ Terr. (geographical designation until 1889)
28 "Ain't that the truth!"
30 Clothing item with hooks
31 Chemical variation
33 Champagne specification
34 Halo and Gears of War
35 Goes on
36 "___ a long story"
38 "Heroides" poet
39 Cosine of 0
44 Bolting down, say
46 Company that merged with Heinz in 2015
47 "Nervous" sort
48 Get ready for a Mr. Universe contest, say
49 Benjamin
50 Like computer data, with "in"
51 Danglers from rear-view mirrors
53 Hit musical with the song "Everything's Coming Up Roses"
56 N.Y.S.E. and Nasdaq: Abbr.
59 Tanning fig.
60 Madre's hermano
61 1970s–'80s cause, for short

by Brian Thomas

ACROSS

1 Metallic waste
6 Isn't a bystander
10 Longtime Syrian leader
15 Preferred seating request
16 Get ready for planting
17 In ___ (developing)
18 Understood
19 Ithaca, to Odysseus
20 Odysseus, to Ithaca
21 Les ___-Unis
22 Patent preceder
23 Girder type
24 Lineage-based women's grp.
25 "___ be my pleasure!"
27 "Star Trek: ___" (syndicated series of the '80s–'90s)
29 Draft org.
30 Pizza chain
31 Stumblebum
33 Rare craps throws
36 Like Mercury among all the planets
41 Legendary Manhattan music club
45 "Here comes trouble!"
46 Distance for Captain Nemo
47 ___ package
48 Big name in mortgages?
49 TV host Ryan
51 Singer Carly ___ Jepsen
52 Hide away
54 Place to go to swim, informally
55 Mythical figure known for ribaldry
57 Writer Edgar ___ Poe
59 Places where streams flow
60 Indirect comment . . . or a hint to this puzzle's circled letters
66 Org. for students in uniform
67 Danish money
68 Blackberrys, e.g., for short
69 Spread in a spread
70 27 Chopin works
71 Bombard
72 Acorn, essentially
73 Deals with
74 Indulged to excess, with "on"

DOWN

1 Like the slang "da bomb" and "tubular, man!"
2 Vaquero's item
3 Award for Washington and Lee
4 Pupil of a lizard, e.g.
5 Becomes established
6 Garden pest
7 Dummkopf
8 "Personally . . ."
9 Worry about, informally
10 The Charioteer constellation
11 Bit of theater detritus
12 Tennis Hall-of-Famer with a palindromic name
13 Arts and hard sciences, e.g.
14 Sides of some quads

26 Pictorial fabric
28 Studying aid
30 Grp. that gets the show on the road
32 Recipient of media complaints, for short
33 Some turkeys
34 [Yawn!]
35 1-1
37 Well-organized
38 Eponymous physicist Ernst
39 Horrid sort
40 Chop ___
42 Made the rounds, say?
43 It varies from black to white
44 Ballpark purchase
49 N.B.A. Hall-of-Famer with four rap albums, informally

50 "The Tale of ___ Saltan" (Rimsky-Korsakov opera)
53 Like some golf shots and most bread
56 City under siege from 2012 to '16
58 "No ___" (bumper sticker)
59 Page 2, 4 or 6, generally
60 Space balls
61 Art Deco notable
62 Dissolute man
63 Butts
64 "Dogs"
65 Abbr. on a brewery sign

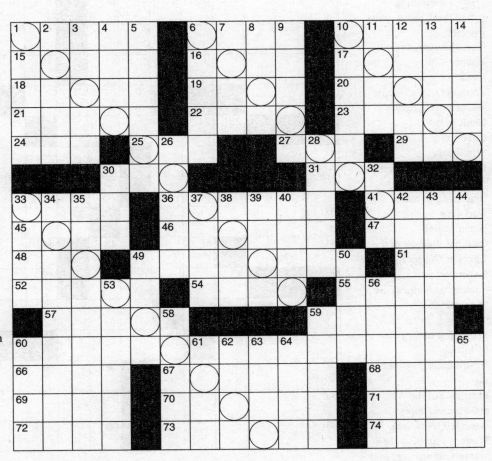

by Jeffrey Wechsler

ACROSS

1 Kept for a rainy day
9 Place where people are going with their drinks?
15 Norman Bates or his mother, in "Psycho"
16 Advice for relaxing
17 Top-level list
18 Judge appropriate
19 Ninny
20 One of the choices on a computer's 17-Across
22 Brown or blacken
23 Welcome at the front door
26 Get dressed (up)
27 Portable workstation
30 ___ it out (fights)
32 Chinua who wrote "Things Fall Apart"
33 Order in the court
34 Concert piece
37 "Here's something for you to think about, you ingrate!"
39 One who spreads discord
41 Shade provider in Thomas Gray's "Elegy Written in a Country Churchyard"
42 Coalition
44 Mindlessly
45 Request during a physical checkup
46 Beginning of many workdays
47 [I don't care]
50 Onetime division of the Chrysler Corporation
52 Sweatshirt part
53 Finding on Snopes.com
54 "Are you ___?"
57 "Ciao"
59 Manage to detach by hitting
63 Have a quick look-see, say
64 Language of the pre-Roman Empire
65 Some IHOP choices
66 Western villain . . . or a hint to four answers in this puzzle

DOWN

1 Spiritual guide
2 "___! 'tis true I have gone here and there" (start of a Shakespeare sonnet)
3 "That so?"
4 Place where plots are hatched
5 The radius runs along it
6 Small
7 Politico who called the press "nattering nabobs of negativism"
8 Incredulous question
9 Worst in a competition
10 Can
11 Animal that shares its name with a king of Thrace in the "Iliad"
12 Sights along the Champs-Élysées
13 Aid for a fugitive
14 Take another shot at
21 Habituate
23 Burgoo, e.g.
24 Kind of purse that sags
25 In public
26 "What are you waiting for?!"
27 Frilly
28 Long
29 "Close call!"
31 A geisha might be found in one
34 Shivering fit
35 Self-referential
36 Place for a king and queen
38 Overdo the flattery
40 Prefix with particle
43 Takedown piece
45 Numbers game
47 Where many cabins are found
48 Comfortable and welcoming
49 "Got it"
51 Will, more emphatically
53 Clothing department
54 Unpleasant find in a sweater
55 ___-Pacific
56 Ding
58 Edge
60 Suggested qty.
61 Inc. alternative
62 Symbol of strength

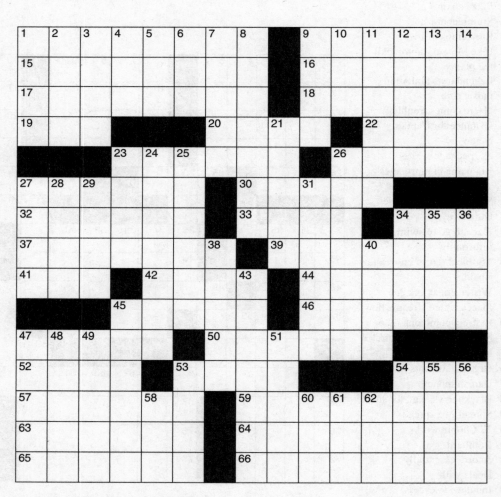

by Nancy Stark and Will Nediger

ACROSS

1 What you might do if you skip a step
5 Like old-fashioned diapers
10 "Selma" director DuVernay
13 Four-star review
14 "Tiny Bubbles" crooner
15 Onetime ruler in the Winter Palace
16 *Insomniac's complaint
19 Japanese lunch box
20 Root beer brand
21 Half-___ (coffee option)
22 Alternative to Tide or Cheer
23 *Leaving dirty dishes on the counter, say
27 ___ cava
28 Firefighter tool
29 Limit
31 Part of a Swiss roll?
33 Ambulance figure, for short
34 Green stone
35 Rain heavily
36 *Sexy detective
38 Bay ___
39 Force on the ground
40 Abbr. in a criminal profile
41 Like the posts at the top of a blog, typically
43 Growling dog
44 Showy neckwear
45 Fifth book of the New Testament
46 *Works like an anti-aging serum
49 West Coaster's summer hrs.
52 Fed-up feeling
53 Certain library loan
54 Lessen, as fears
56 Liquid evidenced by the answers to this puzzle's starred clues?
60 Tiny bit
61 Off the table?
62 Part of N.B.
63 First word of many California city names
64 "___ Anatomy"
65 General ___ chicken

DOWN

1 Group making a reservation?
2 Go-kart, e.g.
3 Ex of the Donald
4 Confined, with "up"
5 Contents of jewel cases, for short
6 Nabokov novel
7 Last year before A.D.
8 1931 boxing movie for which Wallace Beery won a Best Actor Oscar
9 "___ on it!"
10 "Yeah, whatever"
11 With 12-Down, actress Joan whose last name consists of two different conveyances
12 See 11-Down
15 Contraction that starts "Jabberwocky"
17 Cat or top hat, in Monopoly
18 Oil crisis?
24 Completely jumbled
25 Wiped out
26 Ralph who wrote "Only the Super-Rich Can Save Us!"
27 Not stay the same
30 Split tidbit
31 Grounds for discussion?
32 Alliterative ice cream flavor
33 H, as in Athens
34 Highest-grossing film before "Star Wars"
35 ___-12 (N.C.A.A. conference)
37 "As you wish," to a spouse
42 Allen or Hawke
44 Rush-hour sound
45 Actress Hepburn
47 The Krusty ___ (SpongeBob SquarePants's workplace)
48 Egg-shaped
49 Bends at a barre
50 "Book 'em, ___!"
51 Rug rats
55 Rainbow flag initialism
56 Letters at a filling station?
57 Org. with ties to Sinn Fein
58 Part for tuning a guitar
59 Connections

by Erik Agard, Amanda Chung and Karl Ni

ACROSS

1 Happening after doors open on Black Friday
8 Draw
15 Colorful circles
16 Ronan of "Lady Bird"
17 1982 movie starring Julie Andrews
19 Elicited with difficulty
20 Some mortgage adjustments, in brief
23 Run, old-style
24 Skeletons in the closet, so to speak
28 To be, overseas
29 Tighten (up)
31 Money holder
32 Swimmer Ian who won three gold medals in the 2000 Olympics
34 Japanese floor mat
36 Helpful people to know
37 Warning sign
41 Triple ___
42 Collegiate basketball competition, for short
43 Like Natalie Portman, by birth
44 It ended during the Napoleonic Wars: Abbr.
45 Kind of switch
47 Label owned by Sony Music
48 Good earth
50 Formerly
51 Its second ed. contains about 59 million words
52 Miss the mark
53 1% alternative
55 Like many radios
57 A long way off
60 Common sign-off
61 Source of the word "kiwi"
62 River draining 11 countries
63 8:00-9:00 p.m. in prime time, e.g.
64 Deduce
65 Down in the dumps
66 Go down, in a way
67 Like many A.T.M.s
68 Primetime ___

DOWN

1 Western Conference player, informally
2 Shapiro of public radio
3 World AIDS Day mo.
4 More eccentric
5 Soothing succulents
6 1986 #1 Starship hit with the lyric "I'll never find another girl like you"
7 Third-person pronoun
8 Parenthesized comments
9 Food truck offering, maybe
10 Figure, as a sum
11 It may be read to the rowdy
12 Sheet music abbr.
13 Hit CBS series with three spinoffs
14 Spill the ___ (dish out gossip)
18 Line on a leaf
20 Holder of many cones
21 Like some cuisines
22 2008 movie starring Michael Sheen and Frank Langella
25 Movie with graphic violence . . . or what 17-Across, 22-Down or 39-Down each is?
26 Some board game equipment
27 Jazzes (up)
29 Souvenir shop purchases
30 List shortcut
33 Information on a ticket
35 Light on one's feet
38 "ER" role for Paul McCrane
39 1997 movie starring John Travolta and Nicolas Cage
40 Like many pipes nowadays
46 Knock down
49 Like butterscotch
53 Annual Austin festival, for short
54 ___ nut
55 Dictator deposed in 1979
56 Swampland, e.g.
58 Many a university donor, informally
59 "Ratatouille" rat

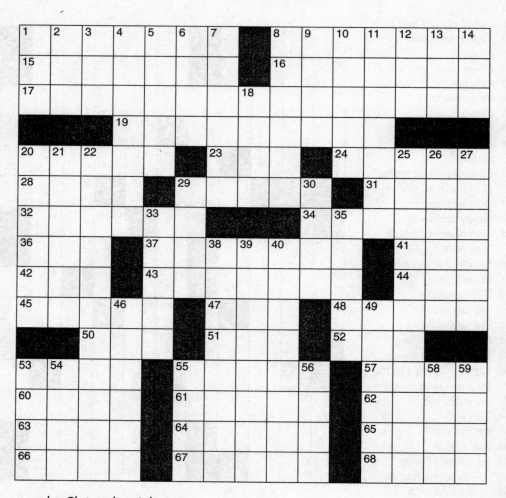

by Christopher Adams

ACROSS

1 Walk in big boots, say
6 Practically
10 Alternative to Venmo
14 A3s, A4s and A8s, in the automotive world
15 Black-and-white item you can consume whole
16 Adjoin
17 Like galoshes weather
18 Ground beef sandwich with Swiss cheese and caramelized onions
20 Success story like Uber or Airbnb
22 "True Detective" and "True Blood" airer
23 Poehler of "Parks and Recreation"
24 Institutions propped up with government support
30 When repeated, start of a cheer
33 Newton who lent his name to three laws of motion
34 "That's my ___!"
35 Da Vinci's "___ Lisa"
36 Catherine who married Henry VIII
37 Gives the cold shoulder
39 McGregor of the "Star Wars" prequels
40 "Just joshin'!"
41 Verb whose past tense is formed by moving the first letter to the end
42 Matrimonial path
43 Chinese path
44 One profiting through litigation, not innovation
47 Granola ___
48 Granola bit
49 Misconceptions about money . . . or a loose hint to 20-, 24- and 44-Across?
57 Discuss one's toilet habits, for example
58 West African republic
60 Something a complainer might raise
61 Easter basketful
62 404 Not Found, e.g.
63 Lodgings
64 Aussies with deep pockets?
65 Poke

DOWN

1 "Wheels"
2 Beach bash
3 Ruler of Valhalla
4 1" version of a 15-Across
5 Mind reader
6 "Didn't bother me at all"
7 1978–79 revolution site
8 Trips up
9 Provocative comments on current events
10 Toyota debut of 1982
11 Help the offense?
12 Classic George Takei role
13 Beginning of a link
19 Orange dish
21 Queen's honour, for short
24 "That's enough out of you!"
25 Universal Studios Japan site
26 Brother of video games
27 Balladeer
28 Less than right
29 Sister
30 "Why do you think that?"
31 Totally
32 Group of talking heads
35 Israel's Golda
37 Role in hide-and-seek
38 It's over your head
42 Chief law officer: Abbr.
44 "Ugh" reviews
45 To boot
46 Scot's headwear
47 Homes for owls
49 Hubs
50 Turgenev who wrote "Fathers and Sons"
51 Deutschland turndown
52 "Othello" schemer
53 Ship of myth
54 Drive-___ window
55 Like walnut shells
56 Smooch, in Britspeak
59 "___ we finished now?"

by Michael Hawkins

116 MEDIUM

ACROSS

1 Volunteer's offer
5 Fivers
9 Nickname for Cleveland Browns fans
14 Talking in a movie theater, e.g.
15 Withered
16 World Golf Hall-of-Famer Lorena
17 Tome
20 Like Guinness
21 Dandies
22 Editorial override
23 Down Under predator
24 Unsavory sort
26 Court org. - or a former court org.
27 D.C. summer setting
28 Palindromic girl's name
30 Often
32 Bonny miss
34 Barely manage, with "out"
36 It's generally not played so much
37 Notable
41 Give a raw deal
44 Have a bug
45 Nashville landmark, familiarly
49 Goon
52 Goose egg
54 Issa of "Insecure"
55 Boston Garden legend Bobby
56 See 51-Down
58 They can carry a tune
60 Crime film genre
62 Noah Webster's alma mater
63 Star ___
64 Request needed to understand four clues in this puzzle
67 Pass
68 One of Thanos's foes in the Avengers movies
69 Vet school subj.
70 It may have a big mouth
71 ___ souci (carefree)
72 Popular bait for catching striped bass

DOWN

1 One who doesn't believe
2 Subject of Hemingway's "Death in the Afternoon"
3 Rubs oil on
4 Label on some packages of jerky
5 Pale wood
6 Sexy, muscular man
7 Gaffe
8 Oozed
9 Bobs and bouffants
10 Doesn't sit idly by
11 Common riddle ending
12 Spoiled
13 Tear-jerker
18 Cry of surprise
19 "Got it"
25 Banned pollutants
29 Frost relative
31 Childish retort
33 Nos. at the beach
35 Watergate-___
38 ___ and Carla (1960s R&B duo)
39 Tina Fey's role on "30 Rock"
40 "The Book of ___" (2010 film)
41 Cadged
42 Wonder Woman, for one
43 Big news regarding extraterrestrials
46 Barbecue griller's purchase
47 Moderate's opposite
48 "We totally should!"
50 Terrier type
51 Says "56-Across!," for example
53 Card count
57 Kind of shirt
59 Cocoon dwellers
61 Geom. figure
65 N.Y.C. subway letters
66 Hems and haws

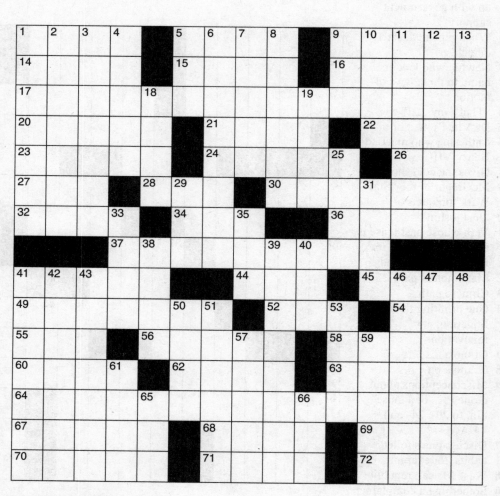

by Damon Gulczynski

ACROSS

1 Goof
4 Mexican resort area, for short
8 Car body option
13 Bets everything one's got
16 Bond wore a white one in "Goldfinger"
17 Commercial holiday mailing
18 Strands at a ski lodge, say
19 *Louis Pasteur, 1885
21 Losing poker player's declaration
24 U2 can call it home
25 *Roald Amundsen, 1906
33 Street cleaning day event
34 "Stat!"
35 Where Apia is found
36 Queens's Arthur ___ Stadium
38 *William Herschel, 1781
42 Half of square dance participants, typically
43 One-named Latin singer
45 "I'll do that job"
47 Letter above a sleeping toon
48 *Howard Carter, 1922
53 Heart and ___
54 Ver-r-ry small
55 Google returns . . . or the answers to the four starred clues
62 Partner of part
63 Enhances, as an original recording
67 Old British biplanes with an apt name
68 Home of the Titans
69 Pick on
70 Unwanted blanket
71 Chicken ___

DOWN

1 Goose ___
2 Reine's husband
3 One issuing red cards, for short
4 The "C" of F.C. Barcelona
5 Others, in a Latin list
6 Wait
7 Length of a quick tennis match
8 Favorable outcome
9 Prez or veep
10 Lucy's man
11 Deuce follower
12 Abstainer's portion
14 Peacock's walk
15 Annual mystery writer's award
16 Pageant topper
20 ___ access
21 Still in one piece
22 Kind of pork on a Chinese menu
23 ". . . am I right?!"
26 Sch. system with campuses in Pullman and Spokane
27 Big part of an elephant
28 Aromatherapy spot
29 Droop
30 Seattle-based retail giant
31 Magic creatures of Jewish lore
32 Pass slowly and carefully
37 Time to remember
39 Bit of Oscar recognition, informally
40 French article
41 Something to confess at a confessional
44 Where it's happening
46 Kind of fly
49 Competitor of Target
50 "Ben-___"
51 Bells and whistles, maybe
52 Exams
55 Dust-up
56 Overhang
57 Verdi's "La donna è mobile," for one
58 Some HDTVs
59 Appear
60 "Let me think . . . huh-uh"
61 Helmut of fashion
64 Topic in parapsychology, for short
65 Vintage car inits.
66 Possible reason for an R rating

by Ross Trudeau

118 MEDIUM

ACROSS

1 Showy accessories
5 Invitation stipulation
9 Goddess in a chariot pulled by peacocks
13 ___ Duncan, Obama education secretary
14 Place where beads are made
15 So-called universal donor type, for short
16 Saying suggesting that worldly possessions should be enjoyed
19 Beloved, in Bologna
20 Division of a hacienda
21 Actress Scala
22 Like Bill Clinton's presidency
25 Iconic introduction in cinema
27 Batman co-creator Bob
28 Longtime Mississippi politico Trent
31 Father of the American Cartoon
32 What one gets after many years of work
33 2008 political catchphrase
36 Instructor's remark after making a mistake
40 Like a sleeper cell?
41 Power ___
43 Head: Ger.
46 Actress Blanchett
47 "A forest bird never wants a ___": Ibsen
48 Insistent refusal
51 Agreed to, in a way
53 Part of some Hebrew men's names
54 Preceder of Edison
57 What goes above and beyond?
58 Where you go for a fresh start . . . or a hint for four answers in this puzzle
63 It's a two-hour drive north of Pittsburgh
64 Noggin
65 European capital
66 Tony and Emmy winner Tyne
67 Length
68 Give an appointment to

DOWN

1 Feature of Cajun Country
2 Goblinlike creature
3 Rain forest menace
4 House rules may not apply here
5 Bucolic call
6 Just for ___
7 ___ Day (supplement)
8 One way to get out of jail
9 The way
10 Puzzle
11 Adjusts, as laces
12 Dumbstruck
14 Like an overcast night sky
17 Number of sides on a triangolo
18 ___ Express (Delhi-to-Agra train)
22 Ring finish, briefly
23 "Where's ___?"
24 Common artwork in New York City subways
26 Fashion editor Wintour
29 First name in dance
30 Convictions
33 The dark side
34 One of a 1970s TV family
35 Court V.I.P.: Abbr.
37 Sleeper that never dreams
38 Quack remedy
39 Literary character who says "I will wear my heart upon my sleeve"
42 French politico Marine Le ___
43 Gnarly, as a tree trunk
44 Mark ___, 1998 P.G.A. Player of the Year
45 What a doodle might be in
47 Subs (for)
49 Man's nickname that sounds like a pest
50 Trying tasks
52 Nautical propeller
55 Cognac age indicator
56 Cool shade
59 What makes a tumbler spin
60 Samovar
61 Doctors Without Borders or Oxfam, in brief
62 "Let's ___!"

by Lewis Rothlein

ACROSS

1 A ewe for you, say
6 Mideast's Gulf of ___
11 Swelling reducer
14 Popped up
15 Some bonds, for short
16 Yule drink
17 Was barely victorious, as in boxing
19 Brooklyn Brown or Newcastle Brown
20 Storage unit
21 Diplomacy
22 Hershey coconut bar
24 Mavens
26 Cole Porter song from "Kiss Me, Kate"
28 Not for kids, say
30 Acquires the film rights to
31 Target numbers
34 Saturn S.U.V.
35 Baseball rarities nowadays . . . or a phonetic hint to the starts of 17-, 26-, 48- and 57-Across
39 ___-lacto-vegetarian
40 More blue
41 Ones who never listen to oldies?
44 Big name in oil
48 As something different to do
51 Mediterranean tourist attraction
52 Bo's'n's quarters
53 Oil or kerosene
55 Bit of work
56 Swear words?
57 Opposite of "consumed daintily"
60 Stephen of "V for Vendetta"
61 Tender spots
62 How many times a clock's little hand goes around in a full day
63 Strongman player on "The A-Team"
64 Not quite a strike
65 Possessed

DOWN

1 Where to order oysters
2 Beethoven's Third
3 Lift : elevator :: ___ : car hood
4 Mil. morale booster
5 On its way
6 Gas brand with a torch in its logo
7 World capital at 9,350 feet
8 "Commonwealth" novelist Patchett
9 Computer image file format
10 Put into categories
11 60 minutes from now
12 Brewskis
13 Casts out
18 Do beat work
23 Everything, with "the"
25 Forest giants
27 Given medicine
29 Do some voice work
32 Actress Thompson
33 "Caught ya!"
35 Often-naive reformer
36 Garment left in a cloakroom
37 Magazine with an Agency of the Year award
38 "Zip-a-___-Doo-Dah"
41 Validate
42 High-end Mercedes line
43 Lonely place, so they say
45 Substitute (for)
46 How curry dishes are often served
47 Pestered
49 A Lion, but not a Tiger, informally
50 External appearance
54 Jared of "Dallas Buyers Club"
58 ___ of Good Feelings
59 "So cute!"

by Alan Arbesfeld

120 MEDIUM

ACROSS

1 Demanding
6 Who said "A woman's perfume tells more about her than her handwriting"
10 Croque-monsieur ingredient
13 ___ View (streaming site)
14 "Dies ___"
15 Beer purchase
16 Kind of alcohol
17 "The Twits" author
18 Nike rival
19 Ornately decorated money?
22 Perfervid
25 Snowcapped, say
26 March meant to end a drought?
30 Oven handle?
31 Adamant refusal
32 Mistake indicator
35 Yellow card displayers
36 Lists of commands
37 Building site code?
38 AC/DC single with the lyric "Watch me explode"
39 Israeli president who was the author of 11 books
40 Commotion
41 Bumper version of a cart?
44 Fireplace receptacle
46 Beginnings
47 What the trees by Walden Pond provided?
51 Frequently cosplayed sci-fi character
52 Socially aware
53 Yellowish color
57 Bend over backward
58 Some
59 Member of an early 20th-century French art movement
60 Pick up
61 [Been there, done that]
62 Let go

DOWN

1 A word before you go
2 ___ milk
3 "I'm trying to work here"
4 Vegan source of protein
5 Four-time Grammy-winning gospel singer Adams
6 Mischievous trick
7 Modern locale of ancient Sumer
8 Home to Interstates H-1, H-2 and H-3
9 Takes a refresher course in
10 Plan (for)
11 Like some elephants
12 George ___, general at the Battle of Chancellorsville
15 Wrist bones
20 Way on Waze: Abbr.
21 Sheep's cry
22 Not with the group
23 Noodle soup
24 New addition to the team
27 Guy in a restaurant
28 Didn't just rent
29 Galvanize
33 "Could you turn on the A.C.?"
34 Weapons for the X-Man Wolverine
36 Dissolve
37 It was once drawn on the street
39 Ballet move
40 Quarterback's option
42 She played Mrs. Which in 2018's "A Wrinkle in Time"
43 What might have a crush on you?
44 America's first ICBM
45 ___ Khan, tiger in "The Jungle Book"
48 Tucson school, informally
49 Twist
50 Cut
54 Strawberry or peach
55 She was tempted
56 Visibly ashamed

by Brendan Emmett Quigley

ACROSS

1 Veronica ___, author of the best-selling "Divergent" series
5 Green and soft, say
10 Movie with famous "dun dun" theme music
14 Measurement that might be a lot?
15 Some Japanese cartoons
17 Profess
18 Menu item #1: A bowlful of Cap'n Crunch that's been on top of the fridge for four years
20 Rhyming opposite of break
21 Officers-to-be
22 Opera term that's sometimes a woman's name
24 Coffee alternative
25 Austin Powers or Jack Bauer
26 Menu item #2: The charred remains of a slice of whole wheat
29 W.C.
30 "___ Flux" (1990s sci-fi series)
32 Kinds
33 Org. whose participants wear helmets
35 Follower of Mary
37 Zip
38 Plea concerning the menu in 18-, 26-, 53- and 64-Across?
42 Chest coverer
43 "Eight more hours and I'm outta here!"
44 "Ya got that right"
46 Subject of a sleep lab study
49 Words to a backstabber
51 Go out for a bit
53 Menu item #3: A Red Delicious, assuming you find sawdust delicious
57 Writing surface
59 Wrath
60 Fail to enunciate
61 Cow sans calf
62 Ben ___, pirate in "Treasure Island"
64 Menu item #4: Something to pour in coffee for a sour surprise
67 "Stat!"
68 Pig, cutely
69 Dot on an ocean map
70 Future-gazer
71 City in West Yorkshire
72 N.B.A.'s Young, familiarly

DOWN

1 Troublemaker
2 Stop sign shape
3 Sacrifice of square footage for location, e.g.
4 ___ Keller, first deaf and blind person to earn a Bachelor of Arts
5 PC alternatives
6 "He still the ___" (lyric in Beyoncé's "Countdown")
7 Word before and after yes, in the military
8 Below-the-belt campaign tactic
9 Long (for)
10 Song one loves, in modern slang
11 Image next to a user name
12 Most socially conscious
13 Comfy pants
16 Not much light can get through it
19 Grammy-winning James
23 Bewildered
26 Wild hog
27 Not satisfied, as expectations
28 "___-daisy!"
31 Actor Idris
34 Media lawyer's specialty
36 Roll with a hole
37 Sound of failure
39 Broken bone revealers
40 Toy for a windy day
41 Ingredient in a melt
45 Kneecap
46 Close chicas
47 Read over
48 Dance done to the 2015 hit "Watch Me"
50 Not new
52 Started listening, with "up"
54 As well
55 It gets bigger in the dark
56 Accident-___
58 The sky, perhaps
61 That woman's
63 Broadcaster of "Wait Wait . . . Don't Tell Me!"
65 1950s prez
66 Guided

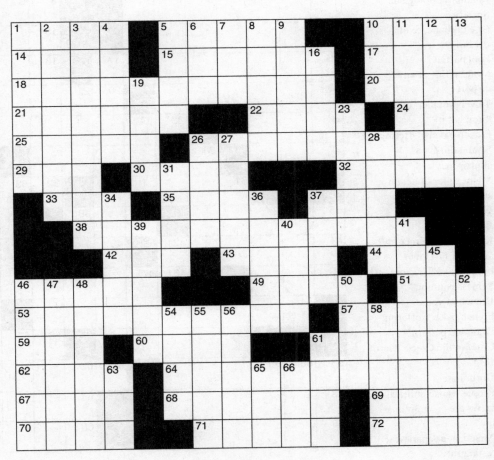

by Alison Ohringer and Erik Agard

ACROSS

1 Head on a plate?
8 Bloviating type
14 Egg-shaped
15 Worth mentioning
16 Global scare
18 Place to go off track?
19 Speak at a level pitch
20 In accordance with
22 King's College of Our Lady of ___ Beside Windsor
23 Image formed by connecting this puzzle's circled letters from A to N and then back to A
27 Lust, but not love
28 Sportscaster in the documentary "Telling It Like It Is"
29 Ref. work begun by the London Philological Society
31 One taking care of the bill
32 Pool parties?
35 Modern line at an airport
38 Towel provider, often
40 "You got it!"
41 French bakery offering
43 Strand during a ski trip, say
45 Major seller of health supplements
46 Peace in the Middle East
48 Keepers of the records?
51 Where a 17-Down becomes a 23-Across
54 Same-sex union?
55 Branch of yoga
56 French bakery offering
58 Diamond pattern
61 Chief in the Creek War of 1813–14
63 Dormmate
64 People whose political views are "Communist lite"
65 Anago, at a Japanese restaurant
66 Has in mind

DOWN

1 Duplicates
2 "Forward!," in Florence
3 Fashionable society
4 Raise one's hand for, say
5 Port north of the Horn of Africa
6 Hand-held console introduced in 1989
7 Teacher of Samuel
8 John and Mark, for two
9 Following
10 Wolf (down)
11 It's always cut short
12 Part of NATO: Abbr.
13 Thousand bucks
17 One that becomes a 51-Across
21 Home of the Rams before 2016: Abbr.
24 Paper clips have lots of them
25 Past the baseline, in tennis
26 Michelle of "Crazy Rich Asians"
28 Spanish word repeated in a welcoming phrase
30 Something to fall back from: Abbr.
31 Air traveler's convenience, informally
33 In good shape
34 A in German 101?
35 Boot brand from Australia
36 En ___ (with all of a court's judges)
37 Engrave
39 Smoothie flavor
42 Its N.Y.S.E. ticker symbol is "X"
44 Entered carefully
47 Comment from a hot bath
48 Sight in a Chinese parade
49 Like Nelson Mandela for 27 years
50 Underline, say
52 Pay for play
53 Bulldog
54 Fail to show up as expected
57 Euro division
58 Married couple?
59 Sushi garnish
60 Indian state whose largest city is Vasco da Gama
62 Lead-in to center

by Alex Eaton-Salners

ACROSS

1 Make known to customs officials
8 Makes a decision on Tinder
14 Sending out a memo, say
16 Mother ___
17 *1956 sci-fi movie with Robby the Robot
19 Big name in classic video games
20 Undergo a chemical change
21 Self-referential
22 *2006 rom-com starring Amanda Bynes and Channing Tatum
27 Curvy letter
28 "Bien sûr!"
29 Obama ___
30 Put 10,000 hours into, it's said
33 Forgets to include
35 *1961 musical for which Rita Moreno won an Oscar
38 "Wouldn't that be nice!"
39 Word often repeated with a different pronunciation
40 ___-Manuel Miranda, creator of "Hamilton"
41 Texter's qualifier
42 British P.M. beginning in 2016
45 *1953 musical with songs by Cole Porter
51 Tucker out
52 Fabulous writer?
53 Parts of the spine
54 What the film answering each starred clue was inspired by
59 Gay of the New Journalism movement
60 Rush of Black Friday shoppers, e.g.
61 Wearable by anyone
62 "I'm laughing so much it hurts!"

DOWN

1 Slander
2 Hams it up on stage
3 Ring figures
4 Large scale of the universe?
5 Et ___ (citation words)
6 Relieved (of)
7 Finish
8 Legendary snake exterminator, for short
9 Actress Raquel
10 Mad as hell
11 Write down
12 Linguistic suffix
13 Took a load off
15 Actor Richard
18 Classic game console, for short
22 Figure (out)
23 "Play that beat!"
24 Only female Israeli prime minister
25 Like many modern black-and-white films
26 Lil ___ X, rapper with the 2019 #1 hit "Old Town Road"
28 Bit of salty language
30 Some advanced degs.
31 Tokyo's former name
32 Cancel, as a fine
33 "Beetle Bailey" dog
34 Herd noise
35 Conflict with the European Theater of Operations, for short
36 German one
37 "Me too!"
38 Category
42 Gave the wrong message
43 Business whose income is computed quarterly?
44 "But of course!"
46 "For goodness' ___!"
47 Reagan attorney general
48 County name in England and five U.S. states
49 Keystone character
50 "Great" creatures
51 Actress Hedren
53 Pelosi and Schumer, informally
54 Fox News commentator Varney, familiarly
55 China's ___ dynasty
56 Ring figure
57 You can bank on it
58 Unit of sunshine

by Evan Mahnken

124 MEDIUM

ACROSS

1 Cry of disgust
4 One cleansed by Jesus
9 Outlet, for one
14 Food fig.
15 President with the same first and last name as his father
16 Amount to give
17 Power increaser
18 First two symbols in a 3-Down
20 Place to find a cluster of stars?
22 Joe Namath and Vinny Testaverde, notably
23 "Watermark" singer, 1988
24 ___ Alpha Theta, first Greek-letter sorority in the U.S.
27 Affected
28 Co. with an image of Mercury in its logo
30 Argentina was named after it
32 Live
34 Assents at sea
35 Onetime competitor of RCA and Columbia
38 Shade of brown
39 Elements of a 3-Down
40 Poison ___
42 Rhyming "Dr."
43 "Hold your horses!"
45 Research institution in Atlanta
46 Shows derision, in a way
48 Expo, today
49 Dovetail (with)
52 Myrrh, for one
54 Rub the wrong way
57 Treasures
59 In the news
61 Final symbol in a 3-Down
64 Palindromic brand in the kitchen
65 Something to lend
66 Longtime Susan Lucci role on "All My Children"
67 Con opener?
68 What the mnemonic "Every good boy does fine" represents
69 "Olympia" painter
70 Georgia, once: Abbr.

DOWN

1 End of every verse of "The Star-Spangled Banner"
2 Online moderator, for short
3 Response to solving this puzzle
4 Bananas
5 Offering on Amazon
6 Capital of the Canary Islands, after "Las"
7 Indie rock genre
8 Commanded
9 Home to a mythical ferry
10 Item sometimes next to a cash register
11 Survey option
12 Butler of renown
13 Minuscule, informally
19 It's more than a fling
21 Pi or phi, in math
25 Perches for some musicians
26 ___ Rock
29 Like curtains and cartoons
31 Center of the Krupp family dynasty
32 Condition with tics, for short
33 Winter Olympics powerhouse: Abbr.
35 Images such as 3-Down
36 Sully
37 Unfriendly
39 Blot on a landscape
41 Rich, savory flavor
44 Raised block of the earth's crust, to a geologist
46 Unruffled
47 Doesn't officially enroll
49 Country with the second greatest number of McDonald's restaurants after the U.S. [2,900+]
50 Home of the Sawtooth National Forest
51 Character who popularized the "mankini"
53 "Neat"
55 Some document transmissions
56 One of 163 in the Burj Khalifa
58 Extremities
60 Princeton Review subj.
62 Bottom line?
63 Alternative to Gain

by Jon Olsen

ACROSS

1 Word found before and after "and," in a phrase
5 Unit for a YouTube video
9 Object
14 Mr. : English :: ___ : Persian
15 Novel on which the film "Clueless" is based
16 Picky ___
17 Matter for the Postal Inspection Service
19 "Is this really necessary?"
20 *Not formally worded
21 *Like the pitcher in a batting order, often
22 Ending with orange or lemon
23 Basis of some scholarships
25 Part of a Snickers bar
26 *Peacocks, but not peahens
28 Mork's birthplace on "Mork & Mindy"
30 Stack
31 A, B, C, D and E, to nutritionists
35 Stop signal
36 What the answers to the starred clues are each anagrams of
39 When doubled, uncritically enthusiastic
40 Joined the Army, say
41 Sheik's peer
43 Bask on the beach
44 *Wandered
48 Post-championship celebration
50 Building by a barn
53 Dark loaf
54 *Like some foreign protests
55 *What keeps a part apart
57 Engraved stone marker
58 Pale-colored beer
60 What Britain voted to Brexit from, for short
61 Cordon (off)
62 Give off
63 Wall St. "500"
64 Gets a Venmo request, say
65 Article's start, in journalism jargon

DOWN

1 Who asked "Would you eat them in a box? Would you eat them with a fox?"
2 Lake Victoria lies on its southern border
3 A little chipper
4 Campus building
5 "Twenty Thousand Leagues Under the Sea" author
6 Public perception
7 Down Under bird
8 Spitball, e.g.
9 Conductor's beat
10 Bring before a superior for reprimand
11 Birth announcement
12 Bottom line figure
13 Clenched, as teeth
18 MuggleNet or The Leaky Cauldron, for "Harry Potter" readers
21 Separate, as stitches
24 *Internet addresses
27 Compassionate "Uncle Tom's Cabin" girl
29 Tears
32 What verb endings indicate
33 Free speech org.
34 Substance for a juicer
36 Killer Bee?
37 Missing button in many an elevator
38 Fuss
39 Meals
42 Argued vehemently (against)
45 Something that requires a special headset to play, informally
46 Lash holder
47 Upper-right keyboard button
49 Next in line
51 "Wouldn't that be nice!"
52 Olympic pool divisions
56 Walk dizzily
58 "My man!"
59 Part of PRNDL

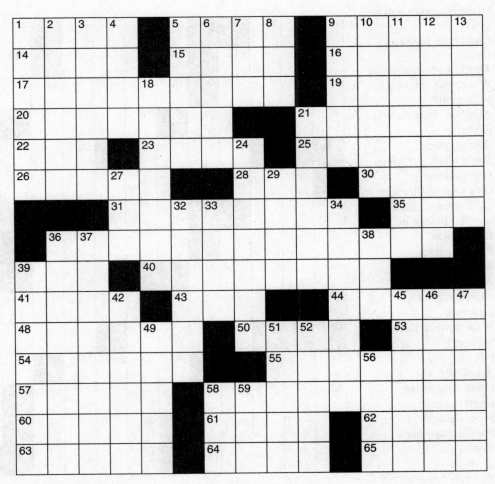

by Joel Fagliano

ACROSS

1 Kind of case in grammar: Abbr.
4 Pandora and others
8 "Autumn frosts have __ July": Lewis Carroll
13 Vichyssoise ingredient
15 __ cheese
16 Summer camp sight
17 Famous Alan whose last name shares three of the four letters of ALAN
18 Greenhouse gas mitigators
20 Events with booths
22 Big Four bank, informally
23 Contraction at the start of a sentence
24 Olympics event since 1964
26 Children's author Lowry
28 Third in a horror series
34 Where you might go for a spell?
35 Abbr. on some natural gas bills
36 Betting game
37 Some S.&L. offerings
39 Intermittently
42 City west of Florence
43 __ Railway, backdrop of "The Bridge on the River Kwai"
45 Fix, as a price
46 Speaker's place
47 Administerer of citizenship tests
52 Lummox
53 What's packed in a backpack
54 Fill
57 Small bite, say
59 Dunk alternative
63 Churchgoer, e.g.
66 Frostbite site
67 Popular sans-serif font
68 __-eyed
69 It can be bounced off someone

70 Like chimneys
71 Uptown, so to speak
72 Notoriously hard thing to define

DOWN

1 "Frozen" character
2 First name in 28-Across
3 "The Last __"
4 Start of a kindergarten song
5 One end of an umbilical cord
6 Prefix with -scope
7 Hard to get
8 Say "Yeah, right!," say
9 Conductor's announcement
10 Over
11 Speck

12 Suffix with bald or bold
14 Co-star of 28-Across
19 Tearjerker?
21 Big __
25 Country straddling the Equator
27 Foundational belief
28 Lifesaving supply
29 Kind of push-up
30 German for 72-Across
31 "Giant Brain" of 1946
32 Answer from behind a door
33 Tide type
34 Israel's Netanyahu, informally
38 Flirts with, in a way
40 "The Ipcress File" novelist
41 Dissonant

44 Back
48 Election after an election
49 Wedding reception cry
50 Variety meat
51 Rial spender
54 Springs for a vacation?
55 Flying start?
56 Athos, Porthos and Aramis, e.g.
58 It may be next to an elevator
60 Sci-fi sage
61 Addict
62 Soil additive
64 One's partner
65 "Cut that out!"

by Julie Bérubé

ACROSS

1 Arm twister?
5 "Glengarry Glen Ross" playwright
10 Butts
14 Start to do well?
15 Its version of 37-Across was popular in the 1970s–'80s
16 Rapper/actor on "Law & Order: SVU"
17 Pro-war sort
18 Hart of "Chicago"
19 "Goodness!"
20 I.C.U. hookups
21 Encroach (on)
23 Particle created by dissolving table salt
24 They're nuts for dessert
26 Intense
28 Fir coat?
29 "___ lighter note . . ."
32 Christmas light locale
33 Full-screen mode exit key
34 Rosalinde's maid in Strauss's "Die Fledermaus"
36 Latin "king"
37 Olympic sport since 1988
40 "___ ever!"
41 India's smallest state
42 Less drunk
46 Ralph who played Voldemort in the Harry Potter films
50 Unidentified date
51 French novelist ___ France
52 Ones making writers write right?: Abbr.
53 MP3-sharing service of the early 2000s
55 Sydney's state: Abbr.
56 ___-sec (wine designation)
58 Sweet cake
59 "Me? Are you kidding?!"
60 ___ Bator
61 Perfume compound
62 Knowledgeable of
63 With 65-Across, another name for 37-Across
64 Sweeties
65 See 63-Across

DOWN

1 Behind the times
2 Not touch
3 It may include sports and weather
4 Neighbor of La.
5 Some schoolteachers, quaintly
6 Resting on
7 Calf coverer
8 Popular Irish girl's name
9 Supermodel Cheryl
10 Carnival host
11 Reaches, as great heights
12 "Is it live or is it . . . ?" sloganeer
13 Jule who wrote the music for "Funny Girl"
21 It might be a blot on your record
22 Superwide shoe spec
25 Skee-Ball locales
27 An ay for an aye, e.g.?
29 Verse from an admirer
30 [Item depicted here]
31 Drink sold by the yard
34 Turned off
35 Bridge experts
38 Element before carbon on the periodic table
39 Musical insensitivity
42 Hastened
43 Nickname for Yale
44 Otto on "The Simpsons," e.g.
45 Lie
46 More rewarding, as a paycheck
47 "Stop! You're doing it all wrong!"
48 ___ Howard, first African-American player on the Yankees (1955)
49 Tailor's skill
54 Mlle., across the Pyrenees
57 Like Mozart's Symphonies Nos. 15, 27 and 32
59 Bit of a bite

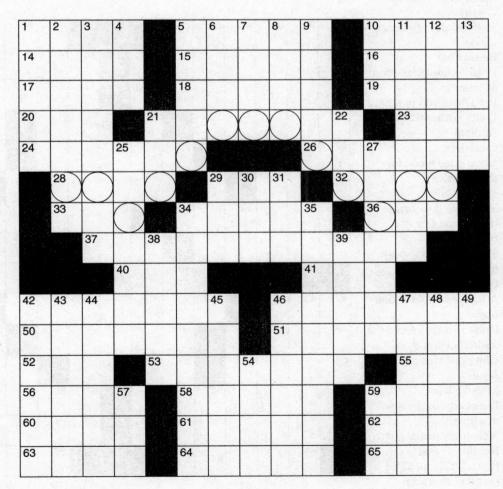

by Stu Ockman

ACROSS

1 Some ranges
7 Verses versus verses events
12 Unassisted
14 Two-masted vessel
16 Qualify
17 The way to do this is the #1 how-to search, according to Google
18 Rungs
19 Children's author Silverstein
21 Actress Headey of "Game of Thrones"
22 Sea dogs
23 Slowpoke
24 Calls for reserves?
25 It may be crushed or shaved
26 Blacksmith's workplace
28 Corruption
29 1998 Winter Olympics locale
31 Be sure of
33 Grade school classroom accessory
34 Pre-Christmas purchase
35 Prefix with science
39 Built up
41 Countless
42 Much-used wood for tool handles
45 Perfect child
47 Shareable doc format
48 Instruction to a typesetter
50 Traveling, so to speak, in basketball
51 Goes pfft!
52 A light one goes a long way
53 Dress that may leave the midriff exposed
54 Glutinous rice cake of Japan
55 Midsize Kias
57 Knocked, like heavy machinery
59 30th anniversary gift
60 Not this or that
61 Fast __ Felson, "The Hustler" character
62 Locking horns

DOWN

1 What an accomplice may be doing
2 Wild and crazy
3 Second person?
4 Gritty films, informally
5 Ironically, they live on every continent except Antarctica
6 Seasoning for une omelette
7 Item of cookware
8 Most common Korean surname after Kim
9 In any way
10 Actress Janet with a Tony, Drama Desk and Olivier Award
11 Eastern faith
13 Like some questions
14 Rod on reels
15 Brewmaster's need
20 It's a sign
23 West Coast air hub, for short
26 Stationary
27 Scout leader?
30 Aladdin's sidekick
32 Opposite of paleo-
34 Bookstore section
36 Like fruit on a tree
37 Kept a close eye (on)
38 Football offense . . . or a hint to six answers in this puzzle
40 Brew with a red triangle logo
41 Racer Unser and son
42 Words before wish or were
43 Siberian land feature
44 Like some pools and arguments
46 Grand tales
49 Threesome
51 Crooner with a ukulele
54 Many a rescue
56 Med. diagnostic
58 Mauna __

by Lewis Rothlein

ACROSS

1 Trial separation?
7 National Do Not Call Registry org.
10 ___ Majesty
13 Blue
14 Beast
16 Form of yoga
17 Freed, but not for free
18 Elvis Presley hit inducted into the Grammy Hall of Fame
20 Angst-ridden music genre
22 Platform for 5-Down
23 Art Deco icon
24 Forum greeting
29 All chief justices of the United States, so far
30 Sub system
31 Disheartened
34 Vacation spot for city slickers
37 Canadian stadium renamed Rogers Centre in 2005
39 Humana competitor
43 ___ Joaquin Valley
44 Gangster group in "Eastern Promises"
47 Handled
49 Booker, for one: Abbr.
50 Have obligations
51 2003 film starring Mark Wahlberg and Charlize Theron
57 Unwraps impatiently
58 First-aid antiseptic
61 Building up
62 More malevolent
63 Vicious of punk rock
64 Avoided elimination in musical chairs
65 Bone/muscle connectors

DOWN

1 Like a professor emerita: Abbr.
2 Slice of history
3 Link
4 Blues singer James
5 Voice-activated assistant
6 Rehnquist's successor on the bench
7 Mrs., in Münster
8 Sawbucks
9 Violin holder
10 "Just play along, please"
11 Put up, as a building
12 L'Oréal hair care brand
14 "Mrs. Doubtfire" plot device - or what the letters in this clue's answer do five times?
15 Went very fast
19 Something a gardener might lean on
20 Sounds of puzzlement
21 Who said "A revolution is not a dinner party"
25 ___ Luck
26 "Phooey!"
27 Small battery
28 Publish
32 Final Four inits.
33 At that point
35 Palme ___ (film award)
36 Cousin of a cassowary
37 Dish often served with wasabi
38 Skateboarder's accessory
40 Big name in cell service
41 "Right away!"
42 Half a sawbuck
43 Hindu aphorisms
45 Beachside view
46 Certain navels
48 Ph.D. hurdle: Abbr.
52 Deep-six
53 Where Samoa Airways is based
54 It begins on Ash Wednesday
55 Rocker Jon Bon ___
56 One-eyed Norse god
59 Never-before-seen
60 Triage centers, for short

by Zhouqin Burnikel

130 Medium

ACROSS

1 Bread used for soup
4 Perspective
9 One to whom you might say "Boo!"
12 "Begone!"
13 Sports replay effect
16 Word after Great or before Street
17 Person behind the curtain?
18 Relatives of rhododendrons
20 -
21 Popular Samsung smartphone
22 "Net" preceder
23 -
26 South American landmark whose name means "old peak"
27 Jeong of "Crazy Rich Asians"
28 Try to win at auction
29 2008 animated film set in ancient China
31 Class with breathing techniques
32 [groan]
35 Hung pieces of art
37 Put in stitches?
38 Doofus
40 -
42 Wears pajamas all day, e.g.
43 Powder holder
44 -
47 Start of a polite request
48 Sound made while clasping oneself
49 Low-hanging clouds
51 Fruit named for a region of France
53 Japanese floor coverings
54 Inert
57 Sgts. outrank them
58 Button-downs?
59 Kind of skirt
60 Cry accompanying a fist pump
61 Parent company of Kool-Aid
62 Not many tracks are found on them, for short

DOWN

1 Superhero with a lightning bolt symbol
2 "Well, ain't that fancy!"
3 "Three Days of the Condor" director
4 Test, in a way
5 "Dagnabbit!"
6 A student might bring this up in an intro class
7 Large military unit
8 Not slouching
9 Buildings with circular floor plans
10 Music genre for Weezer
11 One side of a debate
12 Goodie bag contents
14 ___ fly
15 Toast at a Jewish wedding
19 Raises from the dead?
22 Vandal
24 Go out for a bit
25 Once again
27 Org. disbanded in 1991
28 Angela who played Tina Turner
30 Place name lead-in to -folk or -wich
31 Shepherd's locale
32 Wrinkly fruit
33 Blunder
34 High time in Judaism
36 Part of a race
39 Swells
41 Swimmer's woe
43 Money in Malmö
45 Increase rapidly . . . or a hint to connecting four pairs of answers in this puzzle
46 Moonshiners' equipment
48 One-named singer with an "ö" in her name
49 Speak, as thou might
50 Rae who created "The Misadventures of Awkward Black Girl"
52 Small carp
53 Not kosher, in Jewish law
54 N.C.A.A.'s Big ___ Conference
55 Ball holder
56 Letters between two names

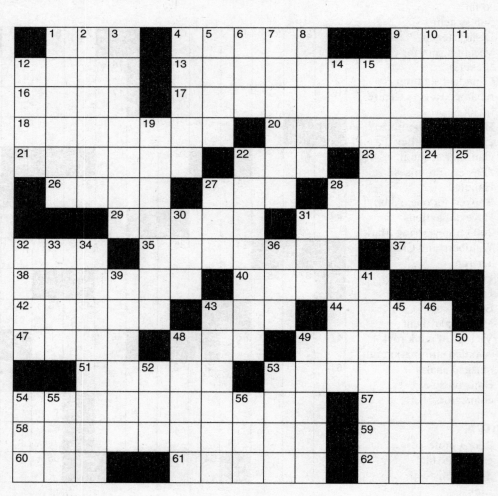

by Jeff Chen

ACROSS

1 Nutrition label unit
5 Air of confidence, in slang
9 Aftermath
13 Distinctive quality
14 Con, across the Pyrenees
15 Take a taxi, informally
16 Alternative to a taxi
17 "Etta ___" (old comic strip)
18 Pizzeria fixtures
19 One for the money
22 Casual greetings
23 Diarist Nin
24 Two for the show
31 Crew member's item
32 Spots
33 Popular Japanese brew
34 Be decisive
35 One way to sway
36 Hardly welcoming
38 Nabokov title character
39 Religion with an apostrophe in its name
41 60 minuti
42 Sticky stuff
43 Three to get ready
48 ___ fuzz
49 Rare outcome of a Scrabble game
50 Four to go
55 Island NW of Oahu
57 Redhead on kids' TV
58 Pioneering computer operating system
59 Pakistan's longest river
60 Reformer Jacob who wrote "How the Other Half Lives"
61 Jazz singer Simone
62 Hyatt hiree
63 Stuff
64 Part of a musical note

DOWN

1 Ancient land conquered by Caesar
2 Naïve sort
3 Domain
4 First first lady
5 Launches an offensive
6 Completed
7 Passages to planes
8 One-eighth of a circle
9 Surfboard/kayak hybrid
10 Act as a lookout for, say
11 Next of ___
12 "The X-Files" extras, briefly
15 Like some crying babies
20 Took cover
21 China's Chou En-___
24 Numbskulls
25 Knock on, as a door
26 Prefix with -dontic
27 Hoopla
28 Muse for Lord Byron
29 Like some currents
30 Tangle
35 "Semper ___" (Marine Corps motto)
36 Militant org. in a 1994 peace agreement
37 Guaranteed to succeed
40 Give a hand
41 To whom Hamlet says "Get thee to a nunnery"
44 Lacking polish
45 Earth tones
46 Completed
47 Syndicated fare
50 Automaker based in Bavaria
51 Send out
52 Not yet out of the running
53 Tree hugger?
54 One might be taken orally
55 Most common Korean surname
56 Santa ___, Calif.

by Alex Eaton-Salners

132 MEDIUM

ACROSS

1 Game with a maximum score of 3,333,360
7 Host Allen of TV's "Chopped"
10 *The outcome of a story might hinge on one
14 Get some air
15 Hotheadedness
16 Brief, abrupt changes in direction
17 *One might say "Home Sweet Home"
18 *Important spot on the body for acupuncture
20 Tempest in a teapot
21 Aid for making a sand castle
22 Vineyard vessel
23 See 42-Across
25 "Victory is ours!"
27 Unlikely homecoming court members
29 Contribute
30 *Viewing angle
31 White-petaled daisy
32 Vault
34 ___ boots
35 Who said "When I'm ready to fight, my opponent has a better chance for surviving a forest fire wearing gasoline drawers"
36 Bet (on)
38 "My heavens!"
42 With 23-Across, modicum
43 Nursing ___
44 Vibe
45 Prominent 1990s Washington duo
48 *Kind of average
50 $C_7H_5N_3O_6$
51 Development centers?
52 Comic actor Seth
53 Fairly small hail size
54 Subtract a year or two from one's age, say
55 Mentally goes [grumble grumble grumble]
57 Gulager of old TV and film
59 With 61-Across, what President Wilson proposed for a lasting peace . . . or what's missing from the answers to the starred clues

61 See 59-Across
64 Fictional schnauzer
65 Area of educ.
66 Nativity scene
67 *School overlooking the Hudson
68 Certain intersection
69 Drill command

DOWN

1 *Locate precisely
2 Good "Wheel of Fortune" buy for CHEESE WHEEL
3 Time to indulge
4 Grp. that trademarked the phrase "Helping Survivors Survive"
5 Provides (for)
6 By birth
7 *Malcolm Gladwell best seller, with "The"
8 Something to run
9 Notarized paper
10 Attire not usually worn outdoors, informally
11 World's most-visited museum
12 Sweet Rosie of old song
13 ___ fly
19 Title usually abbreviated to its first, fifth and sixth letters
21 Certain curtains
23 *Kind of pen
24 Flash of genius, say
26 Conservatory piece
28 *Touchdown follower
33 *Aid in a speaker's presentation
35 Fort ___, Md.
37 Let up
38 Goes on and on and on
39 Visceral shock
40 Author Sarah ___ Jewett
41 *Part of a scatter diagram
43 *Sycophant's reward
45 Hearty laugh
46 Useless
47 Counters
48 Homer's home
49 Rerun
56 Certain cricket match
58 It might be attached to a car
60 Animal feared by Winston in "1984"
61 Survey fig.
62 July 4, 1776, for one: Abbr.
63 *Big moment in a tennis match

by Alex Vratsanos

ACROSS

1 Little something to eat
5 Love handles, essentially
9 Word with pint or plus
13 McFlurry flavor
14 Delight
15 Fawned-over figure
16 Opening night nightmares
17 Times New ___ (popular typeface)
18 Idle, with "off"
19 Talk trash?
22 Nephew of Abraham
23 Bygone Mideast inits.
24 Word with boll or Bowl
28 French novelist Marcel
30 Hairstyle
32 Flurry
33 Recite aphorisms?
36 Swiss city on the Rhine
39 Morn's counterpart
40 No longer in
41 Perform poetry?
44 Ring master
45 C-worthy
46 Old Soviet naval base site
50 Long way to go?
52 Taking after
53 Bordeaux buddy
54 Narrate audiobooks?
58 Native people of southern Arizona
61 First sign of spring
62 Snake eyes or boxcars, in craps
63 Digital image format
64 Brings up
65 Archipelago part
66 Make content
67 Place for a crow's-nest
68 Freshness

DOWN

1 Orange juice specification
2 One on a soapbox
3 Mailed
4 Hydrant hookup
5 Fine meal
6 Exemplar of innocence
7 Run ___ (postpone the bar bill)
8 Del Toro of "The Usual Suspects"
9 Something to see
10 Pledge of allegiance, maybe
11 Menagerie
12 Little help?
14 Typos and such
20 Prepares on short notice
21 Downplay
25 New Mexico resort town
26 Horatian creations
27 There's a bridge at the top of it
29 Operator
30 Green with the 2010 hit "Forget You"
31 Marriott competitor
34 ___ Trueheart, Dick Tracy's love
35 Give quite a shock
36 Slider on an abacus
37 It gets the wheels turning
38 Rain slightly
42 Pitcher's problem
43 "Good riddance!"
47 Appetizer often served with chutney
48 Senses, as trouble
49 Two things in a 747
51 River named for a Plains tribe
52 Head off
55 ___ code
56 Souls, e.g.
57 "Exodus" author
58 Attire in which to retire, briefly
59 Hoppy quaff, for short
60 Convened

by Jules Markey

134 HARD

ACROSS

1 Firearms without serial numbers
10 Capital known as the City of Trees
15 Part of a wedding weekend
16 Something holding up the works?
17 It was discovered on Mars in 2018
19 Some suits
20 Take a furtive look
21 The third of three X's
22 "Cómo es ____ ?" (Spanish for "What's the deal?")
23 Peabrain?
24 Nonreligious observance: Abbr.
25 U-Haul competitor
27 Not up
28 Substantial
30 He works with bugs
32 Lift
33 They're chewable but not meant to be eaten
36 Evening service
37 County in northeast England
38 Old Testament prophet
39 Feature of many a general's statue
40 Political commentator Pfeiffer
41 A caddie may retrieve one
45 To give: Sp.
46 Matched (up)
48 "South Park" brother
49 Hair clump
50 Ancient supercontinent
51 "Shoot!"
52 "What a dang shame"
55 Some bar signs
56 1965 hit by the Kinks
57 "Money says . . ."
58 Perch for a deer hunter

DOWN

1 Seller of staples
2 Martin Luther's crime
3 "Glad to hear it!"
4 They're blue on maps
5 Trig. function
6 Beef
7 The 23rd one took place in 2010
8 Catholic celebration
9 Quenched
10 "It's ____ real"
11 Part of many a rowing club logo
12 "Can I come out now?"
13 Kelp forest resident
14 Magazine that's weekly in France but monthly in the U.S.
18 No later than
23 He has a Wild Ride at Disneyland
24 Oracle's home
26 This or that
28 Totally screw up?
29 Extended warranty fig.
31 Court venue
32 ____ deck (bodybuilder's machine)
33 Deg. that requires the study of calculus
34 Like movie rental stores
35 Workplace kudos
36 Minnelli who married Judy Garland
38 More shabby
40 Hereditary ruler
42 Pfizer drug
43 "Well, that was weird"
44 Put into beta
46 Didn't go anywhere
47 Message on the "cake car" in the climactic scene of "Animal House"
49 Cute-sized
50 It's often spoken with one hand at the edge of one's mouth
51 Falling-out
53 Here's one pour vous
54 Diner's booking, slangily

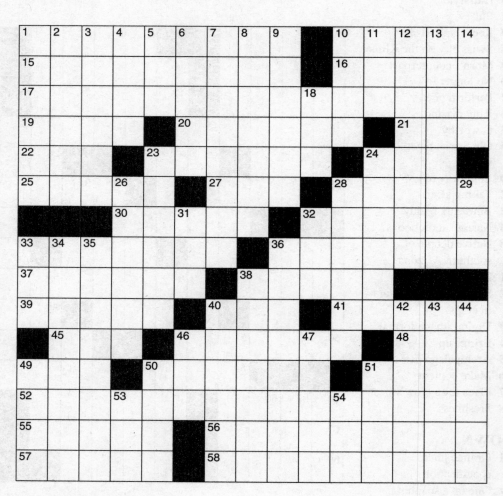

by Greg Johnson

ACROSS

1 Order to stop the presses?
7 In this manner
13 Michael of "Caddyshack"
14 Went berserk
15 Resolve
16 Sore loser
17 ___ Virtue, 2018 Olympic ice dancing gold medalist
18 Tap sites
19 Brightly colored fish
20 According to
21 "Pretty please?"
23 Promised
24 Gangland weapons, quaintly
26 Prepare to divulge a secret, maybe
28 Clink
29 Bona fides from fellow cool people
32 Luxury car of the early 20th century
34 Ones going through the motions?
36 ___ Miguel, largest of the Azores
39 Post on a wall, say
40 Beam
42 Series opener
44 Slacks
46 Prefix with car or conscious
47 "Holy moly!"
48 Poor reception?
49 Fanfare
51 Cold carnival treat
53 Title for Eva Perón
54 Little something to help later on
55 Mate's response
56 Chocolaty Post cereal
57 Ball of yarn, maybe

DOWN

1 Attend without a partner
2 2006 film "___ and the Bee"
3 Is rewarded for service
4 "___ party!"
5 Big insurance acronym
6 With 7-Down, Scottish boys
7 See 6-Down
8 Entry points
9 Comic book sound effect
10 Genre for Fall Out Boy
11 1957 Jimmy Dorsey hit
12 "Well, that was weird"
14 Athletes at the University of Louisiana at Lafayette
16 Early distribution of a piece of software
18 Punishment used by some hit men
22 Parent company of Philip Morris
23 Radio-era dummy
25 Hot rod?
27 Intrude suddenly
30 Alternative to Tempur-Pedic
31 Snoop ___
33 Worrisome comment from a navigator
35 2015 crime film with Emily Blunt and Benicio del Toro
36 Refuses
37 Camper manufacturer
38 Challenge
41 Worker with a seal
43 Uphold
45 "Ta-ta!"
48 Selfish sorts
50 Website with gadget reviews
52 Board appointee, for short
53 ___ fly

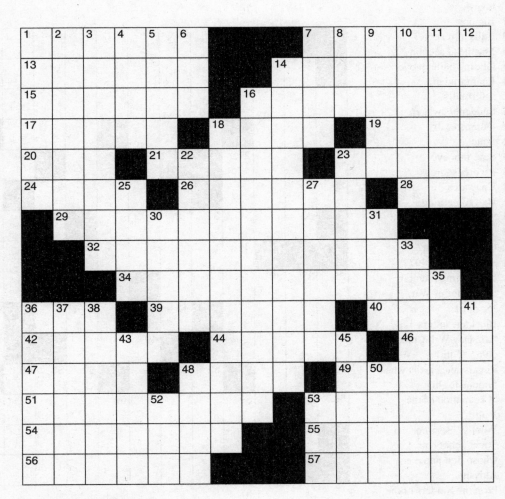

by Ryan McCarty

ACROSS

1 "Pretty good thinking . . ."
12 "Any chance of success, though?"
14 "Things don't always go the way you want"
16 Cry made while holding one's nose
17 Employment form info, for short
18 Bill of the Planetary Society
19 Egypt was once part of it: Abbr.
20 Flue problem
22 Tumult
24 Port north of Kuwait City
26 Word with bird or board
27 Big dos
29 Calls to reserve?
30 Masthead section
32 Gliding ballet move
34 Enamored of, informally
36 Suddenly awaken
39 Dumpster fire
42 Squat
43 Save money
45 Ricotta sources
47 Unawares
49 Had something
50 "You've got the wrong person"
51 CD attachment?
52 Subject of the 1977 best-selling memoir "A Rumor of War," for short
54 Blockage letters
57 "___ Day Will Come" (1963 #1 hit)
58 Renaissance artist who's famous for his "Coronation of the Virgin"
62 Woolly "Sesame Street" character whose first name is Aloysius
63 Prop in "Raiders of the Lost Ark"

DOWN

1 What one may be in the habit for?
2 What regular-season soccer games lack, for short
3 Jeffersons
4 Focuses
5 Equipment for mixologists
6 Word with "first of" or "best of"
7 1979 platinum album with the hit "I'll Never Love This Way Again"
8 Minute, informally
9 Hardly Joe Cool
10 Titaness with a home on the edge of Oceanus
11 Stirs
12 Earthquake that everyone's been waiting for
13 Popular big box stores
14 Get cold feet, with "out"
15 Eliminate
21 Pair of things sold together, in commercialese
23 Baseball announcer's cry
25 Adolescents' support group
27 Pix
28 Charmin alternative
31 When repeated, express disapproval
33 Well-tuned engine output
35 Unwanted growth often related to arthritis
36 Gobble (down)
37 Jim of 1960s TV
38 Rigid
40 Quickly grab
41 Party preps
44 Many Sri Lankans
46 Modern answer source
48 One of a kitchen set
53 Bravo preceder
55 Innocent, perhaps
56 Deception, informally
59 Trim option
60 Little: Fr.
61 Supermarket chain since 1926

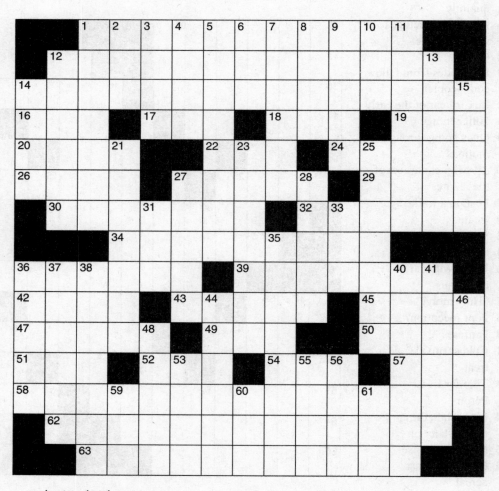

by Ned White

ACROSS

1 Hangs onto something
9 Establishing
15 Bad record
16 "Hello-o-o-o!"
17 Jalapeño, after smoking
18 Like Art Nouveau
19 Aesop's "The ___ and the Grasshopper"
20 Upper-crust sorts, stereotypically
22 Utterly, in modern slang
23 Elect
24 Starbucks competitor
26 Soccer superstar Lionel
29 ___-chic
30 They're loaded with cash
33 Currently
36 "I'm in awe"
37 Fruity liqueur
38 "Ferris Bueller's Day Off" co-star
40 Ending with many fruit names
41 Fried chicken option
43 Openly lament
45 Composition of Indonésie
46 Looping symbols of life
47 "Sweet" locale in T. S. Eliot's "The Waste Land"
49 Pro caregivers, for short
50 Led a parade, musically
52 Title character not requiring an actor
54 Start of many Southwest place names
57 Wayne of soccer fame
59 2016 prequel that earned more than a billion dollars at the box office
61 Lawrence of Arabia portrayer
62 Classic book that begins "At the far end of town where the Grickle-grass grows . . ."

63 Show that won the Outstanding Drama Emmy for each of its first four seasons
64 Worshiper with an inverted pentagram, maybe

DOWN

1 Sight on an Alaskan cruise
2 German route
3 Small peninsula
4 Rafael Nadal's home, in Olympics shorthand
5 Exhibition highlight
6 Adjust to, as on a thermostat
7 Some bottom-dwellers
8 Part of a blended family
9 Invitation qualification
10 Major vessel
11 Cousin of "Gosh darn it!"
12 "Forgive the question . . ."
13 C or D
14 Splits
21 Outlines
23 Agcy. headed by a deputy asst. secretary of labor
25 Like Bugles snacks
26 Colorful parrot
27 Piece played in a conservatory
28 Cart fare
29 Pirated, in a way
31 Transform
32 Rebellion leader of 1786
34 "Haste makes waste," e.g.
35 One with hairy legs
39 Reasons to say "I'm sorry"

42 Many honeymoon locales
44 Whiz
48 "Send My Love" singer, 2016
49 19th-century author whose works are still read word for word
50 Email line
51 "Not one ___!"
53 Site of the 2022 World Cup
54 Rick's wife on "The Walking Dead"
55 Santa ___ (some winds)
56 Barely communicate?
58 Thirst
60 Forever, seemingly

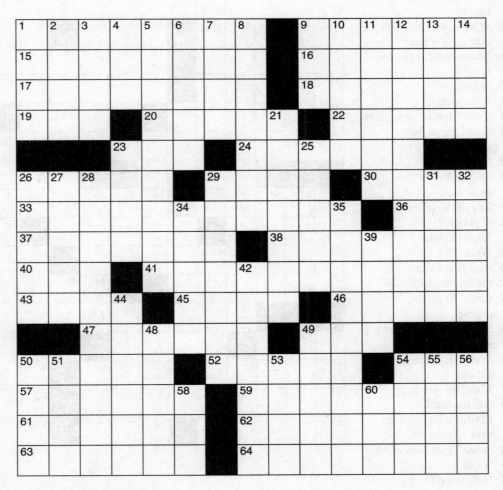

by Howard Barkin

138 HARD

ACROSS

1 Evidence of merit
6 With 38-Across, this whole time
9 Country singer with a cityish name
14 "___ in English is, in the main, just about as sensible as baseball in Italian": H. L. Mencken
15 Cocktail with vodka, cranberry juice and grapefruit juice
17 Doesn't look so well?
18 Carrier with a yin/yang symbol in its logo
19 Lustrous material
21 ___ Drago, opponent of Rocky in "Rocky IV"
22 Actress Aduba of "Orange Is the New Black"
23 Where one might go out to get a bite?
26 Bhagavad-___ (Sanskrit text)
27 Nonsense
31 Extension
34 Collection of superstars
37 Good name for a gardener
38 See 6-Across
39 One of five in "La Bohème"
40 Fairy tale villain
42 U people?
43 Kind of strip
44 Wrinkly fruit
46 Supreme Court nickname, with "the"
52 Cause to groan, maybe
55 Sparks can be seen at its edge
56 Way that someone might get out
57 Make the grade
60 Off-the-wall
61 Pastrami and corned beef
62 Some Deco collectibles
63 "God ___"
64 Hula hoop?
65 Little brats

DOWN

1 Extra help
2 Kind of test for a baby
3 Symbol of change
4 Spider-Man's archenemy
5 Starts something slowly
6 Say "what?," say
7 Pope during the Battle of Ostia
8 Creepy-crawly
9 Stockpile that may be subject to inspection
10 Rapper MC ___ of N.W.A
11 Suitor
12 Former Iraqi V.I.P. Tariq ___
13 Ancient Rome's Circus of ___
16 Piece of equipment in the game cornhole
20 Big Apple media inits.
24 Soup kitchen sight
25 2018 Oscar-nominated picture whose soundtrack sold over one million copies
28 Subway fare?
29 Oliver Twist, for example
30 Part of a Latin trio
31 [I'm still here, you know]
32 Band with the 1980 hit album "Freedom of Choice"
33 Minute amount
35 Sushi bar topping
36 Opposite of excitement
38 No-frills
41 Requirements for voting
42 Nosedives
45 Result of a meltdown?
47 Jermaine who was a six-time N.B.A. All-Star
48 Driver's assignment
49 Totaled
50 Georges of the Romantic era
51 Luster
52 Film site
53 Film site
54 Long green
58 Household name?
59 Auto inspection no.

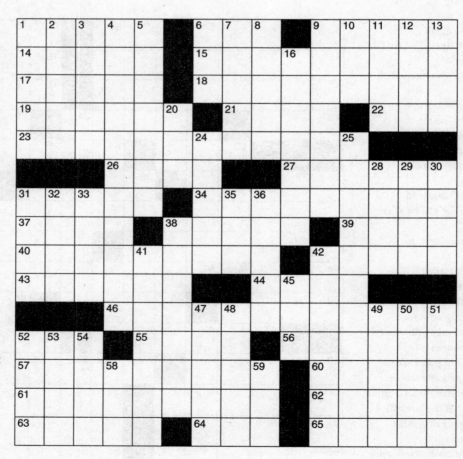

by Debbie Ellerin

ACROSS

1 Outburst after a nefarious plan is hatched
8 Freaks
15 What may be propelled by a propellant
16 Classic song with the lyric "Let's get together and feel all right"
17 Response to a joke
18 Rat
19 Steadfast determination
20 Game where you don't want to reach the top
22 Mac ___ (former Bay Area hip-hop great)
23 Chemical suffix
24 P's
25 Direction to a cellist
26 What "epistaxis" is a fancy medical term for
30 Play detective
31 Epcot's Spaceship Earth, architecturally
33 Big business news
36 Opera with the "Gypsy Song"
37 Treat with an edible container
41 Santa ___
42 Person who's whip-smart?
46 Rightmost option in most menu bars
47 Actor Green of the "Austin Powers" movies
48 "Odi et ___" (Catullus poem)
49 It's not for real
50 Not doubting at all
52 Amoeba, e.g.
53 One might be sent to a passenger's phone
55 Went over
57 Minute Maid drink
58 It comes after "Coming soon . . ."
59 Perfumed
60 Not get hung up on

DOWN

1 Site for a doodle
2 Kook
3 Large numbers
4 Large number
5 An end to smoking?
6 Hilarious sort
7 Like some suits and states
8 Street racers
9 Diarist Nin
10 Live musicians play them
11 Delaware has the lowest mean one in the U.S.: Abbr.
12 Food storage spot
13 Triumph
14 "Come on in!"
21 Pronoun in "America"
25 Girl's name in the U.S. that's a boy's name in Italy
27 Ceramic breakfast accouterment
28 Round parts?
29 Stories that may or may not be true
30 Meager
32 Recognizable figure
33 Sportscaster inducted into the Television Hall of Fame in 2013
34 Having a little of this and a little of that
35 Live-streamed, say
38 Let know
39 Tiny bit
40 Companions
43 ___ Yousafzai, 2014 Nobel Peace Prize winner
44 Performs too broadly
45 King in "Game of Thrones"
47 Nice jacket material
50 Three-player game
51 Meter reading
52 It's hardly worth noticing
54 The 2000s, e.g.: Abbr.
56 Tayside turndown

by Caleb Madison

140 HARD

ACROSS
1 Fratty group
9 "Science may have found a cure for most evils; but it has found no remedy for the worst of them all - the ___ of human beings": Helen Keller
15 Absolutely creamed
16 Dictate
17 What some investments and trained dogs do
18 Top stories
19 Like El Alto, the highest large city (population > 100,000) in the world
20 Kindling
21 One after another?
22 Italian city that's home to the Villa d'Este
23 Nuts
26 More authentic
27 Target, e.g.
29 Shoes that are also water hazards
34 Big heart?
35 Brusque
36 Author of the 2011 political memoir "My Father at 100"
38 Dream
39 "When I was a kid . . ."
46 Less of a mess
47 Middle-of-the-___
48 Anna who played Scheherazade in 1963's "Scheherazade"
49 Spent completely
51 Polar expedition transport
52 Exalt
53 Remove a burden from
54 Delivered
55 Like the apples in apple pie, typically
56 They serve a function

DOWN
1 Cutting
2 Actor with the #1 film performance in Premiere magazine's list of "100 Greatest Performances of All Time"
3 Hardly the silent type
4 Slobber
5 Split
6 Word with will or wage
7 Colored part
8 Second-most populous Swiss canton, after Zurich
9 Start of Kansas' state motto
10 Most small-minded
11 Trigger
12 France's flag, e.g.
13 Trouble for comedians
14 Emphatic agreement
24 Salon, e.g., informally
25 Canine's woe?
28 Something in a pool
29 Gets started
30 Sitcom set in Lanford, Ill.
31 Out but with caveats
32 Pressing
33 Court, in a way
37 Made sparkling, say
40 Silver
41 Photoshop command
42 Salt
43 Main slot on an old PC
44 Codger
45 They're taken while waiting
49 It may be slipped to a doctor
50 Old-fashioned theaters

by Kevin Adamick

ACROSS

1 King or queen
4 Record six-time N.B.A. M.V.P.
15 Northeast sch. in the Liberty League
16 Rather caricatured
17 Understanding responses
18 One involved in a pyramid scheme?
19 Broke down, say
21 End of a Hemingway title
22 Fleck on the banjo
23 Atlanta train system
25 Drink often served chilled
27 Bert's sister in children's literature
28 Dandy headpieces
31 Catch
33 Excessively harsh
35 Philadelphia train system
39 Trio in Greek myth
40 New Deal org.
41 Pope John Paul II's first name
42 Was out
43 Aida in "Aida," e.g.
45 Go preceder
47 Unsightly spots
48 Country music's ___ Brown Band
51 Digs
53 Early customer of Boeing
54 Old Testament kingdom
56 Like the cities Yazd and Shiraz
59 Transport method usually used in the winter
61 One who can see right through you?
64 Author Chinua Achebe, by birth
65 Back-to-back hits
66 "Kate Plus 8" airer
67 Harmless slitherer
68 See 63-Down

DOWN

1 Something that's knitted
2 Here today, gone tomorrow
3 Quite different
4 Latin grammar case: Abbr.
5 Country with the King Hamad Highway
6 Trio abroad
7 Shoshone relatives
8 Player of Cleopatra in "Two Nights With Cleopatra"
9 Who had a #1 hit with "Toot Toot Tootsie (Goo'bye)"
10 Suffix with meth-
11 Spill everything
12 Politico with the 2007 autobiography "Promises to Keep"
13 "The Jungle Book" wolf
14 Put back on
20 Muscle used in bench-pressing
24 Simple dance
26 Things that may be blown
28 Some email pics
29 Photographic memory or perfect pitch, e.g.
30 Master
32 Cincinnati athlete
34 NASA part: Abbr.
36 Outlaws
37 Not too awful
38 Consumables often described with a percentage
44 Comic who said "I open my eyes, remember who I am, what I'm like, and I just go 'Ugh'"
46 Worker on London's Savile Row
48 Weightlessness
49 1943 Churchill conference site
50 Computer programmer
52 Dives
55 Useful thing to keep on hand?
57 "Janie's Got ___" (1989 Aerosmith hit)
58 First in a historical trio
60 Almond ___ (candy)
62 Be short
63 With 68-Across, end of a Hemingway title

by Evans Clinchy

ACROSS

1 Like a drumhead
5 "Forget about it!"
15 Former education secretary Duncan
16 What may hold a body of evidence?
17 Tie securely
18 1970 #1 hit with the lyric "Just call my name"
19 She played Phyllis on TV's "Phyllis"
21 Film director ___ C. Kenton
22 No-goodnik
23 With 33-Down, same old offerings
24 Heavy duty
25 Spock, e.g.: Abbr.
26 One speaking the language Plautdietsch
28 Dictatorial dispatcher on "Taxi"
29 Unfortunate
30 Encyclopedic
31 Dictatorial type
32 "Murder, Inc." Oscar nominee
34 Husky food?
37 Overseas court figure
38 Bush native to the South
41 Santa ___
42 Get down to nothing?
44 Gym bunnies work on them
45 Animal shelter
46 Party divider
47 "Engineered for life" corp.
48 "Wow"-producing look
49 Lack of punch
50 Olivia de Havilland's Best Actress film, 1949
53 Trusting someone you don't know, e.g.
54 Present reality
55 ___ ether
56 Try to win hands down?
57 Gainsay

DOWN

1 Choices in the baby department
2 Body undergoing desertification
3 Ill-conceived
4 Capital in 1979–80 headlines
5 Lead-in to "Los Angeles" or "New Orleans"
6 Magic, on a sports ticker
7 Quiet after the storm, maybe
8 Stain
9 Reacts to a bombshell
10 Sevilla-to-Granada direction
11 Level in an org.
12 A head might go over the top of it
13 Coming in waves?
14 Really embarrassed, maybe
20 Song played at Staples Center after every Lakers victory
24 Department in Picardy
25 Crown
27 "Great" sleuth of kid-lit
28 Jimmy Carter's mother
31 Weight allowance
32 Consoling gestures
33 See 23-Across
34 "Bewitched" witch
35 Barfly's request
36 Spring break preceder, often
38 Pale yellow
39 20th-century novelist who shared first and middle names with poet Emerson
40 With very little hope
42 Theater stage
43 Like theater seating
45 "Leavin' on Your Mind" singer, 1963
48 Stuff in a backpack
49 ___ speak
51 Give the ax?
52 What la Tierra orbits

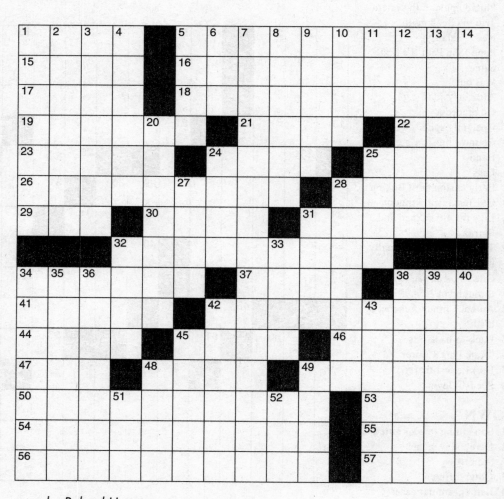

by Roland Huget

ACROSS

1 Phylicia of stage and screen
7 Reduce to tears?
15 Some highway conveniences
17 Unwelcome war report
18 French force
19 Back tracks?
20 ___-relief
21 Blood letters
22 Green org.?
25 Deem to be dumb
31 Quaint means of manipulation
32 Common instruments in jazz combos
33 Cyclist in peak condition?
34 Fine source of humor, with "the"?
35 This was once "art"
36 U.P.S. unit: Abbr.
37 It may come with a price to pay
40 Cousin of a frittata
44 Major tributary of the Missouri
46 Tamarack trees
50 Didn't stand firm in negotiations
51 "Fish Magic" artist
52 Get beaten by

DOWN

1 Aid for clean living
2 Hyundai luxury sedan
3 Blasts inboxes
4 Billionaire, for one
5 "___ sow . . ."
6 Award since W.W. I
7 Outcome in Eden
8 His: Fr.
9 Dressed
10 Glamour rival
11 Bad singers?
12 "Star Wars" saga nickname
13 Driver's aid
14 What makes a top stop?
16 Grammy-nominated blues guitarist in the Louisiana Music Hall of Fame
21 Husky cousins
22 Punt propeller, e.g.
23 Says, informally
24 ___ Toy Barn ("Toy Story 2" locale)
25 Alloy of tin and lead
26 Just slightly
27 Order to a sommelier, maybe
28 Bow out
29 Not out, but not necessarily up
30 Doctors
31 Debussy contemporary
32 1922 Physics Nobelist
33 1959 Kingston Trio hit
37 Explorer alternative
38 Star seeker?
39 Canvas primer
40 City northeast of Kiev
41 Head Stone
42 Biol. branch
43 The New Yorker film critic Anthony
44 +/−
45 Biol. and others
46 Concert piece
47 Kid's cry
48 College final?
49 It's sometimes shown in the corner of a TV screen, for short

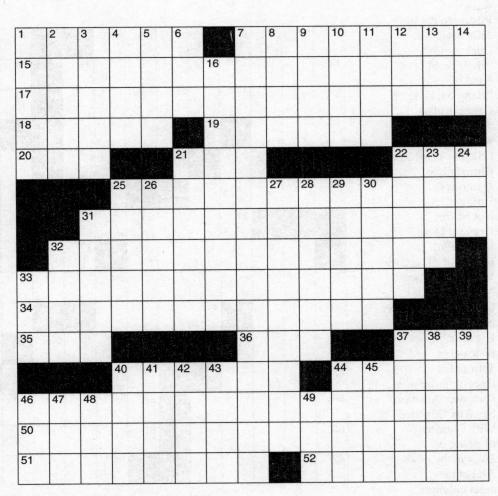

by Martin Ashwood-Smith

ACROSS

1 Spreads
9 Shipping quantity
14 Old-fashioned affair à la "Oklahoma!"
16 Big scrap
17 "Tonight Show" bandleader with a signature 'fro
18 Ancient manuscript
19 Jimmy
20 Something a mother wears
21 Works on the strip?
22 The world's largest one is in South Korea, the second-largest in Sweden
24 See to
25 Sound of moving water
26 Pushes to the limit
28 Joint issue
30 Bush junior?
31 "Hell, yeah!"
35 Kind of
37 "Hang on, hang on"
38 Office drudge
40 Something off the wall?
41 Oakland's Bill ___ Climate Lab
42 Dummies
46 Up
48 Not be free
51 Grateful Dead bassist Phil
52 Robert of "The Girl Who Knew Too Much"
53 One of the 12 tribes of Israel
55 Big inits. in podcasting
56 Termagant
58 Once-popular free computer download
60 Sagal of "Married . . . With Children"
61 #1 going in
62 Twos in the news
63 All but the outer columns, typically

DOWN

1 Where dogs may be put in the backyard
2 Golden Globe winner for "The Wrestler"
3 Bright yellow bouquet
4 Jerk
5 "The fool ___ think he is wise": Shak.
6 Acclaim
7 Personification of Turkey's Weeping Rock
8 Piggy bank contents
9 Canyon maker
10 Keep lubed, say
11 Source of the word "saga"
12 Targets on a hunt
13 Once-common Times Square establishment
15 Bummers
23 Horror movie locale
25 Aforementioned
27 Dome of the Rock, e.g.
29 "Eeep!"
32 Get together
33 Not having many different parts?
34 Alpine region
35 Target of a trap-neuter-return program
36 Vial that a villain might withhold
38 Make a flying jump in the winter
39 Morale booster on base
43 "No problemo"
44 Keen-eyed fisher
45 Does a virtuoso guitar solo, slangily
47 Home of the real-life House of the Seven Gables
49 Condition
50 Like the answer "No."
54 Fetor
57 Start to function?
59 One of the 63-Across: Abbr.

by Josh Knapp

ACROSS

1 Subcompact
8 Subject to an air attack
14 Well-known, now
16 Big name in guitars
17 Put on a pedestal
18 Lock horns
19 Fall foliage color
20 "Girl With a Hoop" painter
22 Banff wildlife
23 First name in cosmetics
25 Common waiting room viewing
26 Fictional race of the distant future
27 Picasso masterpiece with a French title
30 Cousin of a blintz
31 "Hotel Impossible" airer
34 P.M. who won the 1957 Nobel Peace Prize
35 Miraculous solutions
36 Friends, in slang
37 Sir William ___, so-called "Father of Modern Medicine"
38 Runs off at the mouth
39 Guitar-making wood
40 Post-tragedy comment
45 Common question after a name is dropped
46 Salad base
49 ___ war
50 Like some warfare
52 Decision debated for decades
54 Worrisome engine sound
55 Fret about
56 Corsairs and Rangers of the 1950s
57 Things in keys

DOWN

1 Op art pattern
2 It flows for nearly 2,000 miles in Asia
3 Big mushroom producer, in brief
4 "___ war": F.D.R.
5 Frame from a drawer
6 "Jake and ___" (comedy web series)
7 Give a dynamite finish?
8 Form of civil disobedience
9 It's a lift
10 Bled
11 Kings' supporters
12 Dropped like a jaw
13 Book before Daniel
15 Office drones
21 Amoeba feature
24 Gives a lift
26 Lubitsch of old Hollywood
28 State
29 Denoting the style in which one might consider this clue to be written
30 Sympathetic sorts
31 Gets from A to B instantly
32 Says one can make it, say
33 Well
34 Be in store
35 Means of obtaining private information
39 Name in many van Gogh titles
41 "Incredible!"
42 Italian wine
43 Guitar-making wood
44 Ones preparing Easter eggs
46 Presumption
47 "___ problem"
48 In public
51 Ending with Manhattan
53 Bugs on the road

by Michael Wiesenberg

ACROSS

1 Patron for the desperate
7 Ones seeking maximum exposure?
14 ___ blanc (wine variety)
15 Couples' soft spot?
16 Threw
17 A priest, not a beast
18 "The Magpie" and "Grainstack"
19 Bounder
20 Not much, in recipes
21 Early second-millennium year
22 Brushed instrument
23 Vulgarian
24 Stocking stuffer
26 Brace
27 Extremely green
30 "Save Me the Waltz" novelist, 1932
35 2014 U.S. Women's Open winner
36 Band options
40 "And . . . ___!"
41 Enraptured
42 Comedian Marc who recorded a memorable podcast with President Obama
44 Some PCs
45 Bench warmer?
46 Tender
48 Set
49 Green Lantern's archenemy
50 Surrounded, old-style
51 Yet to be imagined
52 Twerp
53 QBs, at times
54 Rush relatives

DOWN

1 Bathos
2 Presidential first name
3 "The Land of Painted Caves" author, 2011
4 Not yet available, as a stock
5 "And how ___ the wise man? as the fool": Ecclesiastes 2:16
6 Modern synonym for 5-Down
7 Aliens
8 Pigmented layer
9 Some PCs
10 Christmas or Easter, for example
11 Main passage
12 Good name for a girl who procrastinates?
13 Like heists and operas
15 Getting totally confused, idiomatically
21 Mojos
24 Eastern mystics
25 Point of view
28 Croque-monsieur ingredient
29 Set
31 Came back strong
32 1978 Robert Altman comedy with Desi Arnaz Jr. and Carol Burnett
33 Department store department
34 Global warming periods?
36 Charges
37 Berth site
38 Fans of pharaohs?
39 Ones with a lot of down time?
43 Long time follower?
45 Who's "got a gun" in a 1989 Aerosmith hit
47 Common newspaper name
48 Chops

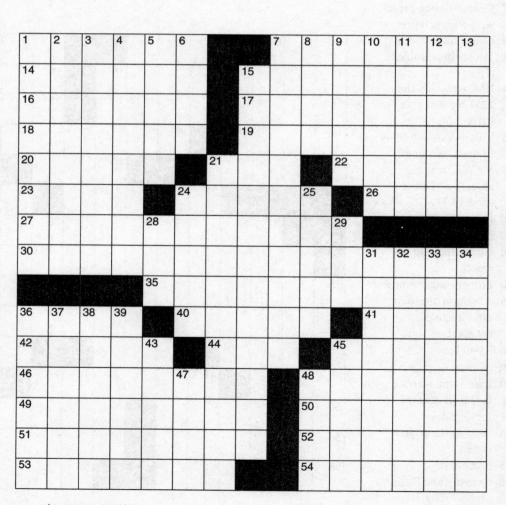

by Byron Walden

ACROSS

1 Far and away one's favorite writer?
7 Mellow R&B track
14 Fly
15 Primitive and backward
16 Items with decorative scrolls
17 Slice from a book?
18 Pay homage, in a way
19 "___ off!" (phrase of homage)
20 Scratches (out)
21 French border region
23 One on the trail, for short
24 Room in Clue
27 20-20 and others
28 Bungling
31 There's one for Best New American Play
32 Extreme
34 500-pound bird hunted to extinction
35 Film character who said "Look, I ain't in this for your revolution, and I'm not in it for you, Princess"
37 A, B or C, but not X, Y or Z
39 ___ caution
40 Knee jerk, e.g.
42 Head shop buy
43 Unite
45 Hue
46 "Woe ___ them that call evil good": Isaiah
47 "The Lost Tapes" rapper
48 Took care of, as guests
50 Z's : sleep :: wavy lines : ___
52 ___ Préval, twice-elected president of Haiti
53 Crude Halloween costume
57 "Drink" for the overly critical
59 Crèche setting
60 Schiller work set to music by Beethoven

61 Little rock
62 Symbol of modern communication
63 Out of retirement?

DOWN

1 Stuff
2 Flush
3 Water source for 11 countries
4 Some blonds
5 Snorkeling mecca
6 ___ Echos (French daily)
7 Pink property
8 Cuts (off)
9 Light air, on the Beaufort scale
10 "It's our time to go!"
11 "Glengarry Glen Ross" co-star, 1992
12 Chill in bed?
13 Pro team with blue-and-orange jerseys
15 Orthodontic device
19 Supposed morning remedy
22 Dusty, fusty or musty
23 British P.M. before and after Addington
24 Blah
25 Lower
26 Statements for the record
29 Aim
30 Steps in a ballroom
33 Puts the kibosh on
36 Underground rock bands?
38 Where Etihad Airways is headquartered
41 ___ Tunes

44 One of the knights of the Round Table
49 Acid/alcohol compound
50 Excited pupil's shout
51 Art genre for Man Ray
52 Punjabi chief
54 Weakens
55 W competitor
56 ___ Vogue magazine
58 Go to waste
59 Day ___

by Ian Livengood

148 HARD

ACROSS

1 Produces heat?
6 Isn't fooling
13 Contents of a bag behind a mound
14 What some women are waist-high in
15 "The Coming of Arthur," e.g.
16 Fictional dog owned by the Winslow family
17 Be of the opinion
18 Fajitas and such
19 Winter hours in Kan.
20 Big dip
22 Gig composition
23 One with a supporting role
24 "Hop-Frog" author, for short
25 Suburb of San Diego
26 "__ Mistress" (1982 horror film)
27 Latin word usually shortened to "c."
28 Rough, loosely woven fabric
29 Crooner with the 1978 platinum album "You Light Up My Life"
30 Groups usually of 13
31 Unhealthily light
32 Grandparents, often
33 Hip attachment?
34 Mechanism for making things disappear in "1984"
38 Fraternal patriotic org.
39 Guards on the gridiron
40 Final menu option, maybe
41 Like conspirators
43 Street with an office
44 458 and 488 on the road
45 Listing
46 Up a tree
47 Arthur Ashe Courage Award and others

DOWN

1 Sight after a blizzard
2 What calves may get caught in
3 Hitherto
4 Pioneering woman in American literature?
5 Staple for sketches, for short
6 Many a West Jordan resident
7 Irish revolutionary Robert
8 Brand of lemon dish liquid
9 Jimbo's sidekick on "South Park"
10 Williams-Sonoma line
11 Calligrapher's grinding mortar
12 Frightful little suckers
14 You can't go over them
16 Petrifying figure
18 Certain home subcontractors
21 Alternative to chow fun
22 Elegant surroundings for kings and queens?
24 Bistro
25 1995 top 10 hit for Hootie & the Blowfish
26 Life __
27 One of a pair that clicks
28 Whirlybird whirlers
29 Clusters of mountains
30 Noted 1950s backup band
32 Bereft
34 The "me" in "Roger & Me"
35 Yellow-flowered primrose
36 Drug company founder of 1876
37 Any of les Nations Unies
39 Latte option
42 Get ready to fight, maybe
43 "Lost" actor Daniel __ Kim

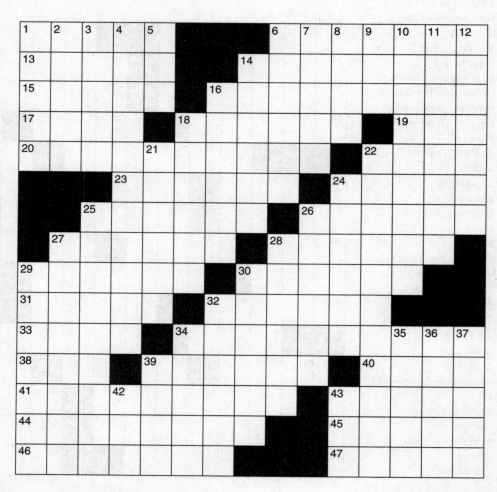

by Damon Gulczynski

ACROSS

1 Sister brand of Scope
6 Like blackjack hands with an ace counted as 11
10 Feature of a modern zoo
14 Athlete who uses steroids
15 Decorative enamelware
17 With 34-, 40- and 60-Across, a somber message for our loyal fans
19 Led astray
20 Agrostologists' study
21 Bud
22 "Whoopee!"
23 Letters before Kitty Hawk
26 Feet, in slang
29 Fruit with yellow skin
34 See 17-Across
37 The Gaels of collegiate sports
38 Actress Issa __ of "The Misadventures of Awkward Black Girl"
39 Shield from the elements
40 See 17-Across
45 Make less flat
46 You might put stock in it
47 Gloaming, to a sonneteer
48 2 letters
50 Pennsylvania and others: Abbr.
52 Inability to sense smells
56 Vigorous reprimand
60 See 17-Across
62 Large marine fish tanks
63 Cardio option
64 "__ Darkness Fall" (L. Sprague de Camp novel)
65 Chew (out)
66 Collects a DNA sample from, say

DOWN

1 Parimutuel calculation
2 Marquis de Sade, e.g.
3 Made like

4 Pause
5 Fancy fabric
6 Long-range guided missile
7 "__ New Hampshire" (state song)
8 Not clear
9 Closet organizer
10 Comfy footwear
11 Responsibility
12 Play money?
13 1980 Oscar nominee directed by Roman Polanski
16 Patronize, as a hotel
18 Later in the text
23 Capital of the Roman province of Africa
24 Coast
25 "Sí" man?

27 Sandwich topped with tzatziki sauce
28 Goes up, up, up
30 __ bath
31 Blow away
32 Comedian who married Joyce Mathews in 1941, divorced her in 1947 and married her again in 1949 "because she reminded me of my first wife"
33 Winter X Games host city
35 Curiosity org.
36 Overhaul
41 Thing with a filament
42 Online course
43 Holiday a month before Passover
44 Pulls out

49 Military group
51 Drinker's bender?
52 Taking unauthorized R&R
53 "Good going!"
54 Shouts of support
55 Crib part
56 Go here and there
57 Bay or gray follower
58 His .366 lifetime batting average is the best ever
59 Yahtzee category
61 Quinceañera invitee

by Peter Gordon

150 HARD

ACROSS

1. Like Michael Strahan of "Live! With Kelly and Michael"
11. Market IDs
15. Mattie Silver's love, in fiction
16. Certain siege defense
17. Trader Joe's competitor
18. Little sweater
19. What you might have for bad eyesight
20. Cross with
22. 1950s gym event
23. Flavoring for springerle biscuits and cookies
25. San Diego Zoo's ___ Cam
26. Grp. headquartered in Ramallah
27. Service branch disbanded in 1978, briefly
28. Meet component
30. Strongly urge
32. "41"
34. "Madam Secretary" star
35. Item on many a patio
38. The Georgia Peach or the Sultan of Swat, e.g.
40. "Sir, you are no gentleman" speaker
41. Member of the grammar police, e.g.
43. Bugs
45. Miss from Metz: Abbr.
46. Be all wet
49. Crib note?
50. Toaster, at times
52. Not focused
54. Company division
55. Want
57. "Being ___" (2015 documentary featuring many wipeouts)
58. Name on 2012 campaign posters
60. Metal staple
62. Completely, after "in"
63. Bridal shop service
64. Puzzle (out)
65. Gondola settings

DOWN

1. Showy trinket
2. Figure on many ancient Greek coins
3. Pronunciation-related
4. Things voyagers bring home
5. First of all
6. Takes out
7. Navy vessel
8. Shouts of victory
9. Port in Lower Saxony
10. Bastille prisoner of 1784–89
11. Person staying near home
12. Discount
13. The "you" in the Neil Diamond lyric "Reachin' out, touchin' me, touchin' you"
14. "Hurry!"
21. Wristwatches may make them
24. Erudite
29. Remnant in a 35-Across
31. 2015 Rock and Roll Hall of Fame inductee
32. Excludes
33. Kind of day
35. Where Arithmancy is an elective
36. "No need to shout!"
37. Houseware purchases that may have suction cups
39. Crony
42. Some commencement dignitaries
44. "w"-like letters in foreign writing
46. French erudition
47. Animal revered by ancient Peruvians
48. Detour markers
51. Contents of a do-it-yourselfer's gun
53. Sauce traditionally made in a mortar
56. Word in many punny Bugs Bunny titles
59. Some R.S.V.P.s
61. Hall figures, for short

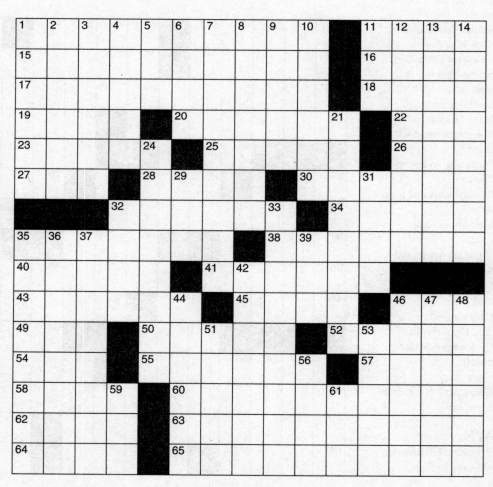

by Doug Peterson and Brad Wilber

ACROSS

1 Blue period?
7 Pet that needs a sitter?
13 Best Actor Oscar nominee for "The Lion in Winter"
14 Oriental blossom
15 Sartre's first novel
16 What you might get a distorted picture from?
17 Tee off
18 Detective fiction author Paretsky
19 Fragrance created by Fabergé
20 Scoring low on the excite-o-meter
21 Rarely missed stroke
23 Fore-and-aft-rigged vessel
24 Country ___ & Suites
26 Fictional biographer
28 "___ Will Be Loved" (Maroon 5 hit)
29 Restaurant critic who lent his name to a brand at the supermarket
32 Show authority?
34 Lightens up, say
36 Service station offering
39 "Beauty and the Beast" lyricist Howard
40 Macabre
42 Obedience school command
44 Foundry supply
46 Rolled item
47 Tribal title
48 Scorecard figures
49 Unpaid interest?
51 Ontario town across from Buffalo
53 Electrify
54 Club that "even God can't hit," according to Lee Trevino
55 It's not common knowledge
56 Worker at a station
57 Dirty

DOWN

1 "Hasn't scratched yet!" product
2 Concluded
3 Ring for dessert
4 Pharmacological amount
5 Bright-eyed
6 Parliamentary vote
7 Horne of "The Lady and Her Music"
8 "I can finally relax!"
9 Nonhuman explorer
10 Woos
11 "This being the case . . ."
12 Get a mouthful?
14 Side lights?
16 Grammy-nominated rock band for "Epic"
18 Setting of many pirate stories
22 Stirs
23 Gave a leg up to?
25 Fly in the ointment
27 At one's disposal
30 Renaissance Faire garment
31 Reputed
33 One who gets no credit?
35 Salt Lake City daily
36 Demand
37 FaceTime device
38 Raised
41 Security system component
43 Shenanigan
45 Gather together for stitching
48 Kind of plane
50 1977 horror film set in Newfoundland
52 Timeline segment
53 Listing on a Rolodex

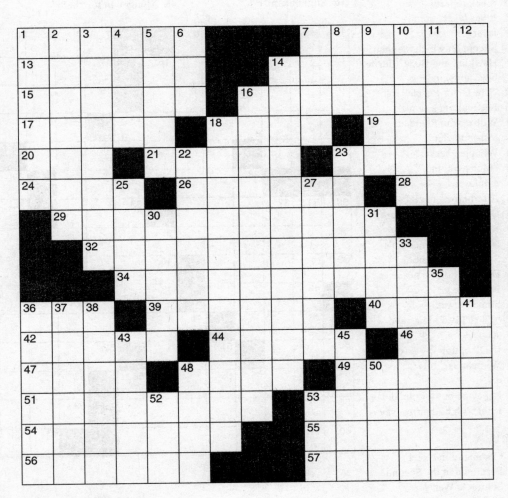

by Patrick Berry

152 HARD

ACROSS

1 Steven who co-created TV's "Sherlock"
7 Remote possibilities
15 Fat fingers?
17 Get the word out, maybe?
18 Big name in fast food
19 Better than, with "a"
20 School group working in harmony?
22 Unspecified power
23 Something to shuck
24 Something to shuck
25 Kind of sauce
27 Thought starter
28 Three-piece
29 It's no surprise
30 "The Paper Chase" novelist
33 Stock report?
34 It has layers upon layers
36 Sitcom on which Stephen Hawking and Buzz Aldrin have appeared
39 "The Color Purple" role
40 Lee making a scene
41 Wilber who founded a fast-food chain
42 Whopper server?
43 "Monsters, Inc." employees
45 Alternatives to clubs
46 Old Lutheran movement
47 Range of sizes, briefly
50 Member of comicdom's S.H.I.E.L.D.: Abbr.
51 Disturber of the peace
52 Exhibit, e.g.
54 Some brewskis
57 "The Naked Maja" and such
58 IHOP option
59 Whitehouse in D.C., e.g.
60 It may be out for blood
61 Hold with both arms, say

DOWN

1 Command in Excel
2 Fort town in the Second Seminole War
3 Circular
4 Clifford Irving's "Autobiography of Howard Hughes," e.g.
5 Sky line
6 Unwelcome Internet activity
7 Six L's
8 One who wasn't high-class, per a 1956 hit
9 Probably gonna, more formally
10 When doubled, a taunt
11 Home to Bellevue U.
12 250-year span in Japan's history
13 California city for which element #116 was named
14 Tick off
16 Slight blemish
21 It may grow between buds
26 Draw out
27 They can't be saved
28 ___ Ragg, Sweeney Todd's assistant
29 "That's O.K., everything's fine"
30 Like Advil or Motrin, for short
31 It's a hard act to follow
32 Took down a peg
35 Dec. 31
37 Medieval steel helmets with visors
38 Alter ego of "Batman" villainess Lorelei Circe
44 Tears apart
45 Mongolian for "hero"
46 Focus of some high-profile 1970s lawsuits
47 Dithers
48 Marilyn of the 5th Dimension
49 Watch's partner
51 Ending for evil or wrong
53 Stand-in for the unnamed
55 Inc. cousin
56 French possessive

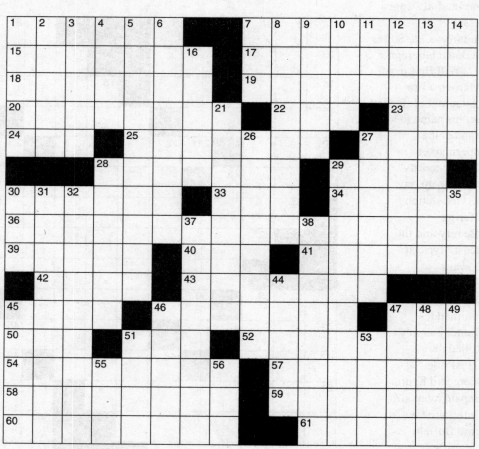

by David Phillips

ACROSS

1 Artificial eyelashes, informally
8 Things with round numbers?
15 Reply to a pushy person
16 Far out?
17 Not flirting with your friend's girlfriend, e.g.
18 Gets crushed by, say
19 "Cats" monogram
20 Peaceful protests
22 Athletic great whose name and jersey number rhyme
23 I Samuel preceder
25 Point ___, Calif.
26 Problem on a record
27 Really get to
29 Yankee opposer
30 Color whose name is French for "mole"
31 It may represent November
33 Quit
35 Seat of Oklahoma's Garfield County
37 They surround lenses
38 Friend on "Friends"
42 Zip, as a Ziploc, say
46 Angel hair toppers?
47 Shout while shaking a pompom
49 Friend of Buckwheat
50 Give out
51 The band fun. and others
53 Look through?
54 Ring letters
55 "Take it easy, bro!"
57 "Odi et ___" (Catullus poem)
58 Beyond the requirement
60 Electronic music genre
62 Bogey
63 Pouring poison into a stream, e.g.
64 Answer to "Capisce?"
65 Spicy cuisine

DOWN

1 Plant seen on the Sistine Chapel ceiling
2 In an ordinary fashion
3 Shower clothes
4 Quotation qualifier
5 Teenage dream?
6 "Star Wars" moon
7 In any way
8 Certain pop music fan of the 2010s
9 Cellular transmitters
10 Bygone sportscaster Hodges
11 ___ Styles, lead character in "Boyz N the Hood"
12 Screwdriver selection
13 Gotham building-climbing tool
14 Expressed derision
21 Sized up
24 One low on dough
26 Big wind
28 Keeps a watch on
30 Kept a watch on?
32 Bagel
34 "Right honourable" sort
36 Behind
38 Treat for a dog
39 Treat for a dog
40 Things you can assume
41 Skate park fixture
43 All over the place
44 California's so-called "Island City"
45 Make public
48 Poker variant
51 Low par
52 Angel hair topper
55 Quicken Loans Arena cagers
56 ___ One (2013 release)
59 Pounded paste
61 Zymurgy, e.g.: Abbr.

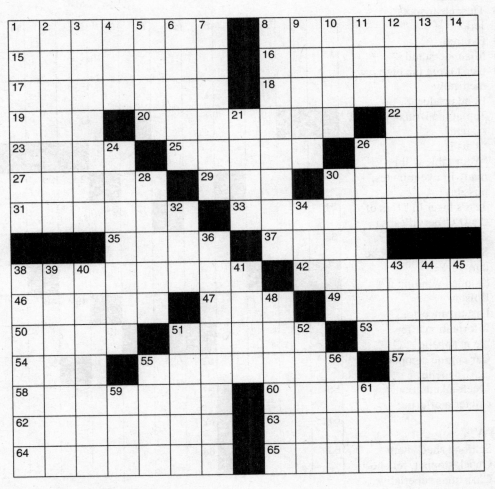

by David Steinberg

154 HARD

ACROSS

1 Edible Asian sprout
12 Something found naturally in tomatoes and potatoes
15 "Like, are you serious?!"
16 Top of an outfit?
17 Furniture item with a rounded back
18 Head
19 Winter coat
20 Seek to explain, in a way
22 Some of them are devoted to gangsters
25 Not close
26 Bob ___, leader of Canada's Liberal Party before Justin Trudeau
27 Org. in the documentary "Citizenfour"
28 They clear spots
31 Jerks
33 Expired
35 Misunderstand
40 One taking the big view, medically
41 Bond producer
42 Top of the British judicial system?
45 "This is ___"
47 "Your table will be ready in five minutes," possibly
48 Tess's lover in "Tess of the D'Urbervilles"
49 Orange snacks
51 Something that may be jam-packed
55 Stopped winging it?
56 Bolster
57 Distant ancestor
61 Information after "Je m'appelle . . ."
62 Car engine component
63 ___-Chapelle
64 Much-joked-about cafeteria offering

DOWN

1 Seafood shack item
2 Quack stopper, for short
3 Christmas superlative
4 Relating to element #56
5 Patrick Stewart's adaptation of "A Christmas Carol," e.g.
6 More after more?
7 Tick
8 Routine responses
9 Pearl Buck heroine
10 Massachusetts' ___ College
11 Hardly a vet
12 Place to get a brew in more than 11,000 U.S. locations
13 Alaska Airlines hub
14 They're history
21 It might help you on your return
22 Assault, as a commanding officer
23 ___ 10
24 Pincered creature
28 How much to be above, as they say
29 Teacher at Oxford
30 Only actor to appear in all eight "American Pie" films
32 Magnum opus of Spinoza
34 ___ subtilior (musical style)
36 Country's ___ Young Band
37 Doctor of book and screen
38 It's found on the side of a highway
39 Passing requirements
42 Ancient Greeks, e.g.
43 Broadway Billy
44 Software text page
46 Warmer, in a way
49 Southeastern European
50 Cold medicine brand
52 Level
53 Sir ___ Ive, designer of the iPad, iPod, iPhone and iMac
54 Qts. and gals.
58 Stretch (out)
59 A.C.C. school
60 Good to go

by Andrew Zhou

ACROSS

1 Too-clever-by-half type
12 Important school fig.
15 Taunt to a head-turner
16 Head-butter
17 Make an Amazon visit, say
18 Thoughtful gift?
19 Lady, for one
20 What a pacer may be experiencing
22 Project Mercury primate
23 Still red, say
25 Flier not found in 49 states
26 Conform to the party line?
27 Salon job, for short
29 Hallmark occasion
33 Chinese Fireball or Norwegian Ridgeback, in Harry Potter
35 Reproductive couple
36 Sharp shooter?
37 Music style featuring accordions
38 They play by themselves
39 Co-star of TV's "thirtysomething"
40 Trickery
41 A unit
43 Years abroad
44 Moose predator
48 Broad in tastes
50 Like silt vis-à-vis sand
51 Years ___
52 "Have some fun!"
55 Fox coverage that may be controversial?
56 What shoulders are often used for
57 Some M.I.T. deg. holders
58 It has many cells

DOWN

1 Hit, old-style
2 Sausalito's county
3 Increase
4 Casting needs
5 Roller on a carriageway
6 ___-hoo
7 Many a Weird Al Yankovic title
8 Cause of a rash response?
9 "Got me"
10 Pick up, as ice cubes
11 Crocheter's purchase
12 Title food in children's literature
13 Crashed
14 Tour gear
21 Relative of Sinhalese
23 Event with goat tying
24 Santa ___ (weather phenomena)
26 Tony
28 Holiday spots?
29 Doofus
30 Lions, Tigers and Bears play in it
31 Cold remedies?
32 Depression shared by soldiers
33 Hills' counterparts
34 Amazonas and Nilo
36 Certain plea, for short
38 Not faking it
40 Legal release
42 Bad things to find in theories
44 Singer's concern
45 Let loose
46 Row with many people
47 "Give it ___!"
48 Monk's on "Seinfeld," e.g.
49 Definitely not step lively
50 Bass parts
53 Turkish chief
54 Set the pace

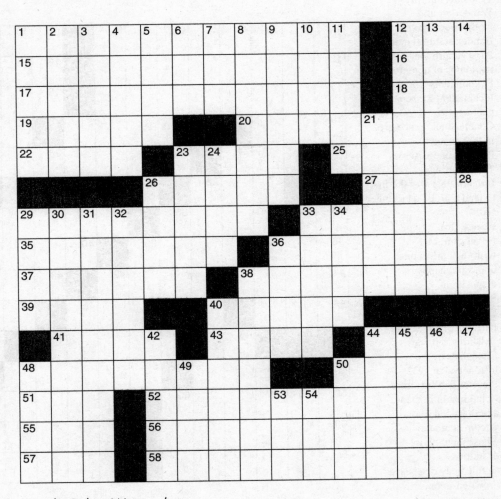

by Robyn Weintraub

ACROSS

1 Give up out of frustration, in slang
9 Person with pressing things to do?
15 [Shrug]
16 Very much
17 Exile
18 Blogging site owned by Yahoo
19 Lose support
20 Look inside
22 "The Glass Bead Game" author
23 10/15, e.g.
25 Table material
27 Garbage
29 Acronym in 1990s news
30 Ingredient in a Dark 'n' Stormy
33 1936 novel family
36 Wander around Hollywood, maybe
38 Banded status symbols
40 Paris suburb that holds the tombs of numerous Fr. monarchs
41 Ideal height for some contact
43 Counterintelligence grp. in 007 novels
44 Partners of 58-Across
45 "CSI" setting
47 Intl. org. that was the first to land a probe on a comet (2014)
48 Cheese dish
50 Novel character with "a comfortable home and happy disposition"
53 Some party wear
56 Shop item
58 Partners of 44-Across
59 "Aladdin" setting
61 Chocolaty treats introduced in 1932
63 Piece of den furniture
64 Relationship in many a Seth Rogen film
65 Sitcom character whose dancing is described as "a full-body dry heave"
66 Frowned-upon construction material

DOWN

1 Portia de ___ (Ellen DeGeneres's wife)
2 In the future
3 Some home remedies
4 Hall of fame on TV
5 Learning center
6 Like all contestants on "The Bachelor"
7 How soda may be sold
8 Highlanders, e.g.
9 Astronomers' std.
10 Parent's reproof
11 Citi Field icon
12 Winners at the Battle of Chickasaw Bayou, for short
13 "___ well"
14 Pericles' domain, in Shakespeare
21 Lots
24 The New Yorker cartoonist Edward
26 Need for sabermetricians
28 Panama Papers revelation
30 Went unchecked
31 Tomb Raider weaponry
32 Go together
33 Self-described "Family City U.S.A."
34 College athlete wearing blue and gray
35 End
37 One of the 12 gifts of Christmas
39 Jason of "How I Met Your Mother"
42 1987 #1 hit with the lyric "Soy capitán, soy capitán"
46 Things played on the floor
48 Black hat wearer
49 Pound
51 ___ Island, Fla.
52 Yo-yos
53 "The Twilight Zone" episode, usually
54 Like some arguments
55 City captured during the Six-Day War
57 "A Series of Unfortunate Events" villainess
60 Word that sounds like a letter of the alphabet that's not in it
62 Results of some four-year programs, for short

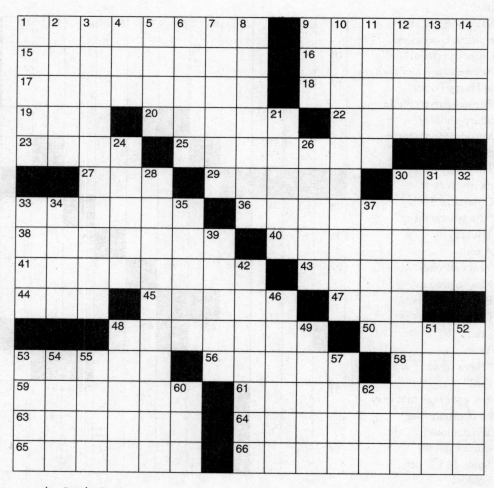

by Paolo Pasco

ACROSS

1 Graveyard hour
7 Dark as dark can be
15 Nova Scotia, once
16 Not excessively
17 A ghostwriter isn't given one
18 Ball
19 Haggis ingredient
20 "What's hangin'?"
21 It comes to a head
22 Ursule, e.g.: Abbr.
23 Means of tracking wildlife
26 Old radio dummy
27 Squeaker in a cage
30 City on the Oka River
31 Arles article
32 Lucky strike
35 Result of holding or hooking
37 Shot-putter's activity
39 Latin word on a diploma
40 Dedicated to
41 Conclusion lead-in
42 Tropical smoothie flavor
45 Double-dipping, e.g.
48 Answering to
49 ___ Balls
50 Healing helper
51 Show that's earned more than 40 Emmys, in brief
52 Lack of anxiety
54 Spreadsheet function
56 Sonnet-ending unit
58 72 of its 108 lines end in "-ore" sounds
59 "The Evangelist" of Christianity
60 Book that doesn't require much time or thought
61 "But still . . ."

DOWN

1 Dynamite
2 Hostile looks
3 A 99¢ burger may be on it
4 "Desperate Housewives" housewife
5 Slangy "True, no?"
6 Questel who voiced Olive Oyl
7 Fitting gifts for puzzle enthusiasts?
8 "Uncle!"
9 Too much, to Marcel
10 See 38-Down
11 Valentino type
12 Fourth-wall breaker
13 Star on the horizon?
14 Work digitally?
22 Fill time at an airport, say
24 Symbols of change, in math
25 Shot from behind the arc, informally
26 Shot putter's supply?
28 Grist for a war of words?
29 Ageless, ages ago
33 It often catches an infection
34 Rail heads
36 "OMG, I'm cracking up!"
37 Place for a stove light
38 With 10-Down, turn in
40 First country in the world with universal suffrage (1906)
43 Product of natural outdoor steeping
44 Onetime motel come-on
45 Refinement
46 Warm welcome?
47 Snoozers
51 Relief pitcher's success
53 Pistolet ou canon
55 "God, home and country" org.
56 Literary monogram
57 Fight call, for short

by Andrew Kingsley

ACROSS

1 Result of a bad trip
10 Signs of life
15 Paper pusher?
16 What some people do to vows
17 1998 Spike Lee film
18 Sunflowerlike flower
19 Royal name in ancient Egypt
20 The Rosetta Stone, for one
21 Engineer's home, for short
22 "I'm not buying it"
24 Small vault
25 Caribbean port
28 Choices, choices
29 Pantheon member
30 They cast no votes
32 Key employer in England?
34 Woodworker's device, informally
37 Advance men?
38 "The Miseducation of __ Hill" (1998 Grammy-winning album)
39 Allen of Hollywood
40 Moscato bianco grape product
41 Ring
43 City across the border from Eilat
47 Max. 3,333,360, in Pac-Man
48 Game also called Five in a Row
50 What three of California's four largest cities share
51 Common name for a chimp
53 Doing mean work?
56 Very loud
57 Light
58 Teacher's implementation
59 Affected by wind or water, say
60 Massage
61 Upset

DOWN

1 Key that's oxymoronic at school?
2 At the original speed, musically
3 Entrap
4 "A Yank at __" (Mickey Rooney film)
5 Substance
6 Gain access, in a way
7 Body-related
8 Fearsome foes
9 Bone-boring tool
10 Stopped lying
11 Almost up
12 Desk feature
13 Grammy-winning LL Cool J song that starts "I've been watching you from afar for as long as I can remember"
14 They clean up well
23 Longtime Indiana senator defeated in 2012
26 Mediterranean vacation spot
27 "Men always hate most what they __ most": H. L. Mencken
29 Public figure?
31 "Whatever Lola Wants," e.g.
33 No longer tied up, say
34 Raucous card game
35 Really must go
36 Best at play
37 Alternators in some internal-combustion engines
39 Acts of a scalawag
42 Put down
44 The Golden Horde, e.g.
45 War cry
46 First name in European politics
48 Ran through
49 Get a handle on
52 Herbal stress reliever from Polynesia
54 "__ Baby" (song from "Hair")
55 Unappealing bowlful

by Mark Diehl

ACROSS

1 Holder of many titles
12 Show with the record for most Emmys won in a single year (12)
14 Encountered trouble
16 Snags
17 What a star may represent
18 Non-Rx
19 Rx abbr.
20 Locales for deep investigations?
25 "We should get going"
29 Home to the naturally pink Lake Retba
30 Attended as an observer
31 It's spanned by the Ponte Santa Trinita
32 Army __
33 Allison Janney's role on "The West Wing"
36 Architect/sculptor with an eponymous New York museum
40 Control and make use of
41 Big name in late-night
42 Topkapi Palace resident
43 Choler
44 Deadline in a western
49 Anticipate
53 Turn lemons into lemonade, so to speak
55 Countercharge
56 Help someone

DOWN

1 M.R.I. alternative
2 "The Zone of Interest" author, 2014
3 Seat of Washoe County
4 Spoil, with "on"
5 Some successful Wharton grads, for short
6 Sports person: Abbr.
7 G
8 They may be graphic
9 Some temperatures
10 Go __ length
11 Bronze
12 Relative of a soul patch
13 Commences
14 Luster
15 Transcribe
21 Get into one's head
22 Tally
23 Mamie Eisenhower hairstyle
24 Grinds
25 Info in a 1-Across
26 Means of divination
27 Put on
28 Showed great happiness
33 It might be yawning
34 Luxury car name since 1935
35 Started, as a generator
37 Lingerie material
38 Speedball component
39 Like atoms with full outer shells
45 Miami Beach architectural style, informally
46 __ vez (again: Sp.)
47 Clay, for one
48 Friend of Bubbles, in an animated film
49 Hang
50 Focus of some prep books
51 Battle of __ (1943 U.S./Japanese conflict)
52 Rouge alternative
54 Thumbnail item

by Julian Lim

ACROSS

1 Small, slim daggers
9 Apple variety
15 Single from Springsteen's "Born in the U.S.A."
16 Major protest
17 Many a Harpo Marx joke
18 Extremely fast?
19 Dip ___ in
20 Get the lead out?
22 "Poor little" one in Coleridge's "To a Young Ass"
23 Automatic, for one
25 Like Egypt
26 Jerks
27 They're followed on message boards
30 "Hmm"
32 Writer who gave his name to an annual award
33 Many vacationers bring them home
34 Question before a personal update
40 Something depicted for goodness' sake?
41 With 48-Across, enters stealthily
42 One-knee plea
46 Entertains at bedtime
47 Color of McCartney's "Sgt. Pepper" uniform
48 See 41-Across
50 Belt line?
51 Sharp's opposite
52 Sharp's handful
54 Captain of fiction
57 Like corduroy
59 Cheese choice
61 As a replacement
62 Simplest sort of deal
63 Insistent retort
64 A good cure for it is sleep, per W. C. Fields

DOWN

1 Where Fermi studied
2 Cut out
3 Place to be avoided
4 Not learned
5 Like a boat's cockpit, usually
6 Drilling sites
7 Plays with emotions?
8 Rocker with the 1976 album "Live Bullet"
9 "I wish *I* had that"
10 On point
11 Common use for pipe cleaners
12 Like tea bags
13 Plunder
14 Words that may elicit a worried gulp
21 Show title shown on a license plate
24 Like much of the Everglades
27 Way up at a ski resort
28 Primary loser to J.F.K. in 1960
29 Longtime nickname in comics
31 Certain sandal
33 First word of Frost's "The Road Not Taken"
35 "Neapolitan Novels" author Ferrante
36 Pleasure principle
37 Frequent chant in 2008
38 Go for it, with "in"
39 Grp. doing private shows?
42 Home of the soccer team that FIFA named the Club of the Century
43 Mother-or-son Philippine president
44 Bit of gang warfare
45 Some wedding parties
46 Hall-of-Fame N.B.A. player known as "The Worm"
49 One of the singing Braxton sisters
53 Mtg.
55 Where Bambara is widely spoken
56 Fit for service
58 Experts in power: Abbr.
60 Symbol of charge density

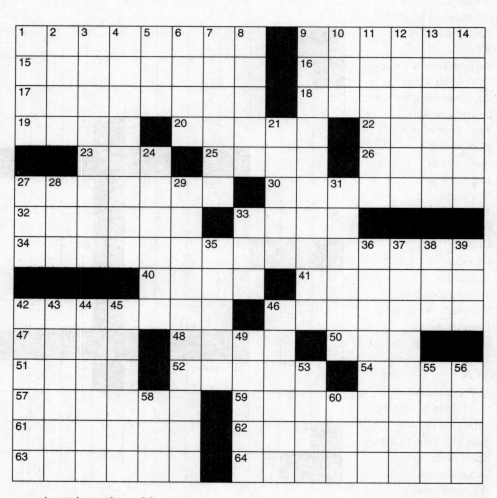

by Kyle Mahowald

ACROSS

1 Longtime "Mike & Mike" airer
10 See 29-Across
15 Utterly
16 Not act conservatively
17 Sets in
18 Widespread unrest
19 Got on a roll?
20 Plot element
21 "Gimme a break" product
22 First name in 39-Down research
24 God with green skin
26 Where "crossword" is "korsord": Abbr.
27 Good-sized combo
29 With 10-Across, player that the Broncos replaced with Peyton Manning
30 Like ___ of corn (really easy)
31 Something given to Apple's Siri
35 Like much locker room language
37 Things to cry over?
38 Samsung Galaxy rival
40 Tabula ___
41 Audio receiver
42 Mountain climbers?
46 Exemplar of ease
47 Hub for All Nippon Airways
50 Sports great with the 1993 memoir "Days of Grace"
51 Place for billiards or bingo
53 Forum rule enforcers, for short
55 Neptune vis-à-vis Saturn
56 Fajita option
57 Halves of twinsets
59 Early growth areas
60 Assurance that you can get bread at a store
61 One with eye patches
62 Well-rooted course?

DOWN

1 Tabasco, por ejemplo
2 Reception annoyance
3 Nudge
4 Hanoi-to-Beijing dir.
5 Chill out
6 Potential reaction to a cat
7 Makes a dead duck
8 "Sure, tell me"
9 Matchless?
10 Actress Polo and others
11 Shoot out
12 Project Gutenberg job
13 Senators' supporters, largely
14 Home to the Royal Opera House
21 Wear for Japan's Coming of Age Day
23 State with the most mountain ranges
25 Big name in projectors
28 Big name in mowers
30 One multiplying by division
32 "Really!"
33 French film award
34 Pristine
35 Panini bread
36 Not in real life, say
38 Finishes
39 Person, e.g.
43 Go after
44 Girl in a Beach Boys hit
45 Saw, say
47 Lumia smartphone launcher
48 The "Velvet" half of jazz's "Velvet & Brass"
49 "___ to the list"
52 Fatten
54 Things laid on scapegoats
57 Hotel waiter?
58 Fed. purchasing agency

by Zhouqin Burnikel

162 HARD

ACROSS

1 Tavern assistant
8 Person typically taking Torts and Contracts
12 Literary reference
13 Roast, e.g.
15 Outsider politician's target
18 Retail giant whose catalog comes in 17 languages
19 "We're doomed!"
20 Wendi ___, ex-wife of Rupert Murdoch
21 Parts of some law profs.' résumés
22 Year in the reign of Antoninus Pius
23 Hudgens and Huxtable
26 Skedaddled
27 Not skedaddle
28 It may have a stretch in it
31 One end of Fla.'s Sunshine Skyway Bridge
33 Currency of West Africa
34 About 3¼ light-years
35 Ice dam locale
36 Juillet's time
37 Picks on
41 Kind of bulb, for short
42 "Can I get an ___?"
43 "You ain't ___!"
46 Strong competition?
49 What's this, Señor?
50 Arm wave or finger snap
53 Hot times?
54 "The application of democracy to love," per H. L. Mencken
55 "Fair point"
56 Some rigs

DOWN

1 Poet who wrote "Tyger! Tyger! burning bright"
2 Hit 2004 sci-fi film with a 2007 sequel
3 Fugitives
4 Some undergrad degs.
5 Part of the conjugation for "avoir"
6 Aquarium decorations
7 Sounds of doom, maybe
8 ___ law
9 Word sung four times before "Born is the King of Israel"
10 The thyroid is part of it
11 Female Action Comics character
12 Inside
14 Network's concern
16 Oscar-nominated actor for "The Aviator"
17 Spitballs, e.g.
24 "Big" comics character
25 Where you may need to read the fine print
29 Liberal political activist Ralph
30 Isaac Asimov's "The Bicentennial Man," e.g.
31 Atlanta women's college
32 Food item cooked "to a light golden color"
38 ___ Stewart, singer of the 1979 #1 hit "Knock on Wood"
39 Add a layer to
40 One of Buddha's 10 disciples
44 Things that lead to Rome?
45 ___ a one
47 Kind of bar
48 Start of Massachusetts' motto
51 One making a report
52 Ancient times, in bygone days

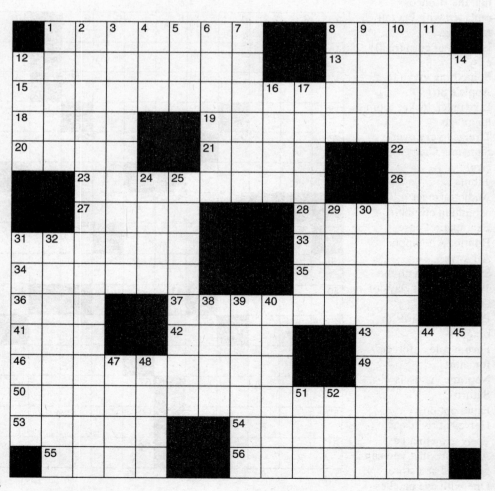

by Todd Gross

ACROSS

1 Fan group?
7 Centerpiece of a holiday gathering
14 The "R" of E.R.
15 No-parking area in a parking lot
16 Holiday cupful
17 Brought out of hibernation
18 Stock
19 Boxing ring producer
20 Worker with a saving plan, for short
21 Dog team's burden
22 With 40-Across, exposed
23 Cricket field shape
24 The American Messenger Co., today
25 Racketeering outfit
26 Drip chamber contents
28 Idled
31 "I'm counting on you!"
33 Harold Hill's portrayer in the original cast of "The Music Man"
35 Bugs
37 Lemon oil source
38 Green on a screen
39 Most important part
40 See 22-Across
41 Wild catch?
42 Rested
43 Party spread
44 Garden assets
45 Test of effectiveness
48 Bright yellow fruit
49 Some Kings' Scholars
50 Exceeding the usual rate
51 Like the papacy of Pius IX, after St. Peter
52 Another name for Michaelmas daisies

DOWN

1 Creates, as trouble
2 Yellow pages?
3 Hostile territory?
4 Took courses
5 Genesis grandson
6 Succumb to gravity
7 Admit defeat
8 Eurasian boundary
9 Dr. Kildare portrayer Ayres
10 Longtime band with the 2015 album "Alone in the Universe"
11 Los Angeles suburb next to San Fernando
12 Very small, as an operation
13 Gradual, as a slope
15 They're good for the long haul
19 Talk show talk
22 Cafeteria utensils
23 "American Me" star, 1992
25 Do well enough
26 Tristram Shandy's creator
27 Came through for
29 High-hat
30 TV drama starring Terrence Howard
32 It begins with All Saints' Day
34 Offers objections to
35 Brewery named for a Dutch river
36 Approaching
40 Principal force
41 Presuppose
43 Two-piece tops
44 Private engagements?
46 First name of 2012's Best Director
47 Misrepresentation
48 1040 preparer, for short

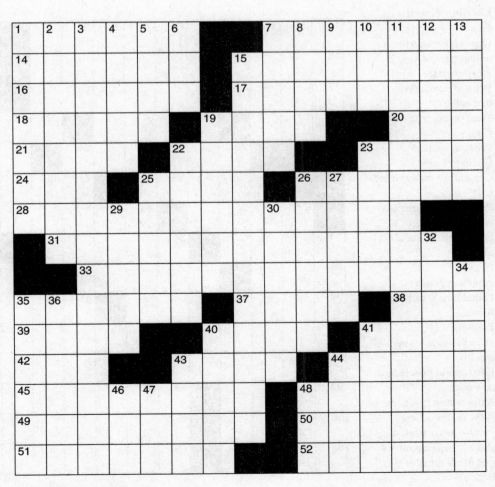

by Patrick Berry

ACROSS

1 "Cut the lip!"
11 Take in just the highlights, say
15 Common wear under a lei
16 Short pants?
17 Rich, sweet-and-sour dessert
18 Thirsts
19 Androids don't use it
20 President during the Korean War
21 Camp David event
23 European race place
25 Guerrilla in "For Whom the Bell Tolls"
26 Flip
27 Cough queller
29 Title teen in a 2007 hit indie film
30 Literature Nobelist ___ Fo
32 Org. whose logo has a talon-gripped key
33 At an impasse
34 Point of computer technology?
35 Went on the fritz
36 Clears
37 Pedestal support
38 Good, to Galba
39 Contents of many culled lists
41 Program that turns out ensigns, for short
43 Green hero of book and film
44 Places
46 Attention getter
48 Football rival of Rutgers
49 Kiss ___
52 Fake-out
53 Tries to unload things quickly
56 Resourceful people find new ones
57 Actor whose first name is the title of a Best Picture he co-starred in, and whose last name is that film's director
58 Bother
59 Grave accents?

DOWN

1 Co-writer of the Surrealist silent film "Un Chien Andalou," 1929
2 With 28-Down, butterlike product of beef fat
3 List in an actor's résumé, informally
4 Short while?
5 Italian border city
6 Cough cause
7 Ones with wedge issues?
8 Prompt to pull over
9 Winner of NBC's "America's Toughest Bouncer" in 1980
10 Are, in Arles
11 Hogtie
12 Detractors' epithet for the Putin regime
13 Setting of the so-called "Seven Islands" of Greece
14 Hot words?
22 It's hair-raising
23 Thirst
24 Sneak peek sent to film critics
26 Band whose "Appetite for Destruction" was the best-selling debut album of all time
28 See 2-Down
29 Rowdy joint
31 First name of 26-Down's frontman
33 IHOP topping option
34 Municipal mainstays: Abbr.
35 The word "shies" in Morse code, entirely
37 Zaire's Mobutu Sese ___
38 Tattoos and piercings
40 Command
42 13th-century B.C. king with 10 namesakes
45 She played Adrian in "Rocky" and Connie in "The Godfather"
47 Cry of excitement
49 City largely destroyed in Operation Charnwood
50 One way to turn a vessel
51 Rx things
54 Accented shout
55 Packed letters?

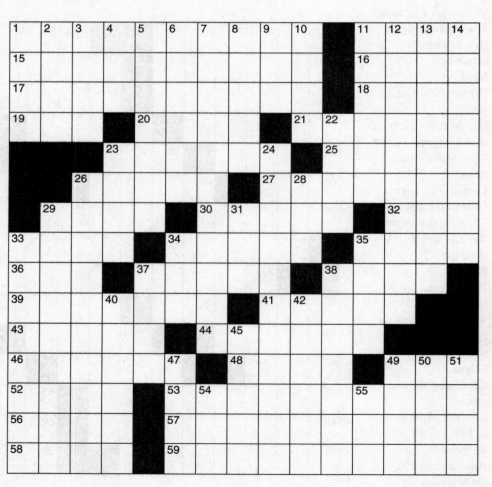

by Kameron Austin Collins

ACROSS

1 Talk
7 Driver's hazards
15 Not divisible, as a job
16 Amelia Earhart, e.g.
17 Good news for wage earners
18 Far Eastern city whose name means "long cape"
19 Org. that covers Springfield in a dome in "The Simpsons Movie"
20 Torpedo
22 Black
23 Office monitor
25 Dough made in the Middle East?
26 Lane in a strip
27 Wedding keepsake
29 Long-running Vegas show
30 Even's opposite
31 Gravy goody
33 Mississippi feeder
35 Backslash neighbor
39 Buddhist memorial dome
40 Like motets
42 Cross words
44 One-on-one basketball play, slangily
46 Sound
47 Feature of un poema
48 Accomplished
50 Damage done
51 It welcomes praise
52 "Wouldn't think so"
54 Pixar specialty, briefly
55 City called the Bush Capital
57 2006 musical featuring a vampire
59 Light blue partner of Connecticut and Vermont
60 Crazy Horse, e.g.
61 "It was my pleasure"
62 They're drawn by the bizarre

DOWN

1 Green grocery choice
2 Brazilian city name that sounds like a U.S. state capital
3 Some southern cookin'
4 Alternative to SHO
5 Celebrate
6 Rapping response
7 Its rosters aren't real
8 1997 comedy with the tagline "Trust me"
9 Odysseus' faithful dog
10 Clout
11 Christmas trio
12 Key of Chopin's étude "Tristesse"
13 Collect lots of
14 Cross states
21 Word with a 35-Across before and after it
24 Separator of the Philippines and Malaysia
26 "Incoming!"
28 Charcuterie, e.g.
30 Nut-brown
32 Tony-winning title role of 1990
34 Country's __ Brown Band
36 Aid in labor management?
37 One handling an OD
38 Get too close, in a way
41 Teases, in older usage
42 French daily, with "Le"
43 Lackey's response
45 Pick
47 Casing job, for short
48 Big supply line
49 Bill collectors?
52 Dimple
53 Something farm-squeezed?
56 Arthur with a Tony
58 Genre for Reel Big Fish

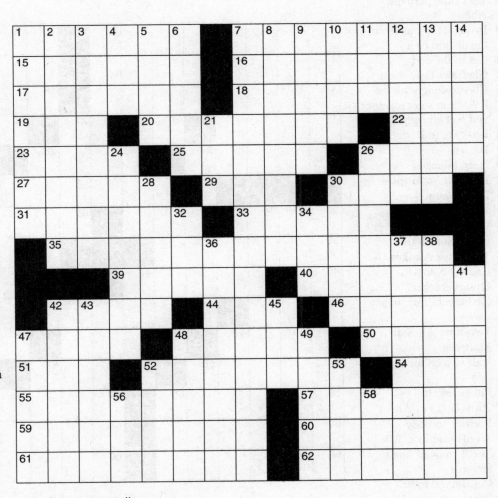

by James Mulhern

ACROSS

1 Postprandial woe
9 Fight memento
15 "That's it . . . too rich for me"
16 Classical record on Norman Bates's turntable in "Psycho"
17 Licorice candy that was originally raspberry-flavored
18 Ross and Spencer
19 John of the Velvet Underground
20 Berlin's ___ Nationalgalerie
22 Promised lands
23 Alex's mom on "Family Ties"
25 Totes
27 Tía's title, perhaps: Abbr.
28 Brought (up), as from the distant past
31 Get in the end
32 Gladiator type
36 Classic song with the lyric "Let's get together and feel all right"
38 Rays are in it
39 Browns
40 Head honchos
42 Pie slice, so to speak
43 Disney aunt
44 Most insensitive
46 "___ Theme," tune from "Star Wars: The Force Awakens"
48 Change colors
49 Oyster cracker?
54 No longer crisp, in a way
56 Two-time All-Star Martinez
58 Half of a comic strip duo
59 Put an end to
61 2008 Tina Fey/Amy Poehler comedy
63 Words said in a rush
64 Small show of one's feelings
65 Considered to be
66 Barren, in a way

DOWN

1 "Broad City," for one
2 N.B.A. star with size 22 shoes
3 "___ enough . . ."
4 Low bars
5 10th-century year
6 Chaplin of "Game of Thrones"
7 Robert ___, F.B.I. director from 2001 to 2013
8 Like many retired Derby winners
9 Like parking meters
10 Singer India.___
11 Pride : lions :: knot : ___
12 It may be a credit to the band
13 "This is too much"
14 Prove one's worth
21 Something that may pop up in the morning
24 Who said "Opportunity is missed by most people because it is dressed in overalls and looks like work"
26 Some claim to have six of them
29 Poor spirits?
30 Loved by
32 Has fun getting towed?
33 Recharging period
34 Like debts
35 Old dope?
37 Director Jacquet of "March of the Penguins"
41 Blue books?
42 Ann Landers, for one
45 Sweeteners
47 M.I.T.'s ___ School of Management
50 Linguistic origin of "mulligatawny"
51 Whisper
52 Ticklish dolls
53 They have coats with white hairs
55 ___ noche (tonight: Sp.)
57 Something that may be found in a pit
60 "___ Mine" (hit of 1957 or 1995)
62 Accounting abbr.

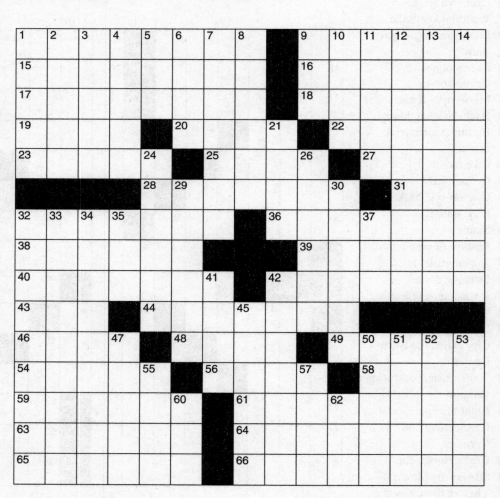

by Erin Rhode

ACROSS

1 Preceder of 64-Across on the calendar
12 It may justify things
15 Ilmenite is the chief one
16 Winner of the first three Fiesta Bowls, for short
17 Airport terminal feature
18 Radio frequency abbr.
19 Scrap
20 Discoverer of New Zealand
21 "I can't believe that!"
22 Liberty's home, for short
23 4-Downs, south of the border
25 Site of Akbar the Great's tomb
28 Article in El País
31 Release?
34 Parts of cross-shaped churches
37 He worked for Hershey in the 1910s–'20s
38 Quaint getaway destination
40 Bring down
41 Officially gives up
42 More compact
44 Dutch oven, e.g.
45 1995 Emmy winner Sofer
46 Less adorned
48 Highway hazard
50 Laverne and Shirley, e.g.
52 Lumber mill employee
55 World of Warcraft figure
58 Bud abroad
59 Port authority?
61 World of Warcraft figure
62 Name that went down in history?
63 Buns, for example
64 Follower of 1-Across on the calendar

DOWN

1 Vitamin a.k.a. riboflavin
2 Story teller
3 Having a scrap
4 Stealthy sort
5 Sweaters and such
6 Got via guile
7 Kirmans, e.g.
8 Certain prayer leader
9 Rapper wrapper?
10 22-Across and others
11 Motion supporter
12 Departs
13 Court legend
14 Dreaded game show sound
21 Antedate
22 Civil War battle site
24 Largest minority in Bulgaria
25 Single chance?
26 Duck lookalike
27 Spots for air traffic controllers
29 They may precede high-speed chases, in brief
30 Peel
32 European city whose name means "eat"
33 Bright swimmer
35 Part of a mean mien
36 One of Utah's state symbols
39 Civil War battle site
43 Like hashish or shoe wax
47 Soul mate?
49 Philosophy
50 Bookkeeper's stamp
51 It's loaded
53 "___ live!"
54 W.W. I battle site
55 With 60-Down, gotten by great effort
56 "Eri tu," but not "Eres Tú"
57 Oz salutation
59 New Mexico State's athletic grp.
60 See 55-Down

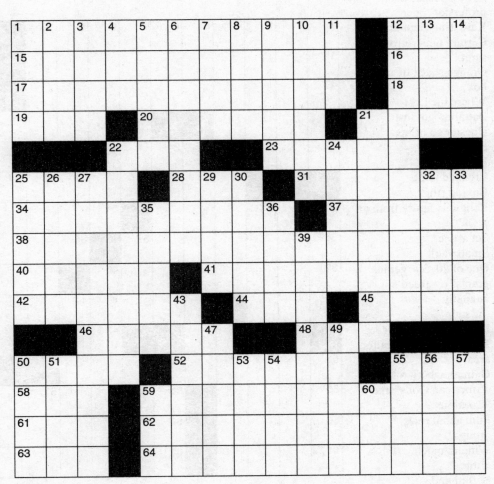

by Barry C. Silk

ACROSS

1 One might have black-and-white standards
11 Treasure hunter's loot, maybe
15 Stay off the water?
16 Unconventional and hippielike, informally
17 Some juvenile records
18 Way: Abbr.
19 Developers work on them
20 Wrong
22 Jazz great Montgomery
23 More than a fraction of a cent
25 Responsibility
26 Outfits for big parts?
29 Station display
31 "The perfect idiot's profession," per Katharine Hepburn
34 Certain upper-growth limit
36 Orange snack in a red box
38 Where the Lost Battalion got lost
39 Doesn't go off as expected
41 Flip-flop, e.g.
42 Crooked joint
43 Boxing ring?
45 Religious figure from on high?
47 Set at sea?
48 Small vault
51 One of 20–30 "genius grants" awarded annually
54 ___ soup
55 Impulse transmitter
56 North Carolina vacation area
59 Gaiman who wrote "American Gods" and "Coraline"
60 Film about rock groups?
61 Without much effort
62 Bellini and Botticelli

DOWN

1 "Yeah, right!"
2 [Fingers crossed]
3 Wins easily
4 War force
5 Pro ___
6 "Out of the Blue" group, for short
7 "Hockey sticks," in cards
8 Buzz, e.g.
9 2011 Best New Artist Grammy winner Bon ___
10 Philippine money
11 His last play was "When We Dead Awaken"
12 "Excuse me?"
13 Classic folk number
14 Heaps
21 Bouquets, quaintly
23 Island known for its spices
24 This year's starlet
26 Sphere of control
27 Org. in "Patriot Games"
28 Like Hemingway vis-à-vis most other writers
30 Exfoliation
31 Tiptop
32 Hung around casually?
33 It may cause sparks to fly
35 Isolated
37 It may be in the bag
40 Went looking for places to shoot
44 First name on the 1970s–'80s Lakers
46 Rugged
48 Swinging joint
49 "The Tin Drum" boy
50 Duck faces, e.g.
51 Salon job, informally
52 Land on the Gulf of Guinea
53 Project with a lot of momentum
54 Like Colt 45 and Mickey's
57 Kind of virus
58 Not haut

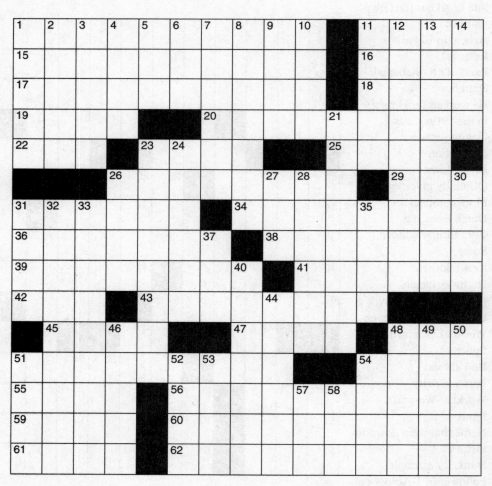

by Josh Knapp

ACROSS

1 Insincerely polite
7 13-Down natives, e.g.
15 Hugh who played TV's House
16 Laid into
17 Wool source
18 Subcontinent-wide
19 One for whom 36-Across has four syllables
21 Many new car drivers
22 Island west of Mull
23 Red stuff to cut through
25 Dim bulbs
26 Off
28 Compromise
30 Trial cover-up
31 Gray head
32 Has the stage
34 What exterior doors typically do
36 See 19- and 57-Across
38 Lyricist who adapted "Pygmalion"
41 Clubs to beat people with?
42 Chrome runners, maybe
45 x, y and z
46 Mozart title starter
48 Devil's deck
50 Lawyer's workload
52 Admission evidence
54 Musical group known for wearing red hats called "energy domes"
55 Recycling bin fill
57 One for whom 36-Across has three syllables
59 Figure-changing agent
61 Calmer?
62 Lesser "Seinfeld" role played by Len Lesser
63 Bomb
64 Early Beatle
65 Going rates

DOWN

1 Beyond slow
2 Sought safety, say
3 Princess in line to the British throne after Beatrice
4 Agents in some therapy
5 When told "I'm sleepy," she sometimes says "I hope you're not driving"
6 Rising generation?
7 The Era of ___ (1964–74 Notre Dame football)
8 Like some angels and arches
9 Really bug
10 Paris fights in it
11 Like many bad words
12 Appended
13 Safari Capital of the World
14 Nine-time presidential contender of the 1940s–'90s
20 Shaving the beard with a razor, in Jewish law
24 Bit of décor in a sports bar
27 It makes a wave
29 Nap
33 Top of the line?
35 Tick, e.g.
36 Fill with anxiety
37 Freeze
38 Like skates and corsets
39 Scrutinize
40 Word repeatedly spelled out by Franklin
42 Make as a heat-and-serve product, say
43 Much-sought-after
44 British floors
47 Time after Time?
49 Think much of
51 Backtrack?
53 Calligraphic messes
56 Creator of the lawyer Perry
58 "Superman" catchphrase starter
60 Grokked

by Matt Ginsberg

ACROSS

1 School for Rory Gilmore of "Gilmore Girls"
5 Item that became trilingual in the late '90s
15 Slavering toon
16 Captain
17 Salty drink?
18 She was "the answer to a prayer" in a 1941 #1 Jimmy Dorsey hit
19 1983 hit for Rufus and Chaka Khan
21 French pronoun
22 Pitch successfully
23 Like salsa
25 Ingredient in a Baltimore Bracer
26 Pros at settling disputes
27 Auto option patented by 3M
28 Cast mate?
30 Italian term of address: Abbr.
31 Leaves out in the open?
33 "No ___!"
36 Shower component
37 Apparent flaw
38 Confessed statements
41 "Wake Up on the Bright Side" sloganeer
44 Louses
45 Medical term for lead poisoning
46 "___ word?"
47 Pool cover
48 Film animation technique
51 Drug smuggler
52 Governor who was the father of another governor
53 Yank with 25 grand slams
54 Polysomnogram finding
55 Bird with a resonant "ha-wah" call

DOWN

1 Balance sheets?
2 Ninth-century pope who was married with a daughter
3 Simba sobriquet
4 A migraine sufferer might have one
5 Level best
6 Aeschylus' play "The Persians" is about one
7 Crossing state lines, perhaps
8 HC(O)NH$_2$, for one
9 Kill
10 Grasp
11 Companion
12 "Swan Lake" heroine
13 "Claude Monet Painting in His Garden at Argenteuil," e.g.
14 Drills
20 Scottish refusal
23 Magazine that published Harry Truman's memoirs
24 Kill
26 Worthless amount
29 2005–07 sitcom about the Gold family, with "The"
31 RICO enforcers
32 They may end with golden goals, for short
33 Job for which you give someone a hand
34 Exhibition locale
35 Rush
36 Former Florida senator Martinez
37 Support for a pilot
38 Gulfs
39 Zipcar alternative
40 Kid-lit character who says "The nicest thing about the rain is that it always stops. Eventually"
42 Trendy pseudocereal
43 Cinerary item
45 Suddenly took notice
47 Locale of the Evert Tennis Academy, familiarly
49 Word that follows pot but precedes pan
50 Clean (up)

by Byron Walden

ACROSS

1 Sharp projections
5 What a capt. may aspire to be
8 Service provider
14 Much-photographed mausoleum site
15 1978 Grammy nominee Chris
16 Be faithful (to)
17 Blotchy, in a way
18 Blotchy, in a way
20 Mimicking
21 "Enfantines" composer
22 "Join the club"
23 Lifesaver, at times
24 Book and film title character surnamed Gatzoyiannis
25 Flame proof?
26 Fancy wrap
28 Measure of econ. health
30 Gear protector
33 Got rich
39 Depression era?
40 One with a smaller Indian relative
41 Hurtful pair in a playground rhyme
42 Show celerity
43 Flop's opposite
44 Mil. roadside hazard
45 78 letters
48 Dixieland sound
51 "10-4"
54 Cole Porter topic
56 "To Helen" writer, in footnotes
57 Feedable thing
58 Abstract Expressionist who married Jackson Pollock
60 Cannery row?
61 Iris feature
62 He's unrefined
63 They're unrefined
64 Brokerage come-on
65 Suffix with green
66 Big name in Renaissance patronage

DOWN

1 Follower of a diet system
2 Twinkle-toed
3 Only living thing that can be seen from outer space
4 Blue
5 Alternative to Geneva
6 Al __
7 Appearing with fanfare
8 Back stroke?
9 "Battlestar Galactica" role
10 Starts suddenly
11 What "Banzai!" literally means
12 Food brand since 1912
13 Fresh styling
19 Who called a date "a job interview that lasts all night"
21 Green around the gills, maybe
27 Shakespearean duel overseer
29 They're often struck in studios
31 Combined
32 Temporary quitting times?
33 Make __ of (botch)
34 Civvies
35 What Google Wallet uses
36 Eternal water-pourers in Hades
37 Chameleon, e.g.
38 Literally, "big water"
46 What some caddies hold
47 __ Norman (cosmetics franchise)
49 21-Across's "Three Pieces in the Shape of __"
50 Circumlocutory
52 Target of the plume trade
53 Western union?
54 War room development
55 Wind-cheating
59 Some camera cells
60 __ College

by Martin Ashwood-Smith and George Barany

ACROSS

1 Those falling head over heels?
9 Little rows
14 Ones with love-hate relationships, say
16 Pop singer Goulding
17 Show on which Adam West voices Mayor Adam West
18 Actress Balaban of "Supernatural"
19 Make a measure of
20 Shift specification: Abbr.
21 Some temple figures
22 César subject
23 Measure (up)
25 Press target, informally
26 Soupçon
27 Is a kiss-up
29 Org. awarding 5-Downs
30 Bass brass
31 Foreign aide
33 Reduced
36 Guts
37 Do-it-yourself wheels
38 W.W. II landing site in Italy
39 Hookups on "House"
40 Tough
42 Malfunctioning
45 Like venison
47 First division, maybe
48 Hindu embodiment of virtue
49 Procedure improving one's looks?
51 "Let me ___ pray thee": Exodus 4:18
52 Picks nits
53 Golfer's error
54 Some small tablets
56 Power of two
57 Hesitant
58 Something to believe in
59 Princess and angel, e.g.

DOWN

1 Move
2 Holders of thoughts?
3 Order back
4 Shelved
5 Supporting strip
6 She anchored "Weekend Update" with Tina, then Seth
7 Scrooge
8 "Bathers at Asnières" and "Parade de Cirque"
9 Game giveaway
10 24-book classic
11 What a troll may perpetuate
12 Preceder of the sound of a gavel
13 Be in shock from a sock
15 Biggest rival of US Foods

23 Recover after being wrecked
24 Year-end tradition since 1966
27 Half of a 2000s stoner-film duo
28 Longtime hair lightener brand
30 Alternative to Flix
32 Kung ___ beef
33 Things that one is good at
34 Be what one isn't
35 Prognostication proclamation
36 Start
38 Music genre for Miriam Makeba
41 Charley Bates's mentor, in literature

42 Musical with the song "There's a Sucker Born Ev'ry Minute"
43 One often accused of being blind
44 Rank and file
46 Something to carve out
48 First lady Barbara's Russian counterpart
50 Last name in the funnies for nearly 50 years
52 "Let's go!"
55 Ariz. doesn't observe it

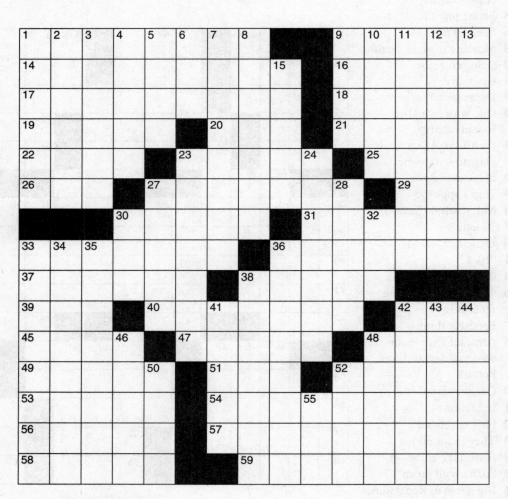

by Debbie Ellerin

ACROSS

1 Gets steamy, with "up"
5 Order to go away
9 Ever
14 Letters on a crucifix
15 Rabbit's friend
16 Grit
17 Teen's fender bender, maybe
20 2001 fantasy/adventure film with three sequels
21 Many an étagère display
22 Gush
23 Lab housing the world's largest machine
24 Luca who "sleeps with the fishes"
25 Symbol of virility
30 Don't delay
31 However
33 "Frozen" princess
34 Match makeup
36 Match
37 "Ellen's Design Challenge" airer
38 One of the eight points of contact in Muay Thai
39 Least apt to offend
41 "Life of Pi" director
42 Longest word in English containing only one vowel
44 Many gases lack them
46 R&B/pop singer Aubrey
47 Readies for an operation
48 Therapist's image
52 Some miniature hors d'oeuvres
54 Concern in family planning
56 Inuit for "house"
57 Simon of the stage
58 Hostile to
59 Roughhouse?
60 Eponyms of the week?
61 270°

DOWN

1 Goes on perfectly
2 Target of the Occupy movement
3 Brains
4 Twisted sorts
5 Figure in a dark suit
6 They're held at both ends when eating
7 Sister co. of Verizon Wireless
8 "How Deep Is Your Love" Grammy winners
9 Principal, e.g.
10 Catacomb component
11 Turn and a half on the ice
12 Shoppers' headache
13 "I'm in!"
18 Cry after "One, two, three," maybe
19 Rail hubs?
23 Intolerantly pious
24 Takes pleasure (in)
25 Deep in thought
26 "Yeah, right!"
27 Like the Bahamas, Barbados and Belize
28 Cuts through
29 "Two thumbs way up!" and such
32 Like losers' looks
35 Get
40 Doughnutlike
43 Kind of pass in basketball
45 Make furniture-safe, in a way
47 Relatives of sprains
48 Relative of a spoonbill
49 Just about
50 African tree cultivated for its nuts
51 Like-minded voters
52 Muslim judge of North Africa
53 Bit of improv
55 Driver of a bus.

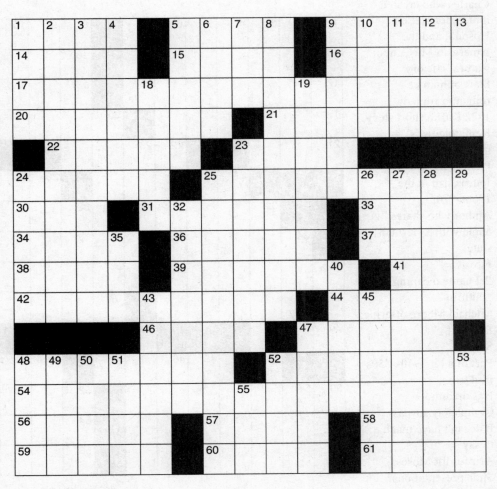

by John Guzzetta

ACROSS

1 Ridiculous imitation
8 Basis of a patent
15 Traffic report source, often
16 Something John Adams and John Quincy Adams each had
17 Change, as allegiances
18 "Mean Girls" screenwriter
19 Close to, colloquially
20 Sell
21 Means of communication since 1817, in brief
22 Some receptions
24 Wonder
27 Surgeon's tool
29 Charles who created murals for Harlem Hospital and the American Museum of Natural History
32 Start of many a romantic comedy
34 1922 Kafka short story
35 Hematologist's measure
36 Pioneer in New Journalism in the 1960s–'70s
37 Author who shares his name with a German state
38 Fire away
39 Pet name meaning "faithful"
40 Michael Moore offering, for short
43 Sea ___
47 Part of a hit 1940s–'50s film trio
50 Has dreams
52 Completely surpass
53 It doesn't have much to say
54 Armful for Moses
55 Slide presentations?
56 Hedge fund employee

DOWN

1 Santa ___
2 They might be ill
3 Feature of CNN or Fox News
4 Hindu goddess often portrayed with her husband Shiva
5 Work on a lead, maybe
6 Part of a square
7 That there
8 F and G, but not H
9 Wife in Jonathan Franzen's "The Corrections"
10 Meander
11 It adds stress: Abbr.
12 "Glass half empty" sort
13 Emily Dickinson's "Ended, ___ it begun"
14 Writer Sedaris
20 Like motel walls, it often seems
23 Host
25 Refuses to
26 Grade sch. class
27 Ladder's counterpart
28 Track things
29 Sprayer
30 "___ pray"
31 Author of the "Mostly Ghostly" book series
32 Attribute as the cause of
33 Sprayed, in a way
34 Start of a Hamlet monologue
35 Child support, for short?
39 Sparring partners?
40 Dull-witted
41 Boots
42 Peak
44 Ready
45 Zodiac symbol
46 One sitting on a celestial throne
48 Goya's "Duchess of ___"
49 Grind down
50 Legal org.
51 Kind of card
52 Itinerary abbr.

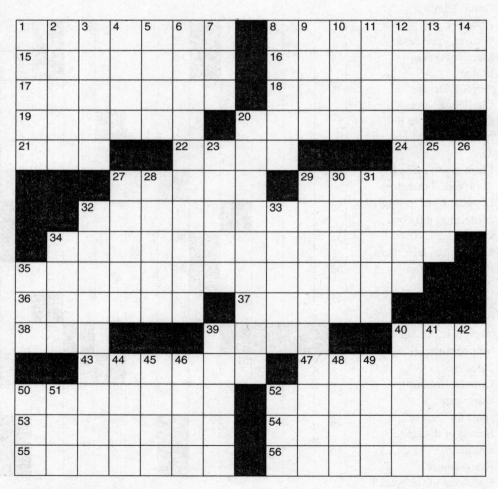

by Lily Silverstein

ACROSS

1 Conflicts with combat
8 TED talk, e.g.
15 Going around the world?
16 Where people live well beyond the city limits
17 Eponym of an annual Golden Globe award for lifetime achievement
18 Parts of abdomens
19 Event where kids ask lots of questions, informally
21 Hardly deliberate
24 Female antelope
25 Student monitors, for short
26 Like the tops of many porticoes
28 Crib piece
30 Home of Charlie Chan
34 Mortal
36 Recited prayers
38 Second City subway org.
39 You might be thrown on it
41 Narrow inlet
42 Average producer
44 Paradise
46 Recital numbers
47 Sammy who wrote the lyrics to "Ain't That a Kick in the Head"
49 Italian dictators
50 Frustrated cry
52 Impressed cry
54 Dunham of "Girls"
55 Real hack?
60 Resembling a heavy curtain, say
61 Christie's event
65 Temple of Artemis city
66 "Ah, got it"
67 Least hopping
68 Chameleon, e.g.

DOWN

1 Put away
2 "Army of ___" (recruiting slogan)
3 "Spotlight" director McCarthy
4 Twists
5 ___-bodied
6 Sore
7 Some women on "Mad Men"
8 Injured: Fr.
9 Added cost of selling overseas
10 Confessional word
11 Charge that may be high
12 "Evolving the way the world moves" sloganeer
13 Compost heap bit
14 Undemanding
20 Colorful swallow?
21 Some mixtapes
22 Playground comeback
23 Opposite of fine print?
27 Locale for a 39-Across
29 Direct
31 Shooting star?
32 U.S. athlete who won more gold medals at the 1980 Winter Olympics than all but two non-U.S. countries
33 Patriotic chant
35 Martial arts weapons that are two sticks connected by a chain
37 Somewhat
40 Div. of the Justice Department
43 Moved like a 20-Down
45 There's nothing to it
48 "I was robbed!"
51 Come about
53 Mount
55 Armisen of "Portlandia"
56 Hip-hop's ___ Fiasco
57 Ottoman honorific
58 Start and end of many a flight
59 The Miners of the N.C.A.A.
62 What makes nose noise?
63 :-D alternative
64 Source of fleece

by Brendan Emmett Quigley

ACROSS

1 Spontaneous public gathering
9 Balance sheet data
14 For whom the Collegiate School was renamed in 1718
16 Sushi bar brew
17 Like Cirque du Soleil performers
18 Paris attraction?
19 Coin collectors?
20 As follows
22 Co. with the slogan "We move the world"
23 Precisely
24 Chuckleheads
26 "Red, White & ___" (2005 rock album)
27 Canonflex or Leicaflex, for short
28 1,000 or 1,000,000
29 Profits
31 Manipulative use of the Force
34 Coup d'___
35 Like a young Jay Gatsby
36 Someone always good for a few pints?
42 Boehner's successor as House minority leader
43 The Japanese captured it in 1941
44 Flight component
46 Procrastinator's favorite word
47 Jay Gatsby's beloved
49 New brunette, say
50 Terminal requests
51 Coup d'___
52 Dwarf warrior in "The Lord of the Rings"
53 Part of many a diary
55 Sticker in a nursery
58 Feeling toward a supervillain
59 Activity for when there's nothing going on?
60 Dapper
61 Back in the day

DOWN

1 Saturnalia events
2 2012–16 host of the Grammys
3 Soaring expense?
4 Certain weanling
5 Nerve centers
6 "Lady Marmalade" Grammy winner of 2001
7 ___ bread
8 Member of a holiday team
9 Morse "Toto," totally
10 Telegraph extension?
11 Shoulder-to-hip belt
12 One who's green after seeing red
13 Stain-free
15 Auto-reply message?
21 Media giant since 1982
24 Get some help with transportation
25 21-Down runs them
26 Shaggy Scottish dog
28 Gives credit
30 Sound of power
32 Red English cattle
33 Figure in the high 60s
36 Y lookalike
37 Genre of some of Yoko Ono's art
38 "My anger got the best of me"
39 Nimbleness
40 Scandalous Manet painting of 1863
41 Knocked for a loop
45 Yank, in Yucatán
48 Facilitates
49 Relatives of stilettos
51 Cry of surprise
52 Ski boots and such
54 Like bodybuilders' bodies
56 Is for a group?
57 Word with soup or salad

by David Phillips

ACROSS

1 Porcine paramour
11 Yesterday, so to speak
15 Product with a Crispy Buffalo variety
16 Underwater breather
17 Tremendous
18 Beginning to morph?
19 Brady bunch, briefly
20 Some zoo employees
21 Harmonious
22 Blubbers
23 Some red giants
24 Little 'un
27 They had rolls to play, once
29 Disappearing exclamations
30 Foe of Big Boy and Little Face
33 Tremendously
34 Bothers
35 Bothers
36 Good news for business
38 Combined
39 Turn on
40 Shot measure
41 Meshes
43 One for whom "hello" is "hej"
44 Geezers
45 Tough spots
46 What "it" is found in
49 Symbol del cristianismo
50 Haughty
53 Artist Magritte
54 It takes turns making dinner
55 Extra, in ads
56 Reminder that sticks?

DOWN

1 Sound from a cheater
2 Israel's Olmert
3 Staple of Memorial Day services
4 Instrument that's cradled, for short
5 Full of butterflies
6 Under water
7 Touches
8 Mushy foods
9 '50s campaign nickname
10 2014 World Cup winner: Abbr.
11 Weapon used in the Vietnam War
12 Seriously under the weather
13 Fix as 20-Across might do
14 Schemes
21 "And who ___?"
22 Hot, salty snack
23 Lord & Taylor rival, informally
24 Go over
25 John Paul II, e.g.
26 Do some ferreting
27 Magical duster
28 Founder of Rhyme $yndicate Records
30 Webster wrote many of them: Abbr.
31 Traffic director
32 Nieuwpoort's river
34 Counterpart of moi
37 Some antlered animals
38 "No, no, really . . ."
40 He succeeded two queens
41 Capital up the coast from Cape Coast
42 Hurt with a horn
43 Hoist on a ship
45 Dashes off
46 Pacific dietary staple
47 Settled
48 Jubilation
50 "Leaves and Navels" artist
51 Comic's nightmare?
52 Eli Manning, on the field

by Kelly Clark

178 HARD

ACROSS
1 Player's fee
5 Plant used in tanneries
10 Topps tidbit
14 Bandleader whose band was the New Orleans Gang
16 River into which the Big Sandy and the Little Sandy flow
17 It goes station to station
18 Private jet, maybe
19 Flummoxed
20 Delights
22 What many do at tax season
23 Cough drop brand
25 Nerves-of-steel type
27 Human member of an old TV trio
28 Sixth graders, typically
32 Whatever
33 Filing centers
34 Jailer, sailor and tailor
35 Book collection?
37 Charlton's "The Ten Commandments" co-star
40 1979 film that ends with Peter Sellers walking on water
41 Big do
42 Long-distance call?
43 Albert Einstein and others
45 Rush
46 Address loudly and at length
50 "People who fight fire with fire usually end up with __": Abigail Van Buren
51 Oscar nominee for "The Aviator"
53 Actress sister of Francis Ford Coppola
55 Disorderly conduct
56 Balanced
57 Door plate, maybe
58 Aid for the forgetful, maybe
59 CAT scan units

DOWN
1 Fodder for dairy cattle
2 Junction injunction
3 Super __
4 With 41-Down, women's fashion brand
5 Luxury hotel facility
6 Some garden ornaments
7 Lapel attachment
8 Religious agreement?
9 Deep scarlet shade
10 Pacifier
11 Horror film remake released on 6/6/06
12 They feature dogfights
13 Game pieces
15 Eminem song about an obsessed fan
21 Device used by Anubis to determine a soul's fate
24 Hymn set to music by Vivaldi and Haydn
26 Psychic mediators
29 Casting lady
30 Olympic-level
31 Ethyl acetate, for one
33 Hillary's mate
34 Eldest Bennet sister in "Pride and Prejudice"
35 1970 Simon & Garfunkel hit
36 Joined the force
37 "Yentl" setting
38 Came out with
39 Dials down
40 Note that sounds like a direction to think
41 See 4-Down
44 Far __
47 Flatten, in a way
48 __ Ramsay, hero of "The Black Stallion"
49 Brown of publishing
52 Put away
54 Symbol of Tut's power

by Patrick Berry

ACROSS

1 "Come again?"
10 They're put in for work
15 Brand whose first commercial featured a cable car
16 Large-scale detail
17 Trust issue?
18 "Bleeding Love" singer Lewis
19 Non-humanities acronym
20 When repeated, spouse's complaint
21 Walter ___, Dodgers manager before Tommy Lasorda
22 "The Fox and the Hound" fox
23 Dish that often has pea pods
25 Medium for many 13-Down
26 Emmy-winning Susan Lucci role
28 "On the hoof," in diner lingo
29 "Yeah, why not!?"
30 Kim Jong-un, for one
32 Gendered "Seinfeld" accessory
34 Shake off
36 Sticky stuff
37 Person with a lot on his plate?
41 [I find this mildly amusing]
45 Confederate
46 Rush, e.g.
48 Corners
49 Federal div. concerned with gas consumption
50 They may be settled over drinks
52 Burn
53 Shakes off
55 "If you ask me . . . ," for short
56 Give a Yelp review, say
57 Hometown of Columbus
58 "Let's do this!"
60 Secluded spaces
61 "Let's do this!"
62 Yom Kippur War leader
63 America, informally

DOWN

1 Took by force
2 Done for
3 Was on the cast of
4 ___ U.S.A.
5 Sr. stress source
6 Reznor of Nine Inch Nails
7 What blowhards blow
8 On end, to Donne
9 Concert needs, for short
10 Good for sledding, say
11 Gender-neutral possessive
12 Entertainment for general audiences?
13 Collection at the Musée d'Orsay
14 Nonactor with cameos in more than 20 Marvel movies
21 Playground comeback
23 ___ Fierce (onetime Beyoncé alter ego)
24 Certain grenade, for short
27 Batman?
29 "Neat-o-rific!"
31 Aquarium fish
33 People thinking on their feet?
35 Road sign silhouette
37 No-goodniks
38 Song that starts "Hate New York City / It's cold and it's damp"
39 Slowly picked up
40 Comeback
42 Battled
43 Model
44 Early Judaic sect
47 End
50 The Antichrist, with "the"
51 They may grab a bite
54 Lisbon lady
56 Beatles title girl with a "little white book"
58 Boring thing
59 Came down with

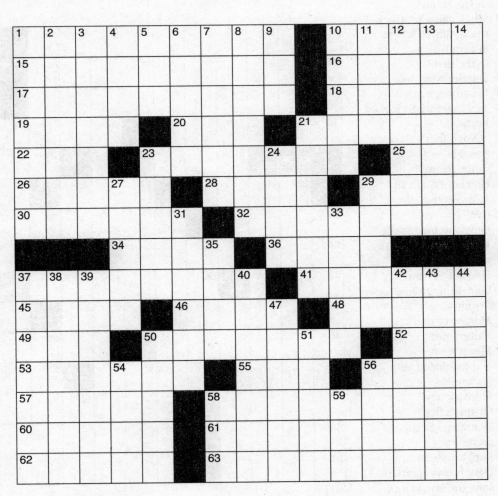

by Paolo Pasco

ACROSS

1 Like a Navy seal
11 Tall tale producer?
15 Colorful ornamental with a trunk
16 Very large, informally
17 One-stop shopping spot
18 Battleship guess
19 Advance look, commercially
20 Backing for a cartoonist
22 ___ Williams, Potsie player on "Happy Days"
24 ___-on-Thames (regatta site)
25 Little bits
27 Wet blanket?
29 Subject of the biography "Lightning in His Hand"
30 Girl's name in which the last three letters are equivalent to the first?
31 Quality wool source
33 It's an imposition
34 Acupuncturist's supply
36 Feeling
38 "OMG, that's enough!"
39 Came (from)
41 Hawkeye State city
42 John Wayne title role
44 Quick on the uptake
45 Washington Sq. Park squad
46 One not yet one, say
48 Something to live for
50 Primitive
52 Marcos of the Philippines
56 Minor flaw
57 Old-fashioned auto feature
59 Front money?
60 Obama's first Homeland Security secretary
61 Supportive cries
62 Dark brown quartz sometimes sold as a gemstone

DOWN

1 One might be involved in a sting
2 Like la mer
3 Stick with it
4 High
5 Most TV Land programming
6 Paralyzes, in a way
7 Education's ___ Tech
8 "What do you call a fake noodle? An impasta," e.g.
9 Foreign term of address
10 Ones put on retainer?
11 "Not another bite for me!"
12 Imprinting tool
13 Like Alzheimer's disease
14 Plot lines
21 Believe in
23 Frederick Forsyth thriller "The ___ File"
25 Four-for-four Super Bowl-winning QB
26 2.5%
28 Seeing right through
30 Thus
31 All the suspects in "The Usual Suspects"
32 ___ Land, 1954 Kirk Douglas sci-fi role
35 Currency in Freetown
37 Accept
40 Animato
43 Edmond ___, the Count of Monte Cristo
45 "Your call"
47 Mountain lakes
49 Lollapalooza
51 53rd "state quarter" locale
53 Capriole
54 "Two Years Before the Mast" author
55 Leaving nothing out
58 ___ Tower Gardens, National Historic Landmark in Florida

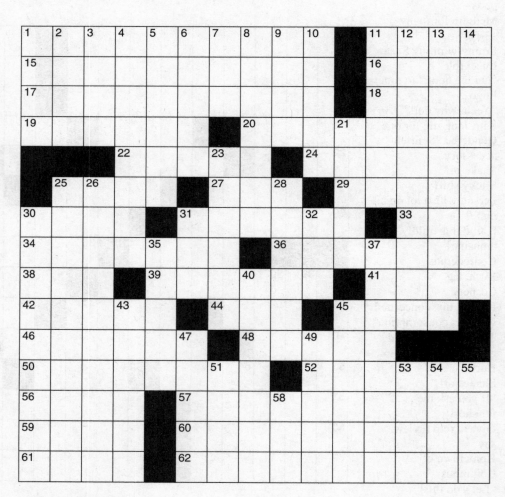

by Mark Diehl

ACROSS

1 Social app with the slogan "the world's catalog of ideas"
10 City with the world's largest clock face
15 Hypnotized
16 Joan of Arc quality
17 Kale or quinoa, it's said
18 Phone charger feature
19 Father of Fear, in myth
20 Many sisters
22 This, in Taxco
23 A crane might hover over one
24 "Good thinking!"
26 Active ingredient in marijuana, for short
28 City in central Israel
29 Through
31 Place for bowlers
35 Ornamental garden installation
37 Quick tennis match
38 Part of a devil costume
39 Fuming
41 "You don't want to miss it!"
42 Bit of bronze
43 Statue outside Boston's TD Garden
44 Lunk
45 Watering holes
48 Eye-opening problem?
52 First name in gossip
53 Knee jerk, perhaps
55 Political accusation
56 Bill Clinton or George W. Bush, informally
58 Only highest-grossing film of the year that lost money
60 Stocking stuff
61 Spots that might smear
62 Pirouetting, perhaps
63 Bought or sold, e.g.

DOWN

1 Fibonacci, notably
2 Temper
3 Pickup points
4 Statistician's tool
5 Say irregardless?
6 Nickname for a two-time Wimbledon winner
7 State
8 Variety of quick bread
9 Multimedia think piece
10 Stephen Curry was one in '15 and '16
11 Like some seals
12 Feature of the 1876 or 2000 presidential election
13 Cup or bowl, but not a plate
14 2012 thriller with John Goodman and Alan Arkin
21 Straight men
25 Boobs
26 4.0, maybe
27 They're straight
30 Chick's tail?
31 Party person
32 Bacteriologist's discovery
33 What emo songs may convey
34 Org. doing pat-downs
36 "Tommyrot!"
40 Large letter in a manuscript
41 Hare-hunting hounds
46 Painter Veronese
47 European country whose flag features a George Cross
48 Relieve, in a way
49 Child of Uranus
50 Passing concern?
51 Off
52 Informal move
54 It's water under the bridge
57 Successful campaign sign
59 Cut of the pie chart: Abbr.

by Andrew Kingsley

ACROSS

1 Where to belt one down and belt one out
11 Latch (onto)
15 Not-so-firm affirmative
16 Yasmina ___, two-time Tony-winning playwright
17 Ones hitting snares
18 Fabric finish?
19 Political pundit Perino
20 "Qué ___?" ("How are you?": Sp.)
21 Demanding occupations?
23 Means of forecasting
25 It may be spiked in winter
27 Hamper
28 Sushi order
30 ___ Minor
32 Owner of Flix, in brief
33 Airhead
37 Mo. with All Saints' Day
38 Cleans up
39 Way down in Wayne Manor
42 Relative of -ish or -ory
43 Deliverer of the U.N. General Assembly speech "Atoms for Peace"
45 Musician with the 2016 album "The Ship"
46 View from the Ponte alla Carraia
47 On, in Orléans
48 Lugs
50 Terrain maker
52 Belt
56 Bandage
58 Monogram for Christ
60 Postcard printing process, for short
61 Essential element
62 Essential element
65 Treat since 1912
66 Popular ice pop
67 Danny Ocean's wife
68 Group that rejected its 2006 Rock and Roll Hall of Fame induction

DOWN

1 Little buddy
2 Biblical name meaning "exalted father"
3 Get together after school?
4 Often-replaced reference works
5 Suffix with Québec
6 Last name of a comic strip title teen
7 Alternative to Dasani or Deer Park
8 Obscure
9 Put it to
10 ___ Sea (Bay of Whales locale)
11 Hibachi feature
12 Song lyric following "But as long as you love me so"
13 Opening for an E.P.A. worker?
14 Opportunity, e.g.
22 Title princess of a comic opera
24 Wooley of "Rawhide"
26 Helldiver, e.g.
29 Like the Arctic Ocean vis-à-vis the Atlantic
31 Set of seven countries, informally
33 Great point
34 Something hammers hit
35 Gives a gloss
36 Gerontologist's subject
40 Accordingly
41 Landscape alternative
44 Alternative to Nytol
46 11-Down buildup
49 Community spirit
51 Like talk, it's said
53 Maker of the Pocket Fisherman and Electric Food Dehydrator
54 Midway, e.g.
55 Dixie cakes
57 Some PC keys
59 One of about 1,000 in Lux.
63 Severe soreness
64 ___ Midway

by Jim Page

ACROSS

1 Ultimate necessity
8 Needs grease, maybe
14 Cup holder
15 School whose mascot is Riptide the Pelican
16 Became untied
17 Intro to Comp Sci, for Data Structures, e.g.
18 Push away
19 Giant in sports entertainment
20 Made new?
21 Something you might take a pass on
22 Valuable diamond
24 Hosp. readout
25 Bigwig
28 One ___ (multivitamin)
29 Highly sought-after things
31 Foucault's "This Is Not ___"
32 This
36 Certain powerful engines, briefly
37 Warrants
38 Newswoman Burnett
39 Guiding light?
40 Writes to briefly?
43 Replies of understanding
44 Month with two natl. holidays
45 Auto name discontinued in 1986
48 One is a prize for scoring
50 Endowed with from the start, as money
52 Nobody special
53 Mace and shield, e.g.
54 Took for a ride
55 Hopeful
56 Closely following
57 Order that's rarely followed?

DOWN

1 Play
2 Fair, e.g.
3 Key
4 Gem
5 Place for a long run, maybe
6 Big ___ Conference
7 Summer Olympics event
8 "A Prairie Home Companion" broadcast site
9 Becomes a traitor
10 "Where Is the Life That Late ___?" ("Kiss Me, Kate" number)
11 One with connections to traveling speakers?
12 Largest sesamoid bones
13 Et ___ (footnote abbr.)
14 Not one's best effort, in coachspeak
21 Ache
23 They can turn red in a flash
26 Contract employee?
27 Actor with the title role in "Robin Hood: Men in Tights"
28 Loan figs.
29 Beam
30 Some linemen: Abbr.
31 Just do it
32 Baseball exec Epstein
33 What to call Judge Judy
34 Words of longing
35 Some help from above
39 Southernmost city on I-35
40 Looms
41 Wolverine of Marvel Comics, e.g.
42 Derisive reaction
44 Reno, for one
46 They're not pros
47 Animal in un parc zoologique
49 Old "Red, White & You" sloganeer
50 Small nail
51 River to the Seine
52 "What you can get away with," according to Andy Warhol

by David Liben-Nowell

ACROSS

1 They get picked up at clubs
5 Engages in a bit of back-and-forth
10 Bread and drink
14 First name in court fiction
15 Goddesses guarding the gates of Olympus
16 Mediterranean pizza topping
17 V feature
19 Charlie Bucket's creator
20 Double-dipping, e.g.
21 One on the Lee-ward side?
22 Not working
24 Political writer/blogger Klein
25 Hits with a big charge
26 Name-dropper's word
27 Volunteer's place: Abbr.
28 Lib. arts major
30 Start to drift, say
32 Wacky morning radio team
36 Refuse
37 Like many roasted potatoes
39 Pollen ___
40 Secluded spot
41 Up until, in poetry
42 "Dona ___ Pacem" (Latin hymn)
46 Man-to-man alternative
47 Kind
50 Blow away
51 Buddy from the block
52 Homologous
54 Singer with the 1954 album "Frontier Ballads"
55 Nascar Hall-of-Famer Jarrett and others
56 Lack life
57 Means of inheritance
58 Waxed
59 Hopper full of dirt?
60 Latin word on Missouri's state seal

DOWN

1 Something to get a spot out of?
2 Secrets
3 Utters unthinkingly
4 Give background information
5 Refuse
6 Key to the city, e.g.
7 Courtroom activity
8 Oversize hip-hop tops
9 Witness
10 Old letters in the mail
11 Starting time?
12 Alternative to Wi-Fi
13 Four-time All-Star third baseman of the 1960s–'70s
18 Dump, e.g.
23 Some sorority women
24 Historic institution on the Jubilee River
29 One of Us?
31 Slightly
32 Chess situation in which any move is a bad move
33 Witness
34 Directive that has some teeth to it?
35 Visitors' announcement
38 Signaled
43 Light shades
44 Motivate
45 Not one-sided, in a way
48 Free from faults
49 Second-largest body in the asteroid belt
53 Neighbor of Victoria: Abbr.
54 "Poppycock!"

by Damon Gulczynski

ACROSS

1 Really huge number
10 Bridge pair, briefly?
15 In a foreboding manner
16 Bane of cereal grain
17 Sufficiently good
18 Sauce often made with lemon juice
19 TiVo remote button
20 Not go to
21 Jerks
22 Lose, as a carrier might with a call
24 New York restaurateur with a Tony Award
26 Doomed
27 Round of four
29 B-ball
31 ___ Dolly ("Winter's Bone" heroine)
32 Contraction in Hamlet's soliloquy
34 1972 blaxploitation film with a soundtrack by Curtis Mayfield
36 Gun point?
40 Fur-lined cloak
41 Tight hold
43 A.L. or N.L. East: Abbr.
44 Some sports cars
45 Six-time U.S. Open champ
47 Get one's fill?
51 "That was exhausting!"
53 Ammonia and others
55 Longtime TV figure known for his garage
56 Dawgs
58 Liver by the Loire?
60 Sculptor who described art as "a fruit that grows in man"
61 "A Dog of Flanders" author
62 Bails
64 Beehive Blender brand
65 It fell in 2016 for the first time since 1919
66 Reviewers of scientific papers
67 Cause of rebellion, maybe

DOWN

1 Thanksgiving table decorations
2 A in physics class?
3 Adolescent program, slangily
4 Goddess who saved Odysseus
5 Records
6 Doesn't show oneself, say
7 So-called "Shakespeare of the Prophets"
8 Veterans
9 Host of the web series "Emoji Science"
10 Junior posthumously inducted into the Football Hall of Fame
11 Victorians
12 Searches for oneself
13 Mustard and others
14 Dirty look
21 Rewarded for waiting
23 Climber's aid
25 Decorate
28 Blacken a bit
30 Baseball commissioner during the steroid era
33 Robot arm movers
35 Navratilova, to 45-Across, e.g.
36 "Well, la-di-frickin'-da!"
37 It has big screens for small films
38 Apple operating system that's also a geographical name
39 One to one, say
42 Seemingly everywhere
46 ___ l'oeil
48 Hideous foe of Popeye
49 Strips, as a ship
50 Valve with a disc at the end of a vertically set stem
52 Like the Atlantic Ocean, slightly, from year to year
54 Barely drink
57 They may ring after parties
59 She, in Venice
62 Project
63 Stop: Abbr.

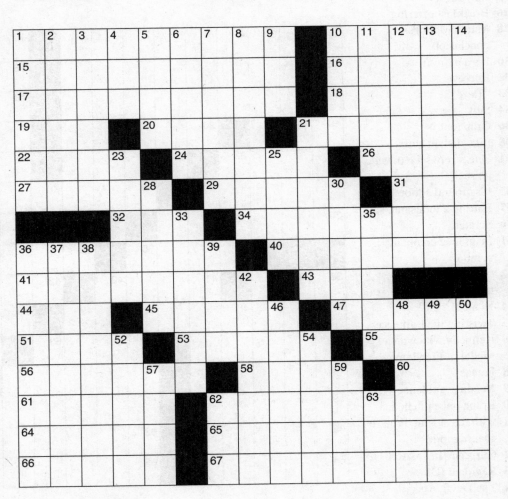

by Kristian House

ACROSS

1 Got smart
10 Section of a golf bag
15 Capital where "hello" is pronounced "johm riab sua"
16 Two cents' worth
17 He played Moe Greene in "The Godfather"
18 "Capeesh?"
19 Title for Romulus
20 Block at an airport, perhaps
21 Move very freely
22 Very dark
24 Drone base
25 Animal whose name is derived from the Latin for "ghosts"
26 Breakfast offering
28 March Madness conclusion
30 It's a natural
32 Burrow
33 "Tabs"
34 Suit
36 Grab (onto)
38 Like distant stars
41 One rarely seen outside its shell?
43 It's around a foot
47 Batting a thousand, say
50 Scratch
51 Insurance company symbol
52 "No __!" ("Sure thing!")
54 Noah of "ER"
55 Twisting the knife, say
56 Kennedy who won a Medal of Freedom
58 Fracas
59 Needing guidance
60 Brand once pitched with the slogan "You're soaking in it"
62 Currency in 15-Across
63 Regional IDs
64 The Devil, e.g.
65 "Ha ha, what a dork!"

DOWN

1 Comment made with an eye roll
2 Soil scientist's measure
3 Banished
4 Object of controversial hunts
5 Modern brain-scanning procedure, for short
6 Late Jurassic, e.g.
7 Cheating
8 Lacking courtesy
9 Frustrating exchange
10 Leeway
11 What a goose may stand on
12 Unbeatable
13 Small lollipops with collectible wrappers
14 Exercised control over
23 Dearest
27 Like Y's
29 Gentle rising and falling, of a sort
31 In the offing
35 Piece of brunch-making equipment
37 "Look who's being catty!"
38 Light carriage
39 Trouble getting started
40 Non-PC sort
42 Rarer than rare
44 Going out with a hot model?
45 Everywhere
46 She famously said "I'm single because I was born that way"
48 Rapper with the 1995 hit "I Wish"
49 Faucet brand
53 "If you want to sulk, go right ahead"
57 Crazy, in a 2010 Shakira hit
61 Common palindromic text

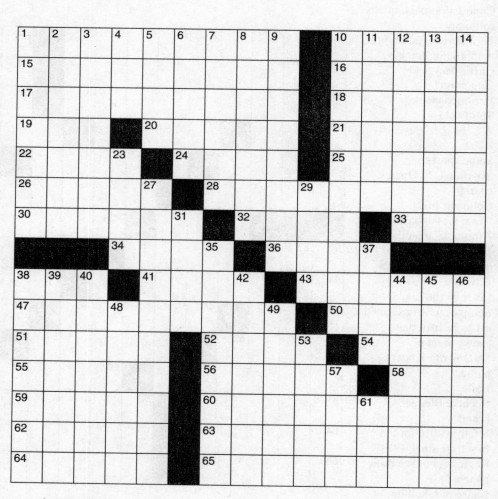

by Peter Wentz

ACROSS

1 Handle things
5 Try out
9 Additional
14 With nobody playing, say
16 Retro stereo component
17 Life preserver?
18 Katherine of NBC's "State of Affairs"
19 Observes closely
20 Girl adopted by Silas Marner
21 Anxious
22 Anti-___ League (Progressive Era organization)
24 Blade brand
26 On the program
28 Feels deep sympathy
32 Site of Oscar Wilde's trials
34 By and by
35 Sound effects pioneer Jack
36 Mandatory courses
37 Eponym of Bible history
39 Ehrich ___ a.k.a. Harry Houdini
40 Was unconsciously disturbing?
41 "I, Claudius" figure
43 Blathers
45 Component of some biodiesels
50 Ones coming ashore
51 Put away for someone
53 Drafted
54 One with changing needs
55 It may be off the charts
56 Like some physicians
57 Fuses
58 Person offering you a fortune
59 Command that a dog shouldn't follow

DOWN

1 Section of a botanical garden
2 School zone?
3 Top of the winter
4 Swords, in Sèvres
5 PC-linking program
6 It's hard to find in a crowd
7 8:00–9:00 on TV, e.g.
8 Proverbial certainty
9 Shakespeare character who coins the term "primrose path"
10 Winner of back-to-back Best Rock Instrumental Grammys in 1980 and 1981
11 The ordinary folk
12 "Scientists dream about doing great things. ___ do them": James A. Michener
13 Capacity
15 Gigli and pici, for two
23 "Dear ___" (1960s–'70s radio program)
25 Longtime "Voice of the New York Yankees"
27 Easter stock
28 Does some grilling
29 Quarters' quarters?
30 Group that almost can't fail?
31 Added to a plant
33 Treat with violent disrespect
35 Become dull
38 Lives the high life
39 Go downhill
42 Chicago Sun-Times columnist Richard
44 Soft options?
46 Brainy high school clique
47 Cosmic path
48 Former Trump Organization member
49 Like Ziegfeld girls
50 Thick of things, in a manner of speaking
52 Kid Cudi's "Day 'n' ___"

by Patrick Berry

188 HARD

ACROSS
1 First name in fantasy fiction
6 Payola payoff
10 Branch extension
14 Subject for une chanteuse
15 When repeated, singer of the 1987 #1 hit "Head to Toe"
16 Exclamation sometimes said with a hand over the mouth
17 One in la-la land
19 Clichéd gift for a prisoner
20 Christ's end?
21 For instance
22 Snack brand first produced at Disneyland in the 1960s
24 Street __
26 Alternative to a snap
28 Asia's __ Darya River
29 Structural support
31 Stephen who was nominated for a 1992 Best Actor Oscar
32 Title sometimes shortened by removing its middle letter
34 Dish that often includes anchovies
37 Website for people interested in "cultivating" a relationship?
38 "Lemme be straight with you . . ."
39 Good-for-nothing
40 Letterhead abbr.
41 5½-point type
45 Falcons, on scoreboards
46 Staple of Victorian architecture
49 Square
50 McCarthy in Hollywood
52 Break down, maybe
54 Terse admission
55 For the ages
56 Some kitchen utensils
59 Court psychologist's ruling

60 Where Arthur Ashe played college tennis
61 Book before Philemon
62 Summer coolers
63 Round end, of a sort
64 Curry of the N.B.A.

DOWN
1 Educational foundations
2 Lend
3 One day's drive, maybe
4 N.F.C. South pro
5 They're graded in geology class
6 Spot for autograph seekers
7 Top
8 One who works a lot?
9 Bulldog rival
10 Spelling with lines
11 "Whew!," upon arriving home
12 Cry before rage-quitting
13 Plaster of paris, essentially
18 King James, e.g.
23 Country that's home to Dracula's Castle
25 Tickets, in slang
27 Pupil
30 They're often said to be sitting or moving
33 Claim
35 Angst-ridden and moody
36 Currency of Peru
37 Place to do some shots?
38 It has rules for writing

39 San Diego suburb known as the "Jewel of the Hills"
42 Wing it?
43 Get misty
44 Catch in a net
47 Deplete
48 One exposed by a flip-flop
51 Summer coolers
53 Counter orders?
57 Bitter __
58 Card

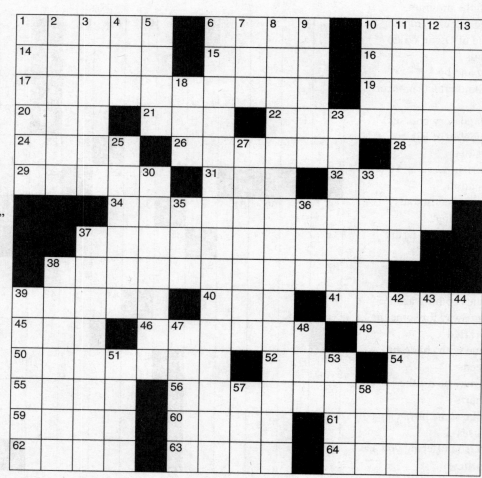

by Andrew J. Ries

ACROSS

1 One making waves over the waves
10 Bridge support
14 Lothario's activity
16 Wearing red to a Chinese funeral, e.g.
17 It has no life
19 Very well-pitched
20 Become flowery
21 Fat: Fr.
22 Cuff
23 Company that makes Tamiflu
24 Mailed or faxed
26 Head of Hogwarts
28 Salon job
30 Says "Top o' the morning," say
32 Shoshone language relative
33 Quite removed (from)
36 Manager honored at Cooperstown in 2013
40 Marker
41 Kitchen drawers?
43 Pilates class sights
45 Southern African game
46 Give a raise?
50 Zoom (along)
52 Many are named after M.L.K.
54 Sit (down) heavily
55 Bond femme fatale
57 Prestidigitator's word
58 Summoning statement
60 Cousin of a kite
61 Modern parents may try to limit it
62 Jazz combo?
63 Broadway star who was on Nixon's list of enemies

DOWN

1 Playground set
2 Painter Jean-___ Fragonard
3 Certain Cornhusker
4 Film setting?
5 Drawn together
6 "Huckleberry Finn" character
7 Conductor who has a hall at Tanglewood named after him
8 Worthy of reference
9 Lego competitor
10 Administer, as a shot
11 "The Consolation of Philosophy" author
12 Aeschylus, Sophocles and Aristophanes
13 College recruitment org.
15 Camera manufacturer whose slogan is "Be a Hero"
18 Shout of surprise
22 Genre that "The Long Goodbye" is based on
25 "Cake Boss" network
27 World capital with 40 islands within its city limits
29 Breakfast spot?
31 Cannon shot in Hollywood
33 Word shouted before "Fire!"
34 Material for mounting photos
35 Get perfectly pitched, in a way
37 Midwest college town
38 Farm butter
39 Openings in the computer field?
42 Longtime "Meet the Press" moderator
44 Places for pilots
45 Digs around
47 Cesario's lover in literature
48 Serious
49 Worked the field, in a way
51 "Yet that thy brazen gates of heaven may ___": Shak.
53 Pianist McCoy ___, member of the John Coltrane Quartet
55 Hearing command
56 Brief moments
57 Start of a classic boast
59 c, in a text

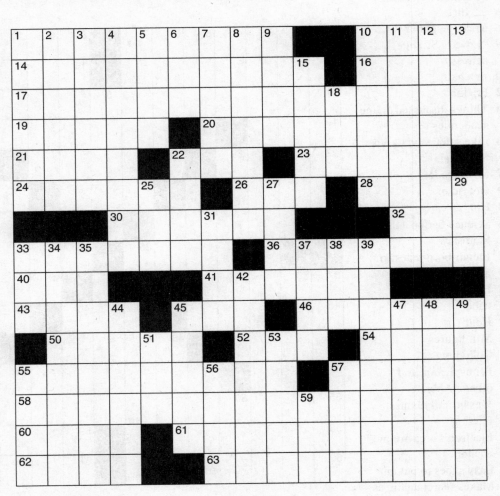

by Andrew Zhou

ACROSS

1 Collection of high lights?
8 Something a dog might fetch
15 Capital of the French department of Loiret
16 Smokeless explosive
17 Youngest-ever Nobel Prize recipient
19 Pennsylvania county named for an animal
20 Delights
21 Cab alternative
22 Cold shower?
24 Missouri and Arizona
25 Fast-food menu information: Abbr.
26 ___ dirt
28 Mich. neighbor
29 "Love Is Strange" actress
30 In a ball
32 Frickin'
34 Things discussed at une académie
36 Like safeties vis-à-vis field goals
37 Missed a lot
40 Got rid of
43 Hot
44 Science fiction author Stanislaw
46 Indian-born maestro
47 Spanish pronoun
48 Head of an Indian tribe
50 Hold
51 Mil. figures
52 Colloquy
54 Pennsylvania and others: Abbr.
55 Was brutally honest
58 Firedog
59 Electron's area around an atom
60 Easy shoes to put on
61 Makes secret again, as court documents

DOWN

1 "I wasn't expecting it, but . . ."
2 Skipping sounds
3 "Seriously . . ."
4 New Deal power agcy.
5 Colt 45, e.g., informally
6 Writer Nin
7 Classic film whose soundtrack is famously composed entirely of strings
8 One going around the block?
9 Shakes
10 Portfolio parts, for short
11 Many an email attachment
12 Italian food named after a queen
13 Amazon, e.g.
14 Curbs
18 Clearing
23 Things corporations and fire trucks both have
25 [Emergency!]
27 Like kiwi fruits
29 Engine sound
31 Cool, in slang
33 Drain
35 Pacific Island group
37 Dishes sometimes served with Riojas
38 Blink of an eye
39 ___-A
41 Like the Olympic flame
42 Fairy tale figures
45 "Someone who allows you to see the hope inside yourself," per Oprah
48 Dakota dialect
49 Olympic skier Phil or Steve
52 Modern know-it-all
53 Bull Run victors
56 Double ___
57 "I already have other plans," often

by Mary Lou Guizzo

ACROSS

1 Golf handicap of zero
8 Like some garages
14 Where Forrest Gump played college football
15 Everything included
16 "Funky Cold Medina" rapper
17 Gives a walk-through, say
18 Fig. on a quarterly report
19 Test pattern?
21 Certain flight pattern
22 1970s TV spinoff
24 Some mouse cells
25 Broadway score?
26 Weigh station sight
27 Place to go when you're not going to the races, for short?
28 Joneses (for)
29 Creamy chilled soup
33 Source of break-dancing beats
35 N.B.A. M.V.P. who has hosted "Saturday Night Live"
36 Inroad
37 New Agey sounds
38 Facial option at a spa
42 "Everyone's private driver" sloganeer
43 Kind of walk
45 River of forgetfulness
46 Jerk
47 "The Chalk Garden" playwright, 1955
49 Shipload
50 1983 hit song that mentions Santa Monica Boulevard
52 Arcane matters
54 Lazy bum
55 Access
56 Playwright Eve
57 Pinch-hitter

DOWN

1 Figures in ribald Greek plays
2 Make a decent person out of?
3 Stochastic
4 Vigoda of "The Godfather"
5 Shire of "The Godfather"
6 "Get outta here!"
7 Collaborative computer coding event
8 Plants sometimes used to make flour
9 Letter of the law?
10 Not you specifically
11 Exchange words
12 Creature that Dalí walked on a leash in public
13 Puts back in the original state
15 Weapon that's thrown
20 Swedish-based maker of infant carriers
23 Seedy place to drink
25 "I'm down with that"
27 Quattuor doubled
28 Rip off
30 Reply that's a bit of a humblebrag
31 Contestants in a war of words?
32 BJ's competitor, informally
33 Major blood protein
34 Cry before taking the plunge
36 Pointless
39 Make it
40 What it always starts with?
41 College where Rutherford B. Hayes was valedictorian
43 Less tanned
44 "OMG!," old-style
45 Component of the combo drug Sinemet
47 Actress Daniels or Neuwirth
48 Practice exam?
51 ___ d'Isère (French ski resort)
53 Spam's place

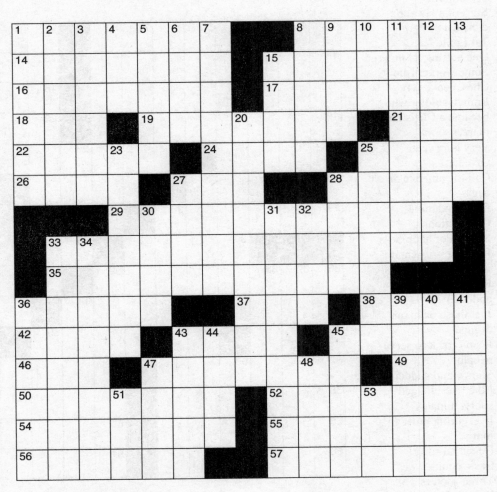

by James Mulhern

ACROSS

1 One of a pair of cuddlers
9 Desired response to a 3-Down
15 Handel bars
16 Bartender's stock
17 Participates in quid pro quo
18 Edward Gorey's "The Gashlycrumb ___"
19 In trouble for base violations?
20 1982 international chart-topper by Trio with a repetitive title
21 Digits in flats, maybe
22 Noted challenges for movers
24 About 92% of britannium
25 Start of a lawyer's conclusion
27 Tar liquid
28 One getting hammered
29 Some workers along Chesapeake Bay
31 Roman soldier who became a Christian martyr
33 Very long span
35 Grinder
36 Call to someone on deck
40 Like sand dunes
44 G.I. portions
45 Symbol of happiness
47 Iraklion is its capital
48 First Chinese dynasty
49 Relating to the abdomen
51 Just those of Juan's things?
52 It's on track to serve people
54 Showy and sudden
56 Like live-blogged sports updates
57 Everything must go in it
58 Deceitful sorts
59 Basic count
60 Three-footers
61 Hoarder's squalor

DOWN

1 Western wear
2 Major export of Western Australia
3 Series of bloopers
4 Puts away under pressure?
5 ___ deck
6 ___ deck
7 Where a mud engineer works
8 Awful rating
9 Showboat
10 Billy the Kid, e.g.
11 Rear
12 Howard Hughes, for one
13 Taking seriously
14 Subject of the 2013 film "The Fifth Estate"
23 Chris of CBS's "The Good Wife"
26 Kind of diagram
28 Motive that makes sense
30 Spelling pro?
32 Decker or Dickerson of the N.F.L.
34 {}, in mathematics
36 Off-road racer
37 Huffington of The Huffington Post
38 March interrupter, maybe
39 Purchased
41 Take to term
42 Headliners at le Palais Garnier, e.g.
43 Spelunker's activity
46 Place for an anchor
49 Brand once advertised with the line "They never get on your nerves"
50 Addition sign
53 Give up
55 Subway Series squad

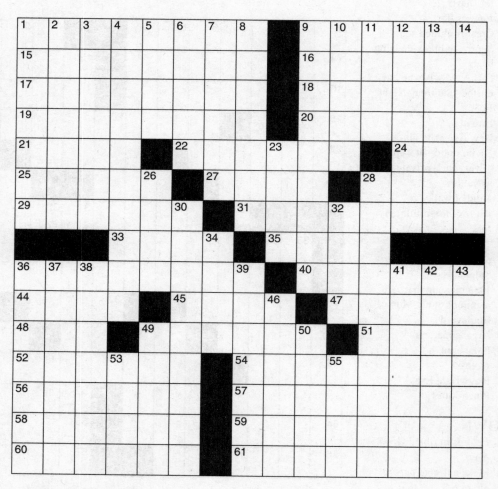

by David Woolf

ACROSS

1 Yoda, e.g.
11 Communication problem?
15 Last of a series of nicknames
16 Zero
17 Billy Crystal's role in "The Princess Bride"
18 Enigma machine decoder Turing
19 It's not a welcome sign
20 Facebook and others
21 Primary funding sources, briefly
22 Facebook, for one
23 Org. whose symbol is an eagle atop a key
24 How garden vegetables may be planted
26 Upset
28 Manicure destroyer
29 Hot Wheels garages?
33 Rhoda's TV mom
34 Emerald ___ borer
37 Expert savers
38 Constitution Hall grp.
39 Marathon champ Pippig
40 Mesozoic Era period
42 Home of Queen Margrethe II
44 Rank below marquis
47 "Let's do it!"
48 Sch. whose first building was Dallas Hall
51 Matches, at a table
53 "Caravan of Courage: An ___ Adventure" (1984 "Star Wars" spinoff)
54 Some Siouans
55 Bayh of Indiana politics
56 Flock gathering place
57 Group getting its kicks?
59 Rep
60 "I could use some help here . . ."
61 First name in architecture
62 Place to test the water

DOWN

1 Harry Potter's father
2 Alchemist's concoction
3 Frito-Lay chip
4 "Bleah!"
5 El Capitan platform
6 Literary hero whose name is Turkish for "lion"
7 Parts of a flight
8 2012 Republican National Convention host
9 Connection concerns, for short
10 "Toy Story" dino
11 Show impatience with
12 Developing company?
13 Wrapper that's hard to remove?
14 It's tailored to guys
24 Drinks with domed lids
25 Interest for a cryptozoologist
27 Impasse
28 Quadrant separator
30 "___ serious?"
31 Lab report?
32 Pay termination?
34 Nielsens measure
35 Fancy glasses
36 Malady with many "remedies"
41 Legal precedents
43 Get by
45 Awaken
46 Get support from
48 Photosynthesis opening
49 Interest of a mycologist
50 Quotidian
52 Old dummy
54 "Wait, I know that!"
57 Some savers' assets
58 Main hub for Virgin America, for short

by Robyn Weintraub

194 HARD

ACROSS

1 Eighty-sixes
7 Rhetorical creation
15 Green
16 First Palme d'Or-winning film directed by a woman (1993)
17 "That thought already occurred to me"
19 Let fate decide, say
20 Subatomic particles with zero spin
21 Kind of cabbage
22 Pillory
26 Pump option, for short
27 Marinara sauce ingredients
32 Structures with excellent insulation
34 Telemarketing tactic
36 Try to find oneself?
38 Warming
39 David Fincher thriller of 2014
41 Had a list
42 Bid on a hand unsuited for suit play, maybe
43 Cusk-___ (deepest living fish, at 27,000+ feet)
45 Rockets
46 Leaders in robes
48 Screens
53 Onetime Fandango competitor
58 One with a long stretch to go?
60 Blaring
61 Fisher for compliments on one's dress?
62 "Les Misérables" extra
63 Managed

DOWN

1 Infatuated, old-style
2 Italian city where Pliny the Elder and Younger were born
3 Matrix specifications
4 "Sob"
5 Type of mobile phone plan
6 Take to living together, with "up"
7 Austrian philosopher Rudolf
8 "Phew!"
9 One might turn on it
10 Per
11 Modern flight amenity
12 Main ingredient of rémoulade
13 Composer of many limericks, for short
14 "À ___ la Liberté" (1931 René Clair film)
18 Period of a revolution?
22 San ___
23 Urge
24 It's all the same
25 Einstein-___ bridge (wormhole)
27 Game's turning point?
28 Brand of sponge
29 Cousin of a skate
30 Neuter
31 Places for runners
33 First word in many temple names
35 Something odd in roulette?
37 Pricing model for many apps
40 Newspaper name that becomes a beverage if you insert an "a" after its fifth letter
44 "___ a little!"
47 State fair attractions
48 Uphill climb, say
49 Drone's place
50 Breaking a comb, in Japan, e.g.
51 "I agree," in slang
52 Toni Morrison novel
54 Menu bar heading
55 Plot feature in "Hansel and Gretel"
56 Old brand in the shaving aisle
57 Puzzle designer Rubik
59 Young women's grp.

by Julian Lim

ACROSS

1 Connections
4 Connections to the sternum
8 Not assured at all
13 "You can figure as well as I can"
16 Treasure
17 Cream song with the lyric "Dance floor is like the sea, / Ceiling is the sky"
18 Things that may be compressed
19 Excluded category in the Paleo diet
20 Little treasure
21 Now
22 Kind of wave
23 Wasabi go-with in sushi meals
24 List heading
25 People who are in them are out, in brief
26 Shavit with the 2013 best seller "My Promised Land"
27 Where Spike Lee earned his M.F.A.
30 Little: Fr.
31 Not identifying with one's assigned sex
34 1851 Sojourner Truth speech
35 Online addresses, in part
36 "Ur hilarious!"
37 Bit of evasion
38 Still
39 Two or three sets, say
42 Where the Taj Mahotsav festival is held
44 Either director of "Inside Llewyn Davis"
46 Part of MSG
47 Fit
49 Info in a Yelp listing: Abbr.
50 Either half of a 1973 "duel"
51 Lacked options
52 Ask

54 Tribe whose name means "long tail"
55 Dessert so-called for its portions of flour, butter, eggs and sugar
56 Purchase at a golf pro shop
57 Purchases at a golf pro shop
58 Flushed

DOWN

1 "Don't you doubt me!"
2 "You cheated!"
3 Round containers?
4 Bet (on)
5 Subj. of many antiglobalization protests
6 Threat of a strike, in labor negotiations
7 Lead
8 Birdbrained
9 Birdbrain
10 Typical "S.N.L." start
11 Something you can control the volume with?
12 "Me?" follower
14 "___, boy!"
15 Terse and unadorned, as writing
23 Part of MGM's motto
26 "Babalú" bandleader
28 Ones ranking above knaves
29 Not realized
31 Fashion mogul Gunn
32 ___ Marcos, Tex.

33 Some "CSI" figs.
34 App with over 200 free stations
35 Place to play with toys
36 Things that might be batted at a ball
39 Approach
40 Something not many people laugh at
41 Blew it
43 Floral symbol of patience
45 ". . . but I could be wrong"
46 Comedian Maron
48 Superlatively
50 Contends (for)
53 Clément Marot poem "A ___ Damoyselle Malade"

by Natan Last

ACROSS

1 Something that might be built around a police station
8 Hen tracks
15 Came aboard, in a way
16 Long-running Joel McHale show on E!
17 Not free
18 Seedy place
19 Bengali who won the 1913 Literature Nobel
20 Small glass disk used as an ornament in a stained-glass window
21 Melted munchie
22 Kind of bean
23 Follower of a team
24 Rear
25 Source of anago sushi
27 Golf units: Abbr.
28 Roughly half of all binary code
29 "Friendly staff" or "For a limited time only"
31 Swallowing worry in an old wives' tale
36 Potential libel defendant
37 Next __
38 Latin trio leader
41 No-brainers?
42 Call from the lobby, perhaps
43 "Utopia" writer, 1516
45 "__ thou love me?": Juliet
46 Completely block
47 "The difference between ordinary and extraordinary," per Vladimir Horowitz
49 Steve Buscemi's role in "Reservoir Dogs"
50 Reveal
51 Triple-platinum Lady Gaga hit of 2011
52 Longtime fitness guru Jack
53 Keep close relations?
54 Part of a physical
55 Common dorm room decorations

DOWN

1 Words of explanation
2 Something sweet potatoes provide
3 Brightly colored marine fish
4 Three albums bound together, e.g.
5 Hero-worship, say
6 Jazz pianist Allison
7 Raid target
8 Forte
9 Directive in tennis after odd-numbered games
10 On a pension: Abbr.
11 Lent symbols
12 Unclear, as thinking
13 Put off guard
14 Blender settings
20 Goes without a leash
22 A child can have a blast with it
25 People ruled by an elective monarchy
26 __ al Khaymah (one of U.A.E.'s seven emirates)
30 Isolate
32 Go head-to-head with?
33 Doctor's patient, e.g.
34 Create a tunnel beneath
35 "The Brady Bunch" bunch
38 Shot glass?
39 Béchamel sauce with Gruyère added
40 Font of knowledge
44 Brilliance
46 Easily outscores
48 What calisthenics improve
49 One up front?
51 High-pitched cry

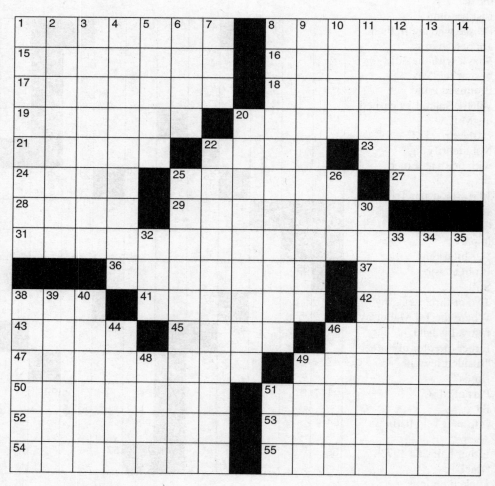

by Mark Diehl

ACROSS

1 Ones making the rules?
16 "Thanks"
17 Passage between Sicily and the toe of Italy
18 Laughfests
19 Take home, perhaps?
20 ___ scripta (statutes)
21 Blyth of "Mildred Pierce"
22 Word before or after "what"
23 Org. opposed to weaving?
25 Scottish refusal
27 Band from the East
29 "1984" concern
38 Pre-buffet declaration
39 Take legal action, say
40 Sheep-counting times
41 Gendered Spanish suffix
42 Prize for Pizarro
43 Gulf War ally
46 Occasion for dragon dances
48 Cousin of a zebra
51 Something that might interrupt a flight, for short
53 "Little ___"
55 Frequent flier
57 Didn't mince words
60 It's of no concern to a usurer
61 Showed caution, in a way

DOWN

1 Perfume named for Baryshnikov
2 Shirley of "Goldfinger"
3 It comes with strings attached
4 Cross words
5 "Mila 18" novelist
6 Abbr. after many a military name
7 Twenty: Prefix
8 Faboo
9 Go, for one
10 Whistle blower?
11 Model X maker
12 "___ complicated"
13 Labor day highlight
14 Batman co-creator Bob
15 Memphis-based record label
22 Large beer mug
24 "Stay"
25 Ad follower?
26 Hopeless
28 Doesn't need a thing
29 Server's bread and butter
30 Round openings in domes
31 Shredded
32 French thinker?
33 Sounds during a massage
34 Arteries: Abbr.
35 Definitive disclaimer
36 Just slightly
37 Seas overseas
44 "Bird on ___" (Mel Gibson/Goldie Hawn comedy)
45 Picked up on
46 Tin anniversary
47 ___-deux
48 Fictional title character who declares "How puzzling all these changes are!"
49 Sub standard?
50 Way up
51 Hit the ground
52 Transparent sheet
54 More than more
55 Org. with many banned Super Bowl ads
56 "Before ___ you go . . ."
58 Clue follower: Abbr.
59 What's left on a farm?

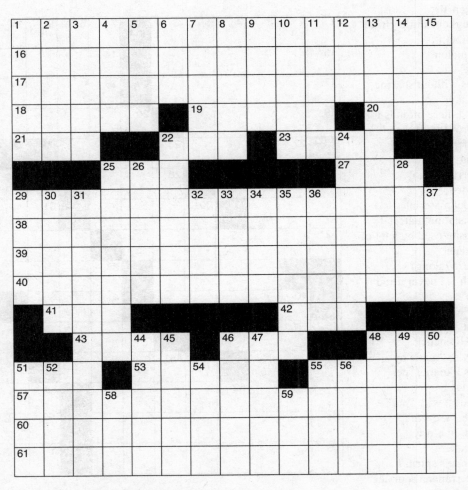

by Martin Ashwood-Smith

198 HARD

ACROSS

1 Rugby rival of Harvard
7 It operates Hamburger U.
15 Like many offshore rescues
16 Visiting only a short time
17 1955 R&B hit for Bo Diddley
18 "Ri-i-ight"
19 Buff
20 17-Across, to the self-titled "Bo Diddley"
21 Took care of
22 Free of shampoo, say
24 Shut (up)
25 "Cleopatre" artist
26 Directory listings: Abbr.
27 A place antelope lope
29 Kittenish
30 Maugham's title girl of Lambeth
31 Suspicion
32 Live
34 Uses without sharing, in slang
37 What there often is for improvement
38 Golfer nicknamed Long John
39 Interruption of service?
40 Model material
41 Translation material
42 Website used by a lot of artisans
43 Breeze (along)
44 "Huh . . . never mind then"
46 One of "the highest form of literature," per Hitchcock
47 They're "made by fools like me," per Kilmer
49 Parades, with "out"
51 Rollback events
53 Start, in a way
54 Squeaker
55 Lift one's spirits?
56 Subterranean scurrier
57 Played first

DOWN

1 Unhand or disarm?
2 Oscar winner before "Grand Hotel"
3 1974 National Book Award winner by Thomas Pynchon
4 Daughter and half sister of Oedipus
5 Shows a preference
6 Shared computer syst.
7 One who goes on to try to conquer the Universe?
8 Language akin to Yupik
9 ID
10 End of a lap
11 They may reduce sentences, for short
12 "And how!"
13 Four-time N.B.A. scoring champion in the 2010s
14 Vessel opener
20 Still matter?
23 Tough nut to crack
24 Court position
25 Prefix with village
27 Front-and-center section
28 Like fringe festival fare
30 It has a Marxist-Leninist ideology
33 Car payment?
34 Bêtes noires
35 Aid in studying a culture
36 Dump
38 Equipment for a rock band
40 Gewgaw
42 Coat
43 Design info
44 Davis of film
45 Really put one's foot down
47 Berth place
48 Repute
50 Was reckless, in a way
52 K'ung Fu-___
53 41-Across is a topic in it, briefly

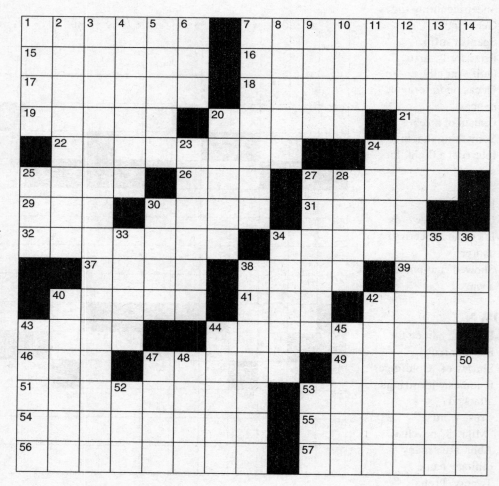

by James Mulhern

ACROSS

1 Like the national currency known as the tala
7 Axilla
13 "Hold on there now!"
15 Chasm
16 Powerful pitch
17 Settled with
18 London locale: Abbr.
19 Like the outer core of the earth
21 Certain logic gate
22 One Direction member Payne
24 The Flying Dutchman, e.g.
25 Limb-entangling weapon
26 One nearly cut Bond in half in "Goldfinger"
29 Rise up
30 1983 double-platinum album by Duran Duran
31 Everyday productivity enhancer, in modern lingo
33 Fictional character whose name is French for "flight of death"
36 Leading newspaper that took its name from a stage comedy
37 It's nothing, really
38 One making introductions
39 "You can't make me!"
44 Queen dowager of Jordan
45 Beyond repair
46 Ago, in an annual song
47 Animal with horns
48 Norman ___, first Asian-American to hold a cabinet post
50 Abbr. in an office address
51 Princess cake and others
53 Simply not done
56 Show disdain for, in a way
57 Subject of some PC Magazine reviews

58 Mixed forecasts?
59 N.F.L. Hall-of-Famer nicknamed "The Kansas Comet"

DOWN

1 Singer Twain
2 Blood lines
3 "Are you ___?!"
4 Cries that might be made while hopping on one foot
5 Slight interruption
6 Sure-to-succeed
7 One with commercial interests, for short
8 Nothing, in Nantes
9 Chant often heard toward the end of an N.B.A. season

10 Rick's, for one
11 Speech habits unique to an individual
12 The first one was delivered in 1984
13 "___ Stop the Rain" (1970 hit)
14 Fright night?
20 Pusillanimous
23 More festive
25 Views
27 Hiker's climb
28 Six-time Hugo Award winner Ben
29 Invoice word
32 Actress Sherilyn who was an Emmy nominee for "Twin Peaks"
33 Common ingredient in furniture polish

34 "No doubt!"
35 NASA spacecraft designed for travel to Mars
36 Units at a horse race
40 Whiskered animals
41 With 54-Down, longtime Long Island home of Theodore Roosevelt
42 Lays to rest
43 Frigid temps
45 They may have bullets
48 Main thrust
49 Field
52 The Nikkei 225 is one of its indexes: Abbr.
54 See 41-Down
55 Some lines of Milton

by Mary Lou Guizzo and Jeff Chen

200 HARD

ACROSS

1 Pickup trucks from a foreign-owned company made and sold only in North America
13 Familiar story line
15 Durable, as a wristwatch
17 Goes no further
18 Moon, in Montreuil
19 Imitation
21 Ford contemporary
22 To some degree
23 Jugged ___ (old British delicacy)
24 Jazzman Montgomery
25 White sheets
26 Second part of a historic trio
27 Some prizes on "The Price Is Right"
28 Dance with high kicks
29 They're put in barrels
32 Keeps a mock rivalry going, say
33 "___ in Moscow" (1959 children's book)
34 Funereal tempo
35 Air spirit, in folklore
36 Metallic stickers
37 "Golly Gosh Oh ___" (Conway Twitty song)
40 Entertainment Weekly interviewee
41 Niche religions
42 Low lament
43 ___ Parker, director and star of 2016's "The Birth of a Nation"
44 Not staged
45 Land line?
46 Sitcom mom whose kids were named Becky, Darlene and D.J.

49 $100 purchase in Monopoly
50 Something played at 1980s parties

DOWN

1 Ticket waster
2 Eat fast, slangily
3 Dresses down
4 Niche religions
5 Dovekies, e.g.
6 "This is ___"
7 Single-rotation skating jumps
8 Covers
9 Ruins the reputation of
10 Discombobulated
11 Small carp

12 Hit hard
14 Add value to
16 Winemaking byproduct
20 Monetary resources
22 Go down toward home?
25 Campus newbie
26 Symptoms of guilt
27 Liqueur in a margarita
28 Bready bunch?
29 Pitch, e.g.
30 Affirmed's rival for the Triple Crown
31 Protégé of Stalin
32 Compiler of an 1855 reference work
34 "The Jack ___ Show," 1959–85

36 Start of a Spanish greeting
37 Australian monitor lizard
38 Show some leniency
39 Starter follower
41 Is a quick learner?
42 His house in Giverny is now a museum
45 Smuggler's hideaway
47 Monarch's reign, perhaps
48 Cool ___

by Patrick Berry

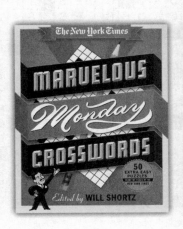

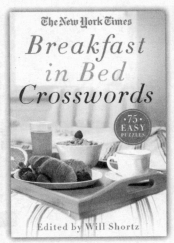
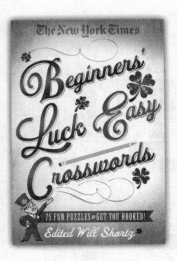

1

```
L P S . A L T O . . R E F E R
I R K . B A R N . S O M A L I
M A I N S T A Y . E G O I S M
I D E E . K I X . M E T R E S
T A R H E E L . F I R E S . .
. . R L S . L O P . S H E D
A R G U E . B E R R A . A V E
R O O . G O O D D O G . K E N
I D O . Y U R T S . L E E R Y
D E S K . T A O . C O M . .
. E N A C T . H O W C O M E
M E D I N A . P O L . E R A S
C L O V I S . H O U S E S I T
A L W E S T . D E M I . O N E
T E N S E . . S Y N C . N E E
```

2

```
L E T S . A M A J . S K U N K
A U R A . T A L E . A N N O Y
I R O N . E T A T . L I B E L
C O N S U M E R P R O F I L E
. . . A P P . M O A N E R .
N A M . O O F . W T S . T E D
A V I A N . A G E S . O H I O
C O N T E N T P R O V I D E R
H I D E . E A S E . C L A I M
O R B . D H L . D A H . Y O S
. E M E R I L . M I C . . .
C O N C L U S I V E P R O O F
O L D I E . T M A N . A M S O
A G E N T . I B I D . M A L E
L A R G E . C O N S . P R O S
```

3

```
S E W S . T A X I . E C L A T
O A H U . I V A N . S H A P E
D R A M A T I C L I C E N S E
A T M . T A S T E D . E D E N
S H O O I N . O T T E R . .
. A L I T . A N Y H O W
S H I F T C H A N G E . O N O
L I D S . E P A . O S L O
U R L . F L O R I D A K E Y S
E E Y O R E . R O L E
. F O A L S . G O D E E P
P I A F . V A N I S H . G R U
S A N D I E G O C H A R G E R
A G O A T . O R E O . D O C S
T O N Y S . S T E W . A N T E
```

4

```
N A L A . B O R E . . A J A R
A D A M . U T E S . I R U L E
N O W O R R I E S . S A L O N
. C I R C L E O F L I F E
I N T O T O . S F O . E T E
N A H . E S S O . F R A T
D I E T S . E L L E . S A L T
I L L S . R E A I R . E Y E R
A S I A . A M F M . S A M O A
. O R B S . S A C K . O N S
O W N . A T E . R A H R A H
H A K U N A M A T A T A
A G I N G . P R I D E R O C K
R E N T S . T E L L . E R I E
A R G O . Y A L E . S C A R
```

5

```
S C R U B . S L A M . M O S
P R U N E S . L O B E . A A H
F U N I N T H E S U N . C S I
S E T . G O O D S . O N A I R
. M A L T . A R O U S E
I C I C L E . S P L A T
M A D E I N T H E S H A D E
O R E S . I O N . C R A W
. B A C K I N T H E B L A C K
. H I R E S . L A U G H S
T E R E S A . B E N E .
U S E R S . E P I C S . O O H
P I C . E Y E I N T H E S K Y
A G O . R E N T . S E A L E D
C N N . S A Y S . E R O D E
```

6

```
L A B S . H A R S H . C R A P
I D V E . A K I T A . L I R E
B E I N G M C C O Y . I D E A
. T E A . K I D . P O E T
. S A C R I F I C E M C F L Y
S U M A T R A . N I L
A M I . H A R T S . T O P A Z
F O N T . S E W O N . P I N E
E S S A Y . D O N U T . P I E
. P A M . I M A M E S S
R U N A W A Y M C B R I D E
O T I S . R U E . I S R
B E E B . I C E M C Q U E E N
O R C A . A C T O R . S A L E
T I E R . H A S T Y . E M I T
```

7

R	A	S	P	S		S	C	R	E	W		W	I	T
E	L	T	O	N		E	L	U	D	E		H	M	O
B	E	A	T	L	E	M	A	N	I	A		A	P	U
E	X	I	T		M	I	D		T	V	S	T	A	R
L	A	D	Y	D	I				W	E	A	N	S	
		M	A	R	C	H	M	A	D	N	E	S	S	
M	I	N	O	R		L	A	I	R		T	R	I	O
I	S	O	U	T		E	R	S		S	A	V	O	R
F	L	I	T		J	A	D	E		I	L	E	N	E
F	A	S	H	I	O	N	C	R	A	Z	E			
	M	E	E	T	S			G	E	T	S	A	T	
B	A	L	D	I	E		M	O	O		T	A	R	A
A	B	A		S	P	R	I	N	G	F	E	V	E	R
J	A	W		S	H	I	N	E		D	R	E	S	S
A	D	S		O	S	A	K	A		A	S	D	O	I

8

A	C	T	S		C	U	B	A	N		D	E	J	A
N	Y	E	T		A	S	I	A	N		E	V	E	L
N	A	S	L		F	E	N	C	E		L	E	T	S
E	N	T	E	R		D	D	E		P	I	N	T	O
	P	O	I	N	T	I	L	L	I	S	M			
A	N	I		F	O	O		L	A	T		O	N	T
S	O	L	D	T	O			C	H	E	R	I	E	
T	R	O	I		R	A	I	S	E		L	E	N	D
R	A	T	E	S		I	N	E		P	O	S	E	D
O	D	S		N	F	L	S	T	A	R		O	R	Y
	L	O	O	M		A	T	O	B					
	G	E	O	R	G	E	S	S	E	U	R	A	T	
P	R	I	N	T		N	U	I		D	A	F	O	E
J	E	N	G	A		T	E	D		O	V	A	R	Y
S	W	E	E	T		S	T	E		F	O	R	T	E

9

H	D	T	V	S		U	S	O	F	A		N	I	L
A	E	I	O	U		L	E	A	S	T		O	R	E
H	A	R	U	M	S	C	A	R	U	M		S	O	D
A	L	E	C		H	E	M			F	L	I	N	G
	H	E	A	R	Y	E	H	E	A	R	Y	E		
C	A	L		D	Q	S		L	O	E	W	E		
A	S	A	D	A			D	S	L		F	E	E	L
M	A	K	E	M	I	N	E	A	D	O	U	B	L	E
O	P	E	L		O	O	F			G	L	O	M	S
	G	U	S	T	O		C	A	R		B	O	T	
A	L	E	X	V	A	N	H	A	L	E	N			
D	O	N	E	E		O	V	A		A	G	A	R	
O	N	E		L	O	G	G	I	N	G	I	N	T	O
R	E	V		T	R	E	A	T		A	V	A	I	L
E	R	A		E	B	O	N	Y		B	E	T	T	E

10

A	T	E	A	M		O	L	D	I	E		L	A	M
T	I	A	R	A		F	E	E	D	S		I	W	O
M	A	R	K	R	U	F	F	A	L	O		Z	A	P
		S	I	N		T	R	Y		B	A	K	E	
T	A	J		T	W	I	S	T		A	I	M	E	D
A	S	A	L	A	R	K		H	O	P	K	I	N	S
T	I	M	E	L	I	N	E		T	E	E	N		
A	D	E	S		T	O	R	C	H		R	N	A	
	E	S	S		T	W	I	N	E		B	E	R	G
	S	T	Y	E		N	O	R	M	A	L	C	Y	
A	N	T	H	O	N	Y		T	W	I	R	L	E	R
I	B	E	A	M		A	T	E	I	N		I	D	O
S	A	W	N		S	C	I		S	G	T			
L	E	A		J	O	H	N	B	E	L	U	S	H	I
E	R	R		A	S	T	E	R		E	T	H	I	C
S	S	T		B	O	S	S	A		S	U	E	M	E

11

C	A	P	P		I	M	I	N	G		S	C	A	M
L	U	L	U		N	O	L	I	E		T	O	G	A
A	R	A	B		P	O	I	N	T	G	U	A	R	D
P	A	Y	G	R	A	D	E		G	O	A	L	I	E
S	E	A	A	I	R		B	O	O	R				
	M	D	T		P	A	I	N	T	G	U	N		
H	O	S	E	S		B	E	N	N	Y		R	N	A
A	R	T	S		P	A	N	D	G		P	A	I	N
S	E	E		P	R	I	U	S		S	A	N	T	A
P	O	P	G	R	O	U	P		F	U	N			
	H	I	L	L		E	N	G	E	L	S			
S	A	F	E	C	O		P	E	A	G	R	E	E	N
P	A	R	T	Y	G	I	R	L	S		A	N	N	A
A	B	E	T		U	B	O	L	T		V	I	D	I
M	A	Y	O		E	M	M	Y	S		Y	E	L	L

12

A	S	Y	E	T		B	E	B	O	P		E	S	T
S	E	E	M	E		O	T	O	E	S		N	T	H
P	A	S	T	H	I	S	T	O	R	Y		D	E	I
E	C	O		E	N	S	U	E			I	W	I	N
C	O	R	D	E	D			R	A	T	F	I	N	K
T	O	N	I		Y	I	N		M	A	S	S	E	S
S	K	O	S	H		N	O	Y	E	S		E	M	O
		C	A	S	H	M	O	N	E	Y				
B	O	T		V	E	D	A	Y		S	E	G	A	R
I	N	A	F	O	G		D	O	G		A	R	I	E
T	A	X	I	C	A	B		E	S	H	A	R	P	
E	L	S	E		Y	U	B	A	N		B	T	U	
S	I	C		B	U	N	N	Y	R	A	B	B	I	T
A	N	A		I	S	O	U	T		F	R	A	M	E
T	E	M		N	E	W	M	E		U	R	G	E	D

13

C	A	L	F		R	O	S	Y		R	A	I	D	S
A	R	I	E		O	P	I	E		E	P	C	O	T
B	U	Z	Z	W	O	R	D	S		P	R	E	G	O
	G	A	Z	A		Y	E	N	T	A		A	B	U
P	U	R	E	S	T		B	O	B	S	A	G	E	T
O	L	D	S	A	W	S			S	T	B	E	D	E
W	A	S		B	I	L	G	E			U	S	S	R
		P	I	X	I	E	D	U	S	T				
O	A	T	H			T	O	A	S	T		F	U	M
R	E	H	E	A	T			M	E	R	G	I	N	G
C	R	E	W	N	E	C	K		R	E	E	S	E	S
H	A	M		G	L	O	A	T		E	L	S	A	
A	T	A	L	L		S	H	O	R	T	C	U	T	S
R	O	G	U	E			E	L	I	E		A	R	E	A
D	R	I	V	E		C	O	L	A		P	E	N	D

14

A	B	R	A			A			A	B	L	E	
L	A	O	S			A	V	A		M	A	I	D
T	T	O	P		A	C	E	L	A		A	T	O	I
A	T	F		A	M	E	R	I	C	A		T	N	T
R	E	G	A	L	E	D		A	D	S	A	L	E	S
	D	A	N	E	S		A		C	A	M	E	L	
J	A	R	T	S		A	L	A		P	A	D	M	E
A	N	D	I		A	R	E	N	A		T	R	E	S
N	E	E		A	N	T	E	N	N	A		E	S	T
D	Y	N	A	S	T	Y		E	N	M	A	S	S	E
J	E	S	S	I	E				E	E	N	S	I	E
		F	A	C	E	P	L	A	N	T				
A	F	R	A	M	E	B	U	I	L	D	I	N	G	S
B	R	O	S		D	A	N	C	E		C	O	O	K
S	O	O	T		E	N	T	E	R		S	W	A	Y

15

C	A	P		D	E	E	R		D	O	D	G	E	D
R	I	O		I	D	L	E		O	R	I	O	L	E
E	S	P		R	U	M	M	A	G	E	S	A	L	E
E	L	U	D	E		U	R	N		C	L	A	P	
P	E	L	I	C	A	N	S	T	A	T	E			
	A	E	T	N	A			P	E	R	I	L	S	
R	A	T	S		A	D	O	S		E	N	D	O	W
A	L	I		S	T	I	L	T	O	N		I	R	A
S	T	O	V	E		R	E	U	P		P	O	E	M
P	O	N	I	E	D		D	E	B	I	T			
	S	K	I	N	N	Y	D	I	P	P	E	R		
A	U	D	I		S	A	O			S	E	R	T	A
W	H	A	T	S	M	Y	N	A	M	E		O	U	T
E	U	R	O	P	A		O	P	E	C		O	D	E
S	H	E	R	Y	L		S	E	N	T		F	E	D

16

A	B	S	E	N	T		S	W	A	L	L	O	W
D	O	O	D	A	H		K	A	R	A	O	K	E
E	X	C	U	S	E	S	E	X	C	U	S	E	S
N	Y	C			M	E	D			R	E	D	
	E	S	T	E	R			D	Y	E			
M	A	R	C	U	S	A	U	R	E	L	I	U	S
A	T	B	A	T		N	A	P		C	H	E	
C	R	A	M		G	R	O	W		H	E	H	E
A	I	L		B	A	A			S	E	D	U	M
W	A	L	R	U	S	M	U	S	T	A	C	H	E
	A	M	P			N	E	U	R	O			
	S	A	P		P	I	G			F	D	A	
J	U	S	T	T	H	E	T	W	O	O	F	U	S
U	P	T	O	N	O	W		A	S	L	E	E	P
G	E	O	R	G	E	S		Y	O	D	E	L	S

17

B	I	G	I	F		S	K	I	N		W	E	S	T
A	R	E	S	O		T	A	C	O		E	X	P	O
B	A	L	L	P	L	A	Y	E	R		R	E	I	N
A	N	T	E		E	R	A		T	E	R	R	E	
	P	A	R	K	V	I	S	I	T	O	R			
G	E	T	B	U	S	Y		E	B	A	N			
A	T	A	L	L		H	E	E		L	E	A	K	
T	R	I	A	L	C	O	U	R	T	J	U	D	G	E
E	E	L	S		A	S	H		I	C	A	R	E	
	T	O	N	S		M	I	L	K	M	A	N		
J	A	Z	Z	P	I	A	N	I	S	T				
A	D	I	O	S		U	S	E		B	A	A	S	
P	E	N	N		O	N	T	H	E	B	E	N	C	H
A	L	E	E		R	O	S	A		B	A	N	T	U
N	E	S	S		S	T	O	P		Q	U	E	S	T

18

S	L	O	T		A	X	I	S		B	A	S	K	S
T	A	S	E		P	I	T	T		D	I	N	A	H
R	U	I	N		R	I	G	A	M	A	R	O	L	E
I	R	E	N	E		I	S	A	Y		W	E	D	
P	A	R	I	S	H	P	R	I	E	S	T	S		
		S	T	O	O	L	S			A	U	T	O	
C	A	B		A	R	M	S		F	O	X	I	E	R
S	T	A	R	T	U	P		C	A	P	I	T	A	L
I	M	B	U	E	S		D	E	N	T		S	L	Y
S	O	Y	S		P	R	O	T	I	P				
	B	E	R	N	I	E	S	A	N	D	E	R	S	
F	L	U		H	O	L	A		G	I	N	U	P	
R	O	M	E	O	R	O	M	E	O		D	E	L	A
A	M	P	E	D		T	O	T	O		D	R	E	D
T	E	S	L	A		S	N	A	P		Y	O	R	E

19

```
C A S T   L A T H   C L A S P
A S H E   A C H Y   H U M O R
S T A N   T E E M   E M P T Y
H U D D L E   G N O M E
I T O   A R G O   W I N D U P
N E W T S   R O S E S   O N E
    B A E   O D I S T   W I G
S C O U R   U S E   R U N T S
P O X   P A T H S   Y A W
A R E   O N S E T   L E A F S
S P R A I N   P A P A   R E A
    G N A S H   A B I D E S
C A R A T   H E W N   O D D S
P R I M E   O R E S   T O M E
A M B E R   E D D Y   A G E D
```

20

```
C C T V   C A S C A   J O S H
O H O H   U S U A L   A L L A
M E W S   B A B Y P O W D E R
P E N   V I S   H O S T E D
A R C T I C O C E A N   I V E
Q U A I D   N H L   A D M E N
S P R E E S   E A R   R E D S
    R O Y A L N A V Y
L A D E   D R S   J E R K E D
E V A D E   A E C   R O L L E
G O T   C O B A L T S T E E L
I N S I T U   A W E   E V E
B L U E O N B L U E   A N A T
L E N S   C A U S E   J E T E
E A S T   E D G E D   A X E D
```

21

```
C O B R A   B R A S H   C O Y
A R I E S   R O U T E   H M O
C I T Y S L I C K E R   R I G
H O E   A I D S   T O Y O T A
E N S U I N G   A S I A N
    B L U E S T O C K I N G
E M C E E S   W O N   C E O
B O A R D   J A M   P A L E D
B O P   B U Y   L O N E R S
S T U F F E D S H I R T
    C U R R Y   U N K E M P T
G E H R I G   A N D Y   A A A
A M I   S M A R T Y P A N T S
G U N   K A T I E   I N L E T
A S S   S N E A D   G A Y L E
```

22

```
A B B E S   O R E   B A L D
L A R G O   P I T   R O D E O
F R O G M A R C H   O S M I C
A R K   A B A C I   P O I S E
L I E S   C H I C K E N R U N
F O R T E S   A S S E R T
A S S A Y   M A I M   D E S
    B E A R C R A W L
A S P   C I T E   B O A R S
T O U S L E   E A G L E T
T U R K E Y T R O T   E L L O
A T R I A   O O Z E D   S I P
C H I E F   G O O S E S T E P
H E N R Y   A N N   C R A V E
E R G S   S E E   O A R E D
```

23

```
A R M S   A G O R A   S H E D
B E A U   P L I E S   E E R O
C A R P   P O L Y P H E M U S
S P E E D E R S   A G A P E
    R A N I   M O D E L T S
S A M M Y D A V I S J R
U V E A S   E S A I   E Y E
M O R N   D I R T Y   I G O R
O N E   S E C S   S C A R E
    J A C K O F S P A D E S
R A C E W A Y   A T E N
A B O R T   A N E W H O P E
B A Z O O K A J O E   E V I L
I T E M   F R A U D   L A P S
N E N E   C E R T S   P L E A
```

24

```
A J A R   A L O F T   O R S O
P O K E   V E N U E   R E E L
S H I F T G E A R S   C A P S
E N N U I   I L L S   L I E
    E N T E R S A N D M A N
A Z A L E A S   S O N
D O N S   S P A M   R A S T A
A L T   K E Y W E S T   T A B
M A I N E   S E T I   J U R E
    A I M   E T H A N O L
C O N T R O L F R E A K
O R E   A R I A   Z A P P A
L O C K   E S C A P E R O O M
I N C A   S T E V E   T R E E
C O O T   O S T E R   A T T N
```

25

```
A B B I E █ Z I N G █ B L O W
R O L F E █ A S E A █ L I V E
O R A N G E P E E L █ U S E S
A N N O █ S P E D █ H E A R T
R E D T A P E █ █ P U B █ █ █
█ █ █ █ I N D I G O G I R L S
O N D V D █ M O N O R A I L
L I I I I █ P A P P Y █ D U M A
A L L O C A T E █ I S L E T
Y E L L O W L I G H T █ █ █
█ █ E O N █ █ R A I N B O W
M A L T S █ F W I W █ O U Z O
A C E R █ G R E E N A R R O W
T I N A █ R E E F █ C A R N E
E D D Y █ R E P S █ S H O E D
```

26

```
C L O S E █ I T L L █ O G L E
R A Z E D █ S H E A █ N O O K
U M A M I █ O R E S █ B L U E
S P R I N K L E R H E A D █ █
T S K █ B I D E █ █ D I S C O
█ █ S O M E R S A U L T E D
█ T S A R █ I T T █ █ A R E
O T T O M A N E M P I R E █
O R U █ S I G █ R O S S
W I N D T U R B I N E S █ █
L I T E S █ I B I S █ R T E
█ S E A S O N O P E N E R S
R A H M █ U N D O █ N O H I T
A L O E █ M E E K █ C R A T E
G A W D █ O A R S █ E M B E R
```

27

```
P E R T █ A D D A M S █ U S E
A V O N █ C R E D I T █ N A G
V I C T O R Y L A N E █ T U G
E L K █ N E A T █ A M I N O
█ C U R █ D A V I D L E A N
P E A N U T S █ E D Y S █ █
E L V I S H █ C E O █ C I G
T O E T H E P A R T Y L I N E
S I S █ N E W █ O E U V R E
█ █ O F F S █ S O R T I E S
M I C R O L O A N █ T E C
O T H E R █ G O A L █ D A B
M A O █ C L A I R D E L U N E
M L K █ E A G L E D █ E T N A
A Y E █ S P E E D S █ D Y E D
```

28

```
C H A P S █ S W A M I █ V E T
R A J A H █ T A M E R █ I S H
A L A M O █ P R A D A █ J A Y
M O R E T H A N J U N E A U
█ L O O T █ █ L I L Y █
C A R A F E █ M A L A Y S I A
A L A █ F R E E L A N S I N G
S E N T █ L O T █ E N T O
A U G U S T A W I N D █ G E N
S T E R N U M S █ A R C H L Y
█ R I O T █ O R A L █
C O N C O R D M Y F E A R S
L A V █ O R I O N █ T A C I T
A G E █ N E G R I █ E N E M Y
P E R █ E D A M S █ E S S E X
```

29

```
D E S I █ K E B A B S █ K F C
O M A N █ A N O D E S █ I L L
E I F F E L T O W E R █ R O Y
S T E R N E █ T E T █ F O O D
█ T O R █ T H E L O U V R E
S A Y N O T O █ K E R R █ █
P O N T N E U F █ A S K M E
E N E █ A R E N A █ I E D
D E T O O █ S O R B O N N E
█ G R I P █ N E R F G U N
N O T R E D A M E █ I A M
A L O E █ E T A █ B A N I S H
K I N █ P A R I S F R A N C E
E V E █ A T O N O F █ G O A L
D E S █ R E N E W S █ E S T D
```

30

```
T I T H E █ F U S S E S █ A R R
A R I E L █ I N T H A T █ L E O
N E T F L I X Q U E U E █ G A G
G N U █ I C E U P █ X A N A D U
Y E S Y O U █ O O F █ M Y E Y E
█ A T S █ T R O P I C █ █
A V E R █ L E S A G E █ A L S
D E A D S E A █ █ M A R Y K A Y
S E T █ C R U S T Y █ O A T S
█ S U N D E W █ A B S █
K A L E L █ E M I █ B U T W H Y
A L E P P O █ A N D O R █ A A A
Y O N █ T H I N K Q U I C K L Y
A N N █ O N S A L E █ A T E A M
K E Y █ R O U S E D █ L A S S E
```

31

32

33

34

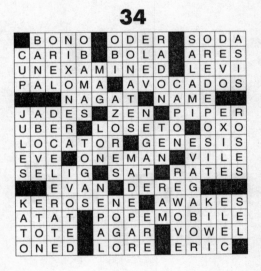

35

36

37

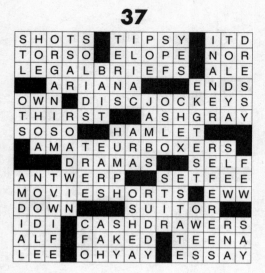

S	H	O	T	S		T	I	P	S	Y		I	T	D
T	O	R	S	O		E	L	O	P	E		N	O	R
L	E	G	A	L	B	R	I	E	F	S		A	L	E
	A	R	I	A	N	A			E	N	D	S		
O	W	N		D	I	S	C	J	O	C	K	E	Y	S
T	H	I	R	S	T		A	S	H	G	R	A	Y	
S	O	S	O		H	A	M	L	E	T				
	A	M	A	T	E	U	R	B	O	X	E	R	S	
		D	R	A	M	A	S		S	E	L	F		
A	N	T	W	E	R	P		S	E	T	F	E	E	
M	O	V	I	E	S	H	O	R	T	S		E	W	W
D	O	W	N		S	U	I	T	O	R				
I	D	I		C	A	S	H	D	R	A	W	E	R	S
A	L	F		F	A	K	E	D		T	E	E	N	A
L	E	E		O	H	Y	A	Y		E	S	S	A	Y

38

H	E	F	T	S		D	T	S		O	A	S	I	S
A	L	L	O	T		I	O	U		B	L	I	N	I
S	L	A	V	E		N	U	E	V	O	L	E	O	N
H	I	S		R	E	A	R		L	E	A	G	U	E
	S	H	A	N	G	R	I	L	A		N	E	T	S
	L	I	S	A		S	O	D	A					
C	P	A	S		D	A	T	A		P	A	S	T	A
A	I	M	L	E	S	S		T	R	E	E	T	O	P
R	E	P	E	L		A	C	H	E		T	R	O	T
			S	O	M	E		T	O	N	I			
P	A	I	D		R	I	V	E	R	B	A	N	K	
O	F	N	O	T	E		I	L	Y	A		G	N	U
R	O	A	D	B	L	O	C	K		M	I	T	E	R
T	O	N	G	A		P	H	I		A	L	I	E	N
S	T	E	E	R		T	E	N		S	L	E	D	S

39

M	T	F	U	J	I		D	A	T	A		G	A	L
P	O	L	L	E	N		O	W	E	N		O	L	E
G	R	O	U	N	D	S	C	R	E	W		R	V	S
	E	E	L		E	A	S	Y		A	E	G	I	S
		A	W	E	D		O	R	L	O	N			
	E	A	T	A	P	E	A	C	H		S	N	A	P
A	S	S	E	T		P	A	N	E		Z	I	T	
S	P	H		T	O	O	L	B	O	X		O	L	A
T	A	B		S	U	P	E		P	A	L	E	S	
I	D	L	E		S	T	A	Y	S	A	W	A	Y	
	R	O	G	E	T		E	T	T	A				
R	I	N	G	S		S	O	A	R		S	K	A	
O	L	D		T	U	N	A	S	A	S	H	I	M	I
A	L	E		E	M	I	T		T	A	I	L	O	R
D	E	S		R	A	P	S		I	G	N	O	R	E

40

P	A	C	K		A	T	L	A	S		M	A	P	S
I	C	O	N		H	A	I	T	I		E	V	I	L
S	U	R	E	W	H	Y	N	O	T		M	A	X	I
A	P	N	E	A		U	N	C	L	E	S	A	M	
			C	R	O	S	S	C	O	U	N	T	R	Y
T	A	B	A	S	C	O		E	M	I	T			
W	R	A	P		H	O	P		G	O	O	F	S	
I	L	L		B	O	N	J	O	V	I		R	I	O
N	O	L	I	E		S	H	E		H	A	L	L	
		R	E	B	A		O	T	H	E	L	L	O	
B	A	C	K	T	O	S	C	H	O	O	L			
G	U	E	S	S	W	H	O		D	P	L	U	S	
A	R	C	O		S	T	A	R	T	A	F	I	R	E
M	A	I	M		T	O	T	H	E		U	C	L	A
E	L	L	E		O	N	I	O	N		L	E	S	S

41

L	E	E	R		O	B	L	A		P	O	U	L	T
A	R	T	E		F	U	E	L		L	U	C	I	E
B	I	T	E	V	A	L	V	E		A	T	L	A	S
S	C	U	B	A		K	I	C	K	S	T	A	R	T
	O	R	B	S		E	M	O						
L	I	L	K	I	M		D	I	Y		W	A	I	L
A	N	O		E	O	S	I	N		T	I	N	N	Y
S	C	R	A	T	C	H	A	N	D	S	N	I	F	F
S	U	R	L	Y		E	L	S	I	E		S	E	T
O	R	E	L		P	A	S		E	L	D	E	R	S
	O	T	C		A	M	I	E						
P	U	N	C	H	B	O	W	L		O	U	G	H	T
A	R	O	A	R		F	I	G	H	T	C	L	U	B
P	L	U	T	O		F	R	A	U		E	E	L	S
A	S	N	E	W		S	E	E	M		S	N	A	P

42

A	T	A	R	I		J	P	O	P		A	D	D
T	I	M	E	D		B	U	O	N	O		F	R	O
I	G	I	V	E		A	R	G	O	T		L	I	E
L	E	G		A	P	B	I	O		A	G	A	V	E
T	R	O	L	L	E	Y	S		S	T	A	C	E	Y
			I	M	D	B		D	O	O	R	D	I	E
	A	L	A		L	A	I	T		F	U	N	D
	S	T	A	N	D	U	P	C	O	M	I	C	S
W	E	E	B		J	E	R	K		E	E	K	
O	R	A	N	G	E	S		T	F	A	L		
R	E	W	E	L	D		G	R	A	N	D	A	M	S
S	N	A	R	E		O	R	A	N	G		S	U	E
H	A	Y		A	S	P	I	C		I	R	A	T	E
I	D	A		M	O	U	S	Y		R	U	N	T	S
P	E	T		S	Y	S	T		L	E	A	S	T	

43

J	E	A	N		P	A	L	M		H	A	S	N	T
O	R	B	S		I	P	S	O		O	C	H	O	A
B	A	B	Y	A	L	B	U	M		T	R	A	M	S
S	T	A	N	C	E			A	F	I	R	S	T	
		C	H	I	L	D	P	R	O	D	I	G	Y	
E	B	B		T	O	R	I	N	O					
T	E	E	N	V	O	G	U	E		T	O	A	S	T
C	A	R	E	E	N			S	I	M	I	L	E	
H	U	M	O	R		A	D	U	L	T	S	W	I	M
		M	O	D	U	L	E			A	P	P		
S	E	N	I	O	R	M	O	M	E	N	T			
A	C	O	R	N	S			P	E	E	W	E	E	
G	O	T	A	T		G	H	O	S	T	T	O	W	N
E	L	A	T	E		T	E	R	I		R	O	O	D
S	I	X	E	R		O	X	E	N		A	S	K	S

44

C	O	D	A		I	D	E	S		B	A	B	E	L
L	A	I	R		N	O	M	E		I	N	U	R	E
U	R	S	A	M	A	J	O	R		G	O	T	A	T
E	S	O	B	E	S	O		G	O	D	D	E	S	S
	B	Y	T	E		T	E	R	I		N	E	G	
G	E	E		C	H	E		S	P	E	E	D	O	
A	R	Y	A	N		O	N	D	O	P	E			
L	A	S	S	O		L	A	O		E	N	O	L	A
	E	R	R	A	N	D		R	Y	D	E	R		
T	R	E	A	T	Y		T	O	P		O	O	F	
W	O	N		H	E	S	S		E	L	O	N		
E	N	M	A	S	S	E		S	C	O	R	N	E	D
E	D	I	C	T		G	R	E	A	T	B	E	A	R
T	E	T	R	A		E	A	R	N		I	L	S	A
S	L	Y	E	R		L	Y	E	S		S	L	E	W

45

	T	R	A	M	P	S		C	H	A	R	T	S	
A	R	A	M	A	I	C		A	I	L	E	R	O	N
P	U	T	O	N	A	H	A	P	P	Y	F	A	C	E
H	E	R	S		N	O	T	I	T		S	U	L	U
I	D	A		P	O	O	L	T	O	Y		M	O	T
D	A	C	H	A		L	A	O		A	B	A	S	E
S	T	E	A	L		D	S	L		W	I	S	E	R
	D	A	T	A		D	A	N	G					
B	R	E	A	K	I	N	T	O	A	S	M	I	L	E
R	E	A	M		S	C	A	M	S		O	N	E	S
A	C	R	E	S		E	R	E		R	U	F	F	S
	O	C	A	L	A		P	E	T	I	T			
F	U	L	L	O	F	G	O	O	D	C	H	E	E	R
E	P	I		G	R	O	W	L	A	T		L	Y	E
E	S	P		S	O	A	N	D	S	O		D	E	B

46

O	D	D	D	U	C	K	S		A	B	R	A	M	S
P	A	R	A	N	O	I	A		N	O	O	G	I	E
A	L	A	N	A	L	D	A		D	H	A	R	M	A
L	E	I	A			F	R	E	E	E	M	A	I	L
S	S	N		D	H	L		R	A	M				
		S	U	E	A	N	N	N	I	V	E	N	S	
W	A	R	H	O	R	S	E		A	I	L	E	Y	
A	L	O	U		S	H	A	P	E		P	S	A	S
S	A	U	N	A		L	A	T	T	E	A	R	T	
P	I	T	T	T	H	E	E	L	D	E	R			
	I	A	M		M	S	N		C	A	M			
D	R	E	S	S	S	I	Z	E		H	U	G	E	
R	A	D	I	S	H		E	D	U	C	A	T	E	S
A	V	E	N	U	E		S	O	N	A	T	I	N	A
B	I	N	G	E	S		T	R	I	D	E	N	T	S

47

A	W	L		I	R	E		T	A	B	A	S	C	O
H	A	I	T	I	A	N		I	G	O	T	C	H	A
O	F	F	S	I	D	E		N	O	T	T	H	A	T
L	E	E	K		I	M	P	S		I	O	N	S	
D	R	S		S	O	Y	A		W	A	C	O		
	T	W	I	G		R	C	A	S		L	Y	E	
T	O	Y	O	T	A		T	O	B	A	C	C	O	S
A	B	L	E		L	A	Y	L	A		L	A	W	S
G	O	E	S	B	A	L	D		S	T	I	F	L	E
S	E	C		E	X	P	O		H	O	P	E		
	H	O	L	Y		W	A	R	P		T	E	D	
N	O	O	N		A	N	T	I		G	E	N	E	
E	P	I	T	A	P	H		O	V	E	R	R	A	N
C	I	C	A	D	A	S		M	E	T	R	I	C	S
K	E	E	P	S	T	O		S	R	A		A	T	E

48

Q	U	A	L	M		T	I	F	F		S	H	A	H
T	A	B	O	O		U	C	L	A		P	A	L	O
R	E	A	C	T		N	O	A	M		I	R	A	N
	A	T	L	A	N	T	I	C	T	I	M	E		
Z	I	P	L	O	C			L	A	Z	B	O	Y	
I	M	A	C		D	E	T	A	I	L		O	S	S
M	E	T	A	L		N	A	P	A	L	M			
A	T	H	L	E	T	I	C	T	R	A	I	N	E	R
	L	O	R	A	I	N		S	K	O	D	A		
A	H	H		V	E	C	T	O	R		E	G	G	Y
T	O	O	K	I	N		K	B	T	O	Y	S		
A	T	O	M	I	C	T	H	E	O	R	Y			
N	A	D	A		H	O	A	X		A	S	H	E	N
D	I	O	R		E	L	H	I		K	O	A	L	A
T	R	O	T		S	L	A	T		E	N	J	O	Y

49

```
AIRS ■ STAN ■ GIANT
NOAA ■ HERA ■ OLDER
TWINPEAKS ■ AKIRA
SANDED ■ ■ AIT ■ ETC
■ ■ DAP ■ FULLHOUSE
SKELETON ■ LED ■ ■ ■
AILS ■ HRS ■ PRESET
ALA ■ BEDHEAD ■ PTA
BOYTOY ■ OPS ■ FORT
■ ■ IRS ■ RESTAREA
QUEENANNE ■ ALT ■
USA ■ FYI ■ ALLSET
AUGER ■ KINGCOBRA
CREPE ■ KNEE ■ FAIR
KYRIE ■ ICES ■ FRET
```

50

```
BLACK ■ SLACK ■ ENT
REBAG ■ TIPPI ■ NIA
AMASS ■ EMBASSIES
VAST ■ ANO ■ STACK
OTHELLO ■ AMERCES
■ ■ ■ ELSINORE ■ ■
STALK ■ CALSTATE
RIGA ■ STALE ■ CHEW
SLAPDASH ■ SHALE
■ ■ ■ BANKNOTE ■ ■
ASCENDS ■ REVERSI
WHALE ■ GAY ■ PITT
GENTLEMEN ■ LOCOS
EEO ■ APING ■ OCCAM
ERN ■ WHILE ■ WHITE
```

51

```
SHO ■ PIPPI ■ FROST
TOPSECRET ■ LUCKY
ONEWAYORANOTHER
PECAN ■ PLOW ■ OWE
■ ■ GUTS ■ ISEE ■ ■
TRU ■ TWOWAYRADIO
WALLSAFE ■ STIRS
INCA ■ STEPS ■ UVEA
SCENT ■ PINGPONG
THREEWAYTIE ■ TEE
■ ■ SAIL ■ APTS ■ ■
AKA ■ BRIO ■ BEECH
SIXWAYSTOSUNDAY
STIEG ■ TREESTUMP
TESTS ■ SADLY ■ COO
```

52

```
ACTII ■ BOAR ■ IDLE
FAINT ■ ALDA ■ CRUX
FRETS ■ HELPMEOBI
ERIE ■ ■ AIDA ■ PET
CINNAMONBUNS ■ ■
TEST(ST)LAB ■ ON(AR)UN
■ ■ PIETA ■ SOME
YOUREMYONLYHOPE
AURA ■ SODOI ■ ■ ■
(W)INS(AT) ■ (R)IPOFF(S)
■ ■ PRINCESSLEIA
OHO ■ SLAY ■ ETSY
WANKENOBI ■ MOTHY
LUTE ■ OMEN ■ ALLEE
SLOG ■ WIRE ■ PEERS
```

53

```
POOH ■ MWAH ■ TAPED
ACNE ■ OHIO ■ OHARA
RUMPROAST ■ LASED
ALITO ■ PLEAD ■ TAB
DAKOTA ■ ELDORADO
ERE ■ IRA ■ SOFABED
■ ■ ENACT ■ CARS ■
■ STILTWALKER ■ ■
MATH ■ ■ OPALS ■ ■
ISRAELI ■ BYU ■ OWE
SKINGAME ■ STONED
CAN ■ ROARS ■ ZALES
AWGEE ■ FAIRYTALE
SAULT ■ ASTO ■ ETAL
TYPOS ■ NEST ■ REDS
```

54

```
HOG ■ ACTAS ■ PAPAL
OTO ■ PAINT ■ IMOUT
(T)OLLP(L)A(Z)A ■ CYSTS
DODOS ■ IMP ■ GEO
OLEO ■ (J)E(O)P(A)R(D)I(Z)E
GENTEEL ■ DEADON
■ ■ REID ■ ALONE
(P)APE(R)AI(R)PLANE ■
LANES ■ POLL ■ ■
ORNATE ■ LAYAWAY
PRES(U)MA(B)L(Y) ■ LACE
■ (O)RA ■ STL ■ MARCO
STING ■ HIDDENGEM
RECTO ■ OGRES ■ ODE
IDEST ■ SEEYA ■ DEN
```

55

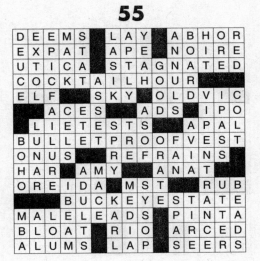

```
DEEMS   LAY   ABHOR
EXPAT   APE   NOIRE
UTICA   STAGNATED
COCKTAILHOUR
ELF   SKY   OLDVIC
  ACES   ADS   IPO
  LIETESTS   APAL
BULLETPROOFVEST
ONUS   REFRAINS
HAR   AMY   ANAT
OREIDA   MST   RUB
  BUCKEYESTATE
MALELEADS   PINTA
BLOAT   RIO   ARCED
ALUMS   LAP   SEERS
```

56

```
MAGIC   ARAL   ACER
ABASH   RODE   SOLE
PULSE   CARGOSHIP
  LENS   SOUPNAZI
QUALITYTIME   BAN
UPN   LOA   TENT
AFT   LOLZ   ASIA
FORKEDLIGHTNING
FRYE   PEAR   RCA
  YOKE   RYE   BOZ
BOW   TEXTMESSAGE
SWEETTEA   SPUR
INABOTTLE   ASTIN
DEVO   LEOX   SHOVE
EDEN   ERNO   SINEW
```

57

```
MEEK   TODO   LUNAR
APSE   UVEA   ATONE
RICE   RAFT   MTWTF
ICANONLYHOPE
ASPICS   CORNEL
  ENSUE   CHOLERA
BERG   PRISONYARD
EXO   IDI   ROE
SPUTNIKONE   BERN
TETHERS   YAYAS
SLEEVE   TESTER
  HIDDENCAMERA
MOREL   ASEA   AXIS
DRILL   MARK   TINT
TROPE   NUDE   ITSA
```

58

```
PAPA   ACT   PRIMER
EVER   NOW   BUREAU
LIAR   CHESSBOARD
TACO   HERO   ANTSY
  NEWYORKCITY
  HARE   COO   JLO
WHEEL   FEW   BOOR
RUPAULSDRAGRACE
AMID   AIR   AUDIO
PEC   HIC   EARN
  ROCKANDROLL
TWEET   OLAF   MAIN
HALLOFFAME   ATVS
URBANE   ROE   REEF
STAYED   MRS   SXSW
```

59

```
OLAV   OFART   SHAH
SOLO   NIMES   COSA
HALLOFFAME   ANTI
ATF   GOTTO   CLERK
HELLOHOWAREYOU
  MOET   BUD
OPAL   STRUM   REP
HILLSTREETBLUES
ONE   THIEF   ELLA
  AAA   PANE
HOLLYWOODACTOR
AREAS   VIOLA   FIR
SIRS   HULLABALOO
TOOK   SLEET   BAJA
ENYA   TERSE   SWAN
```

60

```
AIDS   PLUS   ITEMS
ROUE   RAPT   NASAL
TWEEHOUSE   SUPRA
SALSA   REAM   GRIT
  SWATMACHINE
OAKLEY   RUTTED
WHISKEYMOVE
LAND   EOE   BARS
  WOWEDMOUTHS
SAMSON   AWGOON
QUACKOFDAWN
USNA   READ   EMCEE
ASTRA   ELMERFUDD
SIREN   LAIR   ABIG
HEADY   SINE   SATE
```

61

```
DAWN  STAN  ALOFT
AGRO  ARIA  RAZOR
ROOSEVELT  AMORE
INTERIM  ORGANDY
NYE  ROOT  HOSE
   HARRISON  HOP
COMETS  MAS  WORE
OBAMA  DOG  TYLER
PICS  JOT  ERNEST
ETA  BUCHANAN
  DARN  YELL  PRE
STATION  NIELSEN
HAMID  CLEVELAND
EFILE  ATIE  CLEO
STATS  ADDN  SMEW
```

62

```
AGAVES  SPA  ALLA
IOMOTH  EDU  TEAR
DRYICE  AFROPICK
APPLEPIE  ARRAYS
  OAT  LESSEE
IVE  CELLO  LSATS
DOHA  ASST  SETUP
ELLIOT  KENOBI
STERN  PTUI  TMEN
TARPS  RUSTS  IDS
  IPHONE  OTC
DCAREA  ARTPAPER
ALPACINO  OSCINE
FOOT  KOI  GUILDS
TYPE  URL  APTEST
```

63

```
CANDO  LIMA  EPPS
BLEAK  APOP  ALOE
STARESDOWN  TAPE
 ATTENDS  EASIER
 SFO  FAD  NYE
ARP  FUDGE  AMPED
PEACETIME  MAA
EXPO  SEALS  UPON
 ELI  TIMEPIECE
RERAN  ELENA  RTE
EXP  SAD  SIM
DOLAPS  SEENOTE
STAG  DOWNSTAIRS
EINE  OVID  ENEMY
ACES  IAMS  RADAR
```

64

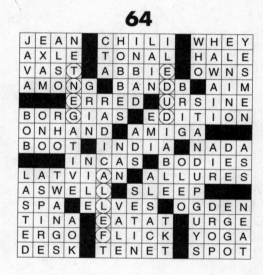

```
JEAN  CHILI  WHEY
AXLE  TONAL  HALE
VAST  ABBIE  OWNS
AMONG  BANDB  AIM
 ERRED  URSINE
BORGIAS  EDITION
ONHAND  AMIGA
BOOT  INDIA  NADA
 INCAS  BODIES
LATVIAN  ALLURES
ASWELL  SLEEP
SPA  ELVES  OGDEN
TINA  EATAT  URGE
ERGO  FLICK  YOGA
DESK  TENET  SPOT
```

65

```
FDA  CASK  CLIOS
ARC  ARIA  GLANCE
TAR  CITYSLICKER
 COOKS  HOP  LAB
BUBBLEWRAP  FINI
BLASE  HUG  SONIA
SATE  FOG  BROGAN
 SUGARCOAT
CRISPS  ALT  RIBS
DAMES  GTO  PARES
RIAS  DUSTJACKET
ANG  BAL  PRESS
CHEVYBLAZER  OWL
KARATS  SEGO  MAO
STYLE  PEST  EXT
```

66

```
MEDALS  ACK  AMOS
IMONIT  MAE  KEPI
CANTERBURYTALES
RITZ  ASPCA  ERA
ALS  THATSASTEAL
 PSAT  SKA
CLEANSLATE  USTA
SPAYS  ALE  ONTAP
TSKS  GOINGSTALE
 SSR  ASSN
NIKOLATESLA  DEA
UZI  ADORN  TBAR
LASTBUTNOTLEAST
LASE  AHS  NIECES
SKYE  LET  TINKLY
```

67

```
J U T S   D A N E   T I T A N S
A S H E   S T A N   O C E L O T
C H E E R L E A D   T E N E T S
O E D   O M A N   T A U T
B R O N C O S   D O L P H I N S
  E G O   D E M O N S   I V A N
  D A F O E   O R A   K N E E L
    T E A M B U I L D I N G
S P E W S   E N T   A N I O N
O D I E   G E T O U T   N T H
P A T R I O T S   B E N G A L S
    T W O S   R U L E   P G A
B A T H O S   L U N I S O L A R
U R B A N E   A T T N   R A M I
G I A N T S   S H U E   O N E S
```

68

```
O S L O   M I A T A   E M U S
S L A V   E C R U S   N A N A
S A V E   R H E T T   U Z I S
O M A R   G O S E E   N E T S
    C H E R   E R I C
J O S H E S   N O I D E A
O R C A S   S S N   N A I L S
C Z A R   A T E O F   T E M P
K O N G   P R A T E   I D O S
    E S P E R A N T O
S A L S A   T A G   A N I S E
A L A   W I C C A N S   M O D
T I P O F T H E I C E B E R G
A B I L I T Y   N A R R A T E
N I N E T Y   A S A N A S
```

69

```
A S H E   P A P A   B E G A T
S H U N   E Y E S O F B L U E
W I N D   P E T I T F O U R S
I N G O T   E M T   N E A T
T Z E   A D D   O E D   S L Y
H O R S D O E U V R E S
  A F T   L A S   M U I R
B O U I L L A B A I S S E
E R R S   G U V   H O C
  M I L L E F E U I L L E
T L C   S A O   F O G   A A A
A E R O   T W O   G E T I T
F R E N C H C H E F   D I M E
T O W E R S U I T E   D O E R
S I S S Y   T O A D   A N D Y
```

70

```
Q U I Z   A M A Z E   C C S
E T R E   K E F I R   H U T
D E K E D   C A R P [IN] G A B [OUT]
    S O Y   N O S   U R S I
A S K   J O E S   L L C S
T H E F O U N T A [IN] O F Y [OUT] H
M I M E   A B O R T S
  V O Y A G E   G E T U P S
    H A R M O N   S U N S
F R O T H [IN] G A T T H E M [OUT] H
L E N O   I S L E   P S Y
A H E M   T E T   Y E T
R A [IN] B O W T R [OUT]   S H E L L
E S C   L I T E R   [IN] B O X
S H H   E X U D E   [OUT] B O X
```

71

```
I V S   R U S E   B O A R D
T I C   C I G A R   I C I E R
T C H O T C H K E   G E S S O
  I N U R E   S C H M A L T Z
  A T L   T B O N E S
C H U T Z P A H   O U I
L I Z A   S L A P   T A L E S
A Y E   Y I D D I S H   A L A
P A R M A   A T T A   O V A L
  I R E   O Y G E V A L T
  B I N D E R   M I L
M E G I L L A H   S I N A I
A L I B I   V E R K L E M P T
D I V A N   E R N I E   P O E
D E E R E   S O A P   S S N
```

72

```
M A M B A   G L O T T I S
S T A U B   B O A R H U N T
G O D R Y   E N S C O N C E
M E S S A G E T   R   A
E M I   S L O B   H   E   D
T A T A   A N A H E I M C A
C N B C   S I D E R O A D S
  E C G   A   E D W I T H
I N T E R L   C   S A L
R A T P O I S O N   N A B S
I G E T I D E A S   S C O T
S   R   N   A G E S   C U P
T   I   G S E C T I O N
G O T O R U I N   A M U C K
I N O N E A C T   L I N E A
G Y M S O C K   E N T R Y
```

73

```
B F A   L O A F     P A S S B Y
O I L G A U G E   E S C A L E
X X F A C T O R   W A R M U P
C A R T E R   R E S P I R E
A T E   D E V I L     P A R K
R E D O   C C S E C T I O N
    U S S R   A L L   M A E
J J C R E W     A A L I N E
A M Y   A A A   O N M E
B B C O M P L E X     E B B S
S A L T     E C O L I   R O T
  R A T P A C K   O K F I N E
O R D E A L   E E R E A D E R
F I E R C E   R A D A R G U N
F E S S E S   D U E S   E P A
```

74

```
T I K I   M E A T   S C I F I
O R A L   I N C H   T O G A S
F I L L I N T H E B L A N K S
U S E   M I S E R Y   L I E U
      M A O   S E E N   T I E
A S S I G N S     A R M E D
S H A D E S O F G R A Y
S E G A   L E O     S A D R
    I N S I D E T H E B O X
  T H R E E   S E A L E G S
H O E   O N C E   E L F
A L A S   S O N A T A   S P A
B E T W E E N T H E L I N E S
I D E A S   D E A R   C A R P
T O R T S   O R B S   E P P S
```

75

```
T H E M   G R O G   Y A C H T
I O T A   E A V E   A G R E E
D A H L   T H E N E R E I D S
E X I L E D   R E N D   S G T
    O S L O   S O L A C E S
G A P   K N E W   K I L O S
U N I X   E X A M I N E
S N A R F   I D A   E X P A T
    A U S T E R E   A O N E
  B R Y C E   S X S W   S O N
L E A S H E D   T O T E
A H I   S T E M   U N R I P E
C A S S I O P E I A   I D O L
E V I T A   O M A R   C O P S
S E N D S   T O N Y   K N E E
```

76

```
L G B T   A C L U   A M A I N
O L I O   W O O T   N A N C E
B U B B L E G U M   T O N O W
S T I E B     O C A R I N A
      J U D A S P R I E S T
E R A S   S E A T A C
G A S P I P E S   T O L L S
A G A I N S T   L A I D O U T
D E P T H   M A R C E C K O
    I M G A M E   S K E W
B A S E B A L L B A T
A M E R I C A   I N E P T
S I T A T   S O D A M I X E R
I N U S E   S H A G   N I N A
L O P E D   Y O L O   E T S Y
```

77

```
J O T   A G E R   P L A S T I C
O N O   B R A E   R I H A N N A
D O D O B I R D   I N S P O T S
I N O U Y E   O H O K   T O T
E E L S   S O S O R E V I E W S
  H I T H E R   V I D E O
B A S S I   A D E   I N S T I R
A N T   L A L A L A N D   U M A
E D S E L S   Y S L   O K R A S
    R E H A B   S A R O N G
S O H E L P M E G O D   O T I S
A N A   L A D E   E S P A N A
N A I L G U N   A L P H A B E T
D I L E M M A   R O T O   L E E
P R E S S E S   S X S W   E R S
```

78

```
  C C S   Q B S   C L E V E R
F O L K   U A E   I O N I A N
B R A I D I N G   N O D O G S
I S M   E L I A   E F I L E
L A B R A T S   B R A V E R Y
A G E E   S H E R A   E T T A
B E R E T   M E M O   S O Y
    L E F T B R A I N
L B J   D A R E   L E A S E
I R O C   S I D E B   C R A G
V I B R A T O   B R A K I N G
  S H E L F   O B I E   A D D
S T U D I O   N O B R A D A Y
E L N I N O   C U E   I N R E
W E T T E D   E T S   L E T
```

79

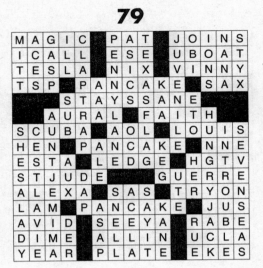

```
M A G I C ▮ P A T ▮ J O I N S
I C A L L ▮ E S E ▮ U B O A T
T E S L A ▮ N I X ▮ V I N N Y
T S P ▮ P A N C A K E ▮ S A X
▮ ▮ S T A Y S S A N E ▮ ▮
▮ A U R A L ▮ F A I T H ▮
S C U B A ▮ A O L ▮ L O U I S
H E N ▮ P A N C A K E ▮ N N E
E S T A ▮ L E D G E ▮ H G T V
S T J U D E ▮ ▮ G U E R R E
A L E X A ▮ S A S ▮ T R Y O N
L A M ▮ P A N C A K E ▮ J U S
A V I D ▮ S E E Y A ▮ R A B E
D I M E ▮ A L L I N ▮ U C L A
Y E A R ▮ P L A T E ▮ E K E S
```

80

```
T H E D A B ▮ C H A N ▮ D U D
M E R I D A ▮ F A T E L I N E
S L I D E R ▮ L G B T I C O N
▮ M E N L O ▮ G A B F E S T
▮ ▮ T E N ▮ H I T A T ▮
G L A M ▮ E G O S ▮ L E P E W
R I R I ▮ T O T ▮ E L V I R A
A B C S ▮ C O L O N ▮ E X I T
D R E S S Y ▮ A U G ▮ R I C E
S A D A T ▮ E V I E ▮ Y E A R
▮ B E C C A ▮ L E V ▮
L A T E R A L ▮ B L O A T
O C E A N I A N ▮ E D I T O R
S A N T E R I A ▮ R E C O D E
S I T ▮ R O R Y ▮ T R E N D Y
```

81

```
A D D R E S S ▮ P O P U P A D
P E R I D O T ▮ O R I N O C O
A V O C (A) D O ▮ W A N D E R S
R O P E ▮ O P E ▮ T I M E
T E S ▮ S I D E R O (A D)
▮ O O H ▮ D E C ▮ E N T
▮ T A R S A L ▮ D A R K R E D
B A T C A V E ▮ O R A N G E S
B R E (A) D E D ▮ N I C E S T
C A N ▮ I A N ▮ N E E
▮ N O T S O B (A D) ▮ M O P
▮ T O I L ▮ T R E ▮ M I L L
L O O N I E R ▮ Z A M U N D A
B A Z O O K A ▮ E L A S T I C
O D Y S S E Y ▮ L O O K S E E
```

82

```
L I A M ▮ T E T E S ▮ F R A T
A C N E ▮ E C O N O ▮ A O N E
P A G E ▮ L O S T L I Q U I D
S N O R K E L S ▮ D R I L L S
E S L ▮ A C A ▮ D E E R E ▮
D O A S L O W B U R N ▮ T H E
▮ H E M ▮ L A S E R T A G
P E P A ▮ S E L ▮ A E R O
B R O M A N C E ▮ S E N ▮
S A W ▮ G O U P A N D D O W N
▮ E D I C T ▮ L A G ▮ N E U
M O R I T A ▮ S C R E A M E D
I N S E A R C H O F ▮ K I N G
S L U G ▮ B R A V E ▮ O K I E
T Y P O ▮ S O W E D ▮ N E E D
```

83

```
S H A G ▮ A G A S P ▮ T I F F
C U J O ▮ R E V U E ▮ R A I L
O L A F ▮ E L E N A ▮ O G L E
T A X L A W S ▮ K G B M O L E
▮ A L E ▮ R A P ▮
N E S T E G G ▮ V A L E T E D
E R E ▮ R O O ▮ E L I
A D A ▮ T O M ▮ D E A ▮ A F T
R O S E ▮ D O W E L ▮ O B I T
S C E N E ▮ R H O ▮ B R I N Y
▮ R O T A R Y C L U B S
P C P ▮ A R A M A I C ▮ C A R
A M E X ▮ T H E M E ▮ B U R Y
P O N Y ▮ ▮ R I G A
A N T Z ▮ C R Y P T ▮ A T O N
```

84

```
E S T A T E ▮ A D S ▮ U R A L
S L A P O N ▮ B O A ▮ P E P E
P (I/A) T T E R ▮ E G G P L A N T
▮ T A I L O R ▮ G A L I L E (O/I)
▮ T E N A C E ▮ U N M A N
B P L U S ▮ N O R I S K
L O A D S ▮ L E C H ▮ (F/C) A T
O L D E ▮ (J/B) E L L Y ▮ P L O W
(B/T) O Y ▮ N E V E ▮ P I A N O
▮ R E T A G S ▮ E L W E S
S A M O A ▮ G E I S E L
C H (I/A) T T E R ▮ S P R A N G
H E C T O R E D ▮ A S G O (O/L) D
M A R E ▮ T E A ▮ T I E R O D
O D O R ▮ E N D ▮ E N R A P T
```

85

```
BUSTED ■ SNOWBALL
EMPIRE ■ CAMELLIA
GALPAL ■ ANGLEFOR
AMIS ■ ILL ■ DEANS
TITHE ■ EDITED ■
■ EDNA ■ MOD ■ HOT
SPEEDO ■ NIL ■ POGO
TILTATWINDMILLS
ALAS ■ BIN ■ YESYES
YEN ■ WAN ■ GALA ■
■ MIDGUT ■ DITSY
SWEAT ■ POE ■ TATA
PITCHOUT ■ WHALER
AFRAIDSO ■ EOLIAN
TIEONEON ■ ROYALS
```

86

```
ADDLE ■ ANDSO ■ HAD
LEVIN ■ COATI ■ RIME
LADPOWERBAL ■ OPEC
■ VIKES ■ BIB ■ OHNO
LAIDIN ■ LADARMORC
ODD ■ TMI ■ SITPAT
PIETY ■ EBBTIDE ■
■ GOWESTYOUNGMAN ■
■ INPHASE ■ EPCOT
FIESTA ■ SSS ■ TOO
LADTACOSA ■ LIVEBY
IMIT ■ ENE ■ JADED ■
NATO ■ LADSUPERBOW
GLOP ■ AIGHT ■ ANIMA
SIR ■ BREES ■ LEGGY
```

87

```
JAMA ■ SOPS ■ PJS
OFAGE ■ PHAT ■ ALAN
BFLATMAJOR ■ LANA
FALSEIDOL ■ FINER
AIMS ■ BEYOURSELF
IRAIL ■ BOTTLE
REP ■ YOYOMA ■ EXED
■ BEAARTHUR ■
RITE ■ TYRANT ■ MAB
IMHERE ■ ERATO
BEARTRACKS ■ ELLA
BATHE ■ THISISWAR
INGA ■ GROWABEARD
TNUT ■ WIKI ■ MARGE
SOY ■ BAES ■ TEED
```

88

```
HERO ■ IBMPC ■ NOSE
ALOU ■ TIARA ■ OD[IOU]S
DUB[IOU]SHONOR ■ TOAT
STEINEM ■ MADONNA
TED ■ ELEA ■ COR ■
■ PEP ■ GRAC[IOU]SME
STARR ■ FEES ■ STAY
LANES ■ END ■ ABUSE
ACDC ■ CADS ■ TINTS
WHY[IOU]GHTA ■ POG ■
■ SEA ■ SVEN ■ IMO
ZINGERS ■ ALADDIN
OBOE ■ MICROLOANS
REAM ■ ENV[IOU]S ■ THEE
ATMS ■ ROSSI ■ SORT
```

89

```
RAHM ■ ESQS ■ SHAKE
OGEE ■ FEET ■ YOUIN
TRADEFAIR ■ DURST
■ EDEN ■ SIEG ■ SOLI
LEBARON ■ ALTERER
OSU ■ OVA ■ MANCAVE
OTT ■ NEKO ■ STA ■
MOTT ■ REEFS ■ THAI
■ ASP ■ DOES ■ OPT
PACKRAT ■ RYE ■ MPS
ONLEASH ■ TERSELY
PTAS ■ SEEN ■ IATE ■
TIMOR ■ FLIPFLOPS
AFOUL ■ ESTO ■ SWAP
BARTS ■ DEED ■ ANYA
```

90

```
EMERALD ■ RAPPELS
LORELEI ■ ITSALIE
HEADLESSCHICKEN
ISTOO ■ ACHE ■ TOUT
■ UKRAINE ■
■ BOTTOMLESSPIT
ALAR ■ BEE ■ SUGAR
LAKEBED ■ PRORATA
ARENA ■ TAO ■ IVAN
■ ENDLESSSUMMER ■
■ INHASTE ■
SMOG ■ DARA ■ LENDS
TOPLESSSWIMSUIT
ONEUNIT ■ ATATIME
PODESTA ■ YACHTER
```

91

```
RIB . MIFF . TAPPED
ONELINER . ORELSE
GATORADE . STRATA
UPTO . NINES . YEN
ETE . HENCE . APSES
. . ROO . HOWTO . .
BADACTOR . HAWKED
OLAF . USERID . IRE
AMY . FLAVOR . OCTA
RASCAL . ONLOOKER
. AREEL . APU . .
TEMPO . RUBIK . PAD
OLE . OATES . IAGO
WIELDS . INESCROW
ESTERS . ONRECORD
DESOTO . NYET . WAY
```

92

```
ATMOST ↓ ↑ ASTROS
REACTOR . SCHNOOK
MANDELA . GRANOLA
ALL . WELLNOW . FIT
NAILS . LEI . LATTE
IDEA . IYAWT . BOER
← YRCGN . UORPS ←
. KEA . O . ORE .
→ POWER . BREAK →
SIMI . OUNDA . ZUNI
ANITA . TYE . BEGIN
LET . BRACERO . USC
ANTIFOG . NATASHA
DUEDATE . INCITES
STROBE ↓ ↑ THRASH
```

93

```
SHUL . ISIS . DYADS
MEGA . SCOT . WAHOO
IRANOMANICELAND
TONIC . BILLET .
HID . CUBALEBANON
SCAPULA . SOS . ERA
. ALERT . KOCH
. UNITEDNATIONS .
SCAR . GLENN .
ALI . LES . ARCADES
MALIESTONIA . ONT
. STMARK . POSSE
PERUSERBIASPAIN
ELIZA . VENT . EGGO
CLOUT . EDGE . LENS
```

94

```
[CAT]TLE . CAPRA . FAT[CAT]
ARES . AIRED . ALEC
LINT . LOATH . GASH
OAT . WILT . DAINTY
GLORIFIES . RNA .
. ADO . IBM . RBI
LITTERBOXES . KIT
ALAS . NAFTA . AIDE
ILK . KITTYCORNER
DYE . NAE . HOE .
. NEE . DONTPANIC
SHOVEL . LOOS . EMO
NOVA . ENDOW . CHAP
OPEN . NOISE . ARMY
[CAT]ERS . STEEL . MUS[CAT]
```

95

```
CABO . HEMI . ANDOR
UPON . AVON . GUIDE
FORA . BIBI . ENRON
FREDDIE . CONCERT
STRAIT . LEROI .
. ROSSI . IRONON
TATER . TVMOM . AWE
AJA . QUEEN . ZIT
LAX . SUDAN . CRIES
CRIMEA . ISSUE .
. EASED . TEASET
BENEFIT . MERCURY
ENOKI . YSER . TRAP
ARIES . MUTE . ELSE
MYRRH . APSO . DYED
```

96

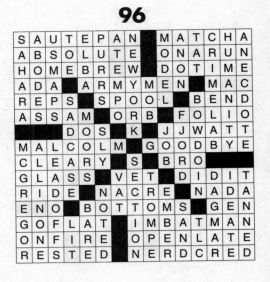

```
SAUTEPAN . MATCHA
ABSOLUTE . ONARUN
HOMEBREW . DOTIME
ADA . ARMYMEN . MAC
REPS . SPOOL . BEND
ASSAM . ORB . FOLIO
. DOS . K . JJWATT
MALCOLM . GOODBYE
CLEARY . S . BRO .
GLASS . VET . DIDIT
RIDE . NACRE . NADA
ENO . BOTTOMS . GEN
GOFLAT . IMBATMAN
ONFIRE . OPENLATE
RESTED . NERDCRED
```

97

```
S L U G   S P L I T S   N B A
O E N O   A L E T A P   A R C
T V P G   S E A A I R   T A N
S Y C O P H A N T   E T U D E
    B E A D S   H A I R
S A G A N     P O D C A S T
C Z A R   I C E A G E   L E O
O U R   A N A G R A M   I M P
O R B   R E B O R N   A S I S
B E A T E R S   A N T S Y
    G O A T   S P O R K
T H E O C   T H E H I L T O N
A I M   O L E A R Y   E R G O
F D A   D E A R I E   T E R R
T E N   E A S E L S   S E E M
```

98

```
A M O S   C A R T S   S P A S
R E N O   A N O U K   T A C K
T E A S   S C E N I C A R E A
  T W O W A Y S A B O U T I T
    H O O       I N N A T E
S K I N O F F M Y B A C K
A R M   A L E E   I H E A R
N O   M Y A N M A R     N O
S C A L Y   Y S E R   R O O
    M A N I S A N I S L A N D
A G O R A S     S A C
L A U G H I N G M A T T E R
F I N E S T H O U R   E D A M
A L T S   O R A T E   N A S A
S Y S T   K A L E S   T Y P O
```

99

```
C I N C H   U G H   S I G M A
A L O H A   F R Y   A R I E L
R O B I N H O O D   Y A N N I
A S I A G O   O R E S   S U V
T E D   A N I M A L H O U S E
    P R O S   F I B
K O N A   R I P E   T E M P O
F A N T A S T I C V O Y A G E
C R E E D   I T O O   E G A D
    N U B   L I E D
B E E T L E J U I C E   T E L
A T M   T E E M   E L T O R O
N A O M I   S P I D E R M A N
D I J O N   S E C   R E E S E
S L I N G   E D Y   S K I E R
```

100

```
C A R O M   E T N A   J A W
A L O N G   A L O O F   E P A
T O T E M   S K Y W R I T E R
A H A B   S E S S I O N S
W A T C H T V     T T O P
B O O   E Y E D   E R M A
A E R I A L R E [CON]   R E E L
  H R E   [CON] E S   I A G O
E M O T I [CON]   Y O Y O M A
S L O P   [CON] T A I N E R
T E L E [CON]   R O S E S   B A M
A G E   T O A L L   I T A L O
G I R A R D I   A R T I S A N
G E A R O I L   N A I L S I T
  S T A L E   D E S T I N Y
```

101

```
S U N   F I R E   M O T H E R
O R I   U R A L   A D W A R E
L I B R E T T O   D E A L I N
  B E G   A P A R T   L E D
H E L L O   T E L E S C O P E
O R E   E A S T   R O A R
L A R G E S T   E C R U
A S S O R T   O P E R A S
  T E E N   E N G L I S H
C I T Y   A R S E   N C O
I N E E D A N A P   N I G H T
U S A   I V A N A   O C T
D I P D Y E   K N O C K O U T
A D O R E R   L O C H   S P A
D E T E R S   E L S E   S I X
```

102

```
J E E P   L O T S   P R A M S
A C D C   D A W N   R E G A L
B O I L   T R I O   O M A N I
  T A K E S T W O T O T A N
Z O M B I E   S Y N E   E G G
I R E   N T S   M I S S E S
O D N I G H T I R E N E
N O U N   E C U   W I N D
  C A R M E N S A N D I E
L F G A M E   T A X   A T E
E R L   M A S C   T E A R E D
G O O V E R T H E E D G E
A T B A T   A I D E   E S A U
T H A N E   S C A N   S A W S
O S L E R   H A M S   A Y E S
```

103

S	P	A	N	■	O	N	I	T	■	D	O	L	L	S
A	L	A	I	■	G	E	S	U	N	D	H	E	I	T
N	A	R	C	■	R	O	O	T	Y	T	O	O	T	Y
■	N	O	O	V	E	N	U	S	E	■	■	N	E	E
M	E	N	L	O	■	■	T	I	T	T	L	E	S	■
I	T	B	A	N	D	S	■	■	■	S	U	E	■	■
M	A	U	S	■	R	A	G	E	■	M	E	S	A	S
E	R	R	■	H	E	A	R	T	H	S	■	E	L	I
S	Y	R	I	A	■	B	E	T	A	■	B	A	I	T
■	■	A	L	T	■	■	A	T	L	A	R	G	E	■
■	C	O	N	T	A	C	T	■	■	I	R	O	N	S
B	A	S	■	■	M	A	R	S	U	P	I	U	M	■
I	N	A	N	U	P	R	O	A	R	■	S	T	E	P
T	A	K	E	S	A	T	U	R	N	■	T	E	N	S
S	L	A	T	S	■	E	T	A	S	■	A	S	T	I

104

W	I	G	■	A	S	C	O	T	S	■	■	P	B	S
I	P	A	G	L	I	A	C	C	I	■	V	I	A	L
D	O	N	O	T	E	N	T	E	R	■	A	L	B	A
E	D	G	E	■	G	O	A	L	■	I	N	O	U	T
■	■	■	S	P	E	E	D	L	I	M	I	T	■	■
L	E	T	O	■	■	■	C	O	L	L	A	R	■	■
B	O	X	■	O	N	E	I	D	A	■	L	I	P	O
O	U	T	O	F	O	R	D	E	R	S	I	G	N	S
A	I	R	Y	■	T	R	O	W	E	L	■	H	E	Y
T	E	A	S	E	R	■	■	■	E	S	T	A	■	■
■	■	S	T	E	E	P	G	R	A	D	E	■	■	■
C	A	M	E	L	■	E	L	A	N	■	N	A	S	H
O	M	A	R	■	R	O	A	D	C	L	O	S	E	D
G	E	L	S	■	I	N	C	O	H	E	R	E	N	T
S	N	L	■	B	Y	E	N	O	W	■	A	T	V	■

105

■	■	I	T	S	A	L	I	E	■	N	O	I	R	■
■	B	R	O	W	N	A	N	D	S	E	R	V	E	■
■	D	U	K	E	A	N	D	D	U	C	H	E	S	S
P	E	R	■	■	T	U	E	S	■	O	R	S	■	■
T	A	G	T	E	A	M	S	■	C	L	U	T	C	H
A	L	L	W	E	T	■	B	A	D	■	E	L	I	■
S	T	E	E	R	■	T	H	A	N	■	B	I	A	S
■	■	R	I	C	E	A	N	D	B	E	A	N	S	■
D	R	A	K	E	A	N	D	J	O	S	H	■	■	■
E	O	N	S	■	M	O	J	O	■	T	A	B	L	E
P	L	Y	■	A	P	R	■	C	A	V	E	A	T	■
P	E	T	A	L	S	■	A	M	A	R	E	T	T	O
■	H	E	P	■	E	D	O	M	■	T	I	N	■	■
S	M	I	T	H	A	N	D	W	E	S	S	O	N	■
P	E	N	N	A	N	D	T	E	L	L	E	R	■	■
A	L	G	A	■	G	O	O	D	S	O	N	■	■	■

106

R	A	G	S	■	W	W	I	■	■	H	E	H	E	■
A	L	E	U	T	I	A	N	■	P	O	R	E	S	■
P	A	T	R	I	C	K	S	T	E	W	A	R	T	■
I	M	S	■	E	K	E	■	O	N	E	S	E	E	D
D	E	W	A	R	S	■	D	A	S	■	■	I	R	A
O	D	I	C	■	■	J	U	D	I	D	E	N	C	H
■	■	A	T	T	U	N	E	D	■	E	R	R	■	■
■	H	U	G	O	W	E	A	V	I	N	G	■	■	■
■	A	G	R	■	T	H	E	B	E	A	N	■	■	■
W	I	L	L	S	M	I	T	H	■	■	S	M	O	G
E	C	O	■	A	R	E	■	H	A	T	E	T	O	■
T	E	C	H	B	R	O	■	J	O	N	■	R	A	P
C	H	A	R	A	C	T	E	R	A	C	T	O	R	■
A	T	R	E	E	■	■	I	T	A	L	I	A	N	O
P	E	E	R	■	X	E	S	■	A	G	E	S	■	■

107

P	R	O	B	E	■	H	A	H	A	■	S	C	A	M
R	O	U	E	N	■	E	G	A	D	■	C	U	B	A
O	O	Z	E	D	■	R	A	N	S	C	A	R	E	D
■	F	O	R	E	W	O	R	D	■	A	M	B	L	E
■	N	A	A	N	■	P	E	R	P	■	■	■	■	■
A	U	G	U	R	Y	■	D	I	C	T	I	O	N	■
S	P	O	T	S	■	B	A	C	H	S	■	C	A	P
A	P	T	S	■	P	I	N	K	O	■	P	U	M	A
P	E	T	■	S	E	R	T	S	■	S	E	L	I	G
■	D	I	C	T	A	T	E	■	S	C	R	I	B	E
■	O	A	T	H	■	S	O	A	K	■	■	■	■	■
E	A	R	L	Y	■	M	A	T	U	R	E	L	Y	■
G	L	A	S	S	W	A	R	E	■	A	D	A	M	S
G	O	G	O	■	O	R	C	A	■	B	U	I	C	K
S	T	U	N	■	O	K	O	K	■	S	P	R	A	Y

108

H	O	R	D	E	■	C	U	R	R	E	N	C	Y	■
A	B	E	A	M	■	S	T	R	E	A	M	B	E	D
J	A	S	M	I	N	E	A	N	D	J	E	A	N	S
■	D	A	N	G	E	R	■	D	A	R	T	S	■	■
T	I	N	■	R	A	B	B	I	■	G	E	O	S	■
B	A	D	G	E	R	S	A	N	D	B	E	A	R	S
A	H	S	O	■	■	R	H	E	A	■	M	S	N	■
■	■	I	C	E	A	N	D	I	N	K	■	■	■	■
P	S	I	■	A	L	S	O	■	■	A	U	D	I	■
C	O	M	E	D	Y	A	N	D	C	R	I	M	E	S
T	W	I	X	■	P	E	C	O	S	■	P	M	S	■
■	S	T	A	T	S	■	U	N	V	O	T	E	■	■
P	E	A	C	E	A	N	D	P	E	P	P	E	R	S
B	A	T	T	E	R	I	E	S	■	E	I	E	I	O
A	R	E	A	M	A	P	S	■	D	E	N	T	S	■

109

```
WHIM_LION__ICANT
PENA_OMOO__NOVAE
MARCHOFPROGRESS
_REAR__SEX_DRAT
SIT_WEBB__EXPO
KOHLS_LIMN__ANGER
EDIE_DELI__LABILE
WINTERWONDERLAND
EDGILY_XIII__ENID
RESTS_LIMB__BUTNO
_SATE__ASTI__POT
TAIL_ATL__OKRA
SPRINGHASSPRUNG
ASADA_ALAI__ANDY
RENEW_LAMB__MEAN
```

110

```
OWLET__IDA__SCALP
CHINMUSIC__LUCIA
HANGEHIGH__OTTER
ETE_NOT__MTCOOK
RAD__HOOKEHORNS
_TADA__KAOS
BONAMI__TOMB__XCI
ROCKESOCKEROBOT
ALE_NOVA__RUNONS
__MIKE__TEXT
KNOCKEDEAD__GIG
REINER__TIM__ANY
ALLOY__STICKEMUP
FLUTE__PINETREES
TYPED__FOG__SASSY
```

111

```
DROSS_ACTS__ASSAD
AISLE_PLOW__UTERO
TACIT_HOME__RULER
ETATS_IDEA__IBEAM
DAR_ITD__TNG__SSS
_UNO___OAF
TWOS_INMOST__CBGB
OHNO_LEAGUE__CARE
MAE_SEACREST__RAE
STASH_THEY__SATYR
_ALLAN__VALES
OBLIQUEREFERENCE
ROTC_KRONER__PDAS
BRIE_ETUDES__PELT
SEED_SEESTO__ODED
```

112

```
LAIDAWAY__BARCAR
ALTEREGO__EXHALE
MAINMENU__SEEFIT
ASS__EDIT__SEAR
_SHOWIN__GUSSY
LAPTOP__DUKES
ACHEBE__WRIT__AMP
CHEWONT__EMONGER
YEW_BLOC__ONAUTO
_SAYAH__NINEAM
SHRUG__DESOTO
HOOD_MYTH__MAD
IMGONE__JARLOOSE
PEEKIN__OLDLATIN
SYRUPS__BLACKHAT
```

113

```
TRIP_CLOTH__AVA
RAVE_DONHO__TSAR
ICANTSLEEPAWINK
BENTO_IBC__CAF
ERA_KITCHENSIN
_VENA__AXE__CAP
FRANC_EMT__JADE
POUR_HOTPI__AREA
ARMY_AKA__NEWER
CUR_BOA__ACTS
MAKESYOUTH__PDT
IRE_DVD__ALLAY
DISAPPEARINGINK
DRIB_EATEN__BENE
SAN_GREYS__TSOS
```

114

```
MADDASH__ATTRACT
AREOLAE__SAOIRSE
VICTOR/VICTORIA
_TEASEDOUT
REFIS_HIE__PASTS
ETRE_TENSE__CLIP
THORPE__TATAMI
INS_REDFLAG__SEC
NIT_ISRAELI__HRE
AC/DC_RCA__LOESS
_NEE_OED__ERR
SKIM_AM/FM__AFAR
XOXO_MAORI__NILE
SLOT_INFER__GLUM
WANE_NOFEE__EMMY
```

115

C	L	O	M	P		N	I	G	H		C	A	S	H
A	U	D	I	S		O	R	E	O		A	B	U	T
R	A	I	N	Y		P	A	T	T	Y	M	E	L	T
	U	N	I	C	O	R	N	S	T	A	R	T	U	P
		H	B	O					A	M	Y			
Z	O	M	B	I	E	B	A	N	K	S		H	I	P
I	S	A	A	C		C	U	E			M	O	N	A
P	A	R	R		S	H	U	N	S		E	W	A	N
I	K	I	D		E	A	T		A	I	S	L	E	
T	A	O		P	A	T	E	N	T	T	R	O	L	L
			B	A	R			O	A	T				
F	I	N	A	N	C	I	A	L	M	Y	T	H	S	
O	V	E	R	S	H	A	R	E		G	H	A	N	A
C	A	I	N		E	G	G	S		E	R	R	O	R
I	N	N	S		R	O	O	S		N	U	D	G	E

116

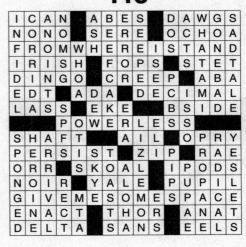

I	C	A	N		A	B	E	S		D	A	W	G	S
N	O	N	O		S	E	R	E		O	C	H	O	A
F	R	O	M	W	H	E	R	E	I	S	T	A	N	D
I	R	I	S	H		F	O	P	S		S	T	E	T
D	I	N	G	O		C	R	E	E	P		A	B	A
E	D	T		A	D	A		D	E	C	I	M	A	L
L	A	S	S		E	K	E			B	S	I	D	E
			P	O	W	E	R	L	E	S	S			
S	H	A	F	T		A	I	L		O	P	R	Y	
P	E	R	S	I	S	T		Z	I	P		R	A	E
O	R	R		S	K	O	A	L		I	P	O	D	S
N	O	I	R		Y	A	L	E		P	U	P	I	L
G	I	V	E	M	E	S	O	M	E	S	P	A	C	E
E	N	A	C	T		T	H	O	R		A	N	A	T
D	E	L	T	A		S	A	N	S		E	E	L	S

117

E	R	R		C	A	B	O		S	E	D	A	N
G	O	E	S	A	L	L	I	N		T	U	X	E	D	O
G	I	F	T	G	U	I	D	E		I	C	E	S	I	N
	R	A	B	I	E	S	V	A	C	C	I	N	E	
I	M	O	U	T			E	I	R	E			
N	O	R	T	H	W	E	S	T	P	A	S	S	A	G	E
T	O	W		A	S	A	P			S	A	M	O	A
A	S	H	E		U	R	A	N	U	S		G	A	L	S
C	H	A	R	O			O	N	I	T		Z	E	E
T	U	T	A	N	K	H	A	M	E	N	S	T	O	M	B
			S	O	U	L			E	E	N	S	Y
S	E	A	R	C	H	R	E	S	U	L	T	S	
P	A	R	C	E	L		R	E	M	A	S	T	E	R	S
A	V	I	A	N	S		T	E	N	N	E	S	S	E	E
T	E	A	S	E		S	M	O	G		P	O	X

118

B	O	A	S		B	Y	O	B		H	E	R	A
A	R	N	E		S	A	U	N	A		O	N	E	G
CANT	T	A	K	E	I	T	W	I	T	H
	C	A	R	A		S	A	L	A		G	I	A
T	W	O	T	E	R	M		JAMES			
K	A	N	E		L	O	T	T		N	A	S	T
O	L	D		Y	E	S	W	E	C	A	N		
	A	S	I	S	A	Y	N	O	T	A	S	I
	O	N	S	I	L	E	N	T		N	A	P
K	O	P	F		C	A	T	E		C	A	G	E
M	E	A	N	S		S	H	O	O	K	O	N
B	E	N		A	L	V	A		E	A	V	E
B	A	C	K	T	O	S	Q	U	A	R	E	O	N	E
E	R	I	E		G	O	U	R	D		R	I	G	A
D	A	L	Y		S	P	A	N		S	L	O	T

119

R	E	B	U	S		A	Q	A	B	A		I	C	E
A	R	O	S	E		M	U	N	I	S		N	O	G
W	O	N	O	N	P	O	I	N	T	S		A	L	E
B	I	N		T	A	C	T		M	O	U	N	D	S
A	C	E	S		T	O	O	D	A	R	N	H	O	T
R	A	T	E	D	R		O	P	T	I	O	N	S	
		Q	U	O	T	A	S		V	U	E		
	D	O	U	B	L	E	H	E	A	D	E	R	S
	O	V	O			S	A	D	D	E	R		
A	G	E	I	S	T	S		W	E	S	S	O	N
F	O	R	A	C	H	A	N	G	E		E	T	N	A
F	O	C	S	L	E		F	U	E	L		E	R	G
I	D	O		A	T	E	L	I	K	E	A	P	I	G
R	E	A		S	O	R	E	S		T	W	I	C	E
M	R	T		S	P	A	R	E		O	W	N	E	D

120

B	O	S	S	Y		D	I	O	R			H	A	M
Y	A	H	O	O		I	R	A	E		C	A	S	E
E	T	H	Y	L		D	A	H	L		A	V	I	A
			B	A	R	O	Q	U	E	B	R	E	A	D
A	R	D	E	N	T			A	L	P	I	N	E	
P	A	R	A	D	E	F	O	R	R	A	I	N		
A	M	A	N	A		I	W	O	N	T		S	I	C
R	E	F	S		M	E	N	U	S		H	T	M	L
T	N	T		P	E	R	E	S		H	O	O	H	A
		C	O	L	L	I	D	E	B	A	R	R	O	W
A	S	H	P	I	T			O	N	S	E	T	S	
T	H	O	R	E	A	U	S	H	A	D	E		
L	E	I	A		W	O	K	E		O	C	H	E	R
A	R	C	H		A	F	E	W		F	A	U	V	E
S	E	E		Y	A	W	N			F	R	E	E	D

121

```
ROTH  MOSSY   JAWS
ACRE  ANIMES  AVOW
STALECEREAL   MAKE
CADETS   ARIA  TEA
AGENT  BURNTTOAST
LOO  AEON    SORTS
  NFL  LAMB  PEP
  FIXBREAKFAST
  BRA  TGIF  YUP
APNEA   ETTU  NAP
MEALYAPPLE  SLATE
IRE  SLUR  HEIFER
GUNN  SPOILEDMILK
ASAP  OINKER  ISLE
SEER   LEEDS  THAD
```

122

```
CABBAGE    GASBAG
OVOIDAL   OFNOTE
PANDEMIC  STABLE
INTONE   ASPER
ETON  BUTTERFLY
SIN  COSELL   OED
   PAYER  STENOS
UBERS  SPA  RIGHT
GATEAU  ICEIN
GNC  SALAAM  DJS
 CHRYSALIS  FRAT
  HATHA  ECLAIR
ARGYLE  REDEAGLE
ROOMIE  PINKOES
SEAEEL  INTENDS
```

123

```
DECLARE  SWIPES
EMAILING  TERESA
FORBIDDENPLANET
ATARI  REACT
META  SHESTHEMAN
ESS  OUI   ERA
 MASTER  OMITS
WESTSIDESTORY
IWISH  TOMATO
LIN  IMO  MAY
KISSMEKATE  TIRE
 AESOP  DISCS
SHAKESPEAREPLAY
TALESE  STAMPEDE
UNISEX  MYSIDES
```

124

```
BAH  LEPER  STORE
RDA  OBAMA  TITHE
AMP  COLONHYPHEN
VIPROOM  EXJETS
ENYA  KAPPA  ARTY
 FTD  SILVER
ONAIR  AYES  EMI
COCOA  :-)  SUMAC
DRE  WHOA  EMORY
  SNORTS  NAT
JIBE  RESIN  MIFF
ADORES  TOPICAL
PARENTHESIS  OXO
AHAND  ERICA  NEO
NOTES  MANET  SSR
```

125

```
SUCH  VIEW  THING
AGHA  EMMA  EATER
MAILFRAUD  MUSTI
INSLANG  UPLAST
ADE  NEED  NOUGAT
MALES  ORK  PILE
 VITAMINS  RED
 STATECAPITALS
RAH  ENLISTED
EMIR  SUN  ROVED
PARADE  SILO  RYE
ANTIUS  HAIRGEL
STELE  BLONDEALE
THEEU  ROPE  EMIT
SANDP  OWES  LEDE
```

126

```
OBJ  APPS  SLAIN
LEEK  BLEU  CANOE
ALDA  CARB[ON/OFF]SETS
FAIRS  CITI  TWAS
  LUGE  LOIS
[S ON/OFF]RANKENSTEIN
BEE  BTU  MONTE
IRAS  [ON]AND[OFF]  PISA
BURMA  SET  AMP
IMMIGRATI[ON/OFF]ICE
  LOUT  GEAR
SATE  NOSH  LAYUP
PERS[ON/OFF]AITH  NOSE
ARIAL  SLOE  IDEA
SOOTY  TONY  ART
```

127

U	L	N	A	■	M	A	M	E	T	■	R	A	M	S
N	E	E	R	■	A	T	A	R	I	■	I	C	E	T
H	A	W	K	■	R	O	X	I	E	■	O	H	M	Y
I	V	S	■	I	M	P	I	N	G	E	■	I	O	N
P	E	C	A	N	S	■	■	S	E	V	E	R	E	■
■	B	A	R	K	■	O	N	A	■	E	A	V	E	■
■	E	S	C	■	A	D	E	L	E	■	R	E	X	■
■	■	T	A	B	L	E	T	E	N	N	I	S	■	■
■	■	D	O	I	■	■	G	O	A	■	■	■	■	■
S	O	B	E	R	E	R	■	F	I	E	N	N	E	S
P	L	U	S	O	N	E	■	A	N	A	T	O	L	E
E	D	S	■	N	A	P	S	T	E	R	■	N	S	W
D	E	M	I	■	T	O	R	T	E	■	N	O	T	I
U	L	A	N	■	E	S	T	E	R	■	I	N	O	N
P	I	N	G	■	D	E	A	R	S	■	P	O	N	G

128

A	M	A	N	A	S	■	■	S	L	A	M	S	■
B	A	L	O	N	E	Y	■	S	K	E	T	C	H	Y
E	N	T	I	T	L	E	■	T	I	E	A	T	I	E
T	I	E	R	S	■	S	H	E	L	■	L	E	N	A
T	A	R	S	■	S	N	A	I	L	■	L	E	T	S
I	C	E	■	I	F	O	R	G	E	T	■	R	O	T
N	A	G	A	N	O	■	B	E	T	O	N	■	■	■
G	L	O	B	E	■	F	I	R	■	N	E	U	R	O
■	■	■	U	R	B	A	N	■	A	T	O	N	O	F
A	S	H	■	T	A	N	G	E	L	O	■	P	D	F
S	T	E	T	■	S	T	E	P	S	■	D	I	E	S
Y	E	A	R	■	S	A	R	I	■	M	O	C	H	I
O	P	T	I	M	A	S	■	C	L	U	N	K	E	D
U	P	E	A	R	L	Y	■	S	O	T	H	E	R	E
■	E	D	D	I	E	■	■	A	T	O	D	D	S	■

129

R	E	C	E	S	S	■	F	T	C	■	H	E	R
E	R	O	T	I	C	■	C	R	E	A	T	U	R	E
T	A	N	T	R	A	■	R	A	N	S	O	M	E	D
■	■	J	A	I	L	H	O	U	S	E	R	O	C	K
E	M	O	■	I	O	S	■	■	E	R	T	E	■
H	A	I	L	C	A	E	S	A	R	■	M	E	N
S	O	N	A	R	■	D	A	U	N	T	E	D	■
■	■	D	U	D	E	R	A	N	C	H	■	■
■	S	K	Y	D	O	M	E	■	A	E	T	N	A
S	A	N	■	R	U	S	S	I	A	N	M	O	B
U	S	E	D	■	S	E	N	■	O	W	E
T	H	E	I	T	A	L	I	A	N	J	O	B
R	I	P	S	O	P	E	N	■	I	O	D	I	N	E
A	M	A	S	S	I	N	G	■	E	V	I	L	E	R
S	I	D	■	S	A	T	■	S	I	N	E	W	S

130

■	S	O	P	■	A	N	G	L	E	■	R	E	F
S	H	O	O	■	S	U	P	E	R	S	L	O	M	O
W	A	L	L	■	S	T	A	G	E	A	C	T	O	R
A	Z	A	L	E	A	S	■	I	C	C	H	U	■
G	A	L	A	X	Y	■	D	O	T	■	A	N	D	A
■	M	A	C	H	■	K	E	N	■	B	I	D	O	N
■	K	U	N	G	F	■	L	A	M	A	Z	E	■
U	G	H	■	M	O	B	I	L	E	S	■	S	E	W
G	O	O	B	E	R	■	L	E	A	S	E	■
L	O	L	L	S	■	K	E	G	■	E	A	R	S
I	F	Y	O	■	B	R	R	■	S	T	R	A	T	I
■	D	A	N	J	O	■	T	A	T	A	M	I	S
S	T	A	T	I	O	N	A	R	Y	■	C	P	L	S
K	E	Y	S	T	R	O	K	E	S	■	H	U	L	A
Y	E	S	■	K	R	A	F	T	■	E	P	S	■

131

G	R	A	M	■	M	O	J	O	■	W	A	K	E
A	U	R	A	■	A	V	E	C	■	C	A	B	I	T
U	B	E	R	■	K	E	T	T	■	O	V	E	N	S
L	E	A	T	H	E	R	W	A	L	L	E	T	■
■	■	H	I	S	■	A	N	A	I	S	■
B	R	O	A	D	W	A	Y	T	I	C	K	E	T	S
O	A	R	■	A	D	S	■	K	I	R	I	N	■
O	P	T	■	F	R	O	■	I	C	Y	■	A	D	A
B	A	H	A	I	■	O	R	A	■	T	A	R	■
S	T	O	P	D	R	O	P	A	N	D	R	O	L	L
■	P	E	A	C	H	■	T	I	E	■
■	A	L	L	W	H	E	E	L	D	R	I	V	E
K	A	U	A	I	■	E	L	M	O	■	U	N	I	X
I	N	D	U	S	■	R	I	I	S	■	N	I	N	A
M	A	I	D	■	S	A	T	E	■	S	T	E	M

132

P	A	C	M	A	N	■	T	E	D	■	P	L	O	T
I	N	H	A	L	E	■	I	R	E	■	J	O	G	S
N	E	E	D	L	E	■	P	R	E	S	S	U	R	E
■	A	D	O	■	S	P	A	D	E	■	V	A	T	■
B	I	T	■	W	E	W	I	N	■	N	E	R	D	S
A	D	D	■	S	T	A	N	D	■	O	X	E	Y	E
L	E	A	P	■	U	G	G	■	M	R	T	■
L	A	Y	O	D	D	S	■	D	E	A	R	G	O	D
■	W	E	E	■	B	R	A	■	A	U	R	A	■
G	O	R	E	S	■	G	R	A	D	E	■	T	N	T
U	T	E	R	I	■	R	O	G	E	N	■	P	E	A
F	I	B	■	S	T	E	W	S	■	C	L	U	■
F	O	U	R	T	E	E	N	■	P	O	I	N	T	S
A	S	T	A	■	S	C	I	■	C	R	E	C	H	E
W	E	S	T	■	T	E	E	■	T	E	N	H	U	T

133

```
NOSH   FLAB   SIZE
OREO   ELATE  IDOL
PANS   ROMAN  GOOF
UTTERRUBBISH
LOT  UAR   COTTON
PROUST  COIF  ADO
   STATEMOTTOES
BASEL  EEN  PASSE
EXPRESSLINES
ALI  SOSO  ODESSA
DETOUR  ALA  AMI
   SPEAKVOLUMES
PIMA  ARIES  ROLL
JPEG  REARS  ISLE
SATE  MAST   SASS
```

134

```
GHOSTGUNS  BOISE
REHEARSAL  EASEL
ORGANICMATERIAL
CEOS  PEEKIN  TOE
ESO  MENDEL  DST
RYDER  SAD  MEATY
   ITGUY  PILFER
DOGTOYS  VESPERS
DURHAM  MICAH
STEED  DAN  DIVOT
 DAR  SYNCED  IKE
MAT  PANGEA  RATS
ITJUSTAINTRIGHT
NEONS  SETMEFREE
IDBET  TREESTAND
```

135

```
GAGLAW    LIKESO
OKEEFE  RANAMOK
SETTLE  BADSPORT
TESSA  KEGS  OPAH
ALA  CANTI  SWORE
GATS  LEANIN  PEN
 HIPSTERCRED
 PIERCEARROW
 TRIALJUDGES
SAO  TAPEUP  GRIN
ALPHA  PANTS  ECO
YIPE  HISS  ECLAT
SNOWCONE  SENORA
NESTEGG  AYESIR
OREOOS   CATTOY
```

136

```
 NOTABADIDEA
 BUTWILLITWORK
WINSOMELOSESOME
UGH  SSN  NYE  UAR
SOOT  DIN  BASRA
SNOW  FETES  LETS
 EDITORS  CHASSE
 NUTSABOUT
SNAPTO  HOTMESS
NADA  STINT  EWES
ABACK  ATE  NOTI
ROM  NAM  SPF  OUR
FRAFILIPPOLIPPI
 SNUFFLEUPAGUS
 TREASUREMAP
```

137

```
OBSESSES  BASING
RAPSHEET  YOOHOO
CHIPOTLE  ORNATE
ANT  WASPS  TOTES
  OPT  MCCAFE
MESSI  BOHO  ATMS
ATTHEMOMENT  OOH
CURACAO  MIASARA
ADE  EXTRACRISPY
WEEP  ILES  ANKHS
  THAMES  RNS
FIFED  GODOT  LAS
ROONEY  ROGUEONE
OTOOLE  THELORAX
MADMEN  SATANIST
```

138

```
BADGE  ALL  URBAN
OPERA  SEABREEZE
OGLES  KOREANAIR
SATEEN  IVAN  UZO
TRANSYLVANIA
 GITA  BUSHWA
ADDON  DREAMTEAM
HERB  ALONG  ARIA
EVILQUEEN  PROFS
MOBIUS  UGLI
 NOTORIOUSRBG
IRK  RENO  ONBAIL
MEASUREUP  GONZO
DELIMEATS  ERTES
BLESS  LEI  SNOTS
```

139

```
MWAHAHA ■ HASACOW
AEROSOL ■ ONELOVE
RIMSHOT ■ TATTLER
GRIT ■ TETRIS ■ DRE
IDE ■■ RHOS ■ ARCO
NOSEBLEED ■ SNOOP
■■ GEODESICDOME
MERGER ■ CARMEN
ICECREAMCONE ■
CLAUS ■ LIONTAMER
HELP ■ SETH ■ AMO
ACT ■ SUREOF ■ BLOB
ETICKET ■ RANLATE
LIMEADE ■ TRAILER
SCENTED ■ SEEPAST
```

140

```
BOYSCLUB ■ APATHY
ATEALIVE ■ DECREE
ROLLOVER ■ ATTICS
BOLIVIAN ■ STICKS
ELEVEN ■ TIVOLI
DERANGED ■ REALER
■ MEGASTORE
CROCS ■ ACE ■ TERSE
RONREAGAN ■
ASPIRE ■ YEARSAGO
NEATER ■ ROADER
KARINA ■ DOGTIRED
SNOCAT ■ IDEALIZE
UNLADE ■ SENTOVER
PEELED ■ CATERERS
```

141

```
BED ■ ABDULJABBAR
RPI ■ CARTOONLIKE
OHS ■ CHEERLEADER
WEPT ■ RISES ■ BELA
■ MARTA ■ NOG ■ NAN
PERIWIGS ■ NAB ■
DRACONIAN ■ SEPTA
FATES ■ FHA ■ KAROL
SLEPT ■ TITLEROLE
■ SET ■ BLOTCHES
ZAC ■ PAD ■ USAIR
EDOM ■ IRANI ■ TBAR
RADIOLOGIST ■ IBO
ONETWOPUNCH ■ TLC
GARTERSNAKE ■ SEA
```

142

```
TAUT ■ NOSIREEBOB
ARNE ■ CRIMESCENE
LASH ■ ILLBETHERE
CLORIS ■ ERLE ■ RAT
USUAL ■ ONUS ■ CMDR
MENNONITE ■ LOUIE
SAD ■ VAST ■ TINGOD
■ PETERFALK ■
TAMALE ■ EARL ■ JEB
ANITA ■ BAREITALL
BODS ■ COTE ■ AISLE
ITT ■ GLAM ■ ANEMIA
THEHEIRESS ■ RISK
HEREANDNOW ■ ENOL
ARMWRESTLE ■ DENY
```

143

```
RASHAD ■ LACERATE
EZPASSTOLLLANES
HEAVYCASUALTIES
ARMEE ■ BSIDES ■
BAS ■ ABO ■ PGA
■ TAKEFORAFOOL
■ FEMININEWILES
■ BARITONESAXES
MOUNTAINBIKER
THREESTOOGES
ARE ■ CTN ■ TAG
■ OMELET ■ OSAGE
AMERICANLARCHES
MADECONCESSIONS
PAULKLEE ■ LOSETO
```

144

```
BROADENS ■ GROSS
BOXSOCIAL ■ MELEE
QUESTLOVE ■ CODEX
PRY ■ HABIT ■ INKS
IKEA ■ TEND ■ SLOSH
TESTS ■ GOUT ■ ROO
■ THATSWHATSUP
■ FAIRLY ■ NOTYET
PENCILPUSHER
ART ■ NYES ■ DODOS
RAISE ■ COST ■ LESH
ALDA ■ ASHER ■ NPR
SCOLD ■ SHAREWARE
KATEY ■ TOPSEEDED
ITEMS ■ WEEKDAYS
```

145

```
MINICAR   STRAFE
ONTHEMAP  IBANEZ
IDEALIZE  TANGLE
RUST RENOIR  ELK
ESTEE  CNN  ELOI
   LAVIE  CREPE
  TRAVELCHANNEL
  LESTERPEARSON
SILVERBULLETS
PEEPS  OSLER
YAPS  ASH  SOSAD
WHO  GREENS  HOLY
AERIAL  ROEVWADE
RATTLE  STEWOVER
EDSELS   ANSWERS
```

146

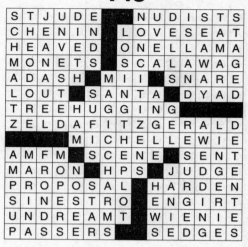

```
STJUDE   NUDISTS
CHENIN  LOVESEAT
HEAVED  ONELLAMA
MONETS  SCALAWAG
ADASH  MII  SNARE
LOUT  SANTA  DYAD
TREEHUGGING
ZELDAFITZGERALD
   MICHELLEWIE
AMFM  SCENE  SENT
MARON  HPS  JUDGE
PROPOSAL  HARDEN
SINESTRO  ENGIRT
UNDREAMT  WIENIE
PASSERS   SEDGES
```

147

```
PENPAL   SLOWJAM
AVIATE  STONEAGE
CELLOS  PAPERCUT
KNEEL  HATS  EKES
  ALSACE  POL
HALL  TIES  INEPT
OBIE  ARRANT  MOA
HANSOLO  VITAMIN
USE  REFLEX  BONG
MERGE  TONE  UNTO
  NAS  HOUSED
ODOR  RENE  SHEET
HATERADE  STABLE
ODETOJOY  PEBBLE
HASHTAG   ARISEN
```

148

```
DRAWS   MEANSIT
ROSIN  MOMJEANS
IDYLL  MARMADUKE
FEEL  TEXMEX  CST
TOTALIDIOT  SETS
  COLUMN  EAPOE
  LAMESA  SATANS
  CETERA  RATINE
MATHIS  COVENS
ASHEN  DOTERS
STER  MEMORYHOLE
SAR  COVERS  EXIT
INCAHOOTS  DELLA
FERRARIS  ATILT
STYMIED   ESPYS
```

149

```
ORALB  SOFT  MOAT
DOPER  CLOISONNE
DUETOBUDGETCUTS
SEDUCED  GRASSES
  PAL  YAY
USS  DOGS  CASABA
THENEWYORKTIMES
IONA  RAE  TARP
CROSSWORDPUZZLE
AERATE  SOUP  EEN
  ABC  RRS
ANOSMIA  RIOTACT
WILLENDTOMORROW
OCEANARIA  TAEBO
LEST  REAM  SWABS
```

150

```
GAPTOOTHED  UPCS
ETHANFROME  MOAT
WHOLEFOODS  PORE
GENE  SOREAT  HOP
ANISE  PANDA  PLO
WAC  DASH  ENJOIN
  BUSHSR  LEONI
HIBACHI  EPITHET
OHARA  PEDANT
GETSTO  MLLE  SOP
WAH  EMCEE  SPACY
ARM  DEARTH  EVEL
RYAN  GUITARSOLO
TOTO  ALTERATION
SUSS  SKIRESORTS
```

151

```
BADDAY    LAPCAT
OTOOLE   TEAROSE
NAUSEA  FUNHOUSE
ANGER  SARA  BRUT
MEH  TAPIN  KETCH
INNS  WATSON  SHE
  DUNCANHINES
  TALKINGHEAD
  GOESONADIET
AIR  ASHMAN  DARK
SPEAK  MOLDS  DIE
KHAN  PARS  HOBBY
FORTERIE  FIREUP
ONEIRON  ARCANA
REDCAP    XRATED
```

152

```
MOFFAT   CHANNELS
ECLAIRS  COPYEDIT
RAYKROC  CUTABOVE
GLEECLUB  NTH  PEA
EAR  ALFREDO  GERM
   TRIFOLD  NORM
OSBORN  MOO  ONION
THEBIGBANGTHEORY
CELIE  ANG  HARDEE
  LIAR  SCARERS
BLTS  PIETISM  SML
AGT  DIN  EVIDENCE
TALLONES  EROTICA
OMELETTE  SENATOR
REDCROSS  NELSON
```

153

```
FALSIES   BARTABS
ISAIDNO   EXURBAN
GUYCODE   LOSESTO
TSE  LOVEINS  ORR
RUTH  REYES  BLOT
EATAT  REB  TAUPE
ELEVEN  DESISTED
   ENID  RIMS
CHANDLER  RESEAL
HALOS  RAH  DARLA
EMIT  TRIOS  XRAY
WBA  CHILLAX  AMO
TOSPARE  DUBSTEP
ONEOVER  ECOCIDE
YESISEE  MEXICAN
```

154

```
BAMBOOSHOOT  MSG
IMEANREALLY  CEO
BARRELCHAIR  CAN
  RIME  ANNOTATE
FBICASES   AFAR
RAE  NSA  ADEXECS
ASSES  RANOUT
GETTHEWRONGIDEA
  HOLIST  EPOXY
PERIWIG  CNN  LIE
ALEC   CHEEZITS
GLASSJAR  ALIT
AID  HOMOERECTUS
NOM  INTAKEVALVE
STE  MYSTERYMEAT
```

155

```
SMARTYPANTS  GPA
MADEYOULOOK  RAM
ORDERONLINE  ESP
TITLE  EDGINESS
ENOS  RARE  NENE
   CONGA  PEDI
BIRTHDAY  DRAGON
OVARIES  NAILGUN
ZYDECO  SOLOISTS
OLIN  WILES
EACH  ANOS  PUMA
CATHOLIC  FINER
AGO  LIVEALITTLE
FUR  EMERGENCIES
EES  SPREADSHEET
```

156

```
RAGEQUIT  GYMRAT
OHIDUNNO  SORELY
SENDAWAY  TUMBLR
SAG  DECOR  HESSE
IDES  DATASET
  ROT  NAFTA  RUM
OHARAS  STARGAZE
ROLEXES  STDENIS
EYELEVEL  SMERSH
MAS  VEGAS  ESA
  RAREBIT  EMMA
TOGAS  LATHE  PAS
ARABIA  MARSBARS
LAZBOY  BROMANCE
ELAINE  ASBESTOS
```

157

```
FIVEAM   JETBLACK
ACADIA   INREASON
BYLINE   GOODTIME
 SUET   SUP  IDEA
STE  IDTAG  SNERD
HAMSTERWHEEL
OREL  LES  TROVE
PENALTY  HEAVING
 SUMMA  FOR  ERGO
   PASSIONFRUIT
TABOO  UNDER  SNO
ALOE  SNL   EASE
SORTDATA  TERCET
THERAVEN  STMARK
EASYREAD  EVENSO
```

158

```
FACEPLANT  ANKHS
STATIONER  RENEW
HEGOTGAME  OXEYE
AMENHOTEP  STELE
RPI  NOSALE  HOP
PONCE  MENU  JOVE
   ANTIS  GAOLER
SHOPVAC  MASHERS
LAURYN   KAREN
ASTI  GANG  AQABA
PTS  GOBANG   SAN
JOCKO  AVERAGING
AROAR  SETABLAZE
CURVE  EROSIONAL
KNEAD  DYSPEPSIA
```

159

```
 CARDCATALOG
 GAMEOFTHRONES
GOTINTOHOTWATER
LASSOES  USSTATE
OTC        TSP
SEALABS  ITSLATE
SENEGAL  SATINON
   ARNO  BRAT
CJCREGG  NOGUCHI
HARNESS  STEPHEN
AGA        IRE
SUNDOWN  PLANFOR
MAKETHEBESTOFIT
 RECRIMINATION
 DOAGOODTURN
```

160

```
PONIARDS  MACPRO
IMONFIRE  UPROAR
SIGHTGAG  STARVE
ATOE  SMELT  FOAL
 ARM  ARAB  TUGS
THREADS  LETSSEE
OHENRY  TANS
WHATSNEWWITHYOU
   HALO  CREEPS
MARRYME  READSTO
AQUA  INTO  POW
DUMB  CARDS  NEMO
RIBBED  AMERICAN
INLIEU  CASHSALE
DOESSO  INSOMNIA
```

161

```
ESPNRADIO  TEBOW
STONECOLD  EMOTE
TAKESHOLD  RIOTS
ATE  TOMB  KITKAT
DIAN  OSIRIS  SWE
OCTET  TIM  ACAN
 VOICECOMMAND
 COARSE  ONIONS
WINDOWSPHONE
RASA  EAR  TBARS
ABC  NARITA  ASHE
PARLOR  MODS  SON
STEAK  CARDIGANS
UTERI  ATMINSIDE
PANDA  BEETSALAD
```

162

```
 BARBACK   ONEL
ALLUSION  HONOR
MAINSTREAMMEDIA
IKEA  ALLISLOST
DENG  LLDS  CLI
 VANESSAS  RAN
 STAY  INNING
STPETE  LEONES
PARSEC  EAVE
ETE  HARASSES
LED  AMEN  LYIN
MRAMERICA  ESTA
ATTENTIONGETTER
NOONS  ADULTERY
 TRUE  TANDEMS
```

163

```
B L A D E S   ■   Y U L E L O G
R E G I N A   ■ F I R E L A N E
E G G N O G   ■ R E A W O K E N
W A R E S ■ B E L L ■   E M T
S L E D ■ L A I D ■   O V A L
U P S ■ G A N G ■ S A L I N E
P A S S E D T H E T I M E ■
■ D O N T L E T M E D O W N
■ R O B E R T P R E S T O N
A N N O Y S ■ R I N D ■ E V A
M E A T ■ B A R E ■ P R E Y
S A T ■ B R I E ■ W O R M S
T R I A L R U N ■ C A S A B A
E T O N I A N S ■ P R I C E Y
L O N G E S T ■ A S T E R S
```

164

```
D O N T S A S S M E ■ S K I M
A L O H A S H I R T ■ T R O U
L E M O N T O R T E ■ Y E N S
I O S ■ R H E E ■ S U M M I T
■ ■ L E M A N S ■ P I L A R
■ G O M A D ■ C O D E I N E
■ J U N O ■ D A R I O ■ N S A
H U N G ■ P I X E L ■ D I E D
O K S ■ S O C L E ■ B O N A
T E N B E S T ■ N R O T C ■
S H R E K ■ S T E A D S ■
Y O O H O O ■ A R M Y ■ C A M
R U S E ■ H O L D S A S A L E
U S E S ■ O L I V E R R E E D
P E S T ■ H E A D S T O N E S
```

165

```
T A T T L E ■ F L A S H E R S
O N E M A N ■ A I R W O M A N
T A X C U T ■ N A G A S A K I
E P A ■ D E S T R O Y ■ J E T
B O S S ■ R I A L S ■ L O I S
A L B U M ■ C S I ■ M O R N
G I B L E T ■ Y A Z O O ■
■ S Q U A R E B R A C K E T ■
■ S T U P A ■ C H O R A L
■ F I E S ■ I S O ■ A U D I O
R I M A ■ A D E P T ■ T O L L
E G O ■ D O U B T I T ■ C G I
C A N B E R R A ■ L E S T A T
O R I E N T A L ■ L A K O T A
N O T A T A L L ■ S T A R E S
```

166

```
F O O D C O M A ■ F A T L I P
A N D I M O U T ■ E R O I C A
R E D V I N E S ■ D I A N A S
C A L E ■ A L T E ■ E D E N S
E L Y S E ■ L U G S ■ S R T A
■ ■ D R E D G E D ■ N E T
W A R R I O R ■ O N E L O V E
A L E A S T ■ S A U T E S
T O P D O G S ■ P E R C E N T
E N A ■ N U M B E S T ■ ■
R E Y S ■ T U R N ■ O T T E R
S T A L E ■ T I N O ■ A R L O
K I B O S H ■ B A B Y M A M A
I M L A T E ■ E M O T I C O N
S E E N A S ■ S E E D L E S S
```

167

```
B L A C K F R I D A Y ■ T A B
T I T A N I U M O R E ■ A S U
W A I T I N G A R E A ■ K H Z
O R T ■ T A S M A N ■ G E E Z
■ ■ M S G ■ G A T O S ■
A G R A ■ L A S ■ S U B L E T
T R A N S E P T S ■ R E E S E
B E D A N D B R E A K F A S T
A B A S E ■ S I G N S O V E R
T E R S E R ■ P O T ■ R E N A
■ B A R E R ■ I C E ■
P A L S ■ S A W Y E R ■ H A G
A M I ■ W I N E S T E W A R D
I M P ■ A N D R E A D O R I A
D O S ■ C Y B E R M O N D A Y
```

168

```
P I R A T E S H I P ■ I D O L
S H O R E L E A V E ■ B O H O
H O M E M O V I E S ■ S Y S T
A P P S ■ E R R O N E O U S
W E S ■ Z I N C ■ O N U S ■
■ ■ F A T S U I T S ■ M A P
A C T I N G ■ T R E E L I N E
C H E E Z I T ■ A R G O N N E
M I S F I R E S ■ S A N D A L
E L L ■ B L A C K E Y E ■
■ L A M A ■ O A R S ■ H O P
M A C A R T H U R ■ M I S O
A X O N ■ O U T E R B A N K S
N E I L ■ G R E E N A L G A E
I D L Y ■ O L D M A S T E R S
```

169

```
GREASY  AFRICANS
LAURIE  RAILEDAT
ANGORA  ALLINDIA
CHEMIST LEASERS
IONA  TAPE  DODOS
AMISS  BEND  ROBE
LEE  ISON  OPENIN
   UNIONIZED
LERNER ACES  PCS
AXES  EINE  TAROT
CASES  STUB  DEVO
EMPTIES PLUMBER
DIETDRUG OPIATE
UNCLELEO TURKEY
PETEBEST SPEEDS
```

170

```
YALE  USPASSPORT
ODIE  TEAMLEADER
GROG  MARIAELENA
AINTNOBODY  TOI
MAKEASALE  LATIN
ANISETTE  FIXERS
TINT  TVWIFE
SIG  FOLIAGE  MAS
   METEOR  WART
CREEDS  LAQUINTA
HEELS  SATURNISM
ANY  BATHINGCAP
STOPMOTION  MULE
MARIOCUOMO  AROD
SLEEPAPNEA  NENE
```

171

```
JAGS  ADM  PASTOR
AGRA  REA  ADHERE
PIED  INKSTAINED
ALA  SATIE  METOO
NET  ELENI  ASH
  BOA  GNP  OIL
AMASSEDAFORTUNE
HURRICANESEASON
AFRICANELEPHANT
STICKSANDSTONES
HIE  HIT  IED
  RPM  DRAWL  YEP
PAREE  EAPOE  EGO
LEEKRASNER  JARS
AREOLA  CAD  ORES
NOFEES  ERY  ESTE
```

172

```
ACROBATS  TIFFS
FRENEMIES  ELLIE
FAMILYGUY  LIANE
ENACT  HRS  LAMAS
CINE  STACK  DELT
TAD  KOWTOWS  WBA
  TUBAS  AUPAIR
SLIMMED  INNARDS
KITCAR  ANZIO
IVS  RUFFIAN  BUM
LEAN  PARTA  RAMA
LASIK  GOI  CARPS
SLICE  IPADMINIS
EIGHT  NOTSOSURE
TENET  PETNAMES
```

173

```
FOGS  SCAT  ATALL
INRI  POOH  MOXIE
TEACHABLEMOMENT
SPYKIDS  BAUBLES
  EMOTE  CERN
BRASI  CHESTHAIR
ACT  THOUGH  ANNA
SETS  AGREE  HGTV
KNEE  NICEST  LEE
STRENGTHS  ODORS
  ODAY  PREPS
INKBLOT  QUICHES
BIOLOGICALCLOCK
IGLOO  NEIL  ANTI
SHACK  GODS  WEST
```

174

```
MOCKERY  NEWIDEA
AMRADIO  ONETERM
REALIGN  TINAFEY
INWITH  PEDDLE
ASL  TEAS  AWE
  CLAMP  ALSTON
  CHANCEMEETING
  AHUNGERARTIST
PLATELETCOUNT
TALESE  HESSE
ASK  FIDO  DOC
  URCHIN  LAMOUR
ASPIRES  ECLIPSE
BITPART  TABLETS
AMOEBAS  ANALYST
```

175

```
HOTWARS █ LECTURE
INORBIT █ EXURBIA
DEMILLE █ SPLEENS
█ TEENJEOPARDY
RASH █ DOE █ RAS █
ARCED █ SLAT █ OAHU
PERSON █ LITANIES
CTA █ JUDOMAT █ RIA
DOWJONES █ XANADU
SOLI █ CAHN █ DUCES
█ GAH █ OOH █ LENA
FLAGRANTFOUL █
RUGLIKE █ ARTSALE
EPHESUS █ ISEENOW
DEADEST █ REPTILE
```

176

```
FLASHMOB █ DEBTS
ELIHUYALE █ ASAHI
ACROBATIC █ HELEN
SOFAS █ THUS █ DHL
TOAT █ BOZOS █ CRUE
SLR █ CUBE █ AVAILS
█ JEDIMINDTRICKS
█ ETAT █ POOR █
UNIVERSALDONOR
PELOSI █ GUAM █ LEG
SOON █ DAISY █ DYER
IDS █ OEIL █ GIMLI
LATCH █ DIAPERPIN
ODIUM █ STREAKING
NATTY █ YEARSAGO
```

177

```
PETUNIAPIG █ ASAP
SHAKENBAKE █ GILL
SUPERDUPER █ ECTO
TDS █ VETS █ INKEY
█ SOBS █ SSTARS
SPROUT █ PIANOS █
POOFS █ DICKTRACY
ALOT █ VEXES █ ADOS
NETPROFIT █ INONE
█ AROUSE █ JIGGER
AGREES █ DANE █
COOTS █ JAMS █ TAG
CRUZ █ ABOVEITALL
RENE █ ROTISSERIE
ADDL █ POSTITNOTE
```

178

```
ANTE █ SUMAC █ STAT
LOUISPRIMA █ OHIO
FUELTANKER █ PERK
ATSEA █ SENDS █ OWE
LUDENS █ ICEMAN
FRAN █ TWEENAGERS
ANY █ NAILSALONS █
█ JOBTITLES █
█ CHARACTERS █ YUL
BEINGTHERE █ FETE
SCREAM █ DEISTS
HIE █ YAPAT █ ASHES
ALDA █ TALIASHIRE
RIOT █ EVENSTEVEN
PANE █ RECAP █ RADS
```

179

```
WHATSTHAT █ HOURS
RICEARONI █ INSET
ESTATETAX █ LEONA
STEM █ NAG █ ALSTON
TOD █ STIRFRY █ OIL
ERICA █ RARE █ SURE
DYNAST █ MANPURSE
█ SHED █ GOOP █
BIGEATER █ TEEHEE
ALLY █ REED █ TRAPS
DOE █ BARBETS █ DIS
EVADES █ IMO █ RATE
GENOA █ BRINGITON
GLENS █ ITSGOTIME
SADAT █ THESTATES
```

180

```
WATERTIGHT █ IMAX
AZALEATREE █ MEGA
SUPERSTORE █ DTEN
PREVUE █ ARTBOARD
█ ANSON █ HENLEY
█ JOTS █ DEW █ TESLA
IONE █ MERINO █ TAX
NEEDLES █ SENSATE
TMI █ ENSUED █ AMES
HONDO █ APT █ NYPD
INFANT █ TODAY
STONEAGE █ IMELDA
WART █ RUMBLESEAT
ANTE █ NAPOLITANO
YAYS █ SMOKYTOPAZ
```

181

```
P I N T E R E S T   M E C C A
I N A T R A N C E   V A L O R
S U P E R F O O D   P R O N G
A R E S   A U N T S   E S T O
N E S T     N E A T I D E A
    T H C   L O D   V I A
H A T T R E E   K O I P O N D
O N E S E T   G O A T E E
S T E A M E D   B E T H E R E
T I N   O R R   A S S
  T A P R O O M S   S T Y E
R O N A   S P A S M   L I A R
E X G O V   C L E O P A T R A
L I S L E   A T T A C K A D S
O N T O E   P A S T T E N S E
```

182

```
K A R A O K E B A R   G L O M
I B E L I E V E S O   R E Z A
D R U M S T I C K S   A T O R
D A N A   T A L   S I T I N S
O M E N S   N O G   D E T E R
  A H I   U R S A   S H O
S P A C E C A D E T   N O V
W I N S B I G   B A T P O L E
E A N   E I S E N H O W E R
E N O   A R N O   S U R
T O T E S   G M C   S T R A P
S W A T H E   I H S   R O T O
P I T H   S I N E Q U A N O N
O R E O   C R E A M S I C L E
T E S S   S E X P I S T O L S
```

183

```
  F R I S B E E   S T I C K S
B R A S T R A P   T U L A N E
G O T L O O S E   P R E R E Q
A L I E N A T E   A N D R E
M I N T E D   B U S   A C E
E C G   W H E E L   A D A Y
  G R A I L S   A P I P E
T H I R T Y T W O A C R O S S
H E M I S   M E R I T S
E R I N   L A S E R   I M S
O H S   J A N   D A T S U N
  O S C A R   B O R N I N T O
A N Y O N E   R I O T G E A R
R O O K E D   A S P I R A N T
T R U E T O   D E S S E R T
```

184

```
T A B S   C H A T S   R Y E S
E R L E   H O R A E   F E T A
A C U T E A N G L E   D A H L
P A R T Y F O U L   R E B
O N T H E F R I T Z   E Z R A
T A S E S   N E E   T E N N
  S O C   G E T B O R E D
Z O O C R E W   S A Y N O T O
U N P E E L E D   S A C
G L E N   E R E   N O B I S
Z O N E   B E N E V O L E N T
W O W   H O M E S L I C E
A K I N   P E T E S E E G E R
N E D S   A R E N T   G E N E
G R E W   H E D D A   E S T O
```

185

```
G A Z I L L I O N   S P E C S
O M I N O U S L Y   E R G O T
U P T O G R A D E   A I O L I
R E C   S K I P   T U G S O N
D R O P   S A R D I   S U N K
S E M I S   H O O P S   R E E
  T I S   S U P E R F L Y
B A Y O N E T   P E L I S S E
I R O N G R I P   D I V
G T S   E V E R T   G A S U P
W H E W   O D O R S   L E N O
H O M I E S   F O I E   A R P
O U I D A   J U M P S S H I P
O S T E R   U S P O S T A G E
P E E R S   T E E N A N G S T
```

186

```
S P I F F E D U P   W O O D S
P H N O M P E N H   I N P U T
A L E X R O C C O   G E T M E
R E X   I C E I N   G L I D E
E V I L   H I V E   L E M U R
M E L O N   T I T L E G A M E
E L E V E N   L A I R   L S D
  E X E C   G L O M
D I M   T A R T   T O E J A M
O N A S T R E A K   M O O L A
G E C K O   P R O B   W Y L E
C R U E L   E T H E L   R O W
A T S E A   P A L M O L I V E
R I E L S   A R E A C O D E S
T A R O T   N E R D A L E R T
```

187

```
C O P E   T E S T     O T H E R
A C A P P E L L A   P H O N O
C E R E A L B O X   H E I G L
T A K E S N O T E   E P P I E
I N A S T E W   S A L O O N
      A T R A   B I L L E D
A C H E S   O L D B A I L E Y
S O O N   F O L E Y   C O R E
K I N G J A M E S   W E I S S
S N O R E D   N E R O
  P R A T E S   C O R N O I L
S U R F S   O N R E S E R V E
W R O T E   D I A P E R B A G
I S L E T   A T T E N D I N G
M E L D S   S E E R   S T A Y
```

188

```
B I L B O   P L U G   T W I G
A M O U R   L I S A   O H M Y
S P A C E C A D E T   R A S P
I A N   S A Y   D O R I T O S
C R E D   V E L C R O   A M U
S T R U T   R E A   M A D A M
    C A E S A R S A L A D
  F A R M E R S O N L Y
  N O T G O N N A L I E
L O U S E   T E L   A G A T E
A T L   T U R R E T   E V E N
M E L I S S A   S O B   I A M
E P I C   E N A M E L W A R E
S A N E   U C L A   T I T U S
A D E S   P E E N   S T E P H
```

189

```
S H O C K J O C K   I B A R
W O M A N I Z I N G   N O N O
I N A N I M A T E O B J E C T
N O H I T   W A X P O E T I C
G R A S   N A B   R O C H E
S E N T T O   L O O   T I N T
    E L I D E S   U T E
A F A R C R Y   L A R U S S A
I O U   A R O M A S
M A T S   G N U   E M B O S S
  M O T O R   S T S   P L O P
O C T O P U S S Y   V O I L A
Y O U V E B E E N S E R V E D
E R N E   S C R E E N T I M E
Z E E S   S T R E I S A N D
```

190

```
S T A R M A P   S L I P P E R
O R L E A N S   C O R D I T E
M A L A L A Y O U S A F Z A I
E L K   T I C K L E S   Z I N
H A I L   S H I P S   C A L S
O L D A S   O N T   T O M E I
W A D D E D   G O S H D A R N
  I D E E S   R A R E R
P I N E D F O R   P U R G E D
A N G R Y   L E M   M E H T A
E S A S   T O T E M   D E E M
L T S   S E M I N A R   R R S
L A I D I T O N T H E L I N E
A N D I R O N   O R B I T A L
S T E P I N S   R E S E A L S
```

191

```
S C R A T C H   T W O C A R
A L A B A M A   B A R N O N E
T O N E L O C   O R I E N T S
Y T D   I N K B L O T   V E E
R H O D A   A A A S   S E A T
S E M I   O T B   H U R T S
    V I C H Y S S O I S E
  G H E T T O B L A S T E R
  L E B R O N J A M E S
F O R A Y   O M S   M A S K
U B E R   P E R P   L E T H E
T U G   B A G N O L D   T O N
I L O V E L A   E S O T E R Y
L I E A B E D   T A P I N T O
E N S L E R   S T A N D I N
```

192

```
B I G S P O O N   H A H A H A
O R A T O R I O   O L I V E S
L O G R O L L S   T I N I E S
O N R E P O R T   D A D A D A
T O E S   P I A N O S   T I N
I R E S T   G R O G   G O N G
E E L E R S   S T G E O R G E
  A E O N   H E R O
B A T T E R U P   R I D G E D
M R E S   C L A M   C R E T E
X I A   C E L I A C   E S O S
B A R C A R   D R A M A T I C
I N G A M E   F I R E S A L E
K N A V E S   O N E T O T E N
E A S E L S   R A T S N E S T
```

193

```
J E D I M A S T E R   S P A M
A L O H A S T A T E   N O N E
M I R A C L E M A X     A L A N
E X I T   A P P S     P A C S
S I T E   N S A   I N A R O W
  R O I L     A C E T O N E
    T O Y B O X E S   I D A
A S H   G O A L I E S   D A R
U T A   J U R A S S I C
D E N M A R K     E A R L
I M G A M E   S M U   S E E S
E W O K     O T O S   E V A N
N A V E   C H O R U S L I N E
C R E D   D O M E A F A V O R
E E R O   S H A L L O W E N D
```

194

```
S C R A P S   S T R A W M A N
M O O L A H   T H E P I A N O
I M W A Y A H E A D O F Y O U
T O S S A C O I N   P I O N S
      S K U N K
D E C R Y   R E G   R O M A S
I G L O O S   R O B O C A L L
E G O S U R F   D E T E N T E
G O N E G I R L   T I L T E D
O N E N O   E E L   S O A R S
      E M I R S
S H O W S   M O V I E F O N E
L I M O U S I N E D R I V E R
O V E R L O U D   E I L E E N
G E N D A R M E   S E E N T O
```

195

```
I N S   R I B S   D I C E Y
D O T H E M A T H   A D O R E
I F E E L F R E E   F I L E S
D A I R Y   G E M   T O D A Y
S I N E   G A R I   T O D O
O R S   A R I   N Y U   P E U
    T R A N S G E N D E R
  A I N T I A W O M A N
  D O M A I N N A M E S
L O L   Z A G   Y E T   G I G
A G R A   C O E N   M O N O
S P A S M   H R S   B A N J O
H A D T O   I N Q U I R E O F
E R I E S   P O U N D C A K E
S K O R T   T E E S   R E D
```

196

```
T V D R A M A   S C R A W L S
H I R E D O N   T H E S O U P
A T A C O S T   R A T H O L E
T A G O R E   R O N D E L L E
S M O R E   M U N G   S L E D
H I N D   C O N G E R   Y D S
O N E S   A D S P E A K
W A T E R M E L O N S E E D S
    T A B L O I D   E X I T
A M O   M O R O N S   P A G E
M O R E   D O S T   D A M U P
P R A C T I C E   M R P I N K
U N C L O A K   Y O U A N D I
L A L A N N E   I N B R E E D
E Y E T E S T   P O S T E R S
```

197

```
M E A S U R I N G S T I C K S
I A P P R E C I A T E T H A T
S T R A I T O F M E S S I N A
H O O T S   S T E A L   L E X
A N N   S A Y   M A D D
    N A E       O B I
T O T A L I T A R I A N I S M
I C O U L D E A T A H O R S E
P U R S U E T H E M A T T E R
S L E E P L E S S N I G H T S
  I T A       O R O
  O M A N   T E T   A S S
A P B   W O M E N   P I L O T
L A I D I T O N T H E L I N E
I N T E R E S T R A T E C A P
T E S T E D T H E W A T E R S
```

198

```
M C G I L L   M I C K E Y D S
A I R S E A   I N A N D O U T
I M A M A N   S U R E S U R E
M A V E N   B S I D E   R A N
  R I N S E O U T   P E N T
E R T E   N O S   V E L D T
C O Y   L I Z A   I D E A
O N S T A G E   B O G A R T S
  R O O M   D A L Y   N E T
  B A L S A   R N A   E T S Y
S A I L   G U E S S N O T
P U N   P O E M S   T R O T S
E B B T I D E S   B O O T U P
C L O S E O N E   I M B I B E
S E W E R R A T   O P E N E D
```

199

```
S A M O A N   . A R M P I T
W H O A W H O A . D I V I D E
H A R D S E L L . R E P A I D
O N T . . M O L T E N . N O T
L I A M . . S H I P . B O L A
L A S E R B E A M . R E B E L
. . . R I O . L I F E H A C K
. L O R D V O L D E M O R T .
L E F I G A R O . N I L .
E M C E E . I W O N T D O I T
N O O R . L O S T . S Y N E
G N U . M I N E T A . S T E
T O R T E S . V E R B O T E N
H I S S A T . E R E A D E R S
S L E E T S . . S A Y E R S .
```

200

```
N I S S A N T I T A N S .
O N C E U P O N A T I M E .
S H O C K R E S I S T A N T
H A L T S . L U N E . S H A M
O L D S . S O R T A . H A R E
W E S . F L O E S . P I N T A
. . T R I P S . C A N C A N
R A M R O D S . B A N T E R S
E L O I S E . L A R G O .
S Y L P H . B A R B S . G E E
I D O L . C U L T S . M O A N
N A T E . R E A L . C O A S T
. R O S E A N N E C O N N E R
. V E R M O N T A V E N U E
. C A S S E T T E T A P E
```

Looking for more Hard Crosswords?

The New York Times

The #1 Name in Crosswords

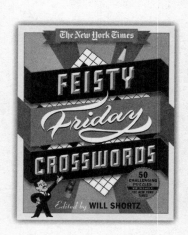

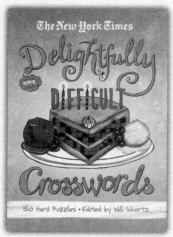